FUNDAMENTAL 2D
GAME PROGRAMMING
WITH JAVA™

TIMOTHY WRIGHT

Cengage Learning PTR

CENGAGE
Learning·

Professional • Technical • Reference

Australia • Brazil • Japan • Korea • Mexico • Singapore • Spain • United Kingdom • United States

CENGAGE Learning

Professional • Technical • Reference

Fundamental 2D Game Programming with Java™
Timothy Wright

Publisher and General Manager, Cengage Learning PTR: Stacy L. Hiquet

Associate Director of Marketing: Sarah Panella

Manager of Editorial Services: Heather Talbot

Senior Acquisitions Editor: Emi Smith

Senior Marketing Manager: Mark Hughes

Project/Copy Editor: Kezia Endsley

Technical Editor: Dustin Clingman

Interior Layout: MPS Limited

Cover Designer: Luke Fletcher

Proofreader: Kelly Talbot Editing Services

Indexer: Kelly Talbot Editing Services

For product information and technology assistance, contact us at **Cengage Learning Customer & Sales Support, 1-800-354-9706**.

For permission to use material from this text or product, submit all requests online at **cengage.com/permissions**.

Further permissions questions can be emailed to **permissionrequest@cengage.com**.

Java is a trademark of Sun Microsystems, Inc. in the U.S. and certain other countries. All other trademarks are the property of their respective owners.

All images © Cengage Learning unless otherwise noted.

Library of Congress Control Number: 2014930065

ISBN-13: 978-1-305-07653-2

ISBN-10: 1-305-07653-2

Cengage Learning PTR

20 Channel Center Street

Boston, MA 02210

USA

Cengage Learning is a leading provider of customized learning solutions with office locations around the globe, including Singapore, the United Kingdom, Australia, Mexico, Brazil, and Japan. Locate your local office at: **international.cengage.com/region**.

Cengage Learning products are represented in Canada by Nelson Education, Ltd.

For your lifelong learning solutions, visit **cengageptr.com**.

Visit our corporate website at **cengage.com**.

Printed in the United States of America
1 2 3 4 5 6 7 16 15 14

To my grams, who always let me play, have fun, think outside the box, and never complained, no matter what kind of mess she had to clean up after I left.

ACKNOWLEDGMENTS

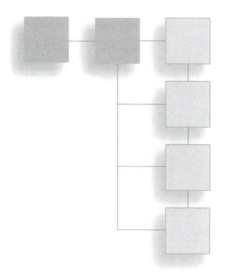

First of all, I would like to thank all of my fellow forum moderators at www.gamedev.net. Your honest and helpful comments gave me the courage to put myself out there and write this book.

Special thanks to Drew Sikora for publishing my early tutorials, and passing on fan mail to keep me going when times were tough. Thanks to John Hattan and to Jason Zink for publishing information. Thanks to everyone who has reviewed the book, helped debug code examples, and fixed all my spelling errors (there were many).

I would like to thank Emi Smith and the rest of the Cengage staff for their help with editing, publishing, and figuring out how to get their Macs to talk with my Windows. I would like to thank Kezia Endsley, my editor, for putting up with all my silly questions, and always being a joy to work with. I would also like to thank Dustin Clingman for the fantastic technical editing, ensuring that the code examples are correct and thoroughly explained.

Most of all, I want to thank my wife, Jimmi. She has been my best friend for over two decades, and without her continued support and belief, none of this would have been possible. I love you baby. Thanks for not taking me out before the book was done. :-)

ABOUT THE AUTHOR

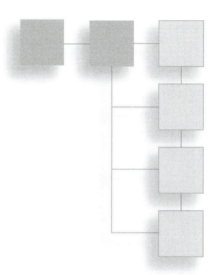

Timothy Wright is a software engineer currently working on the next great indie game. He spent his early adult life as an Army piano player, where he discovered his love of programming. He has a bachelor's degree in computer science and has worked for R&D companies, using optics and lasers, for the last decade. While not working on games or playing them, he enjoys playing poker, cooking good food, and brewing his own beer. With a wife, two daughters, three dogs, two cats, and a foreign exchange student, his weeks are full of drama. Timothy has lived all over the country and spent five years living in Italy, Germany, and traveling Europe. He has been a forum moderator at www.gamedev.net for years, and you can occasionally find him poking about under the name Glass_Knife.

CONTENTS

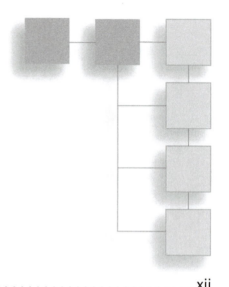

INTRODUCTION

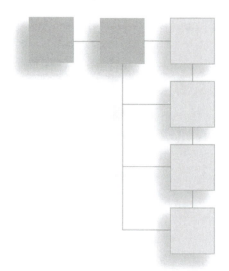

Years ago, when I started my first professional job as a software developer, I was asked to code an applet. At the time, I didn't know a lot about the Java language. Throughout school I used C++ extensively, and while I had done some coding in Java, I viewed it as a slow and dumbed-down version of C++.

At the same time, I was buying and reading as many game programming books as I could get my hands on. One book on artificial intelligence that I was working through had great examples, but they were all C++ and DirectX. Since I was busy learning Java at work, I thought porting the examples to Java would be a good way to learn the language. After all, how hard could Java game programming be?

As I soon discovered, there was very little information available about making games in Java. What I did find centered on applet programming, with virtually nothing on making application-type games. After porting the examples to Java and discovering that it was possible and not difficult, I searched for the tutorial that explained it all. I never did find it, so I wrote my own.

After publishing two tutorials on gamedev.net and writing a software renderer from scratch in Java, I realized that the language had a lot to offer the game community. While working on the next series of tutorials, I ended up with so much information that a book seemed like a much better solution.

That is what you are now reading: one developer's toolkit of code and explanations to help speed up the process of game programming in Java. Hopefully, the following pages can answer all the necessary questions and help you get to the important stuff: making games.

THE BOOK'S ORGANIZATION

This book is split into three sections. The first part, "The Foundations," covers all the concepts you need to create a simple prototype game. The next part, "The Polish," covers the other concepts needed to program a complete game. The last part, "The Complete Game," takes all of the concepts presented and creates a complete game from start to finish. The summary of the content is as follows:

Part I: The Foundations

Chapter 1: Hello World—This chapter creates a frame-rate class, using it to monitor application speed. Then windowed and full-screen game loops are demonstrated.

Chapter 2: Input—This chapter creates classes for monitoring keyboard input, as well as absolute and relative mouse input. Example code demonstrates input handling inside a game loop.

Chapter 3: Transformations—This chapter covers vectors, points, and matrix math, as well as translation, rotation, scaling, and shearing of points and vectors. Matrix transformations, as well as manual methods, are discussed, along with an introduction to Swing's transformation objects.

Chapter 4: Time and Space—This chapter adds a game clock to the loop, allowing for frame-rate-independent object manipulation. Screen mapping is also explored, allowing any screen-space objects to be mapped from normalized device coordinates.

Chapter 5: Simple Game Framework—This chapter uses all the previous code presented to create a simple game framework for use in the remaining examples.

Chapter 6: Vector2f Updates—This chapter updates the `Vector2f` class, first introduced in Chapter 3, with all the necessary linear algebra code needed for inter-section testing.

Chapter 7: Intersection Testing—This chapter covers the math and algorithms necessary to determine whether objects are overlapping or inside each other. Points, circles, lines, and rectangles are used to explore this topic.

Chapter 8: Game Prototype—This chapter uses the code presented so far, along with the simple framework, to create a prototype game. Although it's not yet a complete game, it presents a good idea of all the necessary code needed to make a game.

Part II: The Polish

Chapter 9: Files and Resources—This chapter covers reading and writing XML files, and loading and saving Java property files. It also covers accessing resources contained within archive files on the classpath.

Chapter 10: Images—This chapter covers working with images, creating images from scratch, and working with image files. It also covers using transparency, as well as different methods for drawing, rotating, and scaling images.

Chapter 11: Text—This chapter covers everything you need to draw text using Java's Font library. There are also updates to the input library to support typing.

Chapter 12: Threads—This chapter covers multi-threaded libraries available in Java, and demonstrates creating a non-blocking class, wrapping a non-blocking class with a blocking class, integrating multi-threaded code into a single-threaded game loop, and using a thread pool to speed up resource loading.

Chapter 13: Sound—This chapter covers the problems with the sound support in Java. Both small clip files and large file streaming are explored, as well as using sound controls, such as pan and gain. The sound wrapper library developed in this chapter is used to integrate sound into the game loop with concepts explained in Chapter 12.

Chapter 14: Deployment with ANT—This chapter provides an overview of the ANT build tool, and walks you through the process of creating an extendable build script for game development.

Chapter 15: Collision Detection—This chapter covers determining the intersection point of colliding objects, as well as handling the collision response. Points, lines, rectangles, and circles are explored with many examples to study.

Part III: The Complete Game

Chapter 16: Tools—This chapter develops the tools necessary to make a complete game. Frameworks are developed for windowed games, full-screen games, and Swing editors. The utility library is updated, and a simple Swing editor is created to draw polygons and save them to XML. A sprite class is created, and a simple particle engine is explored.

Chapter 17: Space Rocks—This chapter uses all the code presented to make a complete game from start to finish. Although this game is short and easy, it is complete, with a loading screen, attract mode, gameplay, high-score input and saving, and a deployment ANT script. Hopefully, seeing the work needed to create a complete game will motivate you to finish your own.

Chapter 18: Conclusion—This chapter wraps up the entire book by listing all the code examples. This section presents a list of code examples by chapter, and each example explains the lessons learned, so finding an example is easy.

WHO SHOULD READ THIS BOOK?

This is written for anyone who wants to learn the fundamentals of 2D game programming. While current graphics are evolving very fast, 3D graphics are only a piece of the puzzle. If a programmer does not understand the game loop, input handling, matrix math, intersection testing, collision detection, image rendering, threads, sound, or deployment, 3D graphics are not going to make the game playable. Even though 3D rendering is exciting, learning the fundamentals is important for having a solid foundation and the tools necessary to tackle any situation.

Although this book assumes the reader understands core programming concepts, object oriented software, and the Java programming language, no assumptions are made about previous game programming knowledge.

You should already be familiar with the Java language, as this is not covered in the text.

SOFTWARE AND VERSIONS

This code has been tested on Windows 7 with the latest Java SE 6.0 and Java SE 7.0 versions available at the time of this writing. The Eclipse Helios IDE was used for compiling and execution of the code. The 1.8.2 ANT version was used for deployment.

The source code examples, as well as sound, image, and resource files, are available from:

http://www.indiegameprogramming.com

You can also download them from the book's website, where you can search for the book by title or ISBN:

http://www.cengageptr.com/downloads

CONVENTIONS USED IN THIS BOOK

Monospace font is used for the following:

- Java classes
- Java methods
- Variable names
- Math variables and constants
- Code examples
- Code snippets
- XML
- Command-line output

QUESTIONS OR COMMENTS

Please send any comments, corrections, or questions about the book to the following email address:

indiegameprogramming@gmail.com

The website for the book, with information, updates, corrections, and source code is available at:

http://www.indiegameprogramming.com

PART I

THE FOUNDATIONS

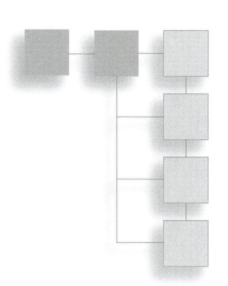

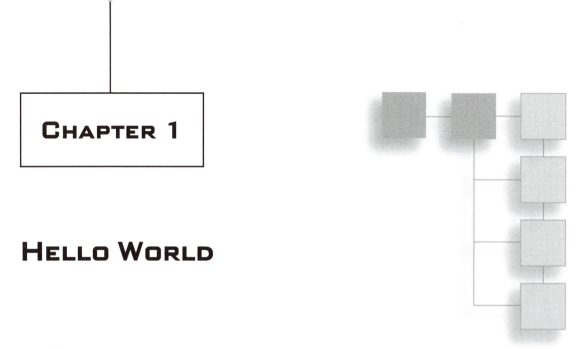

CHAPTER 1

HELLO WORLD

The first step in most programming books is creating a Hello World application that performs a simple function to make sure everything is working. The simplest computer game application is a window with a black background and a tight `while` loop that clears the screen and redraws the black background as fast as possible; however, as simple as this is, it isn't very exciting. Adding a frame rate calculator will measure the application performance and verify that the window is redrawing. Since most examples in this book measure the frame rate, a frame rate calculator is a great place to begin.

USING THE FRAMERATE CLASS

The `FrameRate` class is located in the `javagames.util` package. All the utility code developed in this book goes into the utility package, which you can later turn into a utility library. This class is used to measure the frames per seconds (FPS) of the applications developed in this book. The FPS is stored as a string in the format `"FPS 100"`. This value is calculated every second.

The `initialize()` method needs to be called before the frame rate measurements begin. This method initializes the frame rate string to 0, and the last time to the current time in milliseconds.

The `System.currentTimeMillis()` call returns the number of milliseconds since midnight, January 1, 1970. Depending on the operating system, the accuracy of the time measured can vary. Some versions of Windows, for example, guarantee only 10 milliseconds of accuracy.

The calculate() method should be called once for every rendered frame. To calculate the frame rate, the current time is subtracted from the last time and stored in the delta variable. The frame count is incremented each frame, and when the delta time is over one second, the new FPS are generated. Since the delta variable is rarely exactly one second, 1,000 milliseconds are subtracted from the delta variable to save the extra milliseconds. Once the new frame rate is saved, the frame count is reset and the process begins again.

```java
package javagames.util;

public class FrameRate {

    private String frameRate;
    private long lastTime;
    private long delta;
    private int frameCount;

    public void initialize() {
        lastTime = System.currentTimeMillis();
        frameRate = "FPS 0";
    }

    public void calculate() {
        long current = System.currentTimeMillis();
        delta += current - lastTime;
        lastTime = current;
        frameCount++;
        if( delta > 1000 ) {
            delta -= 1000;
            frameRate = String.format( "FPS %s", frameCount );
            frameCount = 0;
        }
    }

    public String getFrameRate() {
        return frameRate;
    }
}
```

CREATING THE HELLO WORLD APPLICATION

The Hello World application seen in Figure 1.1 is the first game window example. The HelloWorldApp is located in the javagames.render package. Other than clearing and redrawing the background, nothing else is rendered in the window. The HelloWorldApp extends the JFrame class, which is a top level window component from Java's Swing library. This application contains a FrameRate object, which is used to measure the frame rate of the application.

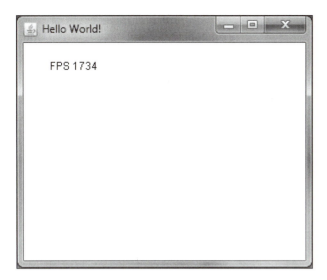

Figure 1.1
The Hello World Application.
© 2014 Timothy Wright.

Because the Swing library is not thread-safe, you should always create and show a JFrame on the Swing event thread. However, the program's main() method is not invoked on the event thread, so it is necessary to use the SwingUtilities class to launch the game window. By using the SwingUtilities class, the GUI components are created on the same thread. It is important to follow Java's guidelines for threading when using Swing components for rendering, because ignoring them can lead to undefined behavior, which is very difficult to debug.

Tip

I know a programmer who once tested whether you really need the SwingUtilities class to launch the game window by commenting out the SwingUtilities code for an application deployed throughout a site. Every few days, someone would report that the application crashed on startup. Not that I would ever do something like that, but it did seem to make a difference. :-)

```
final HelloWorldApp app = new HelloWorldApp();
    SwingUtilities.invokeLater( new Runnable() {
        public void run() {
            app.createAndShowGUI();
        }
});
```

Inside the HelloWorldApp is the GamePanel class that extends a JPanel. This class is used for drawing the graphics to the screen. Overriding the paint method allows the application access to the Graphics object. Note that the panel is cleared with the background color only because the super.paint() method is called. If this method call were removed, the background would not be drawn. The actual code in the onPaint() method doesn't do anything exciting yet. For now it calculates and displays the frame rate.

Notice the call to repaint() inside the paint() method. If the application recursively called paint() from inside itself, the method would never return (until the program threw a stack overflow exception). The repaint() method issues a paint request that will happen as soon as the current paint request is finished. This way the application continuously paints the window as fast as possible.

The createAndShowGUI() method is where the window is actually created and shown. It is important that the preferred size is set on the GamePanel and not on the JFrame. Notice that when the GamePanel is created, its preferred size is set. If the application size is set on the JFrame, some of the drawing area will be taken up by the frame and the drawing area will be a little smaller. Setting the size on the panel ensures it is exactly the specified size.

After setting up the window, but before showing it, the frame rate class is initialized. This is necessary to set the initial start time of the class so the first frame rate calculation will be correct. Once the application is visible from calling setVisible(true), the paint method is called, which continually calculates the frame rate and repaints itself until it is shut down.

Tip

You can find the full source code on the book's website at http://www.indiegameprogramming.com. It also includes updates and corrections, and other information relevant to the book.

The HelloWorldApp example code is as follows:

```
package javagames.render;

import java.awt.*;
import javax.swing.*;
import javagames.util.*;

public class HelloWorldApp extends JFrame {

    private FrameRate frameRate;

    public HelloWorldApp() {
        frameRate = new FrameRate();
    }
```

```
protected void createAndShowGUI() {
    GamePanel gamePanel = new GamePanel();
    gamePanel.setBackground( Color.BLACK );
    gamePanel.setPreferredSize( new Dimension( 320, 240 ) );
    getContentPane().add( gamePanel );
    setDefaultCloseOperation( EXIT_ON_CLOSE );
    setTitle( "Hello World!" );
    pack();
    frameRate.initialize();
    setVisible( true );
}

private class GamePanel extends JPanel {
    public void paint( Graphics g ) {
        super.paint( g );
        onPaint( g );
    }
}

protected void onPaint( Graphics g ) {
    frameRate.calculate();
    g.setColor( Color.WHITE );
    g.drawString( frameRate.getFrameRate(), 30, 30 );
    repaint();
}

public static void main( String[] args ) {
    final HelloWorldApp app = new HelloWorldApp();
    SwingUtilities.invokeLater( new Runnable() {
        public void run() {
            app.createAndShowGUI();
        }
    });
}
}
```

USING ACTIVE RENDERING

The previous example uses a technique called *passive rendering*. The application redraws itself in the paint() method, but it is the Swing library that decides when to call that method. The event dispatch thread handles the rendering of the Swing components and it is out of your hands. Although this is fine for normal applications, it is not recommended for games.

To handle the rendering, a `BufferStrategy` class can be used, but this requires some changes to the structure of the application. This will allow the application to put the rendering code in a separate thread and be in control of the entire process.

There are three reasons to get the game code out of the `paint()` method. The first is that there should not be any long executing or blocking code in the `paint()` method because it will block the GUI from receiving paint events. The second is that the rendering code needs to be in a different thread for full-screen exclusive mode. And the third, and most important reason, is that the rendering code is faster when the drawing is handled from scratch. In order to take advantage of active rendering, both windowed and full-screen, a custom rendering thread is created.

There is no practical way to put the drawing code in the paint method of a `JPanel`, as you saw in the first example, but call that code from a custom rendering thread. In order to handle the painting in a custom loop, you can use a `BufferStrategy` class. This class is used to perform double-buffering and page-flipping.

Double-buffering, illustrated in Figure 1.2, is used to keep the actual drawing of an image from being seen while the drawing is taking place. By drawing an image in memory and then copying the entire image at once, the process of drawing is not seen.

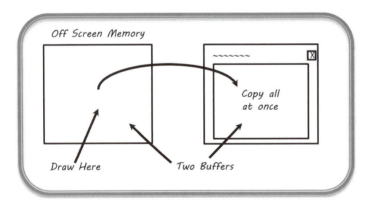

Figure 1.2
Double-Buffering.
© 2014 Timothy Wright.

Page-flipping, which can be used in full-screen exclusive mode, uses the same idea, but instead of copying an image, it maintains two off-screen images and simply swaps a video pointer from one buffer to the other. This way, whichever image is not drawn to the screen can be cleared and redrawn. When the drawing is complete, the pointers are swapped again, drawing the new image to the screen. See Figure 1.3.

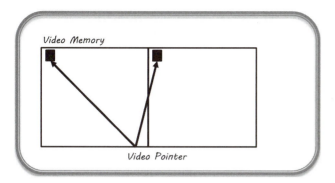

Figure 1.3
Page-Flipping.
© 2014 Timothy Wright.

By using a `BufferStrategy` class, it doesn't matter if the program is full-screen and using page-flipping, or if it is windowed and using double-buffering—it is handled behind the scenes. To use the `BufferStrategy` in a render loop, a graphics object is created using the `getDrawGraphics()` method. This graphics object will draw to the off-screen surface. Once the graphics object is available, it is used exactly like the graphics object passed in the `paint()` method of the `JPanel` class.

It is important to call `contentsLost()` to make sure the off-screen surface is available. Some operating systems let users Alt-Tab away from full-screen applications, causing the off-screen image to be unavailable.

The `show()` method performs either double-buffering/image copying or page-flipping/pointer swapping to display the image. Notice that the code is wrapped in a `try/finally` block. Unlike other painting code, because this graphics object has been created, it must be disposed of when the render loop is finished. Not calling the `Graphics.dispose()` method can cause a memory leak and crash the program.

Caution

Always make sure to call `dispose()` to clean up the graphics object.

```
// The bs object is a BufferStrategy object, and
// will be explained later in the chapter
public void gameLoop() {
    do {
        do {
            Graphics g = null;
            try {
                g = bs.getDrawGraphics();
```

```
            g.clearRect( 0, 0, getWidth(), getHeight() );
            render( g );
        } finally {
            if( g != null ) {
                g.dispose();
            }
        }
    } while( bs.contentsRestored() );
    bs.show();
} while( bs.contentsLost() );
}
```

CREATING A CUSTOM RENDERING THREAD

In addition to using the previous code to perform custom rendering, you need a custom rendering thread. To focus on only the threading issues, the RenderThreadExample, located in the javagames.render package, doesn't actually draw anything to the screen, it just prints out "Game Loop" where the rendering code should go. The next example combines the RenderThreadExample and the previous code to create an active rendering application.

The first thing to notice in the RenderThreadExample is that it implements a *runnable* interface. The runnable interface contains a single method: public void run(). This method contains the render loop, and is called only once. When it returns, the thread is finished and cannot be used again. To keep the code in the run method from exiting until the application is done, the Boolean running variable keeps the run method repeating.

```
private volatile boolean running;
```

Notice the volatile keyword with the declaration of the variable. Because this variable is a primitive type and is accessed from multiple threads, it is necessary to tell the compiler to always read this variable from memory. Without the keyword, the variable may be optimized with a cached value by the Java Virtual Machine (JVM), and the thread would be unable to stop.

Also, notice the sleep() method from the RenderThreadExample, which is used to slow the application down to a more reasonable speed. The sleep method takes a millisecond value and then suspends itself for that amount of time, allowing other threads to utilize the CPU.

Once the application is shut down, the render thread should stop. By adding a window listener, the program can respond to the window closing event. In this case, the program calls `onWindowClosing()`. If your program needs to shut down resources and close files that are no longer needed, this is the place to do it.

```
app.addWindowListener( new WindowAdapter() {
   public void windowClosing( WindowEvent e ) {
      app.onWindowClosing();
   }
});
```

To shut down the rendering thread, the `running` variable is set to `false`. However, the render thread may have just read the value of the `running` variable, and be asleep. To make sure that the thread has stopped, the `join()` method is called. This method will wait until the thread has ended and the `run` method has returned. If a timeout value is not passed into the `join()` method, this will block forever until the thread ends, so make sure the thread is going to end if you don't provide a timeout.

Lastly, the program must be shut down by hand with the `System.exit(0)` call. Previously, when the `JFrame.EXIT_ON_CLOSE` flag was set in the `JFrame`, the program would terminate. Now that the application is handling the shutdown, the program will not end unless the `exit` method is called. If the application hangs after shutting down, it is usually because the programmer forgot to call `System.exit()`.

```
package javagames.render;

import java.awt.event.*;
import javax.swing.*;


public class RenderThreadExample extends JFrame implements Runnable {

   private volatile boolean running;
   private Thread gameThread;

   public RenderThreadExample() {

   }

   protected void createAndShowGUI() {

      setSize( 320, 240 );
      setTitle( "Render Thread" );
      setVisible( true );

      gameThread = new Thread( this );
      gameThread.start();
   }

   public void run() {
      running = true;
      while( running ) {
```

```
            System.out.println( "Game Loop" );
            sleep( 10 );
        }
    }
    private void sleep( long sleep ) {
        try {
            Thread.sleep( sleep );
        } catch( InterruptedException ex ) { }
    }
    protected void onWindowClosing() {
        try {
            System.out.println( "Stopping Thread..." );
            running = false;
            gameThread.join();
            System.out.println( "Stopped!!!" );
        } catch( InterruptedException e ) {
            e.printStackTrace();
        }
        System.exit( 0 );
    }
    public static void main( String[] args ) {
        final RenderThreadExample app = new RenderThreadExample();
        app.addWindowListener( new WindowAdapter() {
            public void windowClosing( WindowEvent e ) {
                app.onWindowClosing();
            }
        });
        SwingUtilities.invokeLater( new Runnable() {
            public void run() {
                app.createAndShowGUI();
            }
        });
    }
}
```

CREATING AN ACTIVE RENDERED WINDOW

The rendering code can be moved from the event dispatch thread to the custom game thread by using active rendering. The Window class and the Canvas class are the two classes available to allow the creation of a BufferStrategy. By adding the canvas, you can access the buffer strategy and force the size of the canvas to exactly the size required, just like the JPanel example in the Hello World application.

Because the render loop does all the painting for this application, the `setIgnoreRepaint()` flag can be set on the `JFrame`. Calling `Canvas.createBufferStrategy()` by passing in the desired number of buffers and then calling `Canvas.getBufferStrategy()` creates the buffers necessary for active rendering. Because the application is handling the drawing, there is no need to respond to repaint methods. The `Component.setIgnoreRepaint()` method takes care of ignoring extra paint messages.

Tip

There is a weird error that happens if the `BufferStrategy` is created before the window has been laid out:

```
Exception in thread "AWT-EventQueue-0"
java.lang.IllegalStateException: Component must have a valid peer
```

Calling the `pack()` method can solve this. Be aware if the previous exception is thrown; make sure the `Component` is visible or has been packed before attempting to create the `BufferStrategy`.

The game loop now performs rendering as discussed in the previous section. Using the `getDrawGraphics()`, `contentsLost()`, `show()`, and `dispose()` methods, the render loop controls the application painting. Once the graphics object is available, and the previous screen has been cleared, the scene can be rendered. The `ActiveRenderingExample` code can be found in the `javagames.render` package.

```java
package javagames.render;

import java.awt.*;
import java.awt.event.*;
import java.awt.image.*;
import javax.swing.*;
import javagames.util.*;


public class ActiveRenderingExample extends JFrame implements Runnable {

    private FrameRate frameRate;
    private BufferStrategy bs;
    private volatile boolean running;
    private Thread gameThread;

    public ActiveRenderingExample() {
        frameRate = new FrameRate();
    }

    protected void createAndShowGUI() {

        Canvas canvas = new Canvas();
        canvas.setSize( 320, 240 );
```

```
        canvas.setBackground( Color.BLACK );
        canvas.setIgnoreRepaint( true );
        getContentPane().add( canvas );
        setTitle( "Active Rendering" );
        setIgnoreRepaint( true );
        pack();

        setVisible( true );
        canvas.createBufferStrategy( 2 );
        bs = canvas.getBufferStrategy();

        gameThread = new Thread( this );
        gameThread.start();
    }

    public void run() {
        running = true;
        frameRate.initialize();
        while( running ) {
            gameLoop();
        }
    }

    public void gameLoop() {
        do {
            do {
                Graphics g = null;
                try {
                    g = bs.getDrawGraphics();
                    g.clearRect( 0, 0, getWidth(), getHeight() );
                    render( g );
                } finally {
                    if( g != null ) {
                        g.dispose();
                    }
                }
            } while( bs.contentsRestored() );
            bs.show();
        } while( bs.contentsLost() );
    }

    private void render( Graphics g ) {
        frameRate.calculate();
        g.setColor( Color.GREEN );
        g.drawString( frameRate.getFrameRate(), 30, 30 );
    }
```

```
    protected void onWindowClosing() {
        try {
            running = false;
            gameThread.join();
        } catch( InterruptedException e ) {
            e.printStackTrace();
        }
        System.exit( 0 );
    }

    public static void main( String[] args ) {
        final ActiveRenderingExample app = new ActiveRenderingExample();
        app.addWindowListener( new WindowAdapter() {
            public void windowClosing( WindowEvent e ) {
                app.onWindowClosing();
            }
        });
        SwingUtilities.invokeLater( new Runnable() {
            public void run() {
                app.createAndShowGUI();
            }
        });
    }

}
```

CHANGING THE DISPLAY MODE

In order to create a full-screen application, the display mode needs to be changed. The DisplayModeTest, as shown in Figure 1.4, uses Swing components. This example is also located in the javagames.render package. If you have never done any Swing programming, some of the code may look strange. There are so many books and tutorials available, and since it would take a book larger than this one to explain everything Swing has to offer, just go with it.

Figure 1.4
Display Mode Application.
© 2014 Timothy Wright.

This example application lists all available screen resolutions, which allows users to switch to full-screen mode and back using any of the available display modes. Not only does this example show programming with Swing components, this code could also be used to create an initial startup game screen before switching to the full-screen game. This would enable users to configure the system using normal Swing components.

This example also contains an inner class called DisplayModeWrapper. Although I am not a fan of inner classes, this one makes the example easier to present in a single file. I prefer to have only one class in each file, and creating classes inside other classes so they can access private methods smells funny, but in the interest of brevity, I will look the other way. The wrapper class uses the equals() method to only compare the width and height of the display modes and not the bit-depth or refresh rate. Depending on the operating system, there may be many modes that differ only by bit-depth and refresh rate:

- 640×480   32 bit   59 Hz
- 640×480   32 bit   60 Hz
- 640×480   32 bit   75 Hz
- 640×480   16 bit   59 Hz
- 640×480   16 bit   60 Hz

Since the program creates the display mode as 32 bits and ignores all others, the 16-bit modes are not available. To let the software decide which refresh rate to use, the REFRESH_RATE_UNKNOWN value is used. This way, only one display mode of 640×480 is used and the others are skipped.

The constructor contains the code necessary to save the current display mode. This mode matches the display mode for the user's system before the software is launched. This display mode will be used to leave the full-screen mode when the application returns to windowed mode.

```
public DisplayModeExample() {
   GraphicsEnvironment ge =
     GraphicsEnvironment.getLocalGraphicsEnvironment();
   graphicsDevice = ge.getDefaultScreenDevice();
   currentDisplayMode = graphicsDevice.getDisplayMode();
}
```

The getMainPanel() method creates the Swing components. These include a combo box listing the available display modes, a button to switch to full-screen mode, and another button to switch back to windowed mode. The `listDisplayModes()` method returns a list of display modes in the wrapper class discussed previously. Not only does the wrapper allow searching the list for modes matching the width and height, it overrides the `toString()` method to produce an easy to read list of values in the combo box.

The `onEnterFullScreen()` method first checks to make sure full-screen is supported, switches to full-screen, and then changes the display mode. The `getSelectedMode()` method actually creates a new `DisplayMode` with an unknown refresh rate so the default refresh rate is used.

```java
// DisplayModeExample.java
protected void onEnterFullScreen() {
    if( graphicsDevice.isFullScreenSupported() ) {
        DisplayMode newMode = getSelectedMode();
        graphicsDevice.setFullScreenWindow( this );
        graphicsDevice.setDisplayMode( newMode );
    }
}
```

The `onExitFullScreen()` method returns the display to windowed mode with the saved display mode. These method calls are in reverse order from entering full-screen mode. Because the display mode can be changed in full-screen mode only, it must be switched before the display mode is changed, and cannot be set back to windowed mode until the original display mode is reset.

```java
package javagames.render;

import java.awt.*;
import java.awt.event.*;
import java.util.*;
import javax.swing.*;


public class DisplayModeExample extends JFrame {
    class DisplayModeWrapper {
        private DisplayMode dm;
        public DisplayModeWrapper( DisplayMode dm ) {
            this.dm = dm;
        }
        public boolean equals( Object obj ) {
            DisplayModeWrapper other = (DisplayModeWrapper)obj;
            if( dm.getWidth() != other.dm.getWidth() )
                return false;
```

```java
            if( dm.getHeight() != other.dm.getHeight() )
                return false;
            return true;
        }

        public String toString() {
            return "" + dm.getWidth() + " x " + dm.getHeight();
        }
    }

    private JComboBox displayModes;
    private GraphicsDevice graphicsDevice;
    private DisplayMode currentDisplayMode;

    public DisplayModeExample() {
        GraphicsEnvironment ge =
            GraphicsEnvironment.getLocalGraphicsEnvironment();
        graphicsDevice = ge.getDefaultScreenDevice();
        currentDisplayMode = graphicsDevice.getDisplayMode();
    }

    private JPanel getMainPanel() {
        JPanel p = new JPanel();
        displayModes = new JComboBox( listDisplayModes() );
        p.add( displayModes );
        JButton enterButton = new JButton( "Enter Full Screen" );
        enterButton.addActionListener( new ActionListener() {
            public void actionPerformed( ActionEvent e ) {
                onEnterFullScreen();
            }
        });
        p.add( enterButton );
        JButton exitButton = new JButton( "Exit Full Screen" );
        exitButton.addActionListener( new ActionListener() {
            public void actionPerformed( ActionEvent e ) {
                onExitFullScreen();
            }
        });
        p.add( exitButton );
        return p;
    }

    private DisplayModeWrapper[] listDisplayModes() {
        ArrayList<DisplayModeWrapper> list = new
            ArrayList<DisplayModeWrapper>();
        for( DisplayMode mode : graphicsDevice.getDisplayModes() ) {
            if( mode.getBitDepth() == 32 ) {
```

```
            DisplayModeWrapper wrap = new DisplayModeWrapper( mode );
            if( !list.contains( wrap ) ) {
                list.add( wrap );
            }
        }
    }
    return list.toArray( new DisplayModeWrapper[0] );
}
protected void createAndShowGUI() {
    Container canvas = getContentPane();
    canvas.add( getMainPanel() );
    canvas.setIgnoreRepaint( true );
    setDefaultCloseOperation( EXIT_ON_CLOSE );
    setTitle( "Display Mode Test" );
    pack();
    setVisible( true );
}
protected void onEnterFullScreen() {
    if( graphicsDevice.isFullScreenSupported() ) {
        DisplayMode newMode = getSelectedMode();
        graphicsDevice.setFullScreenWindow( this );
        graphicsDevice.setDisplayMode( newMode );
    }
}
protected void onExitFullScreen() {
    graphicsDevice.setDisplayMode( currentDisplayMode );
    graphicsDevice.setFullScreenWindow( null );
}
protected DisplayMode getSelectedMode() {
    DisplayModeWrapper wrapper =
        (DisplayModeWrapper)displayModes.getSelectedItem();
    DisplayMode dm = wrapper.dm;
    int width = dm.getWidth();
    int height = dm.getHeight();
    int bit = 32;
    int refresh = DisplayMode.REFRESH_RATE_UNKNOWN;
    return new DisplayMode( width, height, bit, refresh );
}
public static void main( String[] args ) {
    final DisplayModeExample app = new DisplayModeExample();
    SwingUtilities.invokeLater( new Runnable() {
        public void run() {
```

```
            app.createAndShowGUI();
        }
    });
  }
}
```

ACTIVE RENDERING IN FULL-SCREEN DISPLAY MODE

The FullScreenRenderingExample, located in the javagames.render package, contains the active rendering framework and the display mode code to switch to full-screen mode, creating a simple full-screen game framework. This example contains a lot of code presented in previous sections. In addition to setting the background color directly to the JFrame and ignoring repaint, the setUndecorated() flag is enabled. Because the application switched from windowed to full-screen mode in the previous example, this wasn't set; but when using full-screen only, the JFrame should be undecorated.

After saving the current display mode, switching to full-screen, and changing the display mode, the buffer strategy is created using the JFrame methods instead of the Canvas methods shown in the windowed example.

Even though the keyboard hasn't been covered yet, you need some way to exit the program. Because the JFrame is undecorated, there are no controls to close the window. The following code will shut down the application when users press the Escape key:

```
// FullScreenRenderingExample.java
addKeyListener( new KeyAdapter() {
  public void keyPressed( KeyEvent e ) {
    if( e.getKeyCode() == KeyEvent.VK_ESCAPE ) {
      shutDown();
    }
  }
});
```

In this example, the display mode is hard coded to 800×600, 32 bit for simplicity. In an actual production application, the available display modes would be enumerated as shown in the previous example. Make sure you change this code if this display mode isn't supported on your system.

```
private DisplayMode getDisplayMode() {
    return new DisplayMode(
      800, 600, 32, DisplayMode.REFRESH_RATE_UNKNOWN );
}
```

Because there is no way to close the window, there is no need for a window listener. When the Escape key is pressed and the example is shut down, the display mode is returned to normal after the game loop is shut down.

```java
package javagames.render;

import java.awt.*;
import java.awt.event.*;
import java.awt.image.*;
import javax.swing.*;
import javagames.util.*;


public class FullScreenRenderingExample
            extends JFrame implements Runnable {

    private FrameRate frameRate;
    private BufferStrategy bs;
    private volatile boolean running;
    private Thread gameThread;
    private GraphicsDevice graphicsDevice;
    private DisplayMode currentDisplayMode;

    public FullScreenRenderingExample() {
        frameRate = new FrameRate();
    }

    protected void createAndShowGUI() {

        setIgnoreRepaint( true );
        setUndecorated( true );
        setBackground( Color.BLACK );

        GraphicsEnvironment ge =
            GraphicsEnvironment.getLocalGraphicsEnvironment();
        graphicsDevice = ge.getDefaultScreenDevice();
        currentDisplayMode = graphicsDevice.getDisplayMode();
        if( !graphicsDevice.isFullScreenSupported() ) {
            System.err.println( "ERROR: Not Supported!!!" );
            System.exit( 0 );
        }

        graphicsDevice.setFullScreenWindow( this );
        graphicsDevice.setDisplayMode( getDisplayMode() );

        createBufferStrategy( 2 );
        bs = getBufferStrategy();

        addKeyListener( new KeyAdapter() {
            public void keyPressed( KeyEvent e ) {
```

```java
                if( e.getKeyCode() == KeyEvent.VK_ESCAPE ) {
                    shutDown();
                }
            }
        });

        gameThread = new Thread( this );
        gameThread.start();
    }

    private DisplayMode getDisplayMode() {
        return new DisplayMode(
            800, 600, 32, DisplayMode.REFRESH_RATE_UNKNOWN );
    }

    public void run() {
        running = true;
        frameRate.initialize();
        while( running ) {
            gameLoop();
        }
    }

    public void gameLoop() {
        do {
            do {
                Graphics g = null;
                try {
                    g = bs.getDrawGraphics();
                    g.clearRect( 0, 0, getWidth(), getHeight() );
                    render( g );
                } finally {
                    if( g != null ) {
                        g.dispose();
                    }
                }
            } while( bs.contentsRestored() );
            bs.show();
        } while( bs.contentsLost() );
    }

    private void render( Graphics g ) {
        frameRate.calculate();
        g.setColor( Color.GREEN );
        g.drawString( frameRate.getFrameRate(), 30, 30 );
        g.drawString( "Press ESC to exit...", 30, 60 );
    }
```

```
protected void shutDown() {
    try {
        running = false;
        gameThread.join();
        System.out.println( "Game loop stopped!!!" );
        graphicsDevice.setDisplayMode( currentDisplayMode );
        graphicsDevice.setFullScreenWindow( null );
        System.out.println("Display Restored...");
    } catch( InterruptedException e ) {
        e.printStackTrace();
    }
    System.exit( 0 );
}

public static void main( String[] args ) {
    final FullScreenRenderingExample app = new
        FullScreenRenderingExample();
    SwingUtilities.invokeLater( new Runnable() {
        public void run() {
            app.createAndShowGUI();
        }
    });
}
}
```

RESOURCES AND FURTHER READING

Martak, Michael, "Full-Screen Exclusive Mode API," 1995, http://docs.oracle.com
/javase/tutorial/extra/fullscreen/index.html.

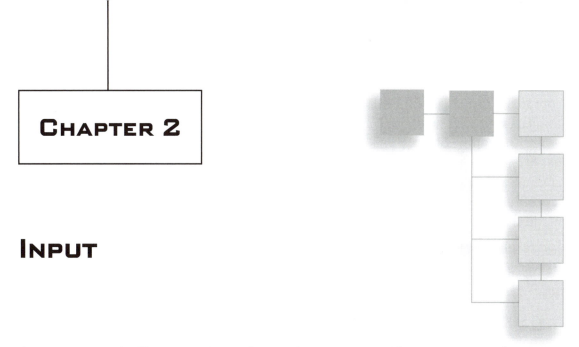

CHAPTER 2

INPUT

As you can see in Figure 2.1, input is very important to video games. It is the reason games are not the same as movies, and it is the topic of this chapter. Although many people place more effort on looks, no matter how spectacular a game looks, if the controls are jumpy, awkward, or difficult, the players can get very frustrated.

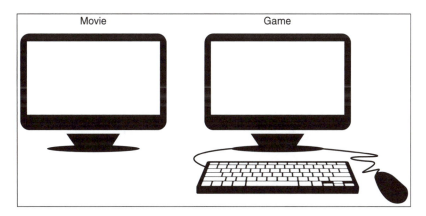

Figure 2.1
Difference Between a Movie and a Game.
© 2014 Cengage Learning.

Although there are many input devices available today, this book covers the two most common: the keyboard and the mouse.

HANDLING KEYBOARD INPUT

In most applications, the software doesn't need to handle the keyboard events. Any components, such as text fields, handle the typing and notify the software when something changes. But most computer games use the keyboard, not for typing, but for game input. Depending on the game, there may be typing, but the keyboard buttons may also be used as direction keys and laser triggers. Many computer games have different input configurations and some even allow users to map the keys however they want. Regardless of how the game uses the keyboard (and it could be an entirely new way), the usual method of listening to keyboard events does not fit the game loop program design.

Swing components allow listeners to be added that implement the `KeyListener` interface:

- `void keyTyped(KeyEvent e)`—Key was pressed and released
- `void keyPressed(KeyEvent e)`—Key was pressed
- `void keyReleased(KeyEvent e)`—Key was released

When a key is pressed, the `keyPressed()` method is called. As expected, the `keyReleased()` method is called when the same key is released. The `keyTyped()` method is called only after a key is pressed and released. The action keys and modifier keys, such as Shift or the arrow keys, do not generate a `keyTyped()` event. This event will be explored in Chapter 11, which covers text.

The problem is, the keyboard is a piece of hardware maintained by the operating system. The operating system, and not the software, generate and dispatch keyboard events to whatever applications have focus. There is nothing stopping the user from switching from a game window to a web browser and checking email. Because of this, all the keyboard events arrive on a different thread and need to be made available to the game loop.

Most games follow some kind of structured loop:

```
while( true ) {
    processInput();
    updateObjects();
    // other stuff...
    renderScene();
}
```

If the input was handled outside of the game loop, the state could change at any time. Also, multiple keys may be down simultaneously, so handling each event by itself doesn't let the user combine keys. To simplify input processing, the keyboard events are saved and made available to the game loop.

When storing the state of the keyboard, it is important to understand how the state of the keyboard is shared with the program. Because the keyboard is a very complicated piece of hardware, not only are the string characters available, but each key, even those that do not represent a character, such as the Shift key, are made available through virtual key codes. Every key on the keyboard is mapped to a key code located in the KeyEvent class. Here are some example values:

- KeyEvent.VK_E—The E key
- KeyEvent.VK_SPACE—The spacebar
- KeyEvent.VK_UP—The up arrow key

Each of these constants maps to a numerical value passed to the key listeners inside the KeyEvent object. The KeyEvent.getKeyCode() method returns the virtual key code for whatever keyboard key generated the event.

The SimpleKeyboardInput class, located in the javagames.util package, does very little. This class implements the KeyListener interface so it can monitor keyboard events. It keeps a Boolean array of 256 keys, which are all the virtual key codes that need to be sampled. It stores the state of the key—true if down, false otherwise—in the key state array. Finally, after using the synchronized keyword to protect the key state array when it is being accessed from multiple threads, it gives access to the current key state with the keyDown(int keyCode) method.

```
package javagames.util;

import java.awt.event.*;

public class SimpleKeyboardInput implements KeyListener {

    private boolean[] keys;

    public SimpleKeyboardInput() {
        keys = new boolean[ 256 ];
    }

    public synchronized boolean keyDown( int keyCode ) {
        return keys[ keyCode ];
    }

    public synchronized void keyPressed( KeyEvent e ) {
        int keyCode = e.getKeyCode();
        if( keyCode >= 0 && keyCode < keys.length ) {
            keys[ keyCode ] = true;
        }
    }
```

```
public synchronized void keyReleased( KeyEvent e ) {
    int keyCode = e.getKeyCode();
    if( keyCode >= 0 && keyCode < keys.length ) {
        keys[ keyCode ] = false;
    }
}

public void keyTyped( KeyEvent e ) {
    // Not needed
}
}
```

Tip

Don't forget that you can find the full source code on the book's website at http://www
.indiegameprogramming.com.

The `SimpleKeyboardExample` class, located in the `javagames.input` package, is a simple test using the keyboard input class, replacing the rendering code with input processing code. Notice that the `SimpleKeyboardInput` is added to the application with the `addKeyListener()` method. Inside the game loop, instead of clearing the image and displaying the frame rate, the game loop checks for the spacebar or the arrow keys and prints out a message whenever the keys are pressed.

When checking the spacebar, the example uses a variable to save the state of the key, only printing to the console once every keypress. The arrow keys, however, continuously print their state to the console until they are released.

```
package javagames.input;

import java.awt.event.*;
import javax.swing.*;
import javagames.util.*;


public class SimpleKeyboardExample extends JFrame implements Runnable {
    private volatile boolean running;
    private Thread gameThread;
    private SimpleKeyboardInput keys;
    private boolean space;
    public SimpleKeyboardExample() {
        keys = new SimpleKeyboardInput();
    }

    protected void createAndShowGUI() {

        setTitle( "Keyboard Input" );
```

```
        setSize( 320, 240 );
        addKeyListener( keys );
        setVisible( true );

        gameThread = new Thread( this );
        gameThread.start();
    }

    public void run() {
        running = true;
        while( running ) {
            gameLoop();
        }
    }

    public void gameLoop() {
        if( keys.keyDown( KeyEvent.VK_SPACE ) ) {
            if( !space ) {
                System.out.println( "VK_SPACE" );
            }
            space = true;
        } else {
            space = false;
        }
        if( keys.keyDown( KeyEvent.VK_UP ) ) {
            System.out.println( "VK_UP" );
        }
        if( keys.keyDown( KeyEvent.VK_DOWN ) ) {
            System.out.println( "VK_DOWN" );
        }
        if( keys.keyDown( KeyEvent.VK_LEFT ) ) {
            System.out.println( "VK_LEFT" );
        }
        if( keys.keyDown( KeyEvent.VK_RIGHT ) ) {
            System.out.println( "VK_RIGHT" );
        }
        try {
            Thread.sleep( 10 );
        } catch( InterruptedException ex ) { }
    }

    protected void onWindowClosing() {
        try {
            running = false;
            gameThread.join();
        } catch( InterruptedException e ) {
```

```
                e.printStackTrace();
         }
         System.exit( 0 );
    }

    public static void main( String[] args ) {
        final SimpleKeyboardExample app = new SimpleKeyboardExample ();
        app.addWindowListener( new WindowAdapter() {
            public void windowClosing( WindowEvent e ) {
                app.onWindowClosing();
            }
        });
        SwingUtilities.invokeLater( new Runnable() {
            public void run() {
                app.createAndShowGUI();
            }
        });
    }

}
```

KEYBOARD IMPROVEMENTS

Although the keyboard input class allows access to the keyboard state in the game loop, there are some problems with the implementation. The first is that if the keyboard key isn't down when the game loop code executes, the keypress can be missed. Although it is not likely to happen with these simple examples, once the application gets more intensive and the game loop requires more time to process all the code, the game loop could slow down enough to miss input. For now, just know that it could be an issue. A solution to keep events from being missed is discussed in Chapter 11.

The second problem is that it is difficult to test when a key is pressed for the first time. If 20 keys need to be tracked, and some of those change behavior based on the game state, it could become a very messy problem trying to keep track of all those states using code similar to this:

```
// SimpleKeyboardExample.java
if( keys.keyDown( KeyEvent.VK_SPACE ) ) {
    if( !space ) {
        System.out.println( "VK_SPACE" );
    }
    space = true;
} else {
    space = false;
}
```

To update the KeyboardInput class to keep track of initial keypresses as well as the keyboard state, an array of integer values is added. These values will keep track of how many frames the key has been pressed. The code implementing the KeyListener interface doesn't change at all, but the keyDown() method no longer pulls the value from the boolean keys array.

The poll() method, synchronized to protect the shared keys array, transfers the keyboard state from the boolean array to the integer array. If the key is down, the value is incremented, otherwise it is set back to zero. The keyDown() method now checks if the value is not zero and a new method, keyDownOnce(), returns true when the value is exactly one.

```java
package javagames.util;

import java.awt.event.*;

public class KeyboardInput implements KeyListener {

    private boolean[] keys;
    private int[] polled;

    public KeyboardInput() {
        keys = new boolean[ 256 ];
        polled = new int[ 256 ];
    }

    public boolean keyDown( int keyCode ) {
        return polled[ keyCode ] > 0;
    }

    public boolean keyDownOnce( int keyCode ) {
        return polled[ keyCode ] == 1;
    }

    public synchronized void poll() {
        for( int i = 0; i < keys.length; ++i ) {
            if( keys[i] ) {
                polled[i]++;
            } else {
                polled[i] = 0;
            }
        }
    }

    public synchronized void keyPressed( KeyEvent e ) {
        int keyCode = e.getKeyCode();
        if( keyCode >= 0 && keyCode < keys.length ) {
            keys[ keyCode ] = true;
        }
    }
```

```
    public synchronized void keyReleased( KeyEvent e ) {
        int keyCode = e.getKeyCode();
        if( keyCode >= 0 && keyCode < keys.length ) {
            keys[ keyCode ] = false;
        }
    }

    public void keyTyped( KeyEvent e ) {
        // Not needed
    }
}
```

This new class can be used by replacing the game loop code from the previous example with the code that follows. The code needed to check for a single press of the spacebar is greatly simplified.

Note

Don't forget to call the KeyboardInput.poll() method every frame!

```
// replacing the game loop
public void gameLoop() {

    keys.poll();

    if( keys.keyDownOnce( KeyEvent.VK_SPACE ) ) {
        System.out.println( "VK_SPACE" );
    }
    if( keys.keyDown( KeyEvent.VK_UP ) ) {
        System.out.println( "VK_UP" );
    }
    if( keys.keyDown( KeyEvent.VK_DOWN ) ) {
        System.out.println( "VK_DOWN" );
    }
    if( keys.keyDown( KeyEvent.VK_LEFT ) ) {
        System.out.println( "VK_LEFT" );
    }
    if( keys.keyDown( KeyEvent.VK_RIGHT ) ) {
        System.out.println( "VK_RIGHT" );
    }
    try {
        Thread.sleep( 10 );
    } catch( InterruptedException ex ) { }
}
```

HANDLING MOUSE INPUT

The `SimpleMouseInput` class, located in the `javagames.util` package, is very similar to the keyboard input class developed in the previous section. The mouse buttons are handled in the same way as the keyboard keys. The class implements the `MouseListener` interface that contains the following methods:

```
mouseClicked(MouseEvent e)
mouseEntered(MouseEvent e)
mouseExited(MouseEvent e)
mousePressed(MouseEvent e)
mouseReleased(MouseEvent e)
```

Two of the methods in this interface, `mouseEntered()` and `mouseExited()`, deal with mouse cursor movement. The other three are for the mouse buttons. Just like the keyboard listener, the pressed and released methods track the state of the mouse buttons, while the clicked method is ignored. To determine which mouse button was pressed, the mouse event contains the following method:

```
public int MouseEvent.getButton()
```

The value returned from this method maps to the following constants:

```
MouseEvent.NOBUTTON = 0
MouseEvent.BUTTON1 = 1
MouseEvent.BUTTON2 = 2
MouseEvent.BUTTON3 = 3
```

The button number starts at one instead of zero, which represents no button, and it is necessary to subtract one from the button number to reference the mouse button array. Other than this little difference, the mouse buttons are treated the same as the keyboard keys, including a `buttonDown()` and `buttonDownOnce()` method.

There are other mouse states available to the program, such as the position and state of the mouse pointer. Along with the `mouseEntered()` and `mouseExited()` methods from the `MouseListener` interface, the mouse input class also implements the `MouseMotionListener` interface.

```
mouseDragged(MouseEvent e)
mouseMoved(MouseEvent e)
```

All four of these methods—entered, exited, dragged, and moved—capture the position of the mouse while informing the program if the mouse is entering or leaving the component listening for mouse events. The following method gets the current position of the mouse:

```
public Point MouseEvent.getPoint()
```

When the mouse input is polled, this value is copied over and made available to the game loop. The current mouse position is available with the following method:

```
public Point SimpleMouseInput.getPosition()
```

Lastly, to monitor the input from the mouse scroll wheel, the input class implements the MouseWheelListener:

```
mouseWheelMoved(MouseEvent e)
```

The following method returns the clicks of the mouse wheel. If the number is negative, the wheel has been moved away from the user. If the value is positive, the wheel has been moved toward the user.

```
public int MouseWheelEvent.getWheelRotation()
```

This value is also saved in the poll() method, and is made available to the game loop from the following method:

```
public int SimpleMouseInput.getNotches()
```

The code for the SimpleMouseInput class is shown here:

```java
package javagames.util;

import java.awt.*;
import java.awt.event.*;


public class SimpleMouseInput
implements MouseListener, MouseMotionListener, MouseWheelListener {

    private static final int BUTTON_COUNT = 3;

    private Point mousePos;
    private Point currentPos;
    private boolean[] mouse;
    private int[] polled;
    private int notches;
    private int polledNotches;

    public SimpleMouseInput() {
        mousePos = new Point( 0, 0 );
        currentPos = new Point( 0, 0 );
        mouse = new boolean[ BUTTON_COUNT ];
        polled = new int[ BUTTON_COUNT ];
    }

    public synchronized void poll() {

        mousePos = new Point( currentPos );
```

```
        polledNotches = notches;
        notches = 0;

        for( int i = 0; i < mouse.length; ++i ) {
            if( mouse[i] ) {
                polled[i]++;
            } else {
                polled[i] = 0;
            }
        }
    }

    public Point getPosition() {
        return mousePos;
    }

    public int getNotches() {
        return polledNotches;
    }

    public boolean buttonDown( int button ) {
        return polled[ button - 1 ] > 0;
    }

    public boolean buttonDownOnce( int button ) {
        return polled[ button - 1 ] == 1;
    }

    public synchronized void mousePressed( MouseEvent e ) {
        int button = e.getButton() - 1;
        if( button >= 0 && button < mouse.length ) {
            mouse[ button ] = true;
        }
    }

    public synchronized void mouseReleased( MouseEvent e ) {
        int button = e.getButton() - 1;
        if( button >= 0 && button < mouse.length ) {
            mouse[ button ] = false;
        }
    }

    public void mouseClicked( MouseEvent e ) {
        // Not needed
    }

    public synchronized void mouseEntered( MouseEvent e ) {
        mouseMoved( e );
    }
```

```
public synchronized void mouseExited( MouseEvent e ) {
    mouseMoved( e );
}

public synchronized void mouseDragged( MouseEvent e ) {
    mouseMoved( e );
}

public synchronized void mouseMoved( MouseEvent e ) {
    currentPos = e.getPoint();
}

public synchronized void mouseWheelMoved( MouseWheelEvent e ) {
    notches += e.getWheelRotation();
}
}
```

The SimpleMouseExample, shown in Figure 2.2 and located in the javagames.input package, adds many new things to the first example. Using the active rendering example code as a starting point, and adding the keyboard and mouse input classes, this example shows not only all three types of mouse input, but also the first example of drawing to the screen with the Graphics object.

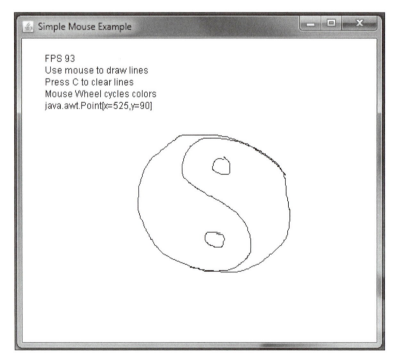

Figure 2.2
Simple Mouse Example.
© 2014 Timothy Wright.

The first thing to notice is the method calls when the GUI is created. These calls add KeyboardInput and SimpleMouseInput as listeners to the components. Note that although the keyboard is added to both the JFrame and the Canvas, the mouse is only added to the Canvas. When the application first starts up, it will not process keyboard events if they have not been added to the JFrame. Once the canvas object receives focus, it will receive keyboard input, but until it is selected the keyboard input is received only by the JFrame. In the game loop, the following method call has been added:

```
public void processInput()
```

Inside this method, both the keyboard and mouse are polled to make their data available. When the mouse button is first pressed, the drawing flag is set. For each frame that the left mouse button is down, a new point is added to the line's data structure. When the button is released, the flag is cleared, and a null object is added to the list, marking the end of the line. This way, the data structure can hold all the lines at the same time.

When the C key is pressed, the lines are cleared from the data structure. This lets the users start over if they are lacking artistic skills (like me)! There is also new code added to the render method. Besides displaying the frame rate, as well as directions for using the application, the current mouse position is displayed as a string.

The mouse scroll wheel is used to select a color index. The following code uses the modulus operator and the absolute value to keep the index a valid value no matter how large or small the index gets.

```
// SimpleMouseExample.java
colorIndex += mouse.getNotches();
Color color = COLORS[ Math.abs( colorIndex % COLORS.length ) ];
g.setColor( color );
```

The % operator will keep the value between (–3, 3). Because the modulus operation of a negative value is either zero or a negative value, the absolute value is used to keep the array index between (0, size –1).

Finally, the lines are drawn. Because null values are inserted into the data structure, code is added to make sure lines are drawn only if neither point is null.

```
package javagames.input;

import java.awt.*;
import java.awt.event.*;
import java.awt.image.*;
import java.util.*;
```

```java
import javagames.util.*;
import javax.swing.*;


public class SimpleMouseExample extends JFrame
            implements Runnable {

    private FrameRate frameRate;
    private BufferStrategy bs;
    private volatile boolean running;
    private Thread gameThread;

    private SimpleMouseInput mouse;
    private KeyboardInput keyboard;
    private ArrayList<Point> lines = new ArrayList<Point>();
    private boolean drawingLine;

    private Color[] COLORS = {
        Color.RED,
        Color.GREEN,
        Color.YELLOW,
        Color.BLUE
    };
    private int colorIndex;

    public SimpleMouseExample() {
        frameRate = new FrameRate();
    }

    protected void createAndShowGUI() {

        Canvas canvas = new Canvas();
        canvas.setSize( 640, 480 );
        canvas.setBackground( Color.BLACK );
        canvas.setIgnoreRepaint( true );
        getContentPane().add( canvas );
        setTitle( "Simple Mouse Example" );
        setIgnoreRepaint( true );
        pack();

        // Add key listeners
        keyboard = new KeyboardInput();
        canvas.addKeyListener( keyboard );

        // Add mouse listeners
        mouse = new SimpleMouseInput();
        canvas.addMouseListener( mouse );
        canvas.addMouseMotionListener( mouse );
```

```
        canvas.addMouseWheelListener( mouse );

        setVisible( true );
        canvas.createBufferStrategy( 2 );
        bs = canvas.getBufferStrategy();
        canvas.requestFocus();

        gameThread = new Thread( this );
        gameThread.start();
    }

    public void run() {
        running = true;
        frameRate.initialize();
        while( running ) {
            gameLoop();
        }
    }

    private void gameLoop() {
        processInput();
        renderFrame();
        sleep( 10L );
    }

    private void renderFrame() {
        do {
            do {
                Graphics g = null;
                try {
                    g = bs.getDrawGraphics();
                    g.clearRect( 0, 0, getWidth(), getHeight() );
                    render( g );
                } finally {
                    if( g != null ) {
                        g.dispose();
                    }
                }
            } while( bs.contentsRestored() );
            bs.show();
        } while( bs.contentsLost() );
    }

    private void sleep( long sleep ) {
        try {
            Thread.sleep( sleep );
        } catch( InterruptedException ex ) { }
    }
```

```
private void processInput() {

    keyboard.poll();
    mouse.poll();

    if( keyboard.keyDownOnce( KeyEvent.VK_SPACE ) ) {
        System.out.println("VK_SPACE");
    }
    // if button is pressed for first time,
    // start drawing lines
    if( mouse.buttonDownOnce( MouseEvent.BUTTON1 ) ) {
        drawingLine = true;
    }
    // if the button is down, add line point
    if( mouse.buttonDown( MouseEvent.BUTTON1 ) ) {
        lines.add( mouse.getPosition() );
        // if the button is not down but we were drawing,
        // add a null to break up the lines
    } else if( drawingLine ) {
        lines.add( null );
        drawingLine = false;
    }
    // if 'C' is down, clear the lines
    if( keyboard.keyDownOnce( KeyEvent.VK_C ) ) {
        lines.clear();
    }

}

private void render( Graphics g ) {

    colorIndex += mouse.getNotches();
    Color color = COLORS[ Math.abs( colorIndex % COLORS.length ) ];
    g.setColor( color );

    frameRate.calculate();
    g.drawString( frameRate.getFrameRate(), 30, 30 );
    g.drawString( "Use mouse to draw lines", 30, 45 );
    g.drawString( "Press C to clear lines", 30, 60 );
    g.drawString( "Mouse Wheel cycles colors", 30, 75 );
    g.drawString( mouse.getPosition().toString(), 30, 90 );

    for( int i = 0; i < lines.size() - 1; ++i ) {
        Point p1 = lines.get( i );
        Point p2 = lines.get( i + 1 );
        // Adding a null into the list is used
        // for breaking up the lines when
```

```
            // there are two or more lines
            // that are not connected
            if( !( p1 == null || p2 == null ) )
                g.drawLine( p1.x, p1.y, p2.x, p2.y );
        }
    }

    protected void onWindowClosing() {
        try {
            running = false;
            gameThread.join();
        } catch( InterruptedException e ) {
            e.printStackTrace();
        }
        System.exit( 0 );
    }

    public static void main( String[] args ) {
        final SimpleMouseExample app = new SimpleMouseExample();
        app.addWindowListener( new WindowAdapter() {
            public void windowClosing( WindowEvent e ) {
                app.onWindowClosing();
            }
        });
        SwingUtilities.invokeLater( new Runnable() {
            public void run() {
                app.createAndShowGUI();
            }
        });
    }

}
```

RELATIVE MOUSE MOVEMENT

There is one problem with the current mouse input class shown in Figure 2.3. At first it may seem obvious, but the program only receives mouse events when the mouse is in the window. Once the mouse leaves the window, the coordinates where the mouse pointer is are no longer valid in the application. To make this worse, when in full-screen mode, the mouse simply stops when it reaches the edge of the screen and doesn't continue registering events. Depending on the needs of the application, relative mouse movement may be needed. Fortunately, it isn't hard to update the mouse input class to support relative mouse movement.

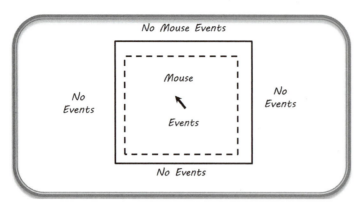

Figure 2.3
Window-Only Mouse Events.
© 2014 Timothy Wright.

The `RelativeMouseInput` class, located in the `javagames.util` package, builds on the class from the previous example and adds relative mouse movement. To accomplish this, the `Robot` class is used to keep the mouse in the center of the window. The Swing component that listens for mouse events is included to calculate the center of the window and convert from relative window coordinates to absolute screen coordinates. If the mouse cursor is always in the center of the window, then it can never leave, and the window will always receive mouse events. The following code centers the mouse:

```
// RelativeMouseInput.java
private Point getComponentCenter() {
    int w = component.getWidth();
    int h = component.getHeight();
    return new Point( w / 2, h / 2 );
}

private void centerMouse() {
    if( robot != null && component.isShowing() ) {
        Point center = getComponentCenter();
        SwingUtilities.convertPointToScreen( center, component );
        robot.mouseMove( center.x, center.y );
    }
}
```

The center of the window is computed at runtime so even if the window is resized, the mouse will stay in the center. The relative center point must be converted to absolute screen coordinates. The upper-left pixel in a window is (0,0) no matter where the window is located on the desktop. If moving the window around the desktop changed the value of the upper-left pixel, graphics programming would be very difficult. Although it makes drawing easier by using relative pixel values, positioning the mouse to the relative center of the window does not take into account the location of the window and could place the mouse cursor so far away from the window that it would stop receiving mouse events. Converting to screen coordinates using the SwingUtilities class solves this problem.

It is important to realize that re-centering the mouse works because when the mouse's new position and the current position are the same, asking the Robot class to reposition the mouse to the same location does not generate new mouse events. If this behavior ever changes, the relative mouse class will always generate mouse events, even when the mouse isn't moving. Checking if the current and new positions are different before requesting a re-center would solve this problem if the mouse behavior ever changes in the future.

A flag is added to the RelativeMouseInput class to allow both relative and absolute mouse movement. It is possible that a game will need both absolute and relative mouse modes at some point, so the class allows switching this at runtime. New code has been added to the mouseMoved() method. If in relative mode, the distance is computed as the difference from the center and then the mouse cursor is re-centered. Because the mouse coordinates and component coordinates are both relative values, there is no need to convert these values. Finally, during the poll method, the mouse position can be either relative or absolute. The delta variables are reset inside the poll method along with all the other variables.

```
package javagames.util;

import java.awt.*;
import java.awt.event.*;
import javax.swing.*;


public class RelativeMouseInput
implements MouseListener, MouseMotionListener, MouseWheelListener {

    private static final int BUTTON_COUNT = 3;

    private Point mousePos;
    private Point currentPos;
    private boolean[] mouse;
    private int[] polled;
    private int notches;
    private int polledNotches;

    private int dx, dy;
    private Robot robot;
    private Component component;
    private boolean relative;
```

```java
public RelativeMouseInput( Component component ) {
    this.component = component;
    try {
        robot = new Robot();
    } catch( Exception e ) {
        // Handle exception [game specific]
        e.printStackTrace();
    }

    mousePos = new Point( 0, 0 );
    currentPos = new Point( 0, 0 );
    mouse = new boolean[ BUTTON_COUNT ];
    polled = new int[ BUTTON_COUNT ];
}

public synchronized void poll() {
    if( isRelative() ) {
        mousePos = new Point( dx, dy );
    } else {
        mousePos = new Point( currentPos );
    }
    dx = dy = 0;

    polledNotches = notches;
    notches = 0;

    for( int i = 0; i < mouse.length; ++i ) {
        if( mouse[i] ) {
            polled[i]++;
        } else {
            polled[i] = 0;
        }
    }
}

public boolean isRelative() {
    return relative;
}

public void setRelative( boolean relative ) {
    this.relative = relative;
    if( relative ) {
        centerMouse();
    }
}

public Point getPosition() {
    return mousePos;
}
```

```
public int getNotches() {
    return polledNotches;
}

public boolean buttonDown( int button ) {
    return polled[ button - 1 ] > 0;
}
public boolean buttonDownOnce( int button ) {
    return polled[ button - 1 ] == 1;
}

public synchronized void mousePressed( MouseEvent e ) {
    int button = e.getButton() - 1;
    if( button >= 0 && button < mouse.length ) {
        mouse[ button ] = true;
    }
}

public synchronized void mouseReleased( MouseEvent e ) {
    int button = e.getButton() - 1;
    if( button >= 0 && button < mouse.length ) {
        mouse[ button ] = false;
    }
}

public void mouseClicked( MouseEvent e ) {
    // Not needed
}


public synchronized void mouseEntered( MouseEvent e ) {
    mouseMoved( e );
}
public synchronized void mouseExited( MouseEvent e ) {
    mouseMoved( e );
}

public synchronized void mouseDragged( MouseEvent e ) {
    mouseMoved( e );
}

public synchronized void mouseMoved( MouseEvent e ) {
    if( isRelative() ) {
        Point p = e.getPoint();
        Point center = getComponentCenter();
        dx += p.x - center.x;
        dy += p.y - center.y;
        centerMouse();
    } else {
```

```
            currentPos = e.getPoint();
        }
    }

    public synchronized void mouseWheelMoved( MouseWheelEvent e ) {
        notches += e.getWheelRotation();
    }
    private Point getComponentCenter() {
        int w = component.getWidth();
        int h = component.getHeight();
        return new Point( w / 2, h / 2 );
    }

    private void centerMouse() {
        if( robot != null && component.isShowing() ) {
            Point center = getComponentCenter();
            SwingUtilities.convertPointToScreen( center, component );
            robot.mouseMove( center.x, center.y );
        }
    }

}
```

The `RelativeMouseExample`, located in the `javagames.input` package and shown in Figure 2.4, tests the new functionality of the updates to the mouse input class.

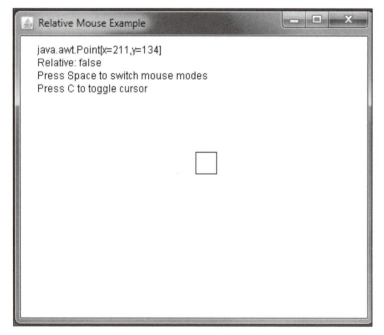

Figure 2.4
Relative Mouse Example.
© 2014 Timothy Wright.

The following code is used to disable the mouse cursor by setting the cursor image to an empty cursor created at runtime.

```java
// RelativeMouseExample .java
private void disableCursor() {
    Toolkit tk = Toolkit.getDefaultToolkit();
    Image image = tk.createImage( "" );
    Point point = new Point( 0, 0 );
    String name = "CanBeAnything";
    Cursor cursor = tk.createCustomCursor( image, point, name );
    setCursor( cursor );
}
```

The render() method of this example displays the help text, calculates the frame rate, and draws the rectangle on the screen. Inside the processInput() method, the spacebar toggles the mouse mode from absolute to relative. The C key is used to show or hide the mouse cursor. When the current mouse position is used to update the square position, the relative values are added to the position, while the absolute values replace the previous values. The code ensures that the square never leaves the screen, wrapping its location if it goes too far in either direction.

```java
package javagames.input;

import java.awt.*;
import java.awt.event.*;
import java.awt.image.*;
import javagames.util.*;
import javax.swing.*;


public class RelativeMouseExample extends JFrame
            implements Runnable {

    private FrameRate frameRate;
    private BufferStrategy bs;
    private volatile boolean running;
    private Thread gameThread;
    private Canvas canvas;
    private RelativeMouseInput mouse;
    private KeyboardInput keyboard;
    private Point point = new Point( 0, 0 );
    private boolean disableCursor = false;

    public RelativeMouseExample() {
        frameRate = new FrameRate();
    }
```

```java
protected void createAndShowGUI() {

    canvas = new Canvas();
    canvas.setSize( 640, 480 );
    canvas.setBackground( Color.BLACK );
    canvas.setIgnoreRepaint( true );
    getContentPane().add( canvas );
    setTitle( "Relative Mouse Example" );
    setIgnoreRepaint( true );
    pack();

    // Add key listeners
    keyboard = new KeyboardInput();
    canvas.addKeyListener( keyboard );

    // Add mouse listeners
    // For full screen : mouse = new RelativeMouseInput( this );
    mouse = new RelativeMouseInput( canvas );
    canvas.addMouseListener( mouse );
    canvas.addMouseMotionListener( mouse );
    canvas.addMouseWheelListener( mouse );

    setVisible( true );
    canvas.createBufferStrategy( 2 );
    bs = canvas.getBufferStrategy();
    canvas.requestFocus();

    gameThread = new Thread( this );
    gameThread.start();
}

public void run() {
    running = true;
    frameRate.initialize();
    while( running ) {
        gameLoop();
    }
}

private void gameLoop() {
    processInput();
    renderFrame();
    sleep( 10L );
}

private void renderFrame() {
    do {
        do {
            Graphics g = null;
```

```
            try {
                g = bs.getDrawGraphics();
                g.clearRect( 0, 0, getWidth(), getHeight() );
                render( g );
            } finally {
                if( g != null ) {
                    g.dispose();
                }
            }
        } while( bs.contentsRestored() );
        bs.show();
    } while( bs.contentsLost() );
}

private void sleep( long sleep ) {
    try {
        Thread.sleep( sleep );
    } catch( InterruptedException ex ) { }
}

private void processInput() {
    keyboard.poll();
    mouse.poll();

    Point p = mouse.getPosition();
    if( mouse.isRelative() ) {
        point.x += p.x;
        point.y += p.y;
    } else {
        point.x = p.x;
        point.y = p.y;
    }

    // Wrap rectangle around the screen
    if( point.x + 25 < 0 )
        point.x = canvas.getWidth() - 1;
    else if( point.x > canvas.getWidth() - 1 )
        point.x = -25;
    if( point.y + 25 < 0 )
        point.y = canvas.getHeight() - 1;
    else if( point.y > canvas.getHeight() - 1 )
        point.y = -25;

    // Toggle relative
    if( keyboard.keyDownOnce( KeyEvent.VK_SPACE ) ) {
        mouse.setRelative( !mouse.isRelative() );
    }
```

```
      // Toggle cursor
      if( keyboard.keyDownOnce( KeyEvent.VK_C ) ) {
         disableCursor = !disableCursor;
         if( disableCursor ) {
            disableCursor();
         } else {
            // setCoursor( Cursor.DEFAULT_CURSOR ) is deprecated
            setCursor( new Cursor( Cursor.DEFAULT_CURSOR ) );
         }
      }
   }

   private void render( Graphics g ) {

      g.setColor( Color.GREEN );
      frameRate.calculate();
      g.drawString( mouse.getPosition().toString(), 20, 20 );
      g.drawString( "Relative: " + mouse.isRelative(), 20, 35 );
      g.drawString( "Press Space to switch mouse modes", 20, 50 );
      g.drawString( "Press C to toggle cursor", 20, 65 );

      g.setColor( Color.WHITE );
      g.drawRect( point.x, point.y, 25, 25 );
   }

   private void disableCursor() {
      Toolkit tk = Toolkit.getDefaultToolkit();
      Image image = tk.createImage( "" );
      Point point = new Point( 0, 0 );
      String name = "CanBeAnything";
      Cursor cursor = tk.createCustomCursor( image, point, name );
      setCursor( cursor );
   }

   protected void onWindowClosing() {
      try {
         running = false;
         gameThread.join();
      } catch( InterruptedException e ) {
         e.printStackTrace();
      }
      System.exit( 0 );
   }

   public static void main( String[] args ) {
      final RelativeMouseExample app = new RelativeMouseExample();
      app.addWindowListener( new WindowAdapter() {
         public void windowClosing( WindowEvent e ) {
```

```
            app.onWindowClosing();
        }
    });
    SwingUtilities.invokeLater( new Runnable() {
        public void run() {
            app.createAndShowGUI();
        }
    });
  }
}
```

RESOURCES AND FURTHER READING

"How to Write a Key Listener," 1995, http://docs.oracle.com/javase/tutorial/uiswing/events/keylistener.html.

"How to Write a Mouse Listener," 1995, http://docs.oracle.com/javase/tutorial/uiswing/events/mouselistener.html.

"How to Write a Mouse-Motion Listener," 1995, http://docs.oracle.com/javase/tutorial/uiswing/events/mousemotionlistener.html.

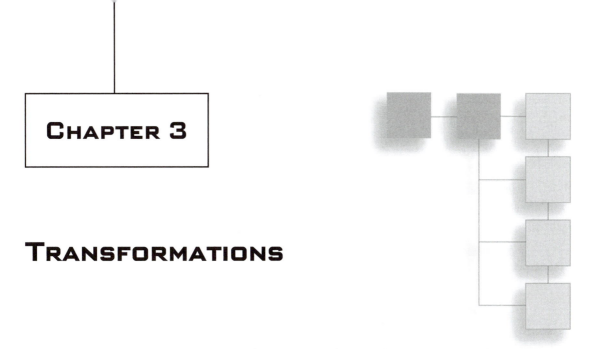

CHAPTER 3

TRANSFORMATIONS

There are four different operations that you can do to a shape in 2D graphics. They are shown in Figure 3.1.

- Translation—Moving an object up, down, left, or right.
- Rotation—Spinning an object around a point.
- Scaling—Growing or shrinking an object.
- Shearing—Shifting an object in one or two directions.

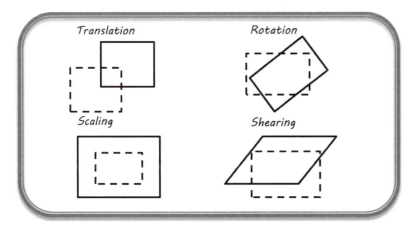

Figure 3.1
Translation, Rotation, Scaling, and Shearing.
© 2014 Timothy Wright.

Each of these operations can be performed in different ways. They can be done by hand, to each coordinate in an object, or they can be concatenated into a matrix and then applied all at once. Each method has advantages and disadvantages, but for learning how these transformations are applied, calculating each coordinate by hand is best.

USING THE VECTOR2F CLASS

The Vector2f class, located in the javagames.util package, is used to represent a location in space, as well as a direction. Notice that the 2D coordinate class has three values: x, y, and w. In order to use the matrix transformations to perform translation, there needs to be an extra coordinate value to get the matrix math to work. So pay no attention to the extra "w" coordinate behind the curtain, it will be explained later.

Note

> Those of you familiar with vector algebra may look at the source code that follows and scream, "Wait! Points and vectors are not the same. Points have a w = 1, but vectors cannot be translated, and should have a w = 0." I will cover that later too, so don't worry. :-)

Translation is very simple. To move the coordinate up, down, left, or right, the distance is added to the coordinate:

```
x = x + tx;
y = y + ty;
```

Scaling is also simple. The coordinate values are multiplied by the scale factor, growing or shrinking them.

```
x = x * sx;
y = y * sy;
```

Shearing is only a little more complicated, shifting values relative to the other coordinate values. Notice the temporary value that's used to keep the old value of x until after it is used to shear the y value. Without the temporary value, the updated values would be used to shear the y value instead of the original values. To shear the values, add to the x value the scaled y value, and to the y value add the scaled x value:

```
float tmp = x + sx * y;
y = y + sy * x;
x = tmp;
```

Rotation is more complicated to understand. Using a temporary value just like the shearing example, rotation is performed as follows:

```
float tmp = x * cos(angle) - y * sin(angle);
y = x * sin(angle) + y * cos(angle);
x = tmp;
```

In order to understand where this equation comes from, it is necessary to understand polar coordinates, which are covered later in this chapter. For now, just assume that it works.

```
package javagames.util;


public class Vector2f {
    public float x;
    public float y;
    public float w;
    public Vector2f() {
        this.x = 0.0f;
        this.y = 0.0f;
        this.w = 1.0f; //!?!
    }
    public Vector2f( Vector2f v ) {
        this.x = v.x;
        this.y = v.y;
        this.w = v.w; //!?!
    }
    public Vector2f( float x, float y ) {
        this.x = x;
        this.y = y;
        this.w = 1.0f; //!?!
    }
    public Vector2f( float x, float y, float w ) {
        this.x = x;
        this.y = y;
        this.w = w; //!?!
    }
    public void translate( float tx, float ty ) {
        x += tx;
        y += ty;
    }
```

```
public void scale( float sx, float sy ) {
    x *= sx;
    y *= sy;
}

public void rotate( float rad ) {
    float tmp = (float)( x * Math.cos( rad ) - y * Math.sin( rad ) );
    y = (float)( x * Math.sin( rad ) + y * Math.cos( rad ) );
    x = tmp;
}

public void shear( float sx, float sy ) {
    float tmp = x + sx * y;
    y = y + sy * x;
    x = tmp;
}

}
```

The VectorGraphicsExample, located in the javagames.transform package and shown in Figure 3.2, draws a polygon ship on the screen and applies translation, rotation, scaling, and shearing using the Vector2f class equations. The initialize() method sets up the polygon ship and calls reset(). The reset() method is responsible for setting all the transformation values back to their starting values.

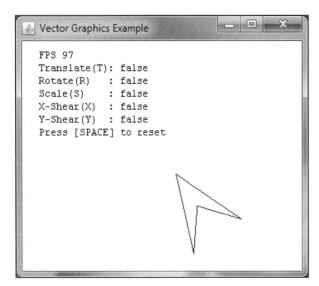

Figure 3.2
Vector Graphics Example.
© 2014 Timothy Wright.

There are keys mapped to the different transformation operations. R for rotation, S for shearing, T for translation, X for x-shearing, Y for y-shearing, and the spacebar to reset the values back to their starting values.

The polygon object is copied into the world list before being transformed. This way, the operations are not cumulative, but happen every frame. Not only does this leave the original model untouched, it allows multiple copies of the original to be used.

Each transformation operation is handled in the same way. First the Boolean value mapped to the specific transformation is checked. If it is true, then that transformation is applied, the bounds are checked, and the step values are adjusted accordingly. After the values are updated, the transformations are applied. Notice that the order of the transformations is important. Changing the order of the operations would change the results on the screen.

Inside the render() method, all the values of the translation flags are displayed. The transformed polygon is then drawn using the drawLine() method of the graphics object. The last point and first point are connected, and then each point is used to draw a line from that point to the previous point, producing a closed polygon.

```java
package javagames.transform;

import java.awt.*;
import java.awt.event.*;
import java.awt.image.*;
import javagames.util.*;
import javax.swing.*;


public class VectorGraphicsExample extends JFrame
            implements Runnable {
    private static final int SCREEN_W = 640;
    private static final int SCREEN_H = 480;

    private FrameRate frameRate;
    private BufferStrategy bs;
    private volatile boolean running;
    private Thread gameThread;
    private RelativeMouseInput mouse;
    private KeyboardInput keyboard;
    private Vector2f[] polygon;
    private Vector2f[] world;
```

```
    private float tx, ty;
    private float vx, vy;
    private float rot, rotStep;
    private float scale, scaleStep;
    private float sx, sxStep;
    private float sy, syStep;
    private boolean doTranslate;
    private boolean doScale;
    private boolean doRotate;
    private boolean doXShear;
    private boolean doYShear;

    public VectorGraphicsExample() {

    }

    protected void createAndShowGUI() {

        Canvas canvas = new Canvas();
        canvas.setSize( 640, 480 );
        canvas.setBackground( Color.BLACK );
        canvas.setIgnoreRepaint( true );
        getContentPane().add( canvas );
        setTitle( "Vector Graphics Example" );
        setIgnoreRepaint( true );
        pack();

        // Add key listeners
        keyboard = new KeyboardInput();
        canvas.addKeyListener( keyboard );

        // Add mouse listeners
        // For full screen : mouse = new RelativeMouseInput( this );
        mouse = new RelativeMouseInput( canvas );
        canvas.addMouseListener( mouse );
        canvas.addMouseMotionListener( mouse );
        canvas.addMouseWheelListener( mouse );

        setVisible( true );
        canvas.createBufferStrategy( 2 );
        bs = canvas.getBufferStrategy();
        canvas.requestFocus();

        gameThread = new Thread( this );
        gameThread.start();
    }
```

```java
public void run() {
    running = true;
    initialize();
    while( running ) {
        gameLoop();
    }
}

private void gameLoop() {
    processInput();
    processObjects();
    renderFrame();
    sleep( 10L );
}

private void renderFrame() {
    do {
        do {
            Graphics g = null;
            try {
                g = bs.getDrawGraphics();
                g.clearRect( 0, 0, getWidth(), getHeight() );
                render( g );
            } finally {
                if( g != null ) {
                    g.dispose();
                }
            }
        } while( bs.contentsRestored() );
        bs.show();
    } while( bs.contentsLost() );
}

private void sleep( long sleep ) {
    try {
        Thread.sleep( sleep );
    } catch( InterruptedException ex ) { }
}

private void initialize() {
    frameRate = new FrameRate();
    frameRate.initialize();
    polygon = new Vector2f[] {
        new Vector2f( 10, 0 ),
        new Vector2f(-10, 8 ),
        new Vector2f(  0, 0 ),
```

```
            new Vector2f( -10, -8 ),
        };
        world = new Vector2f[ polygon.length ];
        reset();
    }

    private void reset() {
        tx = SCREEN_W / 2;
        ty = SCREEN_H / 2;
        vx = vy = 2;
        rot = 0.0f;
        rotStep = (float)Math.toRadians( 1.0 );
        scale = 1.0f;
        scaleStep = 0.1f;
        sx = sy = 0.0f;
        sxStep = syStep = 0.01f;
        doRotate = doScale = doTranslate = false;
        doXShear = doYShear = false;
    }

    private void processInput() {
        keyboard.poll();
        mouse.poll();

        if( keyboard.keyDownOnce( KeyEvent.VK_R ) ) {
            doRotate = !doRotate;
        }
        if( keyboard.keyDownOnce( KeyEvent.VK_S ) ) {
            doScale = !doScale;
        }
        if( keyboard.keyDownOnce( KeyEvent.VK_T ) ) {
            doTranslate = !doTranslate;
        }
        if( keyboard.keyDownOnce( KeyEvent.VK_X ) ) {
            doXShear = !doXShear;
        }
        if( keyboard.keyDownOnce( KeyEvent.VK_Y ) ) {
            doYShear = !doYShear;
        }
        if( keyboard.keyDownOnce( KeyEvent.VK_SPACE ) ) {
            reset();
        }

    }
```

```java
private void processObjects() {
    // copy data...
    for( int i = 0; i < polygon.length; ++i ) {
        world[i] = new Vector2f( polygon[i] );
    }

    if( doScale ) {
        scale += scaleStep;
        if( scale < 1.0 || scale > 5.0 ) {
            scaleStep = -scaleStep;
        }
    }

    if( doRotate ) {
        rot += rotStep;
        if( rot < 0.0f || rot > 2*Math.PI ) {
            rotStep = -rotStep;
        }
    }

    if( doTranslate ) {
        tx += vx;
        if( tx < 0 || tx > SCREEN_W ) {
            vx = -vx;
        }
        ty += vy;
        if( ty < 0 || ty > SCREEN_H ) {
            vy = -vy;
        }
    }

    if( doXShear ) {
        sx += sxStep;
        if( Math.abs( sx ) > 2.0 ) {
            sxStep = -sxStep;
        }
    }

    if( doYShear ) {
        sy += syStep;
        if( Math.abs( sy ) > 2.0 ) {
            syStep = -syStep;
        }
    }

    for( int i = 0; i < world.length; ++i ) {
        world[i].shear( sx, sy );
```

```
            world[i].scale( scale, scale );
            world[i].rotate( rot );
            world[i].translate( tx, ty );
        }
    }

    private void render( Graphics g ) {

        g.setFont( new Font( "Courier New", Font.PLAIN, 12 ) );
        g.setColor( Color.GREEN );
        frameRate.calculate();
        g.drawString( frameRate.getFrameRate(), 20, 20 );
        g.drawString( "Translate(T): " + doTranslate, 20, 35 );
        g.drawString( "Rotate(R)    : " + doRotate, 20, 50 );
        g.drawString( "Scale(S)     : " + doScale, 20, 65 );
        g.drawString( "X-Shear(X)   : " + doXShear, 20, 80 );
        g.drawString( "Y-Shear(Y)   : " + doYShear, 20, 95 );
        g.drawString( "Press [SPACE] to reset", 20, 110 );

        Vector2f S = world[ world.length - 1 ];
        Vector2f P = null;
        for( int i = 0; i < world.length; ++i ) {
            P = world[i];
            g.drawLine( (int)S.x, (int)S.y, (int)P.x, (int)P.y );
            S = P;
        }
    }

    protected void onWindowClosing() {
        try {
            running = false;
            gameThread.join();
        } catch( InterruptedException e ) {
            e.printStackTrace();
        }
        System.exit( 0 );
    }

    public static void main( String[] args ) {
        final VectorGraphicsExample app = new VectorGraphicsExample();
        app.addWindowListener( new WindowAdapter() {
            public void windowClosing( WindowEvent e ) {
                app.onWindowClosing();
            }
        });
```

```
SwingUtilities.invokeLater( new Runnable() {
    public void run() {
        app.createAndShowGUI();
    }
});
    }
}
```

USING POLAR COORDINATES

Cartesian coordinates are represented as a pair of (*x,y*) values. Polar coordinates are represented as an angle and a distance. See Figure 3.3.

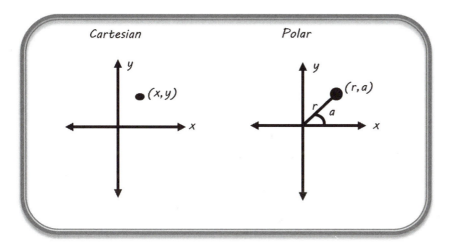

Figure 3.3
Cartesian vs. Polar Coordinates.
© 2014 Timothy Wright.

Instead of an (*x,y*) pair, polar coordinates are in the form (*r,a*), where r is a distance (radius), and a is an angle. Because Java's trigonometric functions use radians, all angles are assumed to be in radians. It is easy to convert between the two representations, however:

```
Math.toRadians( double degrees )
Math.toDegrees( double radians )
```

To convert from the Cartesian coordinates to the polar coordinates, the point can be treated as a triangle, using trigonometry to solve for the desired values.

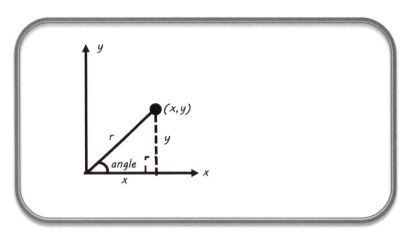

Figure 3.4
Cartesian to Polar Conversion.
© 2014 Timothy Wright.

The distance, as seen in Figure 3.4, can be seen as the hypotenuse of the triangle, and can be found using the Pythagorean theorem:

$$r^2 = a^2 + b^2$$
$$r = \sqrt{a^2 + b^2}$$

The angle can be found using the tangent function:

$$\theta = \tan \frac{y}{x}$$

Converting back from the polar coordinate to the (x,y) pair is also easy:

$$x = r \cos \theta$$
$$y = r \sin \theta$$

It is the previous definition that can be used to derive the rotation equation shown earlier. Rotating from the starting angle some number of radians is the same as adding the desired additional rotation angle to the starting angle. In other words, to rotate a point some number of radians, the equation can be expressed as follows:

$$x' = r \cos(\theta + \varphi)$$
$$y' = r \sin(\theta + \varphi)$$

Trigonometry to the rescue:

$$\sin(\theta + \varphi) = \sin\theta\cos\varphi + \cos\theta\sin\varphi$$
$$\cos(\theta + \varphi) = \cos\theta\cos\varphi - \sin\theta\sin\varphi$$

Replacing the previous equation with this new representation gives:

$$x' = r(\cos\theta\cos\varphi - \sin\theta\sin\varphi)$$
$$y' = r(\sin\theta\cos\varphi + \cos\theta\sin\varphi)$$

Distributing the r values gives:

$$x' = r\cos\theta\cos\varphi - r\sin\theta\sin\varphi$$
$$y' = r\sin\theta\cos\varphi + r\cos\theta\sin\varphi$$

Remembering the following:

$$x = r\cos\theta$$
$$y = r\sin\theta$$

You can substitute the original x and y values, leaving the following:

$$x' = x\cos\varphi - y\sin\varphi$$
$$y' = y\cos\varphi - x\sin\varphi$$

This is the equation presented earlier for rotation of a coordinate in the Vector2f class.

The PolarCoordinateExample, located in the javagames.transform package and shown in Figure 3.5, converts from a Cartesian coordinate to a polar coordinate and back again. The coord variable holds the screen position where the mouse is located, offset by the center of the screen.

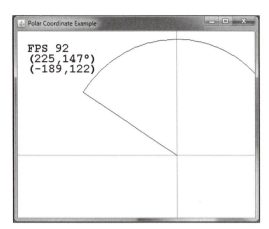

Figure 3.5
Polar Coordinate Example.
© 2014 Timothy Wright.

The conversion happens in the `render()` method. The (*cx,cy*) coordinate represents the center of the screen and the (*px,py*) coordinate offsets the current mouse position from the center of the screen. Because the `y` value is positive in the down direction for screen coordinates, the `py` variable is calculated differently.

```
int px = coord.x - cx;
int py = cy - coord.y;
```

The conversion from the (*px,py*) values to the polar coordinates is stored in the `r` variable for the distance and the `rad` variable for the angle in radians. Because the `Math.atan2()` method returns the angle from (−180, 180), the degrees are adjusted to (0, 360).

```
if( degrees < 0 ) {
    degrees = 360 - degrees;
}
```

The (*sx,sy*) variables hold the conversion from the polar coordinates back to the Cartesian coordinates.

```
double sx = r * Math.cos(rad);
double sy = r * Math.sin(rad);
```

The various values are displayed on the screen so that the converted values can be checked. The starting values and converted values should be the same.

Finally, the curve is displayed using the `drawArc()` method from the graphics object. This method takes the upper-left point, the width and height of the rectangle bounding the arc, and both the starting and ending angles in degrees, not in radians.

Tip

Make sure to convert the radians to degrees before using the drawArc() method.

```java
package javagames.transform;

import java.awt.*;
import java.awt.event.*;
import java.awt.image.*;
import javagames.util.*;
import javax.swing.*;


public class PolarCoordinateExample extends JFrame
            implements Runnable {

    private static final int SCREEN_W = 640;
    private static final int SCREEN_H = 480;

    private FrameRate frameRate;
    private BufferStrategy bs;
    private volatile boolean running;
    private Thread gameThread;
    private RelativeMouseInput mouse;
    private KeyboardInput keyboard;

    private Point coord;

    public PolarCoordinateExample() {

    }

    protected void createAndShowGUI() {

        Canvas canvas = new Canvas();
        canvas.setSize( SCREEN_W, SCREEN_H );
        canvas.setBackground( Color.BLACK );
        canvas.setIgnoreRepaint( true );
        getContentPane().add( canvas );
        setTitle( "Polar Coordinate Example" );
        setIgnoreRepaint( true );
        pack();

        // Add key listeners
        keyboard = new KeyboardInput();
        canvas.addKeyListener( keyboard );

        // Add mouse listeners
        // For full screen : mouse = new RelativeMouseInput( this );
        mouse = new RelativeMouseInput( canvas );
        canvas.addMouseListener( mouse );
```

```java
        canvas.addMouseMotionListener( mouse );
        canvas.addMouseWheelListener( mouse );

        setVisible( true );
        canvas.createBufferStrategy( 2 );
        bs = canvas.getBufferStrategy();
        canvas.requestFocus();

        gameThread = new Thread( this );
        gameThread.start();
    }

    public void run() {
        running = true;
        initialize();
        while( running ) {
            gameLoop();
        }
    }

    private void gameLoop() {
        processInput();
        renderFrame();
        sleep( 10L );
    }

    private void renderFrame() {
        do {
            do {
                Graphics g = null;
                try {
                    g = bs.getDrawGraphics();
                    g.clearRect( 0, 0, getWidth(), getHeight() );
                    render( g );
                } finally {
                    if( g != null ) {
                        g.dispose();
                    }
                }
            } while( bs.contentsRestored() );
            bs.show();
        } while( bs.contentsLost() );
    }

    private void sleep( long sleep ) {
        try {
            Thread.sleep( sleep );
        } catch( InterruptedException ex ) { }
    }
```

```java
private void initialize() {
    frameRate = new FrameRate();
    frameRate.initialize();

    coord = new Point();
}

private void processInput() {
    keyboard.poll();
    mouse.poll();

    coord = mouse.getPosition();
}

private void render( Graphics g ) {
    g.setFont( new Font( "Courier New", Font.BOLD, 24 ) );
    g.setColor( Color.GREEN );
    frameRate.calculate();
    g.drawString( frameRate.getFrameRate(), 20, 40 );

    int cx = SCREEN_W / 2;
    int cy = SCREEN_H / 2;
    g.setColor( Color.GRAY );
    g.drawLine( 0, cy, SCREEN_W, cy );
    g.drawLine( cx, 0, cx, SCREEN_H );

    g.setColor( Color.GREEN );
    g.drawLine( cx, cy, coord.x, coord.y );

    int px = coord.x - cx;
    int py = cy - coord.y;
    double r = Math.sqrt( px*px + py*py );
    double rad = Math.atan2( py, px );
    double degrees = Math.toDegrees( rad );
    if( degrees < 0 ) {
        degrees = 360 + degrees;
    }
    double sx = r * Math.cos( rad );
    double sy = r * Math.sin( rad );
    String polar = String.format( "(%.0f,%.0f\u00b0)", r, degrees );
    g.drawString( polar, 20, 60 );
    String cart = String.format( "(%.0f,%.0f)", sx, sy );
    g.drawString( cart, 20, 80 );

    g.setColor( Color.WHITE );
    g.drawString( String.format( "(%s,%s)", px, py ), coord.x, coord.y );

    g.setColor( Color.BLUE );
```

```
      g.drawArc(
        (int)(cx - r),(int)(cy - r),
        (int)(2*r), (int)(2*r), 0, (int)degrees
      );
    }

    protected void onWindowClosing() {
      try {
        running = false;
        gameThread.join();
      } catch( InterruptedException e ) {
        e.printStackTrace();
      }
      System.exit( 0 );
    }

    public static void main( String[] args ) {
      final PolarCoordinateExample app = new PolarCoordinateExample();
      app.addWindowListener( new WindowAdapter() {
        public void windowClosing( WindowEvent e ) {
          app.onWindowClosing();
        }
      });
      SwingUtilities.invokeLater( new Runnable() {
        public void run() {
          app.createAndShowGUI();
        }
      });
    }

}
```

UNDERSTANDING POINTS AND VECTORS

As shown in Figure 3.6, the differences between points and vectors can be confusing. A point in 2D space is represented as an (x,y) pair. A vector can be represented as two coordinate pairs: an (x,y) coordinate for the start of the vector and another one for the end. However, the first coordinate is often implied as $(0,0)$ and is left out of the representation in the code.

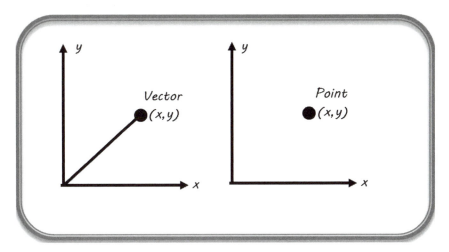

Figure 3.6
Point and Vector Similarities.
© 2014 Timothy Wright.

Note

Because the vector and point can be represented the same way, it can be difficult to understand the difference. Add to that a lazy programmer (like me) who just uses a `vector` class for both vectors and points and it gets even more confusing.

It can help to think about a point as a city and a vector as driving directions.

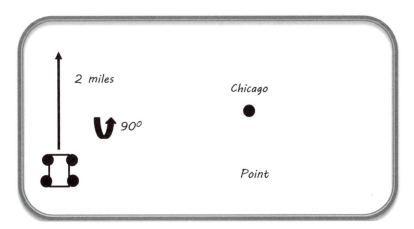

Figure 3.7
Driving Directions, Locations, Vectors, and Points.
© 2014 Timothy Wright.

As seen in Figure 3.7, the city of Chicago is a point. Turning your car 90 degrees to the left and driving straight for two miles is a vector. Starting from anywhere on the Earth, the vector driving directions will place the car somewhere else. Since the car can start from anywhere, just a vector is not enough information to determine a location.

Various mathematical operations can be performed on vectors and points. For example, add these driving directions to a starting point, such as Chicago, and the results are a new point, or a new location. Vectors can be added and subtracted from each other, but because they can start from anywhere, the result is another vector that can also start from anywhere. See Figure 3.8.

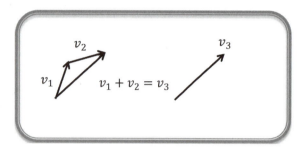

Figure 3.8
Vector Addition.
© 2014 Timothy Wright.

What doesn't make sense is adding two points together:

```
Chicago + New York = ???
```

This causes a lot of confusion when first learning about vectors and points. There are things that are mathematically correct and then there are the things you need to do with vectors and points in the code so that the game works. As discussed previously, to use a matrix to manipulate vectors, an extra w value is added. This is also the reason that a vector and a point can differ by the w value. If the w is equal to one, translation can occur. When the w value equals zero, translation has no effect. Both points and vectors can be represented by the same data structure, just by changing the w value from a one to a zero.

USING MATRIX TRANSFORMATIONS

All of the previous transformations can also be applied using a matrix. There are matrices that represent translation, rotation, scaling, and shearing. These different matrix objects can be multiplied, combining all the different operations into a single matrix that can be used to transform all the points at once. In order to multiply a vector with three elements to a matrix that has 3×3 elements, it is important to understand that matrix multiplication is not like multiplying two numbers.

To multiply two matrices of different sizes, the inside sizes must match. The resulting matrix will have the dimensions of the outside values. In other words, $A \times B * B \times C = A \times C$. The B numbers on the inside must match. The following are valid matrix sizes and their multiplication results:

- $4 \times 2 * 2 \times 3 = 4 \times 3$
- $3 \times 3 * 3 \times 5 = 3 \times 5$
- $1 \times 2 * 2 \times 7 = 1 \times 7$

This is one of the reasons that the extra w value is needed. A $1 \times 2 * 3 \times 3$ matrix operation is not valid. Also, the order of the vector and matrix need to be correct, or the matrix operation doesn't work.

- $3 \times 3 * 1 \times 3 =$ Error, vector can't be a 1×3
- $3 \times 3 * 3 \times 1 =$ Good

Another important point is that matrix multiplication is not commutative. In other words:

```
M1 * M2 != M2 * M1
```

Reversing the multiplication changes the result, which is not the same for other forms of multiplication. Translating and then rotating has a different result from rotating and then translating. It is important to keep this in mind. Multiplying a matrix by another may not produce the same results if the two matrices are switched, although the values could be chosen in such a way to force the results to be the same. Because of this, swapping the vector and the matrix to get the multiplication to work is not a good idea:

```
1x3 vector * 3x3 matrix != 3x3 matrix * 3x1 vector
```

This brings up the next important consideration when working with a matrix: how to properly use row-major or column-major formats.

ROW-MAJOR VS. COLUMN-MAJOR MATRICES

The following transformation matrix is a column-major matrix:

```
[ 1 0 tx ]
[ 0 1 ty ]
[ 0 0  1 ]
```

The vector (*tx, ty,* 1) is the translation vector and goes from the top to the bottom, occupying a column of the matrix.

The following transformation matrix is a row-major matrix:

```
[  1  0 0 ]
[  0  1 0 ]
[ tx ty 1 ]
```

Notice that the transformation vector now goes across the bottom, on the row.

Why is this important? The first reason is that the translation matrices have their values in different places, so mismatching them will cause errors. The second reason, as stated previously, is that M1 * M2 != M2 * M1. This means that order matters. This problem concerns order of operations.

Let C = a concatenation of matrices. If you scale (S), rotate (R), and translate (T), you end up with two different ways of writing the code.

```
C = S * R * T
C = T * R * S
```

Do you do it this way?

```
C = T.mul(R).mul(S);
```

Or this way?

```
C = S.mul(R).mul(T);
```

The answer is, either one is correct, depending on which matrix order is used. If the matrix is stored in row-major form, then matrix concatenation is done left to right. However, if column-major form is used, the matrix concatenation is performed from right to left. Remembering that M * N != N * M, you can see that it is very easy to get something in the wrong place, or do things in the wrong order.

Note

While writing the first version of this chapter, I didn't have much about row major and column major. After the first review, I realized that I had swapped some of the code. I was doing things for row major using column major. After fixing the errors, and re-testing everything, I added this section. :-)

To make it even more complicated, it is easy to write the following code:

```
Matrix3x3f mat = Matrix3x3f.translate( tx, ty );
mat = mat.mul( Matrix3x3f.rotate( rad ) );
```

This does `C = T * R`. It is just as easy to write:

```
Matrix3x3f mat = Matrix3x3f.translate( tx, ty );
mat = Matrix3x3f.rotate( rad ).mul( mat );
```

This does `C = R * T`. But unless the matrix row/column order is specified, there is no way to understand if rotation happens before or after translation. This can be very confusing, so make sure you understand what is going on.

Changing from row major to column major doesn't just involve using a different rotation matrix. The order of vector * matrix is reversed. If row major is used, then the vector is a row, which is a 1×3 matrix. If column major is used, then the vector is a column, which is a 3×1 matrix. The row major is $1 \times 3 * 3 \times 3$, but the column major is $3 \times 3 * 3 \times 1$. I had to update the code to switch from column-major to row-major vector multiplication, and switch the order of the multiplication.

If all of the tutorials available were searched for rotation matrices, there would be some differences. Some libraries, tutorials, and documentation present the matrix transformations as row major, and some as column major. OpenGL, a very popular 3D graphics library, stores the matrix in memory as a single array of data, but some of the documentation shows the values in column-major format. I have seen numerous DirectX documents using row-major format.

Note

I remember when first learning about matrix rotation, I was reading tutorials on a website and I ran across a forum argument where two people were arguing about a rotation matrix. Each poster claimed the other one's minus sign was in the wrong place.

```
[cos(a),-sin(a), 0] [ cos(a), sin(a), 0]
[sin(a), cos(a), 0] [-sin(a), cos(a), 0]
[     0,      0, 1] [      0,      0, 1]
```

Of course, both posters were correct—it was just that one was using a row-major notation, and the other was using a column-major notation. You've been warned. :-)

Having discussed all the general problems that you'll face when first learning about all this stuff, I have glossed over the most complicated part—multiplying two matrices together. The next section presents the matrix class used for all the groovy math stuff (groovy is a technical term).

UNDERSTANDING THE MATRIX3X3F CLASS

The code for adding and subtracting matrices is simple. The values for each index of the two matrices are added or subtracted from each other and placed into the same index. Only matrices of the same width and height can be added together, and you may find that you never actually need to add or subtract a matrix from another matrix.

Multiplication is where things get weird. The top row of the first matrix is multiplied by all three columns of the second matrix. Then the middle row of the first is multiplied by all three columns of the second. Finally, the bottom row is multiplied by all three columns of the second matrix. It is displayed below in two different ways to expose the patterns.

```
   [a, b, c]  [1, 2, 3]
A  [d, e, f] B [4, 5, 6] = C
   [g, h, i]  [7, 8, 9]

   [a*1 + b*4 + c*7, a*2 + b*5 + c*8, a*3 + b*6 + c*9]
C  [d*1 + e*4 + f*7, d*2 + e*5 + f*8, d*3 + e*6 + f*9]
   [g*1 + h*4 + i*7, g*2 + h*5 + i*8, g*3 + h*6 + i*9]

C[0,0] = a*1 + b*4 + c*7
C[0,1] = a*2 + b*5 + c*8
C[0,2] = a*3 + b*6 + c*9
C[1,0] = d*1 + e*4 + f*7
C[1,1] = d*2 + e*5 + f*8
C[1,2] = d*3 + e*6 + f*9
C[2,0] = g*1 + h*4 + i*7
C[2,1] = g*2 + h*5 + i*8
C[2,2] = g*3 + h*6 + i*9
```

Multiplying a vector with three points, [x, y, w], is basically the same as a matrix, except instead of three rows, there is only one. Matrix and vector multiplication for a row-major, $1 \times 3 * 3 \times 3$ matrix is as follows:

```
            [m00, m01, m02]
V[x,y,w] *  [m10, m11, m12]
            [m20, m21, m22]

Vx = m00 * x + m10 * y + m20 * w
Vy = m01 * x + m11 * y + m21 * w
Vw = m02 * x + m12 * y + m22 * w
```

If column-major matrices were used, then the vector is a column, not a row. Matrix and vector multiplication for a $3 \times 3 * 3 \times 1$ column-major vector is as follows:

```
[m00, m01, m02]    [x]
[m10, m11, m12] * V[y]
[m20, m21, m22]    [w]

Vx = m00 * x + m01 * y + m02 * w
Vy = m10 * x + m11 * y + m12 * w
Vw = m20 * x + m21 * y + m22 * w
```

Tip

Make sure to understand all the places the code is different if you choose to switch from the row-major matrix to a column-major matrix. It is easy to miss something. (Trust me!)

The following transformations are multiplied out to show what happens. I have left out multiplication by the zero matrix, because it doesn't matter what you multiply it with; the result is all zeros.

The *identity* matrix, however, is a special matrix that doesn't change the value of another matrix. It is the matrix equivalent of multiplication by one.

```
         [1, 0, 0]    [x]
Identity [0, 1, 0] * V[y]
         [0, 0, 1]    [w]

Vx = 1*x + 0*y + 0*w = x
Vy = 0*x + 1*y + 0*w = y
Vw = 0*x + 0*y + 1*w = w
```

The scale matrix works as expected:

```
       [sx,  0, 0]    [x]
Scale [ 0, sy, 0] * V[y]
       [ 0,  0, 1]    [w]

Vx = sx*x +  0*y + 0*w = sx*x
Vy =  0*x + sy*y + 0*w = sy*y
Vw =  0*x +  0*y + 1*w = w
```

The translation matrix will work only if w = 1. If w = 0, then the operation will not be applied:

```
          [1, 0, tx]    [x]
Translate [0, 1, ty] * V[y]
          [0, 0, 1]     [w]

Vx = 1*x + 0*y + tx*w = x + tx*w
Vy = 0*x + 1*y + ty*w = y + ty*w
Vw = 0*x + 0*y +  1*w = w
```

As discussed previously, the w value is added to make the translation work. If there was no w value, then this transformation would not be possible. Also, notice that w = 0 would cause the translation value to become zero, which would be the correct result for translating a vector.

The shearing matrix is as follows:

```
       [ 1, sx, 0]    [x]
Shear [sy,  1, 0] * V[y]
       [ 0,  0, 1]    [w]
```

$Vx = 1*x + sx*y + 0*w = x + sx*y$
$Vy = sy*x + 1*y + 0*w = y + sy*x$
$Vw = 0*x + 0*y + 1*w = w$

Finally, the rotation matrix is as follows:

```
          [cos(a), -sin(a), 0]    [x]
Rotation [sin(a),  cos(a), 0] * V[y]
          [   0,      0, 1]    [w]
```

$Vx = x*cos(a) + -y*sin(a) + 0*w = x*cos(a) - y*sin(a)$
$Vy = x*sin(a) + y*cos(a) + 0*w = x*sin(a) + y*cos(a)$
$Vw = 0*x + 0*y + 1*w = w$

This also matches the rotation code in the vector class shown previously.

```java
package javagames.util;


public class Matrix3x3f {
    private float[][] m = new float[ 3 ][ 3 ];
    public Matrix3x3f() {

    }
    public Matrix3x3f( float[][] m ) {
        setMatrix( m );
    }
    public Matrix3x3f add( Matrix3x3f m1 ) {
        return new Matrix3x3f( new float[][] {
        { this.m[ 0 ][ 0 ] + m1.m[ 0 ][ 0 ],
          this.m[ 0 ][ 1 ] + m1.m[ 0 ][ 1 ],
          this.m[ 0 ][ 2 ] + m1.m[ 0 ][ 2 ] },
        { this.m[ 1 ][ 0 ] + m1.m[ 1 ][ 0 ],
          this.m[ 1 ][ 1 ] + m1.m[ 1 ][ 1 ],
          this.m[ 1 ][ 2 ] + m1.m[ 1 ][ 2 ] },
        { this.m[ 2 ][ 0 ] + m1.m[ 2 ][ 0 ],
          this.m[ 2 ][ 1 ] + m1.m[ 2 ][ 1 ],
          this.m[ 2 ][ 2 ] + m1.m[ 2 ][ 2 ] } } );
    }
```

```
public Matrix3x3f sub( Matrix3x3f m1 ) {
    return new Matrix3x3f( new float[][] {
    { this.m[ 0 ][ 0 ] - m1.m[ 0 ][ 0 ],
      this.m[ 0 ][ 1 ] - m1.m[ 0 ][ 1 ],
      this.m[ 0 ][ 2 ] - m1.m[ 0 ][ 2 ] },
    { this.m[ 1 ][ 0 ] - m1.m[ 1 ][ 0 ],
      this.m[ 1 ][ 1 ] - m1.m[ 1 ][ 1 ],
      this.m[ 1 ][ 2 ] - m1.m[ 1 ][ 2 ] },
    { this.m[ 2 ][ 0 ] - m1.m[ 2 ][ 0 ],
      this.m[ 2 ][ 1 ] - m1.m[ 2 ][ 1 ],
      this.m[ 2 ][ 2 ] - m1.m[ 2 ][ 2 ] } } );
}

public Matrix3x3f mul( Matrix3x3f m1 ) {
    return new Matrix3x3f( new float[][] {
    { this.m[ 0 ][ 0 ] * m1.m[ 0 ][ 0 ] // ******
    + this.m[ 0 ][ 1 ] * m1.m[ 1 ][ 0 ] // M[0,0]
    + this.m[ 0 ][ 2 ] * m1.m[ 2 ][ 0 ], // ******
      this.m[ 0 ][ 0 ] * m1.m[ 0 ][ 1 ] // ******
    + this.m[ 0 ][ 1 ] * m1.m[ 1 ][ 1 ] // M[0,1]
    + this.m[ 0 ][ 2 ] * m1.m[ 2 ][ 1 ], // ******
      this.m[ 0 ][ 0 ] * m1.m[ 0 ][ 2 ] // ******
    + this.m[ 0 ][ 1 ] * m1.m[ 1 ][ 2 ] // M[0,2]
    + this.m[ 0 ][ 2 ] * m1.m[ 2 ][ 2 ] },// ******
    { this.m[ 1 ][ 0 ] * m1.m[ 0 ][ 0 ] // ******
    + this.m[ 1 ][ 1 ] * m1.m[ 1 ][ 0 ] // M[1,0]
    + this.m[ 1 ][ 2 ] * m1.m[ 2 ][ 0 ], // ******
      this.m[ 1 ][ 0 ] * m1.m[ 0 ][ 1 ] // ******
    + this.m[ 1 ][ 1 ] * m1.m[ 1 ][ 1 ] // M[1,1]
    + this.m[ 1 ][ 2 ] * m1.m[ 2 ][ 1 ], // ******
      this.m[ 1 ][ 0 ] * m1.m[ 0 ][ 2 ] // ******
    + this.m[ 1 ][ 1 ] * m1.m[ 1 ][ 2 ] // M[1,2]
    + this.m[ 1 ][ 2 ] * m1.m[ 2 ][ 2 ] },// ******
    { this.m[ 2 ][ 0 ] * m1.m[ 0 ][ 0 ] // ******
    + this.m[ 2 ][ 1 ] * m1.m[ 1 ][ 0 ] // M[2,0]
    + this.m[ 2 ][ 2 ] * m1.m[ 2 ][ 0 ], // ******
      this.m[ 2 ][ 0 ] * m1.m[ 0 ][ 1 ] // ******
    + this.m[ 2 ][ 1 ] * m1.m[ 1 ][ 1 ] // M[2,1]
    + this.m[ 2 ][ 2 ] * m1.m[ 2 ][ 1 ], // ******
      this.m[ 2 ][ 0 ] * m1.m[ 0 ][ 2 ] // ******
    + this.m[ 2 ][ 1 ] * m1.m[ 1 ][ 2 ] // M[2,2]
    + this.m[ 2 ][ 2 ] * m1.m[ 2 ][ 2 ] } // ******
    });
}
```

```java
public void setMatrix( float[][] m ) {
    this.m = m;
}

public static Matrix3x3f zero() {
    return new Matrix3x3f( new float[][] {
        { 0.0f, 0.0f, 0.0f },
        { 0.0f, 0.0f, 0.0f },
        { 0.0f, 0.0f, 0.0f }
    });
}

public static Matrix3x3f identity() {
    return new Matrix3x3f( new float[][] {
        { 1.0f, 0.0f, 0.0f },
        { 0.0f, 1.0f, 0.0f },
        { 0.0f, 0.0f, 1.0f }
    });
}

public static Matrix3x3f translate( Vector2f v ) {
    return translate( v.x, v.y );
}

public static Matrix3x3f translate( float x, float y ) {
    return new Matrix3x3f( new float[][] {
        { 1.0f, 0.0f, 0.0f },
        { 0.0f, 1.0f, 0.0f },
        {    x,    y, 1.0f }
    });
}

public static Matrix3x3f scale( Vector2f v ) {
    return scale( v.x, v.y );
}

public static Matrix3x3f scale( float x, float y ) {
    return new Matrix3x3f( new float[][] {
        { x,    0.0f, 0.0f },
        { 0.0f,    y, 0.0f },
        { 0.0f, 0.0f, 1.0f }
    });
}

public static Matrix3x3f shear( Vector2f v ) {
    return shear( v.x, v.y );
}
```

```java
    public static Matrix3x3f shear( float x, float y ) {
        return new Matrix3x3f( new float[][] {
            { 1.0f,    y, 0.0f },
            { x,     1.0f, 0.0f },
            { 0.0f, 0.0f, 1.0f }
        });
    }

    public static Matrix3x3f rotate( float rad ) {
        return new Matrix3x3f( new float[][] {
            { (float) Math.cos(rad), (float)Math.sin( rad ), 0.0f },
            { (float)-Math.sin(rad), (float)Math.cos( rad ), 0.0f },
            {                  0.0f,                   0.0f, 1.0f }
        });
    }

    public Vector2f mul( Vector2f vec ) {
        return new Vector2f(
            vec.x * this.m[ 0 ][ 0 ] //
          + vec.y * this.m[ 1 ][ 0 ] // V.x
          + vec.w * this.m[ 2 ][ 0 ],//
            vec.x * this.m[ 0 ][ 1 ] //
          + vec.y * this.m[ 1 ][ 1 ] // V.y
          + vec.w * this.m[ 2 ][ 1 ],//
            vec.x * this.m[ 0 ][ 2 ] //
          + vec.y * this.m[ 1 ][ 2 ] // V.w
          + vec.w * this.m[ 2 ][ 2 ] //
        );
    }

    @Override
    public String toString() {
        StringBuilder buf = new StringBuilder();
        for( int i = 0; i < 3; ++i ) {
            buf.append( "[" );
            buf.append( m[i][0] );
            buf.append( ",\t" );
            buf.append( m[i][1] );
            buf.append( ",\t" );
            buf.append( m[i][2] );
            buf.append( "]\n" );
        }
        return buf.toString();
    }
}
```

Figure 3.9
Matrix Multiplication Example.
© 2014 Timothy Wright.

The `MatrixMultiplicationExample`, located in the `javagames.transform` package and shown in Figure 3.9, demonstrates using matrices to concatenate transformation operations on objects. The reason the matrix is such a powerful tool is because operations such as transformations and rotations can be stored into a single matrix and then applied to objects all at once. Although it is not necessary for a single object, if hundreds or thousands of polygons need to be transformed, the savings can really add up.

Tip

Just for fun, this example also creates some random stars that can be toggled on or off using the "space" bar (get it?).

The *identity* matrix is used as a starting point, and then multiplied by a translation matrix that moves to the center of the screen. The Sun vector is then multiplied by the matrix, placing the Sun's center at the center of the screen. Although it is only a single point, an entire polygon model could be multiplied by the matrix transforming all the coordinates.

The path of the Earth's orbit is drawn as a white circle, and then the Earth is drawn, spinning around the sun. Notice that the same matrix is used. Concatenating the Earth's rotation with the previous matrix allows the Earth to spin around the Sun with only one more rotation and translation. The difference between this example and the previous is important. See Figures 3.10 and 3.11 for the difference between rotating first and translating first.

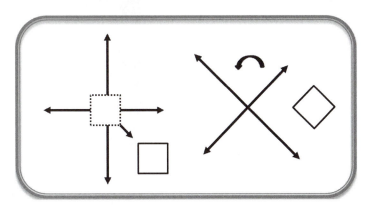

Figure 3.10
Translate -> Rotate.
© 2014 Timothy Wright.

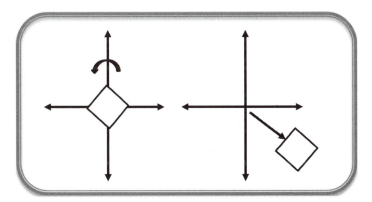

Figure 3.11
Rotate -> Translate.
© 2014 Timothy Wright.

Still using the same matrix, another circle representing the Moon orbits the Earth. Both of these planets orbit the Sun. This is all possible and very easy using matrix multiplication. Make sure to study the code until the results make sense.

```java
package javagames.transform;

import java.awt.*;
import java.awt.event.*;
import java.awt.image.*;
import java.util.Random;
import javagames.util.*;
import javax.swing.*;


public class MatrixMultiplyExample extends JFrame implements Runnable {
    private static final int SCREEN_W = 640;
    private static final int SCREEN_H = 480;

    private FrameRate frameRate;
    private BufferStrategy bs;
    private volatile boolean running;
    private Thread gameThread;
    private RelativeMouseInput mouse;
    private KeyboardInput keyboard;

    private float earthRot, earthDelta;
    private float moonRot, moonDelta;

    private boolean showStars;
    private int[] stars;
    private Random rand = new Random();

    public MatrixMultiplyExample() {

    }

    protected void createAndShowGUI() {
        Canvas canvas = new Canvas();
        canvas.setSize( SCREEN_W, SCREEN_H );
        canvas.setBackground( Color.BLACK );
        canvas.setIgnoreRepaint( true );
        getContentPane().add( canvas );
        setTitle( "Matrix Multiply Example" );
        setIgnoreRepaint( true );
        pack();

        // Add key listeners
        keyboard = new KeyboardInput();
        canvas.addKeyListener( keyboard );
```

```
        // Add mouse listeners
        // For full screen : mouse = new RelativeMouseInput( this );
        mouse = new RelativeMouseInput( canvas );
        canvas.addMouseListener( mouse );
        canvas.addMouseMotionListener( mouse );
        canvas.addMouseWheelListener( mouse );

        setVisible( true );
        canvas.createBufferStrategy( 2 );
        bs = canvas.getBufferStrategy();
        canvas.requestFocus();

        gameThread = new Thread( this );
        gameThread.start();
    }
    public void run() {
        running = true;
        initialize();
        while( running ) {
            gameLoop();
        }
    }
    private void gameLoop() {
        processInput();
        renderFrame();
        sleep( 10L );
    }
    private void renderFrame() {
        do {
            do {
                Graphics g = null;
                try {
                    g = bs.getDrawGraphics();
                    g.clearRect( 0, 0, getWidth(), getHeight() );
                    render( g );
                } finally {
                    if( g != null ) {
                        g.dispose();
                    }
                }
            } while( bs.contentsRestored() );
            bs.show();
        } while( bs.contentsLost() );
    }
```

```java
private void sleep( long sleep ) {
    try {
        Thread.sleep( sleep );
    } catch( InterruptedException ex ) { }
}

private void initialize() {
    frameRate = new FrameRate();
    frameRate.initialize();

    earthDelta = (float)Math.toRadians( 0.5 );
    moonDelta = (float)Math.toRadians( 2.5 );

    showStars = true;
    stars = new int[ 1000 ];
    for( int i = 0; i < stars.length - 1; i += 2 ) {
        stars[i] = rand.nextInt( SCREEN_W );
        stars[i+1] = rand.nextInt( SCREEN_H );
    }
}

private void processInput() {

    keyboard.poll();
    mouse.poll();

    if( keyboard.keyDownOnce( KeyEvent.VK_SPACE ) ) {
        showStars = !showStars;
    }

}

    private void render( Graphics g ) {

    g.setColor( Color.GREEN );
    frameRate.calculate();
    g.drawString( frameRate.getFrameRate(), 20, 20 );
    g.drawString( "Press [SPACE] to toggle stars", 20, 35 );

    if( showStars ) {
        g.setColor( Color.WHITE );
        for( int i = 0; i < stars.length - 1; i += 2 ) {
            g.fillRect( stars[i], stars[i+1], 1, 1 );
        }
    }
    // draw the sun...
    Matrix3x3f sunMat = Matrix3x3f.identity();
    sunMat = sunMat.mul(
        Matrix3x3f.translate( SCREEN_W / 2, SCREEN_H / 2 )
    );
```

```java
        Vector2f sun = sunMat.mul( new Vector2f() );

        g.setColor( Color.YELLOW );
        g.fillOval( (int)sun.x - 50, (int)sun.y - 50, 100, 100 );

        // draw Earth's Orbit
        g.setColor( Color.WHITE );
        g.drawOval( (int)sun.x - SCREEN_W / 4, (int)sun.y - SCREEN_W / 4,
                SCREEN_W / 2, SCREEN_W / 2 );

        // draw the Earth
        Matrix3x3f earthMat = Matrix3x3f.translate( SCREEN_W / 4, 0 );
        earthMat = earthMat.mul( Matrix3x3f.rotate( earthRot ) );
        earthMat = earthMat.mul( sunMat );

        earthRot += earthDelta;

        Vector2f earth = earthMat.mul( new Vector2f() );
        g.setColor( Color.BLUE );
        g.fillOval( (int)earth.x - 10, (int)earth.y - 10, 20, 20 );

        // draw the Moon
        Matrix3x3f moonMat = Matrix3x3f.translate( 30, 0 );
        moonMat = moonMat.mul( Matrix3x3f.rotate( moonRot ) );
        moonMat = moonMat.mul( earthMat );
        moonRot += moonDelta;

        Vector2f moon = moonMat.mul( new Vector2f() );
        g.setColor( Color.LIGHT_GRAY );
        g.fillOval( (int)moon.x - 5, (int)moon.y - 5, 10, 10 );
    }

    protected void onWindowClosing() {
        try {
            running = false;
            gameThread.join();
        } catch( InterruptedException e ) {
            e.printStackTrace();
        }
        System.exit( 0 );
    }

    public static void main( String[] args ) {
        final MatrixMultiplyExample app = new MatrixMultiplyExample();
        app.addWindowListener( new WindowAdapter() {
            public void windowClosing( WindowEvent e ) {
                app.onWindowClosing();
            }
        });
```

```
    SwingUtilities.invokeLater( new Runnable() {
        public void run() {
            app.createAndShowGUI();
        }
    });
    }

}
```

AFFINE TRANSFORMATION

Java has a class, called AffineTransform, that can be used to perform the matrix transformations. Although it is good to not rewrite code, it is also good to study and learn
algorithms to understand them. The code examples will continue to develop libraries
from scratch, but feel free to use the built-in classes.

```
AffineTransform.setToIdentity()
AffineTransform.concatenate(AffineTransform)
AffineTransform.rotate(double radians)
AffineTransform.scale(double sx, double sy)
AffineTransform.translate(double tx, double ty)
AffineTransform.shear(double sx, double sy)
```

Using the AffineTransform class, there are many ways to apply the transformations to
points of data. The following code uses all the available methods:

```
AffineTransform trans = new AffineTransform();
Shape srcShape = new Rectangle();
Shape destShape = null;
Point2D srcPoint = new Point2D.Float();
Point2D destPoint = new Point2D.Float();
Point2D pointSrc[] = new Point2D[] {
        new Point2D.Float(),
        new Point2D.Float(),
        new Point2D.Float()
};
Point2D pointDest[] = new Point2D[3];
double[] doubleSrc = new double[6];
double[] doubleDest = new double[6];
float[] floatSrc = new float[6];
float[] floatDest = new float[6];
int srcOff = 0;
int dstOff = 0;
int numPts = 3; // array is (x,y) pairs...
```

```
// Point -> Point
trans.transform( srcPoint, destPoint );

// Point[] -> Point[]
trans.transform( pointSrc, srcOff, pointDest, dstOff, numPts );

// double[] -> double[]
trans.transform( doubleSrc, srcOff, doubleDest, dstOff, numPts );

// float[] -> float[]
trans.transform( floatSrc, srcOff, floatDest, dstOff, numPts );

// double[] -> float[]
trans.transform( doubleSrc, srcOff, floatDest, dstOff, numPts );

// float[] -> double[]
trans.transform( floatSrc, srcOff, doubleDest, dstOff, numPts );

// Shape -> Shape
destShape = trans.createTransformedShape( srcShape );
```

The last example shown here, transforming one Shape to another, presents difficulty retrieving the transformed coordinates for other operations, such as physics or collision detection. The resulting data can be acquired with a PathIterator, but its usage is a little difficult to understand. Path iteration can return various paths of data:

- SEG_MOVETO–Starting location for a new path

- SEG_LINETO–Second point of a line

- SEG_QUADTO–Two points that specify a quadratic parametric curve

- SEG_CUBICTO–Three points that specify a cubic parametric curve

Notice that three (x,y) pairs may be returned. The following code transforms a rectangle and iterates over the resulting transformation:

```
AffineTransform trans = new AffineTransform();
trans.rotate( Math.PI / 3.0 );
trans.translate( 5.0, 7.0 );
Shape shape = new Rectangle( 0, 0, 100, 150 );
Shape transformed = trans.createTransformedShape( shape );

PathIterator pit = transformed.getPathIterator( null );
float[] seg = new float[6];
while( !pit.isDone() ) {
    int segType = pit.currentSegment( seg );
    String point = "(" + seg[0] + "," + seg[1] +
                   "),(" + seg[2] + "," + seg[3] +
                   "),(" + seg[4] + "," + seg[5] + ")";
    switch( segType ) {
```

```
case PathIterator.SEG_MOVETO:
   System.out.println( "SEG_MOVETO: " + point );
   break;
case PathIterator.SEG_LINETO:
   System.out.println( "SEG_LINETO: " + point );
   break;
case PathIterator.SEG_QUADTO:
   System.out.println( "SEG_QUADTO: " + point );
   break;
case PathIterator.SEG_CUBICTO:
   System.out.println( "SEG_CUBICTO: " + point );
   break;
case PathIterator.SEG_CLOSE:
   System.out.println( "SEG_CLOSE: " + point );
   break;

   }
   pit.next();
}
```

RESOURCES AND FURTHER READING

Akenine-Moller, Tomas and Eric Haines, *Real-Time Rendering,* 2nd Edition, A K Peters, 2002.

Ericson, Christer, *Real-Time Collision Detection*, Focal Press, 2004.

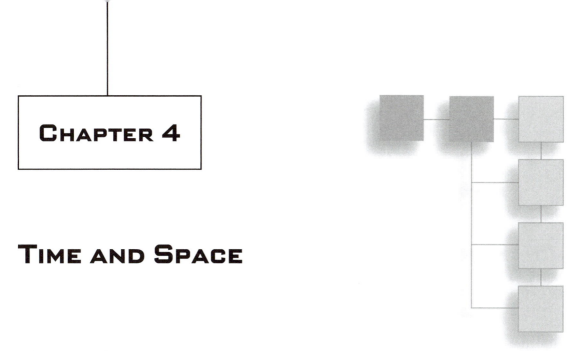

Chapter 4

Time and Space

When I was learning game programming, and I wanted to do something involving physics, I searched for some equations and read some tutorials about movement. I then tried to write some code involving gravity, and I tried to do it correctly, so that the gravity would be the same in my computer program as it is on earth. When I read that gravity is 9.8 m/s^2, I stopped, stared at the computer for a while, and didn't have a clue where to start. I didn't have anything like a meter, and no seconds. I was stumped. It was at this point that I began to realize how difficult computer games could be. The goal of this chapter is to add a timestep to the game loop, allowing for calculations involving time. It also covers screen mapping so any arbitrary coordinate system can be drawn on a window of any size.

Calculating Time Delta

All of the previous examples have been updating the moving objects every frame. This causes different computer speeds to move objects faster or slower depending on the frame rate. See Figure 4.1.

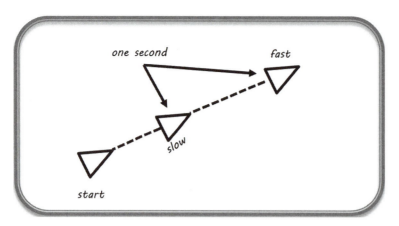

Figure 4.1
Timed Movement.
© 2014 Timothy Wright.

In order to tune parameters and keep the game from being too easy or too difficult, objects need to move at consistent speeds, regardless of the computer processor speed. At some point, a computer will be too old and too slow, but for every other computer, speeds will change. If enough other applications are running, a computer that seems fast one day can be slow the next.

The solution is to calculate the elapsed time between frames and use that value to scale the updates.

```
last_ns = last tick count
curr_ns = current tick count

elapsed_time_ns = curr_ns - last_ns
elapsed_seconds = elapsed_time_ns / 1.0E9
```

Notice that 1 second equals 1.0E9 nanoseconds. Dividing the elapsed time by the number of nanoseconds per second produces the elapsed time per second. Originally, my code used milliseconds, but my processor was so fast that there wasn't enough precision, and nothing moved. Although it may work on a slower computer, stick with the nanoseconds.

The run() method has been updated to calculate the elapsed time:

```
public void run() {
    running = true;
    initialize();
    long curTime = System.nanoTime();
    long lastTime = curTime;
    double nsPerFrame;
```

```
while( running ) {
    curTime = System.nanoTime();
    nsPerFrame = curTime - lastTime;
    gameLoop( nsPerFrame / 1.0E9 );
    lastTime = curTime;
}
}
```

Once the elapsed time for each frame is available, it is used to scale the movement values so the distance moved on the screen does not change based on the frame rate:

```
new position = old position + rate * time delta
```

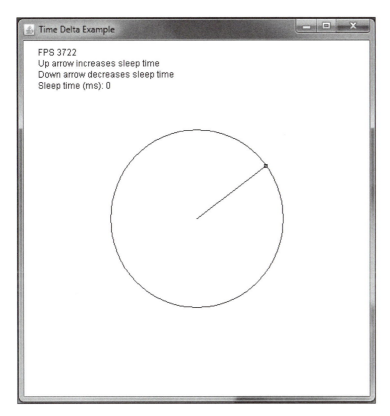

Figure 4.2
Time Delta Example.
© 2014 Timothy Wright.

The `TimeDeltaExample`, shown in Figure 4.2 and located in the `javagames.timeandspace` package, creates a spinning gauge, much like a clock. The hand spins around at a rate of one revolution every four seconds. The arrow keys are used to increase and decrease the frame rate, while making sure that the speed of the rotation doesn't change based on the frame rate.

The first thing to notice is that the canvas is saved as a class variable to resize the clock if the window is resized.

The second thing to notice is that the sleep value is also a variable, so the frame rate can be adjusted while the application is running. When the up or down arrow keys are pressed, the sleep value is adjusted by 10 milliseconds. This value is always less than one second because with the polling keyboard, it will start missing keypresses if the frame rate drops too low (you'll learn how to fix this in Chapter 11, "Text").

The `run()` method has been updated to calculate the time between frames in seconds, and pass that value to the game loop. The game loop can now pass the elapsed time to any of the methods that need it. For this example, there isn't any reason to have the elapsed time when processing input, but it will be needed later.

The `updateObjects()` method is where the new value is used. The step value that is added to the angle is set to PI / 2 radians, or 90 degrees. By multiplying it by the elapsed time, the spinning hand will move at 90 degrees per second. It is easy to see that if one second has passed, the value added to the angle would be PI / 2. If the elapsed time was half a second, the value added would be half, or PI / 4.

```java
private void updateObjects( double delta ) {
    angle += step * delta;
    if( angle > 2 * Math.PI ) {
        angle -= 2 * Math.PI;
    }
}
```

The `render()` method prints out the controls, along with the current sleep time. The code to draw the circle is a little different; it uses the screen width and height to resize the display when the window is resized.

```java
package javagames.timeandspace;

import java.awt.*;
import java.awt.event.*;
import java.awt.image.*;
import javagames.util.*;

import javax.swing.*;


public class TimeDeltaExample extends JFrame implements Runnable {
    private FrameRate frameRate;
    private BufferStrategy bs;
    private volatile boolean running;
    private Thread gameThread;
```

```
private RelativeMouseInput mouse;
private KeyboardInput keyboard;
private Canvas canvas;

private float angle;
private float step;
private long sleep;

public TimeDeltaExample() {

}

protected void createAndShowGUI() {

    canvas = new Canvas();
    canvas.setSize( 480, 480 );
    canvas.setBackground( Color.WHITE );
    canvas.setIgnoreRepaint( true );
    getContentPane().add( canvas );
    setTitle( "Time Delta Example" );
    setIgnoreRepaint( true );
    pack();

    keyboard = new KeyboardInput();
    canvas.addKeyListener( keyboard );

    mouse = new RelativeMouseInput( canvas );
    canvas.addMouseListener( mouse );
    canvas.addMouseMotionListener( mouse );
    canvas.addMouseWheelListener( mouse );

    setVisible( true );
    canvas.createBufferStrategy( 2 );
    bs = canvas.getBufferStrategy();
    canvas.requestFocus();

    gameThread = new Thread( this );
    gameThread.start();
}

public void run() {
    running = true;
    initialize();
    long curTime = System.nanoTime();
    long lastTime = curTime;
    double nsPerFrame;
    while( running ) {
        curTime = System.nanoTime();
        nsPerFrame = curTime - lastTime;
```

```java
            gameLoop( nsPerFrame / 1.0E9 );
            lastTime = curTime;
        }
    }

    private void gameLoop( double delta ) {
        processInput( delta );
        updateObjects( delta );
        renderFrame();
        sleep( sleep );
    }

    private void renderFrame() {
        do {
            do {
                Graphics g = null;
                try {
                    g = bs.getDrawGraphics();
                    g.clearRect( 0, 0, getWidth(), getHeight() );
                    render( g );
                } finally {
                    if( g != null ) {
                        g.dispose();
                    }
                }
            } while( bs.contentsRestored() );
            bs.show();
        } while( bs.contentsLost() );
    }

    private void sleep( long sleep ) {
        try {
            Thread.sleep( sleep );
        } catch( InterruptedException ex ) { }
    }

    private void initialize() {
        frameRate = new FrameRate();
        frameRate.initialize();

        angle = 0.0f;
        step = (float)Math.PI / 2.0f;
    }

    private void processInput( double delta ) {
        keyboard.poll();
        mouse.poll();
```

```java
        if( keyboard.keyDownOnce( KeyEvent.VK_UP ) ) {
            sleep += 10;
        }
        if( keyboard.keyDownOnce( KeyEvent.VK_DOWN ) ) {
            sleep -= 10;
        }

        if( sleep > 1000 ) {
            sleep = 1000;
        }
        if( sleep < 0 ) {
            sleep = 0;
        }

    }

    private void updateObjects( double delta ) {
        angle += step * delta;
        if( angle > 2 * Math.PI ) {
            angle -= 2 * Math.PI;
        }
    }

    private void render( Graphics g ) {

        g.setColor( Color.BLACK );
        frameRate.calculate();
        g.drawString( frameRate.getFrameRate(), 20, 20 );
        g.drawString( "Up arrow increases sleep time", 20, 35 );
        g.drawString( "Down arrow decreases sleep time", 20, 50 );
        g.drawString( "Sleep time (ms): " + sleep, 20, 65 );

        int x = canvas.getWidth() / 4;
        int y = canvas.getHeight() / 4;
        int w = canvas.getWidth() / 2;
        int h = canvas.getHeight() / 2;
        g.drawOval( x, y, w, h );

        // polar -> coords
        float rw = w / 2; // radius width
        float rh = h / 2; // radius height
        int rx = (int)( rw * Math.cos( angle ) );
        int ry = (int)( rh * Math.sin( angle ) );

        int cx = (int)(rx + w);
        int cy = (int)(ry + h);
        // draw clock hand
        g.drawLine( w, h, cx, cy );
```

```
      // draw dot at end of hand
      g.drawRect( cx - 2, cy - 2, 4, 4 );
   }

   protected void onWindowClosing() {
      try {
         running = false;
         gameThread.join();
      } catch( InterruptedException e ) {
         e.printStackTrace();
      }
      System.exit( 0 );
   }

   public static void main( String[] args ) {
      final TimeDeltaExample app = new TimeDeltaExample();
      app.addWindowListener( new WindowAdapter() {
         public void windowClosing( WindowEvent e ) {
            app.onWindowClosing();
         }
      });
      SwingUtilities.invokeLater( new Runnable() {
         public void run() {
            app.createAndShowGUI();
         }
      });
   }
}
```

SCREEN MAPPING

When you're moving objects around using physics equations, there are two things you need that have not been available in the previous examples. Moving 10 m/s means that every second, the object travels 10 meters. The seconds have been added, but what about the meters?

In some of the previous examples, some of the values used are not intuitive and do not behave as expected. This is due to the screen coordinates not matching the Cartesian system taught in school. See Figure 4.3.

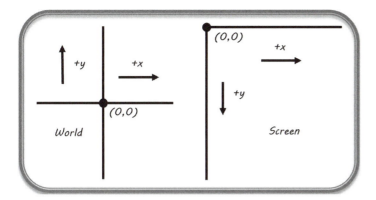

Figure 4.3
World vs. Screen Mapping.
© 2014 Timothy Wright.

It would be nice if you could define objects in any coordinate system, and then map them to the screen. As it turns out, it is simple to do this, using the transformations discussed in the previous chapter. This is important not only to create a coordinate system that behaves as expected, but also to scale the mapped values on the screen so that the size of the window doesn't matter. This can be important for games that have different sized windows on different devices. See Figure 4.4.

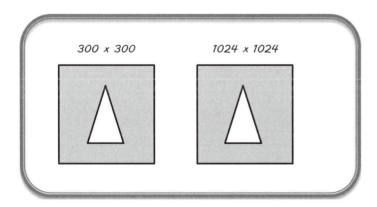

Figure 4.4
Multiple Sizes.
© 2014 Timothy Wright.

The larger window will scale everything, keeping the ratios between objects the same, no matter what size the window occupies. To start, you must define a width and height that define the game world. Many graphic systems use a (−1,1) window. See Figure 4.5.

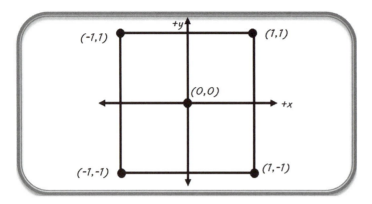

Figure 4.5
Normalized Device Coordinates.
© 2014 Timothy Wright.

This defines an area of 2 × 2 units that will be mapped to the screen, with the units being anything you want. If the game needs meters, call it meters. If the game is a planet game, maybe it's miles or light years. It doesn't matter, but it can help define the size of the objects and allow for a sense of distance on the screen. For this example, assume the units are meters, and the usable area is 2 × 2 meters, or about 6.56 × 6.56 feet.

To map the world area to the screen, you first scale the area to the screen width and height. Next, flip the y-axis. Finally, translate the area so when the values are drawn to the screen they are correct. See Figure 4.6.

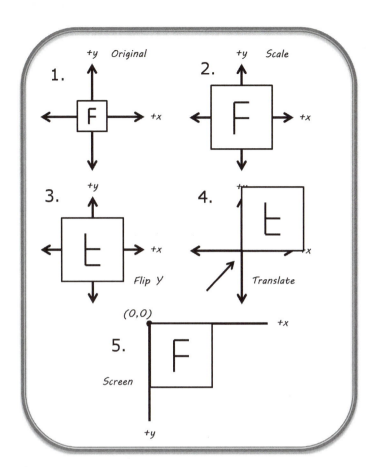

Figure 4.6
Screen Mapping Algorithm.
© 2014 Timothy Wright.

The following code calculates the viewport matrix that's used to transform the world coordinates to screen coordinates. Notice in this example that the scale and translate values are width / 2 and height / 2. This is only because the (−1,1) world coordinates have a width and height of two. If the world area was 5 × 5, for example, then the scale values would be divided by 5, but the translate values are always divided by 2 and the center of the world coordinates is located at (0,0).

```
float worldWidth = 2.0f;
float worldHeight = 2.0f;
float screenWidth = canvas.getWidth() - 1;
float screenHeight = canvas.getHeight() - 1;
float sx = screenWidth / worldWidth;
float sy = screenHeight / worldHeight;
float tx = screenWidth / 2.0f;
```

```
float ty = screenHeight / 2.0f;
Matrix3x3f viewport = Matrix3x3f.scale( sx, -sy );
viewport = viewport.mul( Matrix3x3f.translate( tx, ty ) );
```

Notice in the previous example code that 1 is subtracted from the screen width and height before they are used. This is because the actual pixel values are mapped to the screen, and although the screen width may be 10, the pixels go from 0 – 9, just like an array. If the actual width were used, when the world coordinates were converted to screen coordinates, the last row and column would be drawn off the screen, which is not the desired intent. Setting the screen width to width – 1 and the screen height to height – 1 keeps this from happening.

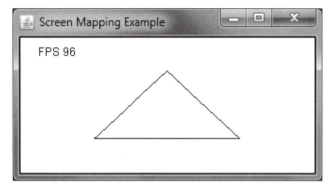

Figure 4.7
Screen Mapping Example.
© 2014 Timothy Wright.

The `ScreenMappingExample`, seen in Figure 4.7 and located in the `javagames. timeandspace` package, is a simple program that allows the screen to be resized while keeping the width/height ratio matched with the window width and height.

There is a triangle array and a copy called `triWorld` to hold the mapped values. The values for the triangle in the `initialize()` method are now small values. Because the world size is 2 × 2, very small values produce a triangle that fills the screen.

The `render()` method creates the viewport matrix and multiplies the triangle points, mapping the values from the world space to screen space. Also, a border rectangle is drawn around the edges. Try removing the −1 from the screen width and screen height calculation, and see what happens to the border rectangle.

```
package javagames.timeandspace;

import java.awt.*;
import java.awt.event.*;
import java.awt.image.*;
```

```java
import javagames.util.*;
import javax.swing.*;


public class ScreenMappingExample extends JFrame
            implements Runnable {

    private Canvas canvas;
    private FrameRate frameRate;
    private BufferStrategy bs;
    private volatile boolean running;
    private Thread gameThread;
    private RelativeMouseInput mouse;
    private KeyboardInput keyboard;

    private Vector2f[] tri;
    private Vector2f[] triWorld;

    private Vector2f[] rect;
    private Vector2f[] rectWorld;

    public ScreenMappingExample() {

    }

    protected void createAndShowGUI() {

        canvas = new Canvas();
        canvas.setSize( 640, 480 );
        canvas.setBackground( Color.WHITE );
        canvas.setIgnoreRepaint( true );
        getContentPane().add( canvas );
        setTitle( "Screen Mapping Example" );
        setIgnoreRepaint( true );
        pack();

        keyboard = new KeyboardInput();
        canvas.addKeyListener( keyboard );

        mouse = new RelativeMouseInput( canvas );
        canvas.addMouseListener( mouse );
        canvas.addMouseMotionListener( mouse );
        canvas.addMouseWheelListener( mouse );

        setVisible( true );
        canvas.createBufferStrategy( 2 );
        bs = canvas.getBufferStrategy();
        canvas.requestFocus();

        gameThread = new Thread( this );
        gameThread.start();
    }
```

```
public void run() {
    running = true;
    initialize();
    long curTime = System.nanoTime();
    long lastTime = curTime;
    double nsPerFrame;
    while( running ) {
        curTime = System.nanoTime();
        nsPerFrame = curTime - lastTime;
        gameLoop( nsPerFrame / 1.0E9 );
        lastTime = curTime;
    }
}

private void initialize() {

    frameRate = new FrameRate();
    frameRate.initialize();

    tri = new Vector2f[] {
            new Vector2f(  0.0f,  0.5f ),
            new Vector2f( -0.5f, -0.5f ),
            new Vector2f(  0.5f, -0.5f ),
    };
    triWorld = new Vector2f[ tri.length ];

    rect = new Vector2f[] {
            new Vector2f( -1.0f,  1.0f ),
            new Vector2f(  1.0f,  1.0f ),
            new Vector2f(  1.0f, -1.0f ),
            new Vector2f( -1.0f, -1.0f ),
    };
    rectWorld = new Vector2f[ rect.length ];
}

private void gameLoop( double delta ) {
    processInput( delta );
    updateObjects( delta );
    renderFrame();
    sleep( 10L );
}

private void renderFrame() {
    do {
        do {
            Graphics g = null;
```

```
            try {
                g = bs.getDrawGraphics();
                g.clearRect( 0, 0, getWidth(), getHeight() );
                render( g );
            } finally {
                if( g != null ) {
                    g.dispose();
                }
            }
        } while( bs.contentsRestored() );
        bs.show();
    } while( bs.contentsLost() );
}

private void sleep( long sleep ) {
    try {
        Thread.sleep( sleep );
    } catch( InterruptedException ex ) { }
}

private void processInput( double delta ) {

    keyboard.poll();
    mouse.poll();

}

private void updateObjects( double delta ) {

}

private void render( Graphics g ) {

    g.setColor( Color.BLACK );
    frameRate.calculate();
    g.drawString( frameRate.getFrameRate(), 20, 20 );

    float worldWidth = 2.0f;
    float worldHeight = 2.0f;
    float screenWidth = canvas.getWidth() - 1;
    float screenHeight = canvas.getHeight() - 1;
    float sx = screenWidth / worldWidth;
    float sy = screenHeight / worldHeight;
    float tx = screenWidth / 2.0f;
    float ty = screenHeight / 2.0f;
    Matrix3x3f viewport = Matrix3x3f.scale( sx, -sy );
    viewport = viewport.mul( Matrix3x3f.translate( tx, ty ) );

    for( int i = 0; i < tri.length; ++i ) {
        triWorld[i] = viewport.mul( tri[i] );
    }
```

```
        drawPolygon( g, triWorld );
        for( int i = 0; i < rect.length; ++i ) {
            rectWorld[i] = viewport.mul( rect[i] );
        }
        drawPolygon( g, rectWorld );
    }

    private void drawPolygon( Graphics g, Vector2f[] polygon ) {
        Vector2f P;
        Vector2f S = polygon[ polygon.length - 1 ];
        for( int i = 0; i < polygon.length; ++i ) {
            P = polygon[i];
            g.drawLine( (int)S.x, (int)S.y, (int)P.x, (int)P.y );
            S = P;
        }
    }

    protected void onWindowClosing() {
        try {
            running = false;
            gameThread.join();
        } catch( InterruptedException e ) {
            e.printStackTrace();
        }
        System.exit( 0 );
    }

    public static void main( String[] args ) {
        final ScreenMappingExample app = new ScreenMappingExample();
        app.addWindowListener( new WindowAdapter() {
            public void windowClosing( WindowEvent e ) {
                app.onWindowClosing();
            }
        });
        SwingUtilities.invokeLater( new Runnable() {
            public void run() {
                app.createAndShowGUI();
            }
        });
    }
}
```

ADJUSTING THE VIEWPORT RATIO

In the last example, the triangle stretches to fill the window, no matter what the size. It is possible to resize the window to push the triangle far from its original size, which is probably not the behavior a windowed game should have. Although it is important to be able to map to different sized viewports, it is also important to keep the ratio the same, so that no matter how large or small the window is, the proportions remain correct.

When you add a ComponentListener, the window will notify the application whenever it is resized. Therefore, no matter what the size, the ratio can stay the same. The ComponentListener has a few interfaces, but only the componentResized() method is necessary for detecting resize events:

```
componentHidden( ComponentEvent e )
componentMoved( ComponentEvent e )
componentResized( ComponentEvent e )
componentShown( ComponentEvent e )
```

Once the resize event is detected, the viewport needs to be adjusted to that the ratio remains the same. Depending on the size of the window and the size of the viewport, some interesting sizes can occur. See Figure 4.8.

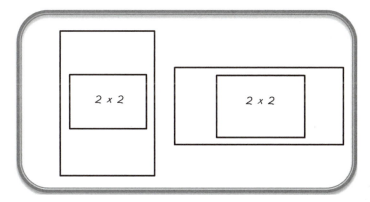

Figure 4.8
Width and Height Ratio.
© 2014 Timothy Wright.

If the adjusted viewport is centered in the current window, then no matter what size the window is, the viewport will grow or shrink to the largest size possible that still maintains the correct aspect ratio.

The new size is found using the ratio of the two windows:

$$\frac{new\ width}{new\ height} : \frac{viewport\ width}{viewport\ height}$$

$$new\ width = new\ height * \frac{viewport\ width}{viewport\ height}$$

$$new\ height = new\ width * \frac{viewport\ height}{viewport\ width}$$

To calculate the new size of the viewport, either the screen width or screen height can be chosen to calculate the other value so that the ratio will remain correct. Although you can perform checks to determine which dimension to use, it is just as easy to pick one, see if the new ratio will fit in the current window, and if it is too big, use the other one.

```
int newW = vw;
int newH = (int)(vw * worldHeight / worldWidth);
if( newH > vh ) {
    newW = (int)(vh * worldWidth / worldHeight);
    newH = vh;
}
```

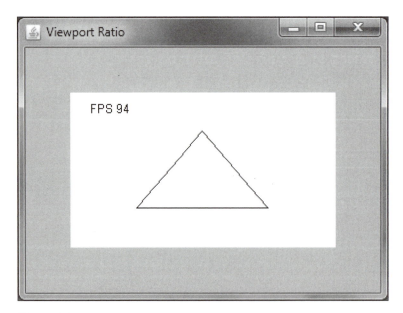

Figure 4.9
Viewport Ratio Example.
© 2014 Timothy Wright.

The ViewportRatioExample, shown in Figure 4.9 and located in the javagames. timeandspace package, maintains the world ratio size regardless of the screen size. The first thing to notice is ComponentAdapter, which is added to the content pane. This listener can also be added to the JFrame instead, but it does not receive resize events until the mouse button is released. Depending on the behavior of your game, this may be necessary, instead of redrawing the window while it is being resized.

```
getContentPane().addComponentListener( new ComponentAdapter() {
    public void componentResized( ComponentEvent e ) {
        onComponentResized( e );
    }
});
```

The ratio of the world is set to a 16:9, a wide screen sized world in the initialize() method. Changing these values will change the ratio of the viewport.

```
worldWidth = 16.0f;
worldHeight = 9.0f;
```

The actual resizing is done by calculating a new (x,y) position and a new width and height for the canvas object. See Figure 4.10.

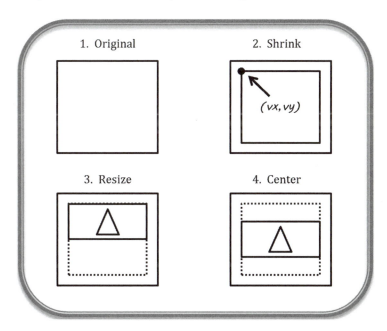

Figure 4.10
Resize and Center Algorithm.
© 2014 Timothy Wright.

The resizing process progresses as follows:

1. Original. The new size is available inside the `componentResized()` event.

2. Shrink. The current size is adjusted. In this case, it is changed to ¾ the current size. The center is calculated by taking the difference of the original size and the ¾ size, and cutting the remaining area in half.

3. The new width and height are calculated using the adjusted smaller size, so there will be a border.

4. The adjusted size is centered in the smaller size just like the previous viewport was centered.

The example code is shown here:

```java
package javagames.timeandspace;

import java.awt.*;
import java.awt.event.*;
import java.awt.image.*;
import javagames.util.*;

import javax.swing.*;


public class ViewportRatio extends JFrame implements Runnable {

    private FrameRate frameRate;
    private BufferStrategy bs;
    private volatile boolean running;
    private Thread gameThread;
    private RelativeMouseInput mouse;
    private KeyboardInput keyboard;
    private Canvas canvas;

    private Vector2f[] tri;
    private Vector2f[] triWorld;
    private float worldWidth;
    private float worldHeight;

    public ViewportRatio() {

    }

    protected void createAndShowGUI() {
        canvas = new Canvas();
        canvas.setBackground( Color.WHITE );
        canvas.setIgnoreRepaint( true );
        getContentPane().setBackground( Color.LIGHT_GRAY );
```

```
    setLayout( null );
    setTitle( "Viewport Ratio" );
    setSize( 640, 640 );
    getContentPane().add( canvas );

    keyboard = new KeyboardInput();
    canvas.addKeyListener( keyboard );

    mouse = new RelativeMouseInput( canvas );
    canvas.addMouseListener( mouse );
    canvas.addMouseMotionListener( mouse );
    canvas.addMouseWheelListener( mouse );

    getContentPane().addComponentListener( new ComponentAdapter() {
        public void componentResized( ComponentEvent e ) {
            onComponentResized( e );
        }
    });

    setVisible( true );
    canvas.createBufferStrategy( 2 );
    bs = canvas.getBufferStrategy();
    canvas.requestFocus();

    gameThread = new Thread( this );
    gameThread.start();
}

protected void onComponentResized( ComponentEvent e ) {
    Dimension size = getContentPane().getSize();
    int vw = size.width * 3 / 4;
    int vh = size.height * 3 / 4;
    int vx = (size.width - vw) / 2;
    int vy = (size.height - vh) / 2;

    int newW = vw;
    int newH = (int)(vw * worldHeight / worldWidth);
    if( newH > vh ) {
        newW = (int)(vh * worldWidth / worldHeight);
        newH = vh;
    }

    // center
    vx += (vw - newW) / 2;
    vy += (vh - newH) / 2;
    canvas.setLocation( vx, vy );
    canvas.setSize( newW, newH );
}
```

```java
public void run() {
    running = true;
    initialize();
    long curTime = System.nanoTime();
    long lastTime = curTime;
    double nsPerFrame;
    while( running ) {
        curTime = System.nanoTime();
        nsPerFrame = curTime - lastTime;
        gameLoop( nsPerFrame / 1.0E9 );
        lastTime = curTime;
    }
}

private void gameLoop( double delta ) {
    processInput( delta );
    updateObjects( delta );
    renderFrame();
    sleep( 10L );
}

private void renderFrame() {
    do {
        do {
            Graphics g = null;
            try {
                g = bs.getDrawGraphics();
                g.clearRect( 0, 0, getWidth(), getHeight() );
                render( g );
            } finally {
                if( g != null ) {
                    g.dispose();
                }
            }
        } while( bs.contentsRestored() );
        bs.show();
    } while( bs.contentsLost() );
}

private void sleep( long sleep ) {
    try {
        Thread.sleep( sleep );
    } catch( InterruptedException ex ) { }
}
```

```java
private void initialize() {
    frameRate = new FrameRate();
    frameRate.initialize();

    tri = new Vector2f[] {
            new Vector2f( 0.0f, 2.25f ),
            new Vector2f(-4.0f,-2.25f ),
            new Vector2f( 4.0f,-2.25f ),
    };
    triWorld = new Vector2f[ tri.length ];

    worldWidth = 16.0f;
    worldHeight = 9.0f;
}

private void processInput( double delta ) {

    keyboard.poll();
    mouse.poll();

}

private void updateObjects( double delta ) {

}

private void render( Graphics g ) {

    g.setColor( Color.BLACK );
    frameRate.calculate();
    g.drawString( frameRate.getFrameRate(), 20, 20 );

    float sx = (canvas.getWidth() - 1) / worldWidth;
    float sy = (canvas.getHeight() - 1) / worldHeight;
    float tx = (canvas.getWidth() - 1) / 2.0f;
    float ty = (canvas.getHeight() - 1) / 2.0f;
    Matrix3x3f viewport = Matrix3x3f.identity();
    viewport = viewport.mul( Matrix3x3f.scale( sx, -sy ) );
    viewport = viewport.mul( Matrix3x3f.translate( tx, ty ) );

    for( int i = 0; i < tri.length; ++i ) {
        triWorld[i] = viewport.mul( tri[i] );
    }
    drawPolygon( g, triWorld );
}

private void drawPolygon( Graphics g, Vector2f[] polygon ) {
    Vector2f P;
    Vector2f S = polygon[ polygon.length - 1 ];
    for( int i = 0; i < polygon.length; ++i ) {
```

```
            P = polygon[i];
            g.drawLine( (int)S.x, (int)S.y, (int)P.x, (int)P.y );
            S = P;
        }
    }

    protected void onWindowClosing() {
        try {
            running = false;
            gameThread.join();
        } catch( InterruptedException e ) {
            e.printStackTrace();
        }
        System.exit( 0 );
    }

    public static void main( String[] args ) {
        final ViewportRatio app = new ViewportRatio();
        app.addWindowListener( new WindowAdapter() {
            public void windowClosing( WindowEvent e ) {
                app.onWindowClosing();
            }
        });
        SwingUtilities.invokeLater( new Runnable() {
            public void run() {
                app.createAndShowGUI();
            }
        });
    }

}
```

Cannon Physics

The CannonExample, shown in Figure 4.11 and located in the javagames.timeandspace package, shoots a square in the air like a cannon ball. It is important to understand how the time delta parameter is used when moving objects.

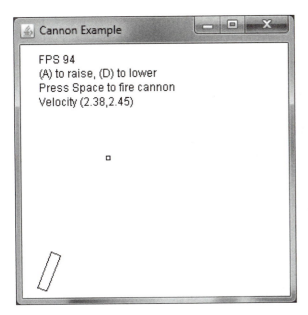

Figure 4.11
Cannon Example.
© 2014 Timothy Wright.

A standard physics equation for finding the position of an object could be done as follows:

$$d = d_0 + vt - \frac{at^2}{2}$$

where (d_0) is the initial position, (v) is the velocity, (a) is the acceleration, (t) is the time, and (d) is the resulting position. The problem with using this equation is that it needs the entire time, not just the time between frames. For the instantaneous time, the following equations are more useful:

$$v = \frac{d}{t}, \quad a = \frac{v}{t}, \quad d = vt, \quad v = at$$

These equations use only the current time, not the entire time. Make sure to pay attention to which time value is needed. If the entire time is required, don't just use the elapsed time.

The initialize() method sets the default values, creates the cannon model, and scales it by 0.75. When the A or D keys are pressed, the cannon is rotated, and the time delta is used to control the rotation. In previous examples, the rotation delta was set to a small value, like 5 degrees. Now it is set to 90 degrees per second and advanced using the time delta.

When the users press the spacebar, a new cannon ball is created. The velocity is calculated by creating a vector on the x-axis of 7.0 units and then rotating it to the correct angle. This could also be calculated using polar coordinates, but I wanted to show another way using matrices.

The cannon ball is transformed to the end of the rotated cannon. The 0.375 value is used because the original cannon length of 0.5 was scaled by 0.75 before the model is used.

The update() function positions and copies the cannon model so it is ready to be rendered. If there is a cannon ball, its position is adjusted. Instead of using a vector for gravity, I am cheating by using a value of −9.8. Now that the viewport mapping is in place, even though positive y values move down on the screen, I can use −9.8 as a gravity parameter. Without mapping the viewport, the y units would be flipped and a positive value for gravity would need to be used to get the bullet to fall, which is just weird.

The render method displays the usual frame rate and instructions. The world space for this example is 5 × 5 meters, which is mapped to the screen. The ratio is not maintained, so resizing the screen causes some weird things with the physics. After applying the viewport transform, the cannon and cannon ball are drawn.

```
package javagames.timeandspace;

import java.awt.*;
import java.awt.event.*;
import java.awt.image.*;
import javagames.util.*;

import javax.swing.*;


public class CannonExample extends JFrame
                implements Runnable {

    private FrameRate frameRate;
    private BufferStrategy bs;
    private volatile boolean running;
    private Thread gameThread;
    private RelativeMouseInput mouse;
    private KeyboardInput keyboard;
```

```java
private Canvas canvas;

private Vector2f[] cannon;
private Vector2f[] cannonCpy;
private float cannonRot, cannonDelta;

private Vector2f bullet;
private Vector2f bulletCpy;
private Vector2f velocity;

public CannonExample() {

}

protected void createAndShowGUI() {

    canvas = new Canvas();
    canvas.setSize( 640, 480 );
    canvas.setBackground( Color.WHITE );
    canvas.setIgnoreRepaint( true );
    getContentPane().add( canvas );
    setTitle( "Cannon Example" );
    setIgnoreRepaint( true );
    pack();

    keyboard = new KeyboardInput();
    canvas.addKeyListener( keyboard );

    mouse = new RelativeMouseInput( canvas );
    canvas.addMouseListener( mouse );
    canvas.addMouseMotionListener( mouse );
    canvas.addMouseWheelListener( mouse );

    setVisible( true );
    canvas.createBufferStrategy( 2 );
    bs = canvas.getBufferStrategy();
    canvas.requestFocus();

    gameThread = new Thread( this );
    gameThread.start();
}

public void run() {
    running = true;
    initialize();
```

```
        long curTime = System.nanoTime();
        long lastTime = curTime;
        double nsPerFrame;
        while( running ) {
            curTime = System.nanoTime();
            nsPerFrame = curTime - lastTime;
            gameLoop( nsPerFrame / 1.0E9 );
            lastTime = curTime;
        }
    }

    private void initialize() {

        frameRate = new FrameRate();
        frameRate.initialize();

        velocity = new Vector2f();
        cannonRot = 0.0f;
        cannonDelta = (float)Math.toRadians( 90.0 );
        cannon = new Vector2f[] {
            new Vector2f( -0.5f, 0.125f ), // top-left
            new Vector2f( 0.5f, 0.125f ), // top-right
            new Vector2f( 0.5f, -0.125f ), // bottom-right
            new Vector2f( -0.5f, -0.125f ), // bottom-left
        };
        cannonCpy = new Vector2f[ cannon.length ];

        Matrix3x3f scale = Matrix3x3f.scale( .75f, .75f );
        for( int i = 0; i < cannon.length; ++i ) {
            cannon[i] = scale.mul( cannon[i] );
        }

    }

    private void gameLoop( double delta ) {
        processInput( delta );
        updateObjects( delta );
        renderFrame();
        sleep( 10L );
    }

    private void renderFrame() {
        do {
            do {
                Graphics g = null;
```

```
            try {
                g = bs.getDrawGraphics();
                g.clearRect( 0, 0, getWidth(), getHeight() );
                render( g );
            } finally {
                if( g != null ) {
                    g.dispose();
                }
            }
        } while( bs.contentsRestored() );
        bs.show();
    } while( bs.contentsLost() );
}

private void sleep( long sleep ) {
    try {
        Thread.sleep( sleep );
    } catch( InterruptedException ex ) { }
}

private void processInput( double delta ) {

    keyboard.poll();
    mouse.poll();

    if( keyboard.keyDown( KeyEvent.VK_A ) ) {
        cannonRot += cannonDelta * delta;
    }
    if( keyboard.keyDown( KeyEvent.VK_D ) ) {
        cannonRot -= cannonDelta * delta;
    }
    if( keyboard.keyDownOnce( KeyEvent.VK_SPACE ) ) {

        // new velocity
        Matrix3x3f mat = Matrix3x3f.translate( 7.0f, 0.0f );
        mat = mat.mul( Matrix3x3f.rotate( cannonRot ) );
        velocity = mat.mul( new Vector2f() );

        // place bullet at cannon end
        mat = Matrix3x3f.translate( .375f, 0.0f );
        mat = mat.mul( Matrix3x3f.rotate( cannonRot ) );
        mat = mat.mul( Matrix3x3f.translate( -2.0f, -2.0f ) );
        bullet = mat.mul( new Vector2f() );
    }
}
```

```java
private void updateObjects( double delta ) {

    Matrix3x3f mat = Matrix3x3f.identity();
    mat = mat.mul( Matrix3x3f.rotate( cannonRot ) );
    mat = mat.mul( Matrix3x3f.translate( -2.0f, -2.0f ) );

    for( int i = 0; i < cannon.length; ++i ) {
        cannonCpy[i] = mat.mul( cannon[i] );
    }

    if( bullet != null ) {

        velocity.y += -9.8f * delta;
        bullet.x += velocity.x * delta;
        bullet.y += velocity.y * delta;
        bulletCpy = new Vector2f( bullet );

        if( bullet.y < -2.5f ) {
            bullet = null;
        }
    }

}

private void render( Graphics g ) {

    g.setColor( Color.BLACK );
    frameRate.calculate();
    g.drawString( frameRate.getFrameRate(), 20, 20 );
    g.drawString( "(A) to raise, (D) to lower", 20, 35 );
    g.drawString( "Press Space to fire cannon", 20, 50 );
    String vel =
        String.format( "Velocity (%.2f,%.2f)", velocity.x, velocity.y );
    g.drawString( vel, 20, 65 );

    float worldWidth = 5.0f;
    float worldHeight = 5.0f;
    float screenWidth = canvas.getWidth() - 1;
    float screenHeight = canvas.getHeight() - 1;

    float sx = screenWidth / worldWidth;
    float sy = -screenHeight / worldHeight;
    Matrix3x3f viewport = Matrix3x3f.scale( sx, sy );
    float tx = screenWidth / 2.0f;
```

```
      float ty = screenHeight / 2.0f;
      viewport = viewport.mul( Matrix3x3f.translate( tx, ty ) );

      for( int i = 0; i < cannon.length; ++i ) {
         cannonCpy[i] = viewport.mul( cannonCpy[i] );
      }

      drawPolygon( g, cannonCpy );

      if( bullet != null ) {
         bulletCpy = viewport.mul( bulletCpy );
         g.drawRect( (int)bulletCpy.x-2, (int)bulletCpy.y-2, 4, 4 );
      }
   }

   private void drawPolygon( Graphics g, Vector2f[] polygon ) {
      Vector2f P;
      Vector2f S = polygon[ polygon.length - 1 ];
      for( int i = 0; i < polygon.length; ++i ) {
         P = polygon[i];
         g.drawLine( (int)S.x, (int)S.y, (int)P.x, (int)P.y );
         S = P;
      }
   }

   protected void onWindowClosing() {
      try {
         running = false;
         gameThread.join();
      } catch( InterruptedException e ) {
         e.printStackTrace();
      }
      System.exit( 0 );
   }

   public static void main( String[] args ) {
      final CannonExample app = new CannonExample();
      app.addWindowListener( new WindowAdapter() {
         public void windowClosing( WindowEvent e ) {
            app.onWindowClosing();
         }
      });
```

```
    SwingUtilities.invokeLater( new Runnable() {
        public void run() {
            app.createAndShowGUI();
        }
    });
    }
}
```

RESOURCES AND FURTHER READING

Sanglard, Fabien, "Game Timers: Issues and Solutions," http://fabiensanglard.net/timer_and_framerate/index.php.

Fiedler, Glenn, "Fix Your Timestep," http://gafferongames.com/game-physics/fix-your-timestep/.

CHAPTER 5

SIMPLE GAME FRAMEWORK

Many of the examples so far have a lot of common code. All of the previous chapters added and updated features to the main game loop in some way. Since there are no more updates to the framework of each example, it is helpful to create a SimpleFramework that can be used as a starting point for all the following examples.

SCREEN-TO-WORLD CONVERSION

The Utility class has been added to the javagames.util package with the following methods for creating viewport-transformation matrices:

```
package javagames.util;

public class Utility {
    public static Matrix3x3f createViewport(
            float worldWidth, float worldHeight,
            float screenWidth, float screenHeight ) {

        float sx = (screenWidth - 1) / worldWidth;
        float sy = (screenHeight - 1) / worldHeight;
        float tx = (screenWidth - 1) / 2.0f;
        float ty = (screenHeight - 1) / 2.0f;
        Matrix3x3f viewport = Matrix3x3f.scale( sx, -sy );
        viewport = viewport.mul( Matrix3x3f.translate( tx, ty ) );
        return viewport;
    }

    public static Matrix3x3f createReverseViewport(
            float worldWidth, float worldHeight,
```

```
                 float screenWidth, float screenHeight ) {
         float sx = worldWidth / (screenWidth - 1);
         float sy = worldHeight / (screenHeight - 1);
         float tx = (screenWidth - 1) / 2.0f;
         float ty = (screenHeight - 1) / 2.0f;
         Matrix3x3f viewport = Matrix3x3f.translate( -tx, -ty );
         viewport = viewport.mul( Matrix3x3f.scale( sx, -sy ) );
         return viewport;
      }


   }
```

Notice that the `createReverseViewport()` translates and scales instead of scaling and translating, performing the reverse of the viewport transformation. This can been used to convert the mouse screen coordinates into world coordinates.

`getViewportTransform()` and `getReverseViewportTransform()` have been added as utility methods, using the canvas size and the world size to create the transformation matrices. `getWorldMousePosition()` is used to transform the screen coordinates into world coordinates. The `getRelativeWorldMousePosition()` method is used when the mouse is set to return relative positions.

```
// SimpleFramework.java
protected Matrix3x3f getViewportTransform() {
   return Utility.createViewport(
   appWorldWidth, appWorldHeight, canvas.getWidth(), canvas.getHeight()
   );
}

protected Matrix3x3f getReverseViewportTransform() {
   return Utility.createReverseViewport(
   appWorldWidth, appWorldHeight, canvas.getWidth(), canvas.getHeight()
   );
}

protected Vector2f getWorldMousePosition() {
   Matrix3x3f screenToWorld = getReverseViewportTransform();
   Point mousePos = mouse.getPosition();
   Vector2f screenPos = new Vector2f( mousePos.x, mousePos.y );
   return screenToWorld.mul( screenPos );
}

protected Vector2f getRelativeWorldMousePosition() {
   float sx = appWorldWidth / (canvas.getWidth() - 1);
   float sy = appWorldHeight / (canvas.getHeight() - 1);
   Matrix3x3f viewport = Matrix3x3f.scale( sx, -sy );
```

```
        Point p = mouse.getPosition();
        return viewport.mul( new Vector2f( p.x, p.y ) );
}
```

Understanding the Simple Framework

The first thing to notice about the `SimpleFramework` class, located in the `javagames.util` package, is all the properties. Although there could be methods to access each individual property, it is easier to just use the default values or change them in the constructor. Since all the properties start with `app`, using code completion in a code editor will bring up a list of available properties. See Figure 5.1.

Figure 5.1
Launch Application.
© 2014 Timothy Wright.

- `appBackground`—The background color of the main game area.

- `appBorder`—The color of the border when the aspect ratio is maintained.

- `appFPSColor`—The color to draw the frames-per-second display.

- `appFont`—The font to use when displaying the frames-per-second.

- `appTitle`—The title of the example.

- `appBorderScale`—The ratio of the game area to border area when the aspect ratio is maintained.

- `appWidth`—The startup width of the window.

- `appHeight`—The startup height of the window.

- appWorldWidth—The width of the world coordinates.
- appWorldHeight—The height of the world coordinates.
- appSleep—The number of milliseconds to sleep each frame.
- appMaintainRatio—True if the aspect ratio should be maintained.

This class has no main() method. Subclasses can use the launchApp() method to add the shutdown window listener and start the application.

```
// SimpleFramework.java
protected static void launchApp( final SimpleFramework app ) {
    app.addWindowListener( new WindowAdapter() {
        public void windowClosing( WindowEvent e ) {
            app.onWindowClosing();
        }
    });
    SwingUtilities.invokeLater( new Runnable() {
        public void run() {
            app.createAndShowGUI();
        }
    });
}
```

Inside the createAndShowGUI() method, the new code checks the aspect ratio property and either initializes the application to stretch the view, or maintains the aspect ratio when the window is resized. See the ViewportRatioExample in Chapter 4, "Time and Space," for more information. The onComponentResized() method is used to resize the canvas when the window is resized and the aspect ratio should be maintained. See Figure 5.2.

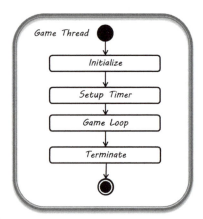

Figure 5.2
Game Thread.
© 2014 Timothy Wright.

The run() method has two methods added to it to allow subclasses the ability to run code before and after the main game loop:

- initialize() is called before the game loop starts.
- terminate() is called after the application is closed.

The initialize() method creates and initializes the frameRate object, the terminate() method is empty, and the game loop is the same. There is nothing performed in the terminate() method, and the game loop remains the same. The three methods used to perform game actions have been made protected so subclasses can override them.

```
protected void processInput(float delta)
protected void updateObjects(float delta)
protected void render(Graphics g)
```

The processInput() method calls the poll methods for the keyboard and mouse. The render() method draws the frame rate, and the updateObjects() method is empty for the time being. See Figure 5.3.

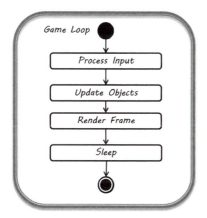

Figure 5.3
Game Loop.
© 2014 Timothy Wright.

```
package javagames.util;

import java.awt.*;
import java.awt.event.*;
import java.awt.image.BufferStrategy;

import javax.swing.JFrame;
import javax.swing.SwingUtilities;
```

```java
public class SimpleFramework extends JFrame implements Runnable {

    private BufferStrategy bs;
    private volatile boolean running;
    private Thread gameThread;

    protected FrameRate frameRate;
    protected Canvas canvas;
    protected RelativeMouseInput mouse;
    protected KeyboardInput keyboard;

    protected Color appBackground = Color.BLACK;
    protected Color appBorder = Color.LIGHT_GRAY;
    protected Color appFPSColor = Color.GREEN;
    protected Font appFont = new Font( "Courier New", Font.PLAIN, 14 );
    protected String appTitle = "TBD-Title";
    protected float appBorderScale = 0.8f;
    protected int appWidth = 640;
    protected int appHeight = 480;
    protected float appWorldWidth = 2.0f;
    protected float appWorldHeight = 2.0f;
    protected long appSleep = 10L;
    protected boolean appMaintainRatio = false;

    public SimpleFramework() {

    }

    protected void createAndShowGUI() {

        canvas = new Canvas();
        canvas.setBackground( appBackground );
        canvas.setIgnoreRepaint( true );
        getContentPane().add( canvas );
        setLocationByPlatform( true );

        if( appMaintainRatio ) {
            getContentPane().setBackground( appBorder );
            setSize( appWidth, appHeight );
            setLayout( null );
            getContentPane().addComponentListener( new ComponentAdapter() {
                public void componentResized( ComponentEvent e ) {
                    onComponentResized( e );
                }
            });
        } else {
            canvas.setSize( appWidth, appHeight );
            pack();
        }
```

```java
    setTitle( appTitle );

    keyboard = new KeyboardInput();
    canvas.addKeyListener( keyboard );

    mouse = new RelativeMouseInput( canvas );
    canvas.addMouseListener( mouse );
    canvas.addMouseMotionListener( mouse );
    canvas.addMouseWheelListener( mouse );

    setVisible( true );
    canvas.createBufferStrategy( 2 );
    bs = canvas.getBufferStrategy();
    canvas.requestFocus();

    gameThread = new Thread( this );
    gameThread.start();
}

protected void onComponentResized( ComponentEvent e ) {
    Dimension size = getContentPane().getSize();
    int vw = (int)(size.width * appBorderScale);
    int vh = (int)(size.height * appBorderScale);
    int vx = (size.width - vw) / 2;
    int vy = (size.height - vh) / 2;

    int newW = vw;
    int newH = (int)(vw * appWorldHeight / appWorldWidth);
    if( newH > vh ) {
        newW = (int)(vh * appWorldWidth / appWorldHeight);
        newH = vh;
    }

    // center
    vx += (vw - newW) / 2;
    vy += (vh - newH) / 2;
    canvas.setLocation( vx, vy );
    canvas.setSize( newW, newH );

}

protected Matrix3x3f getViewportTransform() {
    return Utility.createViewport(
    appWorldWidth, appWorldHeight, canvas.getWidth(), canvas.getHeight()
    );
}

protected Matrix3x3f getReverseViewportTransform() {
    return Utility.createReverseViewport(
```

```
          appWorldWidth, appWorldHeight, canvas.getWidth(), canvas.getHeight()
       );
   }

   protected Vector2f getWorldMousePosition() {
      Matrix3x3f screenToWorld = getReverseViewportTransform();
      Point mousePos = mouse.getPosition();
      Vector2f screenPos = new Vector2f( mousePos.x, mousePos.y );
      return screenToWorld.mul( screenPos );
   }

   protected Vector2f getRelativeWorldMousePosition() {
      float sx = appWorldWidth / (canvas.getWidth() - 1);
      float sy = appWorldHeight / (canvas.getHeight() - 1);
      Matrix3x3f viewport = Matrix3x3f.scale( sx, -sy );
      Point p = mouse.getPosition();
      return viewport.mul( new Vector2f( p.x, p.y ) );
   }

   public void run() {
      running = true;
      initialize();
      long curTime = System.nanoTime();
      long lastTime = curTime;
      double nsPerFrame;
      while( running ) {
         curTime = System.nanoTime();
         nsPerFrame = curTime - lastTime;
         gameLoop( (float)(nsPerFrame / 1.0E9) );
         lastTime = curTime;
      }
      terminate();
   }

   protected void initialize() {
      frameRate = new FrameRate();
      frameRate.initialize();
   }

   protected void terminate() {

   }

   private void gameLoop( float delta ) {
      processInput( delta );
      updateObjects( delta );
```

```
            renderFrame();
            sleep( appSleep );
        }
        private void renderFrame() {
            do {
                do {
                    Graphics g = null;
                    try {
                        g = bs.getDrawGraphics();
                        g.clearRect( 0, 0, getWidth(), getHeight() );
                        render( g );
                    } finally {
                        if( g != null ) {
                            g.dispose();
                        }
                    }
                } while( bs.contentsRestored() );
                bs.show();
            } while( bs.contentsLost() );
        }
        private void sleep( long sleep ) {
            try {
                Thread.sleep( sleep );
            } catch( InterruptedException ex ) { }
        }
        protected void processInput( float delta ) {
            keyboard.poll();
            mouse.poll();
        }
        protected void updateObjects( float delta ) {

        }
        protected void render( Graphics g ) {
            g.setFont( appFont );
            g.setColor( appFPSColor );
            frameRate.calculate();
            g.drawString( frameRate.getFrameRate(), 20, 20 );
        }
        protected void onWindowClosing() {
            try {
                running = false;
                gameThread.join();
            } catch( InterruptedException e ) {
```

```
                e.printStackTrace();
        }
        System.exit( 0 );
    }

    protected static void launchApp( final SimpleFramework app ) {
        app.addWindowListener( new WindowAdapter() {
            public void windowClosing( WindowEvent e ) {
                app.onWindowClosing();
            }
        });
        SwingUtilities.invokeLater( new Runnable() {
            public void run() {
                app.createAndShowGUI();
            }
        });
    }

}
```

USING THE SIMPLE FRAMEWORK TEMPLATE

The SimpleFrameworkTemplate, located in the javagames.util package, can be used as a
starting point for all of the examples that follow. The framework hides the common
code, making it easier to explore the new code in the examples (see Figure 5.4).

Figure 5.4
Simple Framework Template.
© 2014 Timothy Wright.

The template extends the SimpleFramework class. The launchApp() method is used in the
main method to start the application.

```
// SimpleFrameworkTemplate.java
public static void main( String[] args ) {
    launchApp( new SimpleFrameworkTemplate() );
}
```

The constructor is the place to set all of the application's properties. Setting the properties in the initialize() method is too late, because some of them have already been used before the initialize() method is called. Any properties whose default values are acceptable can be removed from the constructor.

Caution

Do *not* set the properties in the initialize() method; do so in the constructor.

Overriding the five following methods allows for custom code to be executed in the game loop:

- initialize()
- processInput(float delta)
- updateObjects(float delta)
- render(Graphics g)
- terminate()

The following example template is used as a base for the examples in the following chapters.

```
package javagames.util;

import java.awt.Color;
import java.awt.Font;
import java.awt.Graphics;

import javagames.util.SimpleFramework;


public class SimpleFrameworkTemplate extends SimpleFramework {
    public SimpleFrameworkTemplate() {
        appBackground = Color.WHITE;
        appBorder = Color.LIGHT_GRAY;
        appFont = new Font( "Courier New", Font.PLAIN, 14 );
        appBorderScale = 0.9f;
        appFPSColor = Color.BLACK;
        appWidth = 640;
        appHeight = 640;
```

```
        appMaintainRatio = true;
        appSleep = 10L;
        appTitle = "FramworkTemplate";
        appWorldWidth = 2.0f;
        appWorldHeight = 2.0f;
    }

    @Override
    protected void initialize() {
        super.initialize();
    }

    @Override
    protected void processInput( float delta ) {
        super.processInput( delta );
    }

    @Override
    protected void updateObjects( float delta ) {
        super.updateObjects( delta );
    }

    @Override
    protected void render( Graphics g ) {
        super.render( g );
    }

    @Override
    protected void terminate() {
        super.terminate();
    }

    public static void main( String[] args ) {
        launchApp( new SimpleFrameworkTemplate() );
    }

}
```

RESOURCES AND FURTHER READING

Code and a Coke 2D framework tutorial; see http://www.cokeandcode.com/main /tutorials/space-invaders-101/.

Java framework for desktop, iOS, Android, and HTML games; see http://libgdx.bad logicgames.com/.

The lightweight Java game library; see http://lwjgl.org/.

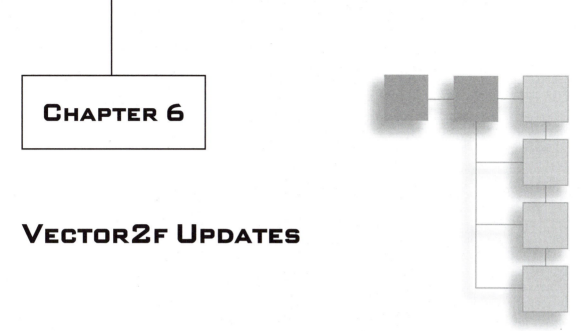

CHAPTER 6

VECTOR2F UPDATES

There are updates to the vector class that you need to be aware of before you move on to the intersection-testing algorithms and concepts. The updates are covered in this chapter.

INV( )

```
public Vector2f inv() {
    return new Vector2f( -x, -y );
}
```

The inv() method returns a new vector that is the inverse of the current vector. The inverse of a vector, as shown in Figure 6.1, is a new vector that points in the opposite direction.

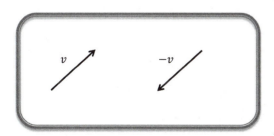

Figure 6.1
Vector Inverse.
© 2014 Timothy Wright.

ADD( )

```
public Vector2f add( Vector2f v ) {
        return new Vector2f( x + v.x, y + v.y );
    }
```

The add() method returns a new vector that is the sum of the current vector and the given vector. See Figure 6.2.

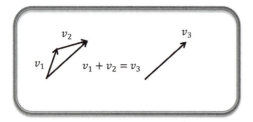

Figure 6.2
Vector Addition.
© 2014 Timothy Wright.

SUB( )

```
public Vector2f sub( Vector2f v ) {
        return new Vector2f( x - v.x, y - v.y );
    }
```

The sub() method returns a new vector that is the subtraction of the given vector and the current vector. Notice in Figure 6.3 that order matters. The arrow of the new vector will point to the first vector in the operation.

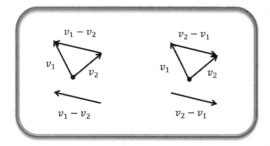

Figure 6.3
Vector Subtraction.
© 2014 Timothy Wright.

Sometimes it is easier to visualize subtraction as adding the inverse of a vector. As shown in Figure 6.4, $V_1 - V_2$ and $V_1 + (-V_2)$ produce the same result.

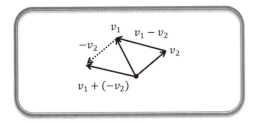

Figure 6.4
Vector Subtraction as Inverse Addition.
© 2014 Timothy Wright.

MUL( )

```
public Vector2f mul( float scalar ) {
     return new Vector2f( scalar * x, scalar * y );
  }
```

The mul() method returns a new vector that is the product of the vector component and the scalar value. Notice in Figure 6.5 that negative values invert the vector.

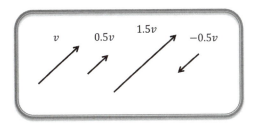

Figure 6.5
Vector Multiplication.
© 2014 Timothy Wright.

DIV( )

```
public Vector2f div( float scalar ) {
     return new Vector2f( x / scalar, y / scalar );
  }
```

The div() method is the same as multiplying by one over the scalar. Notice that no checks are made for dividing by zero.

LEN( ) AND LENSQR( )

```
public float len() {
     return (float)Math.sqrt( x * x + y * y );
  }
```

To find the length of a vector, you use the Pythagorean Theorem. See Figure 6.6.

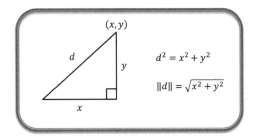

Figure 6.6
Length of Vector.
© 2014 Timothy Wright.

Single lines are used for the absolute value |a|. Double lines are used for the length of a vector ||a||.

$$If \ x > y \ then \ x^2 > y^2$$

```
public float lenSqr() {
    return x * x + y * y;
}
```

Because the square root operation can take many computer cycles, sometimes it is easier to just use the squared length value in comparisons.

NORM( )

```
public Vector2f norm() {
        return div( len() );
    }
```

The norm() method returns a normalized vector that has a length of one, as shown in Figure 6.7. Many graphics equations can be simplified by using a vector with a length of one. The little hat (a caret) above the variable in the diagrams indicates a unit vector.

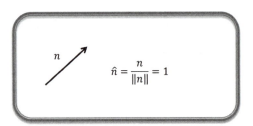

Figure 6.7
Vector Normalization.
© 2014 Timothy Wright.

PERP( )

```
public Vector2f perp() {
      return new Vector2f( -y, x );
   }
```

The perp() method returns a new vector that is perpendicular to the current vector. See Figure 6.8. This is useful for creating a normal vector that is needed in many of the equations in the following chapters. Notice that either $(-y, x)$ or $(y, -x)$ produce a perpendicular vector. The upside down T represents a perpendicular vector.

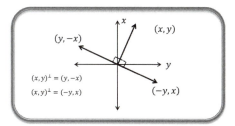

Figure 6.8
Perpendicular Vector.
© 2014 Timothy Wright.

DOT( )

```
public float dot( Vector2f v ) {
      return x * v.x + y * v.y;
   }
```

The dot() method returns the dot product of two vectors. This method of multiplying two vectors is very useful. As shown in Figure 6.9, the dot product projects one vector onto another, forming a right triangle, which is very helpful when testing object intersections.

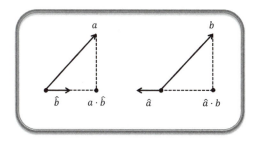

Figure 6.9
Dot Product.
© 2014 Timothy Wright.

The dot product proof, as illustrated in Figure 6.10, is as follows:

$$A * B = ||A|| \, ||B|| \cos(\theta A - \theta B)$$
$$A * B = AB \left[\cos(\theta A) \cos(\theta B) + \sin(\theta A) \sin(\theta B)\right]$$
$$A * B = A\cos(\theta A) \, B \cos(\theta B) + A \sin(\theta A) \, B \sin(\theta B)$$

Reviewing Cartesian polar conversions:

$$A_x = A \cos(\theta A)$$
$$B_x = B \cos(\theta B)$$
$$A_y = A \sin(\theta A)$$
$$B_y = B \sin(\theta B)$$
$$A * B = A_x B_x + A_y B_y$$

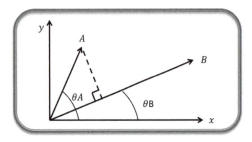

Figure 6.10
Dot Product Angle.
© 2014 Timothy Wright.

The dot product has the following mathematical properties:

$$A * B = B * A$$
$$C * (A + B) = C * A + C * B$$
$$C(A * B) = CA * B$$
$$A * A^{\perp} = 0$$

The last property is important, and is used for the basis of many mathematical proofs. Because the angle between two perpendicular vectors is always zero, their dot product is always zero.

$$A * A^{\perp} = ||A|| \, ||A^{\perp}|| \cos(90°)$$
$$A * A^{\perp} = ||A|| \, ||A^{\perp}|| \, (0)$$
$$A * A^{\perp} = 0$$

The final important point is that the dot product returns a scalar value, not a vector, as shown in Figure 6.11. To project one vector onto another, the vector receiving the projection must be a normal vector and that normal vector needs to be scaled by the dot product.

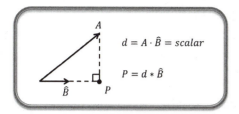

Figure 6.11
Dot Product Scalar.
© 2014 Timothy Wright.

ANGLE( )

```
public float angle() {
      return (float)Math.atan2( y, x );
   }
```

The `angle()` method returns the angle in radians created by the vector, as shown in Figure 6.12. Notice the `atan2()` method is used to handle the cases where x is zero, so no additional checks are needed.

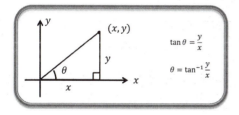

Figure 6.12
Angle.
© 2014 Timothy Wright.

POLAR( )

```
public static Vector2f polar( float angle, float radius ) {
      return new Vector2f(
         radius * (float)Math.cos( angle ),
         radius * (float)Math.sin( angle )
      );
   }
```

The polar() method takes an angle in radians and a radius and returns a vector with the converted x and y coordinates, as shown in Figure 6.13.

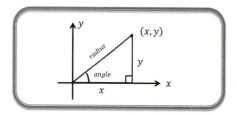

Figure 6.13
Polar.
© 2014 Timothy Wright.

toString()

```
@Override
public String toString() {
return String.format( "(%s,%s)", x, y );
}
```

The last update is helpful for displaying the vector values as strings for debugging.

```
package javagames.util;


public class Vector2f {
    public float x;
    public float y;
    public float w;
    public Vector2f() {
        this.x = 0.0f;
        this.y = 0.0f;
        this.w = 1.0f;
    }
    public Vector2f( Vector2f v ) {
        this.x = v.x;
        this.y = v.y;
        this.w = v.w;
    }
    public Vector2f( float x, float y ) {
        this.x = x;
        this.y = y;
        this.w = 1.0f;
```

```java
    }
    public Vector2f( float x, float y, float w ) {
        this.x = x;
        this.y = y;
        this.w = w;
    }
    public void translate( float tx, float ty ) {
        x += tx;
        y += ty;
    }
    public void scale( float sx, float sy ) {
        x *= sx;
        y *= sy;
    }
    public void rotate( float rad ) {
        float tmp = (float)( x * Math.cos( rad ) - y * Math.sin( rad ) );
        y = (float)( x * Math.sin( rad ) + y * Math.cos( rad ) );
        x = tmp;
    }
    public void shear( float sx, float sy ) {
        float tmp = x + sx * y;
        y = y + sy * x;
        x = tmp;
    }
    public Vector2f add( Vector2f v ) {
        return new Vector2f( x + v.x, y + v.y );
    }
    public Vector2f sub( Vector2f v ) {
        return new Vector2f( x - v.x, y - v.y );
    }
    public Vector2f mul( float scalar ) {
        return new Vector2f( scalar * x, scalar * y );
    }
    public Vector2f div( float scalar ) {
        return new Vector2f( x / scalar, y / scalar );
    }
    public Vector2f inv() {
        return new Vector2f( -x, -y );
    }
    public Vector2f norm() {
```

```java
        return div( len() );
    }

    public float dot( Vector2f v ) {
        return x * v.x + y * v.y;
    }

    public float len() {
        return (float)Math.sqrt( x * x + y * y );
    }

    public float lenSqr() {
        return x * x + y * y;
    }

    public Vector2f perp() {
        return new Vector2f( -y, x );
    }

    public float angle() {
        return (float)Math.atan2( y, x );
    }

    public static Vector2f polar( float angle, float radius ) {
        return new Vector2f(
            radius * (float)Math.cos( angle ),
            radius * (float)Math.sin( angle )
        );
    }

    @Override
    public String toString() {
        return String.format( "(%s,%s)", x, y );
    }

}
```

RESOURCES AND FURTHER READING

Akenine-Moller, Tomas, and Eric Haines, *Real-Time Rendering*, 2nd Edition, A K Peters, 2002.

Ericson, Christer, *Real-Time Collision Detection*, Focal Press, 2004.

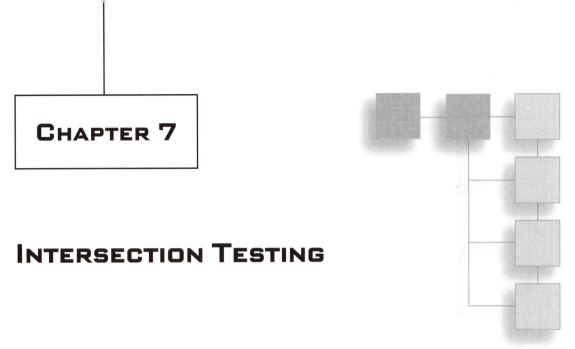

CHAPTER 7

INTERSECTION TESTING

It won't be much of a game if objects fly about the screen but never interact with each other. Regardless of the kind of game, even if it is just to check whether the mouse is hovering over something, at some point intersection testing and collision detection will be necessary. The problem is that these topics can be complicated. Entire tomes of algorithms and math can be found on many shelves and people are still trying to find ways to improve on the algorithms. Most people assume that the huge 3D sandbox games are full of complicated ideas, but that simple (looking) 2D games are easy. After this chapter, it should be obvious that looks can be deceiving.

POINT IN POLYGON TESTING

In order to determine if the mouse pointer is inside an object, two operations are needed. First, it is necessary to convert the mouse position in screen coordinates into world coordinates. This code was covered in Chapter 5, "Simple Game Framework." Second, the objects need to be tested to see if the mouse position in world coordinates is inside the object. Testing if a point is inside a polygon is useful for a variety of situations in computer games.

An algorithm for determining if a point is inside a polygon is easy to understand, but there are lots of concepts that are not obvious at first. The test itself is easy to explain, but hard to implement. You take the point to be tested and extend a ray along the x-axis. Count every time the ray crosses the polygon. If it crosses an even number of times, it is outside. If it crosses an odd number of times, it is inside. See Figure 7.1.

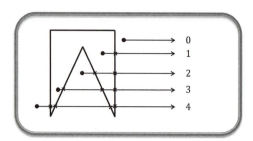

Figure 7.1
Point in Polygon.
© 2014 Timothy Wright.

As shown in Figure 7.1, points 0, 2, and 4 are outside the polygon because they cross an even number of times. Points 1 and 3 are inside because they cross an odd number of times. Because the algorithm needs to know if the ray crosses a polygon line, the test can be broken into four different cases, as illustrated in Figure 7.2.

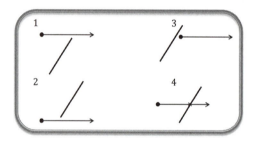

Figure 7.2
Point in Polygon Cases.
© 2014 Timothy Wright.

The first three cases, where the polygon line is either above, below, or behind the point, all evaluate to no intersection. Only number four counts as the ray crossing a polygon line.

```
// PointInPolygonExample.java
private boolean pointInPolygon( Vector2f point, List<Vector2f> poly ) {
        boolean inside = false;
1:      if( poly.size() > 2 ) {
2:          Vector2f start = poly.get( poly.size() - 1 );
3:          boolean startAbove = start.y >= point.y;
4:          for( int i = 0; i < poly.size(); ++i ) {
5:              Vector2f end = poly.get( i );
6:              boolean endAbove = end.y >= point.y;
```

```
7:                    if( startAbove != endAbove ) {
                          // TBD - test ahead or behind
                      }
8:                    startAbove = endAbove;
9:                    start = end;
                  }
              }
10:       return inside;
}
```

The steps for the `pointInPolygon()` algorithm are as follows:

1. Don't bother if there are not at least three lines in the polygon.

2. Start with the last and first points.

3. Set `startAbove` to `true` if the first polygon point is above the y value of the point to check.

4. Loop through all the points in the polygon.

5. Since the code gets the last point in the polygon, start with the first.

6. Set `endAbove` to `true` if the second polygon point is above the y value of the point to check.

7. If both `startAbove` and `endAbove` are equal, then they are either both above or both below the point and there cannot be an intersection.

8. Save the `startAbove` state.

9. Make the end point the start point.

10. Return the result.

In order to determine whether the intersection is ahead or behind the ray, the point-slope equation can be used to solve for the unknown x coordinate value.

$$y - y_1 = m(x - x_1)$$
$$x - x_1 = \frac{y - y_1}{m}$$
$$x = x_1 + \frac{y - y_1}{m}$$
$$where\ m = \frac{\Delta y}{\Delta x} = \frac{y_2 - y_1}{x_2 - x_1}$$

Once the x intersection value is found, it is compared to the point's x value. If the intersection value is smaller than the point's x value, the intersection is behind the point, and no intersection occurs.

```
if( startAbove != endAbove ) {
    float m = (end.y - start.y) / (end.x - start.x);
    float x = start.x + (point.y - start.y) / m;
    if( x >= point.x ) {
        inside = !inside;
    }

}
```

Point in Polygon Special Cases

This algorithm works well as long as the lines of the polygon do not intersect. The two following polygons have crossing lines, and both treat the dark shaded sections that are inside the polygon as if they were outside. See Figure 7.3.

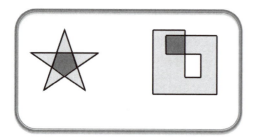

Figure 7.3
Point in Polygon Special Cases.
© 2014 Timothy Wright.

To correctly identify these overlapped sections, the direction where the line crosses the ray can be counted. For every crossing, going from the top to the bottom, the count is incremented and for every crossing, going from the bottom to the top, the count is decremented. If the number of crossings has the same number of clockwise and counterclockwise crossings (the count is zero), then the point is outside. See Figure 7.4.

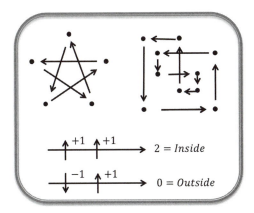

Figure 7.4
Polygon Winding.
© 2014 Timothy Wright.

The complete algorithm with and without winding is as follows:

```java
// PointInPolygonExample.java
private boolean pointInPolygon(
    Vector2f point, List<Vector2f> poly, boolean winding ) {

    int inside = 0;
    if( poly.size() > 2 ) {
        Vector2f start = poly.get( poly.size() - 1 );
        boolean startAbove = start.y >= point.y;
        for( int i = 0; i < poly.size(); ++i ) {
            Vector2f end = poly.get( i );
            boolean endAbove = end.y >= point.y;
            if( startAbove != endAbove ) {
                float m = (end.y - start.y) / (end.x - start.x);
                float x = start.x + (point.y - start.y) / m;
                if( x >= point.x ) {
                    if( winding ) {
                        inside += startAbove ? 1 : -1;
                    } else {
                        inside = inside == 1 ? 0 : 1;
                    }
                }
            }
            startAbove = endAbove;
            start = end;
        }
    }
    return inside != 0;
}
```

Point in Polygon Example

The PointInPolygonExample, located in the javagames.intersection package and shown in Figure 7.5, uses the SimpleFramework class for all the boilerplate code. The poly list holds the polygon created by clicking on the screen. The polyCpy list holds the polygon transformed to screen coordinates. All points inside the polygon are placed into the inside list and all points outside are placed into the outside list. The mouse position is the converted world coordinates. The selected variable is set to true if the mouse is inside the polygon. The winding variable is true when the algorithm should use the winding when testing points.

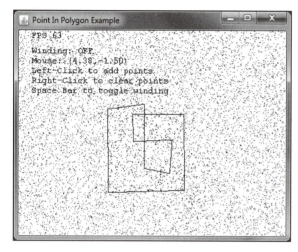

Figure 7.5
Point in Polygon Example.
© 2014 Timothy Wright.

There are a couple of new methods added to the Utility class to draw polygons. The code is the same as used in the previous examples, but it is easier to add it to the Utility class than to copy and paste it in all the examples.

```
package javagames.util;

import java.awt.Graphics;
import java.util.List;
```

```
public class Utility {
    // other methods ...
    public static void drawPolygon(
        Graphics g, Vector2f[] polygon ) {
        Vector2f P;
        Vector2f S = polygon[ polygon.length - 1 ];
        for( int i = 0; i < polygon.length; ++i ) {
            P = polygon[i];
            g.drawLine( (int)S.x, (int)S.y, (int)P.x, (int)P.y );
            S = P;
        }
    }

    public static void drawPolygon(
        Graphics g, List<Vector2f> polygon ) {
        Vector2f S = polygon.get( polygon.size() - 1 );
        for( Vector2f P : polygon ) {
            g.drawLine( (int)S.x, (int)S.y, (int)P.x, (int)P.y );
            S = P;
        }
    }
}
```

In the processInput() method, the mouse position is converted to world coordinates (covered in Chapter 5, "Simple Game Framework"). The spacebar toggles the polygon winding. Left clicks with the mouse add polygon points and right clicks clear the polygon.

The updateObjects() method sets the selected variable if the mouse is inside the polygon. Random points are then tested against the polygon and placed in the appropriate list. The pointInPolygon() method presented previously is used to determine the location of points relative to the polygon. The render() method displays the winding, mouse coordinates in world position, as well as the control descriptions. If the mouse is located inside the polygon, the polygon is drawn green; otherwise, it is drawn blue. All the randomly generated points inside the polygon are drawn green and all the points outside the polygon are drawn red.

```
package javagames.intersection;

import java.awt.*;
import java.awt.event.*;
import java.util.*;
import java.util.List;

import javagames.util.*;
```

```java
public class PointInPolygonExample extends SimpleFramework {
    private static final int MAX_POINTS = 10000;

    private ArrayList<Vector2f> poly;
    private ArrayList<Vector2f> polyCpy;
    private ArrayList<Vector2f> inside;
    private ArrayList<Vector2f> outside;
    private Vector2f mousePos;
    private boolean selected;
    private boolean winding;

    public PointInPolygonExample() {
        appWidth = 640;
        appHeight = 640;
        appTitle = "Point In Polygon Example";
        appBackground = Color.WHITE;
        appFPSColor = Color.BLACK;
    }

    @Override
    protected void initialize() {
        super.initialize();
        // polygon points and lists of point inside
        // and outside the polygon
        poly = new ArrayList<Vector2f>();
        polyCpy = new ArrayList<Vector2f>();
        inside = new ArrayList<Vector2f>();
        outside = new ArrayList<Vector2f>();

        mousePos = new Vector2f();
    }

    @Override
    protected void processInput( float delta ) {
        super.processInput( delta );

        mousePos = getWorldMousePosition();
        // draw polygon for algorithm testing
        if( keyboard.keyDownOnce( KeyEvent.VK_SPACE ) ) {
            winding = !winding;
        }
        if( mouse.buttonDownOnce( MouseEvent.BUTTON1 ) ) {
            poly.add( mousePos );
        }
        if( mouse.buttonDownOnce( MouseEvent.BUTTON3 ) ) {
            poly.clear();
        }
    }
```

```java
@Override
protected void updateObjects( float delta ) {
    super.updateObjects( delta );
    // see if the mouse is inside the polygon
    selected = pointInPolygon( mousePos, poly, winding );
    // test random points against the polygon
    Random rand = new Random();
    inside.clear();
    outside.clear();
    for( int i = 0; i < MAX_POINTS; ++i ) {
        float x = rand.nextFloat() * 2.0f - 1.0f;
        float y = rand.nextFloat() * 2.0f - 1.0f;
        Vector2f point = new Vector2f( x, y );
        if( pointInPolygon( point, poly, winding ) ) {
            inside.add( point );
        } else {
            outside.add( point );
        }
    }
}

private boolean pointInPolygon( Vector2f point, List<Vector2f> poly,
    boolean winding ) {
    // point in polygon algorithm
    int inside = 0;
    if( poly.size() > 2 ) {
        Vector2f start = poly.get( poly.size() - 1 );
        boolean startAbove = start.y >= point.y;
        for( int i = 0; i < poly.size(); ++i ) {
            Vector2f end = poly.get( i );
            boolean endAbove = end.y >= point.y;
            if( startAbove != endAbove ) {
                float m = (end.y - start.y) / (end.x - start.x);
                float x = start.x + (point.y - start.y) / m;
                if( x >= point.x ) {
                    if( winding ) {
                        inside += startAbove ? 1 : -1;
                    } else {
                        inside = inside == 1 ? 0 : 1;
                    }
                }
            }
        }
    }
}
```

```
                startAbove = endAbove;
                start = end;
            }
        }
        return inside != 0;
    }

    @Override
    protected void render( Graphics g ) {
        super.render( g );
        // render instructions
        g.drawString( "Winding: " + (winding?"ON":"OFF"), 20, 35 );
         String mouse =
            String.format( "Mouse: (%.2f,%.2f)", mousePos.x, mousePos.y );
        g.drawString( mouse, 20, 50 );
        g.drawString( "Left-Click to add points", 20, 65 );
        g.drawString( "Right-Click to clear points", 20, 80 );
        g.drawString( "Space Bar to toggle winding", 20, 95 );

        Matrix3x3f view = getViewportTransform();
        // draw test polygon
        if( poly.size() > 1 ) {
            polyCpy.clear();
            for( Vector2f vector : poly ) {
                polyCpy.add( view.mul( vector ) );
            }
            g.setColor( selected ? Color.GREEN : Color.BLUE );
            Utility.drawPolygon( g, polyCpy );
        }
        // draw inside point blue, outside points red
        g.setColor( Color.BLUE );
        for( Vector2f vector : inside ) {
            Vector2f point = view.mul( vector );
            g.fillRect( (int)point.x, (int)point.y, 1, 1 );
        }
        g.setColor( Color.RED );
        for( Vector2f vector : outside ) {
            Vector2f point = view.mul( vector );
            g.fillRect( (int)point.x, (int)point.y, 1, 1 );
        }
    }

    public static void main( String[] args ) {
        launchApp( new PointInPolygonExample() );
    }
}
```

Using an Axis Aligned Bounding Box (AABB) for Intersection Testing

An axis aligned bounding box (AABB) is a rectangle that has edges parallel to the x-axis and y-axis. See Figure 7.6.

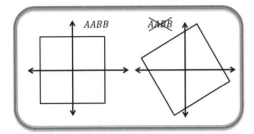

Figure 7.6
Axis Aligned Bounding Box.
© 2014 Timothy Wright.

Because the rectangle is not rotated, it is an easy shape to use for intersection testing. The shape can be represented with only a minimum and a maximum value, as shown in Figure 7.7. Note that AABBs cannot be rotated.

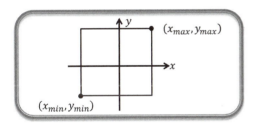

Figure 7.7
AABB Representation.
© 2014 Timothy Wright.

Transforming and drawing an AABB is straightforward.

```
private void drawAABB( Graphics g, Vector2f min, Vector2f max ) {
    Matrix3x3f view = getViewportTransform();

    Vector2f topLeft = new Vector2f( min.x, max.y );
    topLeft = view.mul( topLeft );

    Vector2f bottomRight = new Vector2f( max.x, min.y );
    bottomRight = view.mul( bottomRight );

    int rectX = (int)topLeft.x;
    int rectY = (int)topLeft.y;
```

```
    int rectWidth = (int)( bottomRight.x - topLeft.x );
    int rectHeight = (int)( bottomRight.y - topLeft.y );
    g.drawRect( rectX, rectY, rectWidth, rectHeight );
}
```

Because the shape is not rotated, you simply need to check if there's a point between both x and y minimum and maximum values. That's all that is needed to check if a point is within an AABB.

```
private boolean pointInAABB( Vector2f p, Vector2f min, Vector2f max ) {
    return p.x > min.x && p.x < max.x &&
            p.y > min.y && p.y < max.y;
}
```

Checking if two AABBs overlap is also easy. If any of the values do not overlap, then there is no intersection. See Figure 7.8.

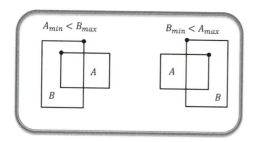

Figure 7.8
AABB Intersection.
© 2014 Timothy Wright.

```
private boolean intersectAABB( Vector2f minA, Vector2f maxA,
    Vector2f minB, Vector2f maxB ) {

    if( minA.x > maxB.x || minB.x > maxA.x ) return false;
    if( minA.y > maxB.y || minB.y > maxA.y ) return false;
    return true;
}
```

USING CIRCLES FOR INTERSECTIONS

Circles are also a useful shape to use for intersections testing. Circles can be represented as a center point and a radius, as shown in Figure 7.9.

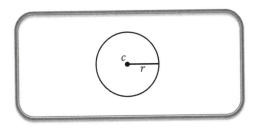

Figure 7.9
Circle Representation.
© 2014 Timothy Wright.

You draw a circle so that it stretches with the size of the window the same way you drew the AABB.

```
private void drawOval( Graphics g, Vector2f center, float radius ) {
    Matrix3x3f view = getViewportTransform();

    Vector2f topLeft =
        new Vector2f( center.x - radius, center.y + radius );
    topLeft = view.mul( topLeft );

    Vector2f bottomRight =
        new Vector2f( center.x + radius, center.y - radius );
    bottomRight = view.mul( bottomRight );

    int circleX = (int)topLeft.x;
    int circleY = (int)topLeft.y;
    int circleWidth = (int)(bottomRight.x - topLeft.x);
    int circleHeight = (int)(bottomRight.y - topLeft.y);

    g.drawOval( circleX, circleY, circleWidth, circleHeight );
}
```

To check if a point is inside a circle, you compare the distance from the point in the center of the circle to the radius, as shown in Figure 7.10. If the radius is larger than the distance, the point is inside the circle.

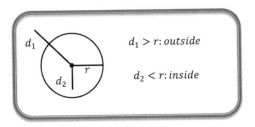

$d_1 > r: outside$

$d_2 < r: inside$

Figure 7.10
Point in Circle.
© 2014 Timothy Wright.

Because the square root method can be slow, it is easier to check the squared distance.

$$if\ a < b\ then\ a^2 < b^2$$

Most of the comparisons using the distance in the following examples use the squared distance for comparison. This is illustrated in the following method:

```
private boolean pointInCircle( Vector2f p, Vector2f c, float r ) {
    Vector2f dist = p.sub( c );
    return dist.lenSqr() < r*r;
}
```

The test to check if two circles overlap is very similar to the point test. If the distance from the circles' centers is larger than the sum of the radii, they do not overlap. See Figure 7.11.

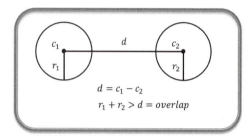

Figure 7.11
Circle Overlap.
© 2014 Timothy Wright.

The code that tests for overlapping circles is as follows:

```
private boolean intersectCircle(
    Vector2f c0, float r0, Vector2f c1, float r1 ) {
    Vector2f c = c0.sub( c1 );
    float r = r0 + r1;
    return c.lenSqr() < r*r;
}
```

Circle AABB Overlap

To determine whether a circle and an AABB overlap, you calculate the distance from the circle to the AABB. The circle's center will either be outside the AABB or inside the AABB. If the circle's center is less than the minimum AABB value, the distance between them is the difference between the minimum and the circle center. If the circle's center is greater than the maximum, the distance between them is the difference between the maximum and the center. If the center is greater than the minimum but less than the maximum, it is located inside the AABB and no further testing is required. See Figure 7.12. Using the calculated distance for each x and y, the closest point on the AABB is found and can be used to test against the circle radius distance exactly like the previous examples.

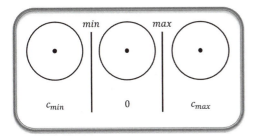

Figure 7.12
Circle AABB Cases.
© 2014 Timothy Wright.

The algorithm can be written as follows:

```
private boolean intersectCircleAABB(
    Vector2f c, float r, Vector2f min, Vector2f max ) {

    float dx = 0.0f;
    if( c.x < min.x ) dx = c.x - min.x;
    if( c.x > max.x ) dx = c.x - max.x;

    float dy = 0.0f;
    if( c.y < min.y ) dy = c.y - min.y;
    if( c.y > max.y ) dy = c.y - max.y;

    float d = dx*dx + dy*dy;
    return d < r*r;
}
```

It is possible to optimize this code by combining the dx and dy variables into a single variable, performing the square and accumulation in the same line. The optimized version is as follows:

```
private boolean intersectCircleAABB(
    Vector2f c, float r, Vector2f min, Vector2f max ) {

    float d = 0.0f;
    if( c.x < min.x ) d += (c.x - min.x)*(c.x - min.x);
    if( c.x > max.x ) d += (c.x - max.x)*(c.x - max.x);
```

```
    if( c.y < min.y ) d += (c.y - min.y)*(c.y - min.y);
    if( c.y > max.y ) d += (c.y - max.y)*(c.y - max.y);
    return d < r*r;
}
```

The `OverlapExample`, as shown in Figure 7.13, and located in the `javagames.` `intersection` package, draws two circles and two AABBs. Those shapes can be clicked on and dragged around. Doing so uses the screen mouse coordinate to world coordinate transformation as well as the previous tests to check the location of the mouse.

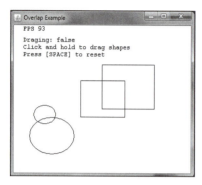

Figure 7.13
Overlap Example.
© 2014 Timothy Wright.

If the shapes intersect, they are drawn blue; otherwise, they are drawn black. The methods for drawing an AABB and a circle presented earlier in the chapter are used to draw the collision shapes so that they will scale with the size of the window.

All of the overlap tests presented—circle-circle, AABB-AABB, and circle-AABB—are used to test if any shape overlaps with any other shape. The AABBs are represented as a minimum value, a maximum value, and a position. The circles are represented by a center and a radius.

```
package javagames.intersection;

import java.awt.*;
import java.awt.event.*;

import javagames.util.*;


public class OverlapExample extends SimpleFramework {
    // mouse variables
    private Vector2f mousePos;
```

```
private Vector2f mouseDelta;
private boolean clicked;
private boolean dragging;
// AABB variables
private Vector2f min0, max0;
private Vector2f min0Cpy, max0Cpy;
private Vector2f rect0Pos;
private boolean rect0Collision;
private boolean rect0Moving;

private Vector2f min1, max1;
private Vector2f min1Cpy, max1Cpy;
private Vector2f rect1Pos;
private boolean rect1Collision;
private boolean rect1Moving;
// circle variables
private Vector2f c0, c0Pos;
private float r0;
private boolean circle0Collision;
private boolean circle0Moving;

private Vector2f c1, c1Pos;
private float r1;
private boolean circle1Collision;
private boolean circle1Moving;

public OverlapExample() {
    appHeight = 640;
    appWidth = 640;
    appTitle = "Overlap Example";
    appBackground = Color.WHITE;
    appFPSColor = Color.BLACK;
}

protected void initialize() {
    super.initialize();

    mousePos = new Vector2f();

    min0 = new Vector2f(  -0.25f,  -0.25f );
    max0 = new Vector2f(   0.25f,   0.25f );

    min1 = new Vector2f(   -0.3f,   -0.3f );
    max1 = new Vector2f(    0.3f,    0.3f );

    r0 = 0.25f;
    r1 = 0.125f;

    reset();
}
```

```
private void reset() {
    rect0Pos = new Vector2f();
    rect1Pos = new Vector2f( 0.25f, 0.5f );
    c0Pos = new Vector2f( -0.60f, -0.60f );
    c1Pos = new Vector2f( 0.6f, 0.6f );
}

@Override
protected void processInput( float delta ) {
    super.processInput( delta );
    // reset objects on spacebar
    if( keyboard.keyDownOnce( KeyEvent.VK_SPACE ) ) {
        reset();
    }
    // convert screen coordinates to world coordinates
    // for intersection testing
    Vector2f pos = getWorldMousePosition();
    mouseDelta = pos.sub( mousePos );
    mousePos = pos;

    clicked = mouse.buttonDownOnce( MouseEvent.BUTTON1 );
    dragging = mouse.buttonDown( MouseEvent.BUTTON1 );

}

@Override
protected void updateObjects( float delta ) {
    super.updateObjects( delta );
    // calculate the AABB minimum and maximum values
    Matrix3x3f mat = Matrix3x3f.translate(
        rect0Pos.x, rect0Pos.y
    );
    min0Cpy = mat.mul( min0 );
    max0Cpy = mat.mul( max0 );

    mat = Matrix3x3f.translate(
        rect1Pos.x, rect1Pos.y
    );
    min1Cpy = mat.mul( min1 );
    max1Cpy = mat.mul( max1 );
    // position the circles
    mat = Matrix3x3f.translate(
        c0Pos.x, c0Pos.y
    );
    c0 = mat.mul( new Vector2f() );
```

```
 mat = Matrix3x3f.translate(
     c1Pos.x, c1Pos.y
);
c1 = mat.mul( new Vector2f() );
      // test for click and drag of objects
if( clicked && pointInAABB( mousePos, min0Cpy, max0Cpy ) ) {
   rect0Moving = true;
}
if( clicked && pointInAABB( mousePos, min1Cpy, max1Cpy ) ) {
   rect1Moving = true;
}
if( clicked && pointInCircle( mousePos, c0Pos, r0 ) ) {
   circle0Moving = true;
}
if( clicked && pointInCircle( mousePos, c1Pos, r1 ) ) {
   circle1Moving = true;
}

rect0Moving = rect0Moving && dragging;
if( rect0Moving ) {
   rect0Pos = rect0Pos.add( mouseDelta );
}
rect1Moving = rect1Moving && dragging;
if( rect1Moving ) {
   rect1Pos = rect1Pos.add( mouseDelta );
}
circle0Moving = circle0Moving && dragging;
if( circle0Moving ) {
   c0Pos = c0Pos.add( mouseDelta );
}
circle1Moving = circle1Moving && dragging;
if( circle1Moving ) {
   c1Pos = c1Pos.add( mouseDelta );
}

rect0Collision = false;
rect1Collision = false;
circle0Collision = false;
circle1Collision = false;
// perform intersection testing
if( intersectAABB( min0Cpy, max0Cpy, min1Cpy, max1Cpy ) ) {
   rect0Collision = true;
   rect1Collision = true;
}
```

```
        if( intersectCircle( c0, r0, c1, r1 ) ) {
            circle0Collision = true;
            circle1Collision = true;
        }
        if( intersectCircleAABB( c0, r0, min0Cpy, max0Cpy ) ) {
            circle0Collision = true;
            rect0Collision = true;
        }
        if( intersectCircleAABB( c0, r0, min1Cpy, max1Cpy ) ) {
            circle0Collision = true;
            rect1Collision = true;
        }
        if( intersectCircleAABB( c1, r1, min0Cpy, max0Cpy ) ) {
            circle1Collision = true;
            rect0Collision = true;
        }
        if( intersectCircleAABB( c1, r1, min1Cpy, max1Cpy ) ) {
            circle1Collision = true;
            rect1Collision = true;
        }
    }

    private boolean pointInAABB( Vector2f p, Vector2f min, Vector2f max ) {
        return p.x > min.x && p.x < max.x &&
               p.y > min.y && p.y < max.y;
    }

    private boolean pointInCircle( Vector2f p, Vector2f c, float r ) {
        Vector2f dist = p.sub( c );
        return dist.lenSqr() < r*r;
    }

    private boolean intersectAABB(
        Vector2f minA, Vector2f maxA, Vector2f minB, Vector2f maxB ) {
        if( minA.x > maxB.x || minB.x > maxA.x ) return false;
        if( minA.y > maxB.y || minB.y > maxA.y ) return false;
        return true;
    }

    private boolean intersectCircle(
        Vector2f c0, float r0, Vector2f c1, float r1 ) {
        Vector2f c = c0.sub( c1 );
        float r = r0 + r1;
        return c.lenSqr() < r*r;
    }
```

```java
private boolean intersectCircleAABB(
    Vector2f c, float r, Vector2f min, Vector2f max ) {
    float d = 0.0f;
    if( c.x < min.x ) d += (c.x - min.x)*(c.x - min.x);
    if( c.x > max.x ) d += (c.x - max.x)*(c.x - max.x);
    if( c.y < min.y ) d += (c.y - min.y)*(c.y - min.y);
    if( c.y > max.y ) d += (c.y - max.y)*(c.y - max.y);
    return d < r*r;
}

@Override
protected void render( Graphics g ) {
    super.render( g );
    // render instructions
    g.drawString( "Draging: " + dragging, 20, 35 );
    g.drawString( "Click and hold to drag shapes", 20, 50 );
    g.drawString( "Press [SPACE] to reset", 20, 65 );
    // render objects
    g.setColor( rect0Collision ? Color.BLACK : Color.BLUE );
    drawAABB( g, min0Cpy, max0Cpy );

    g.setColor( rect1Collision ? Color.BLACK : Color.BLUE );
    drawAABB( g, min1Cpy, max1Cpy );

    g.setColor( circle0Collision ? Color.BLACK : Color.BLUE );
    drawOval( g, c0, r0 );

    g.setColor( circle1Collision ? Color.BLACK : Color.BLUE );
    drawOval( g, c1, r1 );
}
// draw the AABB
private void drawAABB( Graphics g, Vector2f min, Vector2f max ) {
    Matrix3x3f view = getViewportTransform();

    Vector2f topLeft = new Vector2f( min.x, max.y );
    topLeft = view.mul( topLeft );

    Vector2f bottomRight = new Vector2f( max.x, min.y );
    bottomRight = view.mul( bottomRight );

    int rectX = (int)topLeft.x;
    int rectY = (int)topLeft.y;
    int rectWidth = (int)( bottomRight.x - topLeft.x );
    int rectHeight = (int)( bottomRight.y - topLeft.y );
    g.drawRect( rectX, rectY, rectWidth, rectHeight );
}
```

```
// draw the circle
private void drawOval( Graphics g, Vector2f center, float radius ) {
    Matrix3x3f view = getViewportTransform();

    Vector2f topLeft =
        new Vector2f( center.x - radius, center.y + radius );
    topLeft = view.mul( topLeft );

    Vector2f bottomRight =
        new Vector2f( center.x + radius, center.y - radius );
    bottomRight = view.mul( bottomRight );

    int circleX = (int)topLeft.x;
    int circleY = (int)topLeft.y;
    int circleWidth = (int)(bottomRight.x - topLeft.x);
    int circleHeight = (int)(bottomRight.y - topLeft.y);

    g.drawOval( circleX, circleY, circleWidth, circleHeight );
}

public static void main( String[] args ) {
    launchApp( new OverlapExample() );
}

}
```

USING THE SEPARATING AXIS METHOD

The separating axis method for testing if two objects overlap is more complicated than the previous tests, but it can handle any convex shape rotated to any position. Although it will not give the exact collision point by itself, it can be very useful for testing if objects overlap.

The idea is simple: if there exists an axis of separation between two convex polygons, then the objects do not overlap. In other words, if you can draw a line between two shapes, they cannot overlap. See Figure 7.14.

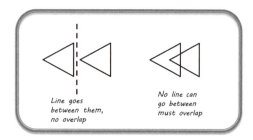

Figure 7.14
Separating Axis Method.
© 2014 Timothy Wright.

There are many examples on the Internet if you are looking for a rigorous mathematical proof of the theorem. For the purposes here, Figure 7.14 shows adequate proof. Keep in mind that this only works for convex polygons. If there are any interior angles greater than 180 degrees, the polygon is concave and the separating axis test will not work. Figure 7.15 shows an example of a failing test due to a concave polygon.

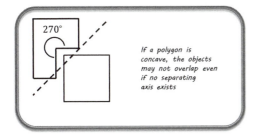

Figure 7.15
Concave Polygon Problems.
© 2014 Timothy Wright.

Tip

If you have a concave polygon, it can always be broken up into multiple convex polygons for testing. See Figure 7.16.

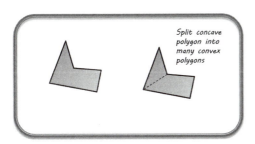

Figure 7.16
Splitting Concave Polygons.
© 2014 Timothy Wright.

It is easy to see how to draw a line between two objects, but this test needs to be done in the code using math. Fortunately, not only is the general case easy, there are some optimizations that can also be applied to symmetrical shapes.

To test if shapes overlap, do the following: for each line segment in both shapes, create a perpendicular normal vector, and project all the points onto the normal using the dot product. See Figure 7.17.

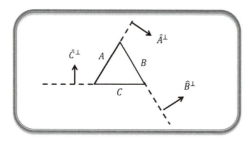

Figure 7.17
Projection Lines.
© 2014 Timothy Wright.

Once the points are projected onto the perpendicular normal, if the projections overlap, then the polygons overlap. If none of the projections contains any overlapping areas, then there is no overlap. See Figure 7.18.

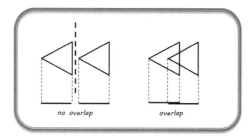

Figure 7.18
Overlapping Projections.
© 2014 Timothy Wright.

Also, as shown in the following examples, if the object being projected is symmetrical, then the radius of each object can be compared to the distance between the two object centers. This test is just like testing for overlapping circles. This concept is shown in Figure 7.19.

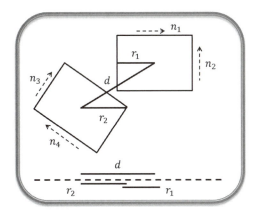

Figure 7.19
Rectangle Overlap.
© 2014 Timothy Wright.

The distance (d) above and the sum of (r_1) and (r_2) are used to determine if the objects overlap. If any one of the tests fails, then the objects do not overlap. If no axis has a separation between objects, then they intersect, provided the objects do not curve about each other. One good thing about this method is that it works in more than two dimensions. In the previous illustration, the only axis that does not have an overlap is (n_3).

USING THE LINE-LINE OVERLAP METHOD

The center of each line can be found using the midpoint formula:

$$midpt = \frac{P_0 - P_1}{2}$$

Using the center of each line, the distance to either endpoint is the radius of the line. That same radius, when normalized to a length of one, is the axis used for the projection. Because the radius of each line, when projected onto itself, is always zero, only the radius of the other line is compared to the projected center distance. See Figure 7.20.

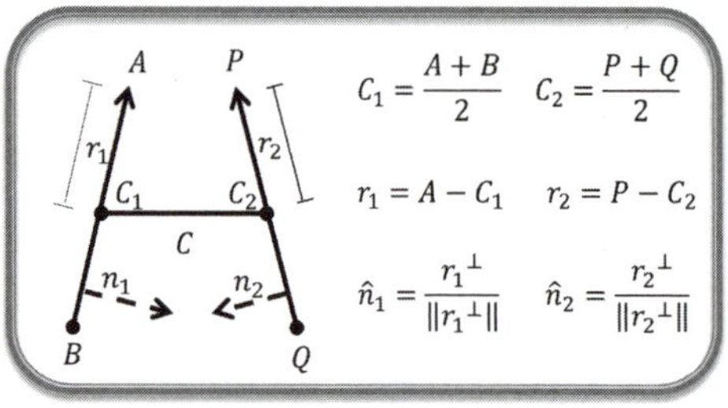

Figure 7.20
Line-Line Overlap.
© 2014 Timothy Wright.

$$if \, |\hat{n}_1 * (C_1 - C_2)| > |\hat{n}_1 * r_2| : no \ overlap$$
$$if \, |\hat{n}_2 * (C_1 - C_2)| > |\hat{n}_2 * r_1| : no \ overlap$$

Because the comparisons are only using distance, which is always a positive value, they use the absolute value to ensure that no negative values are computed.

Figure 7.21
Line-Line Overlap Example.
© 2014 Timothy Wright.

The LineLineOverlapExample, located in the javagames.intersection package and shown in Figure 7.21, stores two lines—P, Q for the initial line and start, end for the second line. The start point is placed when the left mouse button is clicked and the end point follows the mouse pointer.

Inside the updateObject() method, the two lines are checked to see if they overlap using the separating axis method. The two lines are used to find the center, the radius, and each axis normal. Then the projected distance between the centers is compared to the radius of both lines. If the distance is larger than the radius, there is no overlap.

The `render()` method draws both lines. If they overlap, they are drawn as blue lines; otherwise, they are drawn as black.

```java
package javagames.intersection;

import java.awt.*;
import java.awt.event.MouseEvent;

import javagames.util.*;


public class LineLineOverlapExample extends SimpleFramework {
    private Vector2f P, Q;
    private Vector2f start, end;

    boolean overlap = false;

    public LineLineOverlapExample() {
        appWidth = 640;
        appHeight = 640;
        appSleep = 10L;
        appTitle = "Line Line Overlap";
        appBackground = Color.WHITE;
        appFPSColor = Color.BLACK;
    }

    @Override
    protected void initialize() {
        super.initialize();

        P = new Vector2f( -0.6f, 0.4f );
        Q = new Vector2f( 0.6f, -0.4f );
        start = new Vector2f( 0.8f, 0.8f );
        end = new Vector2f();

    }

    @Override
    protected void processInput( float delta ) {
        super.processInput( delta );

        end = getWorldMousePosition();
        if( mouse.buttonDownOnce( MouseEvent.BUTTON1 ) ) {
            start = new Vector2f( end );
        }

    }

    @Override
    protected void updateObjects( float delta ) {
        super.updateObjects( delta );
```

```
        overlap = lineLineOverlap( P, Q, start, end );
    }

    private boolean lineLineOverlap(
        Vector2f A, Vector2f B, Vector2f P, Vector2f Q ) {

        Vector2f C0 = A.add( B ).div( 2.0f );
        Vector2f C1 = P.add( Q ).div( 2.0f );
        Vector2f C = C0.sub( C1 );

        Vector2f r0 = A.sub( C0 );
        Vector2f r1 = P.sub( C1 );

        Vector2f N0 = r0.perp().norm();
        Vector2f N1 = r1.perp().norm();

        float abs1 = Math.abs( N0.dot( C ) );
        float abs2 = Math.abs( N0.dot( r1 ) );
        if( abs1 > abs2 ) return false;

        abs1 = Math.abs( N1.dot( C ) ) ;
        abs2 = Math.abs( N1.dot( r0 ) );
        if( abs1 > abs2 ) return false;

        return true;
    }

    @Override
    protected void render( Graphics g ) {
        super.render( g );

        g.drawString( "Overlap: " + overlap, 20, 35 );
        g.drawString( "Left Click for new line", 20, 50 );

        g.setColor( overlap ? Color.BLUE : Color.BLACK );

        Matrix3x3f view = getViewportTransform();
        Vector2f v0 = view.mul( P );
        Vector2f v1 = view.mul( Q );
        g.drawLine( (int)v0.x, (int)v0.y, (int)v1.x, (int)v1.y );

        v0 = view.mul( start );
        v1 = view.mul( end );
        g.drawLine( (int)v0.x, (int)v0.y, (int)v1.x, (int)v1.y );
    }

    public static void main( String[] args ) {
        launchApp( new LineLineOverlapExample() );
    }
}
```

USING THE RECTANGLE-RECTANGLE OVERLAP METHOD

To test for overlapping rectangles, the same method is used. The center, width, height, and two axis vectors need to be computed for each rectangle. See Figure 7.22.

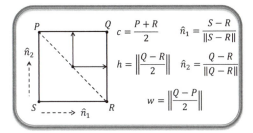

Figure 7.22
Rectangle Overlap Calculations.
© 2014 Timothy Wright.

To project the radius onto an axis, a single vector to the corner cannot be used, because the rotation can cause the projection to be incorrect. See Figure 7.23. You must always project the width and height separately in order to project the correct radius.

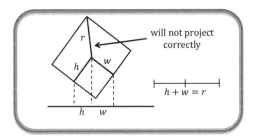

Figure 7.23
Rectangle Radius Projection.
© 2014 Timothy Wright.

The `RectRectOverlapExample`, as shown in Figure 7.24 and located in the `javagames.intersection` package, holds the four points of a base rectangle that is copied for each of the two rectangles tested in the example. Each rectangle testing for overlap has an array of points, a position, and a rotation in radians. The intersection variable holds the state of the separating axis test.

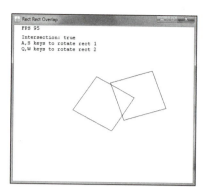

Figure 7.24
Rect-Rect Overlap Example.
© 2014 Timothy Wright.

The processInput() method moves the second rectangle around using the mouse position. The A and S keys rotate the first triangle and the Q and W keys rotate the second triangle.

The updateObjects() method copies each rectangle and then translates and rotates them so they can be tested for overlap.

The rectRectIntersection() method computes the center of each rectangle, the four point axis values, and the width and height of each rectangle. The sum of each width and height are compared to the distance of each center. If they do not overlap, then the objects do not overlap.

The render() method transforms the rectangles to screen coordinates and draws the rectangles in blue if they overlap, and black otherwise.

```
package javagames.intersection;

import java.awt.*;
import java.awt.event.KeyEvent;

import javagames.util.*;


public class RectRectOverlapExample extends SimpleFramework {
    private Vector2f[] rect;

    private Vector2f[] rect0;
    private Vector2f rect0Pos;
    private float rect0Angle;

    private Vector2f[] rect1;
    private Vector2f rect1Pos;
    private float rect1Angle;
```

```java
private boolean intersection;

public RectRectOverlapExample() {
    appWidth = 640;
    appHeight = 640;
    appSleep = 10L;
    appTitle = "Rect Rect Overlap";
    appBackground = Color.WHITE;
    appFPSColor = Color.BLACK;
}

@Override
protected void initialize() {
    super.initialize();
    // set up rectangles for testing
    rect = new Vector2f[] {
            new Vector2f( -0.25f,  0.25f ),
            new Vector2f(  0.25f,  0.25f ),
            new Vector2f(  0.25f, -0.25f ),
            new Vector2f( -0.25f, -0.25f ),
    };

    rect0 = new Vector2f[ rect.length ];
    rect0Pos = new Vector2f();
    rect0Angle = 0.0f;

    rect1 = new Vector2f[ rect.length ];
    rect1Pos = new Vector2f();
    rect1Angle = 0.0f;

}

@Override
protected void processInput( float delta ) {
    super.processInput( delta );
    // convert mouse coordinate for testing
    rect1Pos = getWorldMousePosition();
    // rotate rectangles
    if( keyboard.keyDown( KeyEvent.VK_A ) ) {
        rect0Angle += (float)( Math.PI / 4.0 * delta );
    }
    if( keyboard.keyDown( KeyEvent.VK_S ) ) {
        rect0Angle -= (float)( Math.PI / 4.0 * delta );
    }
    if( keyboard.keyDown( KeyEvent.VK_Q ) ) {
        rect1Angle += (float)( Math.PI / 4.0 * delta );
    }
```

```java
            if( keyboard.keyDown( KeyEvent.VK_W ) ) {
                rect1Angle -= (float)( Math.PI / 4.0 * delta );
            }
        }

        @Override
        protected void updateObjects( float delta ) {
            super.updateObjects( delta );
            // translate objects
            Matrix3x3f mat = Matrix3x3f.identity();
            mat = mat.mul( Matrix3x3f.rotate( rect0Angle ) );
            mat = mat.mul( Matrix3x3f.translate( rect0Pos ) );
            for( int i = 0; i < rect.length; ++i ) {
                rect0[i] = mat.mul( rect[i] );
            }

            mat = Matrix3x3f.identity();
            mat = mat.mul( Matrix3x3f.rotate( rect1Angle ) );
            mat = mat.mul( Matrix3x3f.translate( rect1Pos ) );
            for( int i = 0; i < rect.length; ++i ) {
                rect1[i] = mat.mul( rect[i] );
            }
            // test for intersection
            intersection = rectRectIntersection( rect0, rect1 );
        }

        private boolean rectRectIntersection( Vector2f[] A, Vector2f[] B ) {
            // separating axis intersection algorithm
            Vector2f N0 = A[0].sub( A[1] ).div( 2.0f );
            Vector2f N1 = A[1].sub( A[2] ).div( 2.0f );
            Vector2f CA = A[0].add( A[2] ).div( 2.0f );
            float D0 = N0.len();
            float D1 = N1.len();
            N1 = N1.div( D1 );
            N0 = N0.div( D0 );

            Vector2f N2 = B[0].sub( B[1] ).div( 2.0f );
            Vector2f N3 = B[1].sub( B[2] ).div( 2.0f );
            Vector2f CB = B[0].add( B[2] ).div( 2.0f );
            float D2 = N2.len();
            float D3 = N3.len();
            N2 = N2.div( D2 );
            N3 = N3.div( D3 );

            Vector2f C = CA.sub( CB );
            float DA = D0;
            float DB = D2 * Math.abs( N2.dot( N0 ) );
```

```
      DB += D3 * Math.abs( N3.dot( N0 ) );
      if( DA + DB < Math.abs( C.dot( N0 ) ) ) return false;

      DA = D1;
      DB = D2 * Math.abs( N2.dot( N1 ) );
      DB += D3 * Math.abs( N3.dot( N1 ) );
      if( DA + DB < Math.abs( C.dot( N1 ) ) ) return false;

      DA = D2;
      DB = D0 * Math.abs( N0.dot( N2 ) );
      DB += D1 * Math.abs( N1.dot( N2 ) );
      if( DA + DB < Math.abs( C.dot( N2 ) ) ) return false;

      DA = D3;
      DB = D0 * Math.abs( N0.dot( N3 ) );
      DB += D1 * Math.abs( N1.dot( N3 ) );
      if( DA + DB < Math.abs( C.dot( N3 ) ) ) return false;

      return true;
   }

   @Override
   protected void render( Graphics g ) {
      super.render( g );
      // render instructions
      g.drawString( "Intersection: " + intersection, 20, 35 );
      g.drawString( "A,S keys to rotate rect 1", 20, 50 );
      g.drawString( "Q,W keys to rotate rect 2", 20, 65 );
      // draw rectangles
      g.setColor( intersection ? Color.BLUE : Color.BLACK );

      Matrix3x3f view = getViewportTransform();
      for( int i = 0; i < rect0.length; ++i ) {
         rect0[i] = view.mul( rect0[i] );
      }
      Utility.drawPolygon( g, rect0 );

      for( int i = 0; i < rect1.length; ++i ) {
         rect1[i] = view.mul( rect1[i] );
      }
      Utility.drawPolygon( g, rect1 );


   }

   public static void main( String[] args ) {
      launchApp( new RectRectOverlapExample() );
   }
}
```

OPTIMIZING YOUR TESTS

It is important to always look at the shapes and the tests to see if there are ways to simplify the math. For example, if AABB shapes are used, some information can be hard-coded into the tests. The normalized vectors for AABBs are always of length 1 and always on the x- and y-axis. See Figure 7.25.

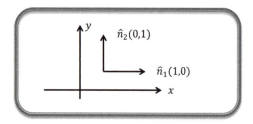

Figure 7.25
Optimizations.
© 2014 Timothy Wright.

Any dot product using these normal vectors will always be:

$$P * n_1 = P_X * (1) + P_y * (0) = P_x$$
$$P * n_2 = P_X * (0) + P_y * (1) = P_y$$

In this case, the x and y values from the point P can be used without even calculating the normal vectors. Optimizations like this can simplify the code, speed up calculations, and keep bugs from creeping in. Always be on the lookout for situations like this.

If the separating axis test is used with AABB rectangles, then the perpendicular normals turn out to be the x-axis and y-axis. The dot product between these normals and the sides of the rectangles reduces to the minimum and maximum (x,y) coordinates. See Figure 7.26.

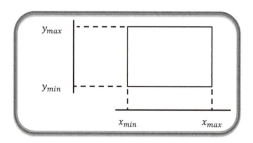

Figure 7.26
AABB Separating Axis.
© 2014 Timothy Wright.

This is exactly how the overlapping rectangle test is done. You were using the separating axis test and didn't even know it. :-)

RESOURCES AND FURTHER READING

Haines, Eric, "Point in Polygon Strategies," *Graphics Gems IV,* ed. Paul Heckbert, Academic Press, pp. 24–46, 1994.

Akenine-Moller, Tomas, and Eric Haines, *Real-Time Rendering,* 2nd Edition, A K Peters, pp. 598–599, 600, 2002.

Arvo, James, "A Simple Method for Box-Sphere Intersection Testing," *Graphic Gems,* ed. Andrew S. Glassner, Academic Press, pp. 335–339.

Ericson, Christer, *Real-Time Collision Detection,* Focal Press, p. 184, 2004.

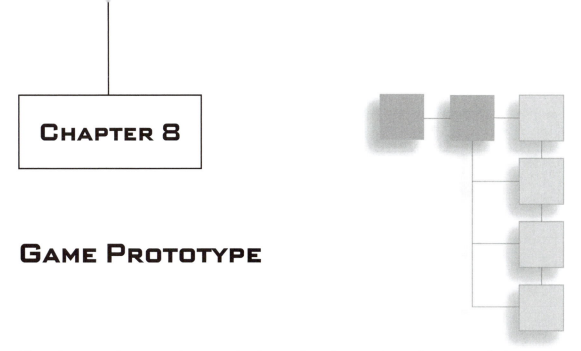

CHAPTER 8

GAME PROTOTYPE

This chapter takes everything you've learned in the previous chapters and shows you how to create a prototype space game. Although there are still too many elements missing to call this a complete game, enough tools are available to create a working prototype.

One problem I had when first learning how to program was that there were so many examples using the various programming concepts—such as loops, variables, inheritance, and polymorphism—but there weren't a lot of examples of doing something real. The examples were either really simple, useless code snippets, or incredibly complicated, poorly written programs that crammed in all the computer science they could, instead of using only what was needed to get the job done. The prototype game in this chapter doesn't try to cram in everything; it instead tries to balance good class design with easy-to-understand code.

Just like any other game, the very first problem wasn't covered in any of the previous chapters. What happens when the space ship flies off the screen?

CREATING A POLYGON WRAPPER CLASS

When making a 2D space ship game, the first big problem to solve is what happens when the ship gets to the edge of the screen. One solution is to keep the ship in the middle of the screen, and move the world around it. Without any support for loading files, and no level editor, this seems a bit ambitious. The second option is to bounce the ship around the screen when it hits the edge. That just seems weird. The third option is to wrap the ship from one side to the other. Let's go with the third method.

There are many ways to solve this problem. One way is to have the ship leave the screen completely and then bring it back on the other side, as shown in Figure 8.1.

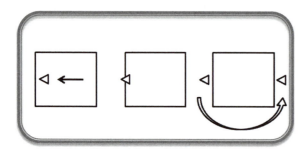

Figure 8.1
Wrap Polygon.
© 2014 Timothy Wright.

Trying this idea out seemed simple enough; you use a bounding box around the ship to test when it leaves the screen and move it to the other side. This method has two issues: one is that it is possible to fly the ship so only a very tiny piece is visible and is very hard to hit, and the second is that the ship can get stuck off-screen. It doesn't happen often, but it can be very hard to hit the objects when most of the polygon is off the screen. Because of these issues, wrapping the objects seems like a better choice than waiting until the entire object is off the screen.

Wrapping the objects so that any part off one side of the screen wraps to the other side is also fraught with peril. It is possible, when you're wrapping an object from one side to the other, for there to be four copies of the same object, as seen in Figure 8.2.

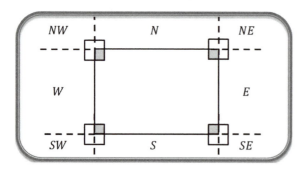

Figure 8.2
Wrapped Copies.
© 2014 Timothy Wright.

Not only is it necessary to draw the four copies, but all four copies need to be checked for collisions. If only the first object is used for collisions, then two objects at opposite corners wouldn't register a collision, even when their drawn objects overlap. See Figure 8.3.

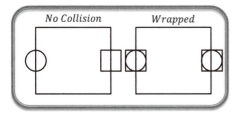

Figure 8.3
Wrapped Copies.
© 2014 Timothy Wright.

Creating a render list that contains copies of each object solves the problem. The objects can be drawn and the entire list can be used to check for collisions.

The objects that wrap never get stuck because once the middle of the object is outside the bounds of the world, it is wrapped by adjusting the position by the width or height of the world. By always placing the wrapped position inside the bounds, the object can never get stuck. See Figure 8.4.

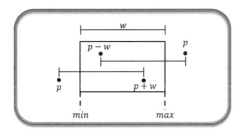

Figure 8.4
Polygon Shift.
© 2014 Timothy Wright.

```
if( p < min )
    p += w;
if( p > max )
    p -= w;
```

Once the position of the object is wrapped, the AABB for the object is computed by finding the minimum and maximum (*x,y*) values, as seen in Figure 8.5.

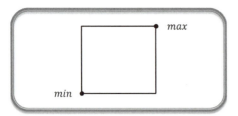

Figure 8.5
Min Max AABB.
© 2014 Timothy Wright.

This bounding box determines if the object is outside the bounds of the screen and needs to be wrapped to the other side.

The PolygonWrapper class, located in the javagames.prototype package, contains methods to wrap polygons and positions. The constructor takes the width and height of the screen in world coordinates and computes the minimum and maximum vector values. The hasLeftWorld() method checks the given position against the minimum and maximum world coordinates. The wrapPosition() method returns a wrapped position if the given position has left the bounds of the world. The wrapped position is adjusted by the width and height of the world so the new position is never outside the bounds of the world. The bounds of the polygon to be wrapped are computed as follows:

```
// PolygonWrapper.java
private Vector2f getMin( Vector2f[] poly ) {
   Vector2f min = new Vector2f( Float.MAX_VALUE, Float.MAX_VALUE );
   for( Vector2f v : poly ) {
      min.x = Math.min( v.x, min.x );
      min.y = Math.min( v.y, min.y );
   }
   return min;
}

private Vector2f getMax( Vector2f[] poly ) {
   Vector2f max = new Vector2f( -Float.MAX_VALUE, -Float.MAX_VALUE );
   for( Vector2f v : poly ) {
      max.x = Math.max( v.x, max.x );
      max.y = Math.max( v.y, max.y );
   }
   return max;
}
```

The wrapPolygon() method computes the minimum and maximum values and uses these to determine if the object needs to be wrapped to the north, south, east, or west. If the object is wrapped to two cardinal directions, such as south and east, it is also wrapped to the north and west. Each of the four diagonal directions is tested.

Each wrapped polygon is copied and added to the render list using the transform method:

```java
// PolygonWrapper.java
private Vector2f[] transform( Vector2f[] poly, Matrix3x3f mat ) {
    Vector2f[] copy = new Vector2f[ poly.length ];
    for( int i = 0; i < poly.length; ++i ) {
        copy[i] = mat.mul( poly[i] );
    }
    return copy;
}
```

The polygon is wrapped to the eight directions by adding or subtracting the width and height of the world. See Figure 8.6.

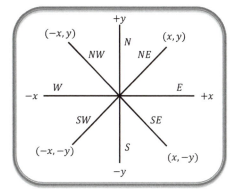

Figure 8.6
Compass Directions.
© 2014 Timothy Wright.

The PolygonWrapper code is as follows:

```java
package javagames.prototype;

import java.util.List;

import javagames.util.Matrix3x3f;
import javagames.util.Vector2f;


public class PolygonWrapper {

    private float worldWidth;
    private float worldHeight;
    private Vector2f worldMin;
    private Vector2f worldMax;
```

```java
public PolygonWrapper( float worldWidth, float worldHeight ) {
    this.worldWidth = worldWidth;
    this.worldHeight = worldHeight;
    worldMax = new Vector2f( worldWidth / 2.0f, worldHeight / 2.0f );
    worldMin = worldMax.inv();
}

public boolean hasLeftWorld( Vector2f position ) {
    return position.x < worldMin.x || position.x > worldMax.x ||
        position.y < worldMin.y || position.y > worldMax.y;
}

public Vector2f wrapPosition( Vector2f position ) {
    Vector2f wrapped = new Vector2f( position );
    if( position.x < worldMin.x ) {
        wrapped.x = position.x + worldWidth;
    } else if( position.x > worldMax.x ) {
        wrapped.x = position.x - worldWidth;
    }
    if( position.y < worldMin.y ) {
        wrapped.y = position.y + worldHeight;
    } else if( position.y > worldMax.y ) {
        wrapped.y = position.y - worldHeight;
    }
    return wrapped;
}

public void wrapPolygon( Vector2f[] poly, List<Vector2f[]> renderList ) {
    Vector2f min = getMin( poly );
    Vector2f max = getMax( poly );

    boolean north = max.y > worldMax.y;
    boolean south = min.y < worldMin.y;
    boolean west = min.x < worldMin.x;
    boolean east = max.x > worldMax.x;

    if( west ) renderList.add( wrapEast( poly ) );
    if( east ) renderList.add( wrapWest( poly ) );
    if( north ) renderList.add( wrapSouth( poly ) );
    if( south ) renderList.add( wrapNorth( poly ) );
    if( north && west ) renderList.add( wrapSouthEast( poly ) );
    if( north && east ) renderList.add( wrapSouthWest( poly ) );
    if( south && west ) renderList.add( wrapNorthEast( poly ) );
    if( south && east ) renderList.add( wrapNorthWest( poly ) );
}

private Vector2f getMin( Vector2f[] poly ) {
    Vector2f min = new Vector2f( Float.MAX_VALUE, Float.MAX_VALUE );
```

```java
        for( Vector2f v : poly ) {
            min.x = Math.min( v.x, min.x );
            min.y = Math.min( v.y, min.y );
        }
        return min;
    }

    private Vector2f getMax( Vector2f[] poly ) {
        Vector2f max = new Vector2f( -Float.MAX_VALUE, -Float.MAX_VALUE );
        for( Vector2f v : poly ) {
            max.x = Math.max( v.x, max.x );
            max.y = Math.max( v.y, max.y );
        }
        return max;
    }

    private Vector2f[] wrapNorth( Vector2f[] poly ) {
        return transform( poly, Matrix3x3f.translate( 0.0f, worldHeight ) );
    }

    private Vector2f[] wrapSouth( Vector2f[] poly ) {
        return transform( poly, Matrix3x3f.translate( 0.0f, -worldHeight ) );
    }

    private Vector2f[] wrapEast( Vector2f[] poly ) {
        return transform( poly, Matrix3x3f.translate( worldWidth, 0.0f ) );
    }

    private Vector2f[] wrapWest( Vector2f[] poly ) {
        return transform( poly, Matrix3x3f.translate( -worldWidth, 0.0f ) );
    }

    private Vector2f[] wrapNorthWest( Vector2f[] poly ) {
        return transform(
            poly, Matrix3x3f.translate( -worldWidth, worldHeight )
        );
    }

    private Vector2f[] wrapNorthEast( Vector2f[] poly ) {
        return transform(
            poly, Matrix3x3f.translate( worldWidth, worldHeight )
        );
    }

    private Vector2f[] wrapSouthEast( Vector2f[] poly ) {
        return transform(
            poly, Matrix3x3f.translate( worldWidth, -worldHeight )
        );
    }
```

```
private Vector2f[] wrapSouthWest( Vector2f[] poly ) {
    return transform(
        poly, Matrix3x3f.translate( -worldWidth, -worldHeight )
    );
}

private Vector2f[] transform( Vector2f[] poly, Matrix3x3f mat ) {
    Vector2f[] copy = new Vector2f[ poly.length ];
    for( int i = 0; i < poly.length; ++i ) {
        copy[i] = mat.mul( poly[i] );
    }
    return copy;
}

}
```

The ScreenWrapExample, as shown in Figure 8.7 and located in the javagames.prototype package, uses the PolygonWrapper class to wrap a square that is moved around the screen. The pos vector holds the position of the square. The poly array holds the square polygon. The renderList holds the copies of the square that are wrapped, as well as the original transformed polygon. The wrapper variable is the PolygonWrapper shown previously.

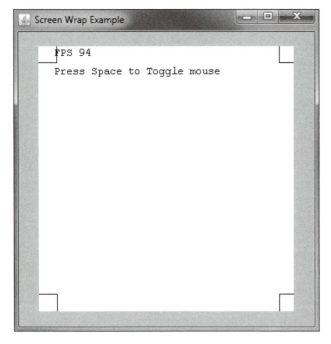

Figure 8.7
Screen Wrap Example.
© 2014 Timothy Wright.

The `initialize()` method creates all the objects and sets the mouse to relative movements so the object can be wrapped around the screen without the mouse leaving the screen. The `processInput()` method moves the square by using the mouse position if the absolute position is used and by adding the relative movement to the current position if relative movement is being used. This method also toggles relative mouse movement with the spacebar.

The `transform()` method creates a copy of the object and transforms it by the given matrix. The `updateObjects()` method clears the render list, wraps and transforms the square, and then uses the `PolygonWrapper` to add any copies of the object to the render list. The `render()` method draws all the objects in the render list to the screen.

```java
package javagames.prototype;

import java.awt.*;
import java.awt.event.KeyEvent;
import java.util.ArrayList;

import javagames.util.*;


public class ScreenWrapExample extends SimpleFramework {

    private Vector2f pos;
    private Vector2f[] poly;
    private ArrayList<Vector2f[]> renderList;
    private PolygonWrapper wrapper;

    public ScreenWrapExample() {

        appBorderScale = 0.9f;
        appWidth = 640;
        appHeight = 640;
        appMaintainRatio = true;
        appTitle = "Screen Wrap Example";
        appBackground = Color.WHITE;
        appFPSColor = Color.BLACK;
    }

    @Override
    protected void initialize() {
        super.initialize();

        mouse.setRelative( true );
        renderList = new ArrayList<Vector2f[]>();
        wrapper = new PolygonWrapper( appWorldWidth, appWorldHeight );

        poly = new Vector2f[] {
            new Vector2f( -0.125f, 0.125f ),
            new Vector2f( 0.125f, 0.125f ),
```

```
        new Vector2f( 0.125f, -0.125f ),
        new Vector2f( -0.125f, -0.125f ),
    };
    pos = new Vector2f();
}

@Override
protected void processInput( float delta ) {
    super.processInput( delta );

    if( mouse.isRelative() ) {
        Vector2f v = getRelativeWorldMousePosition();
        pos = pos.add( v );
    } else {
        pos = getWorldMousePosition();
    }

    if( keyboard.keyDownOnce( KeyEvent.VK_SPACE ) ) {
        mouse.setRelative( !mouse.isRelative() );
        if( mouse.isRelative() ) {
            pos = new Vector2f();
        }
    }
}

@Override
protected void updateObjects( float delta ) {
    super.updateObjects( delta );

    renderList.clear();
    pos = wrapper.wrapPosition( pos );
    Vector2f[] world = transform( poly, Matrix3x3f.translate( pos ) );
    renderList.add( world );
    wrapper.wrapPolygon( world, renderList );
}

private Vector2f[] transform( Vector2f[] poly, Matrix3x3f mat ) {
    Vector2f[] copy = new Vector2f[ poly.length ];
    for( int i = 0; i < poly.length; ++i ) {
        copy[i] = mat.mul( poly[i] );
    }
    return copy;
}

@Override
protected void render( Graphics g ) {
    super.render( g );
    g.drawString( "Press Space to Toggle mouse", 20, 35 );
```

```
        Matrix3x3f view = getViewportTransform();
        for( Vector2f[] toRender : renderList ) {
            for( int i = 0; i < toRender.length; ++i ) {
                toRender[i] = view.mul( toRender[i] );
            }
            Utility.drawPolygon( g, toRender );
        }
    }

    public static void main( String[] args ) {
        launchApp( new ScreenWrapExample() );
    }

}
```

MAKING A PROTOTYPE ASTEROID

The `PrototypeAsteroid` class, also located in the `javagames.prototype` package, represents a rock flying through space. Upon creation, a random velocity and rotation are created. Java's random number generator only returns floating-point numbers between zero and one, so to create random numbers that span an arbitrary range, additional steps are required. For example, to return random numbers from –3 to 7, follow these steps:

1. Calculate the distance between the number range by subtracting the minimum value from the maximum value.

2. Generate a random float from zero to one.

3. Multiply the random number by the distance.

4. Shift the range by adding the minimum.

The steps make it sound a lot more confusing than it actually is.

```
private float getRandomFloat( float min, float max ) {
    float rand = new Random().nextFloat();
    return rand * (max - min) + min;
}
```

The same thing is done to get a random integer. Since the random generator returns a number from zero to `count` minus one, the method is adjusted slightly.

```
private float getRandomRadians( int minDegree, int maxDegree ) {
    int rand = new Random().nextInt( maxDegree - minDegree + 1 );
    return (float)Math.toRadians( rand + minDegree );
}
```

The getRandomRotationDelta() method returns an angle in radians between (5,45) degrees or (–5,–45) degrees, as shown in Figure 8.8.

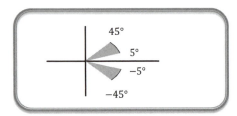

Figure 8.8
Random Rotation Delta.
© 2014 Timothy Wright.

```
private float getRandomRotationDelta() {
    float radians = getRandomRadians( 5, 45 );
    return new Random().nextBoolean() ? radians : -radians;
}
```

There are also setters and getters you can use to access some of the asteroid's properties:

```
public void setPolygon( Vector2f[] polygon );
public void setPosition( Vector2f position );
public Vector2f getPosition();
public void setSize( PrototypeAsteroid.Size size );
public PrototypeAster.Size getSize()
```

The size is an enumerated value:

```
public class PrototypeAsteroid {

    public enum Size {
        Large,
        Medium,
        Small;
    }
    //...
}
```

The update() method is responsible for adjusting the position and rotation of the asteroid. Notice that in addition to adjusting the position and rotation, the PolygonWrapper class is used to wrap the position of the polygon.

The `draw()` method is responsible for drawing the polygon with the given viewport matrix and `Graphics` object. To draw filled polygons, two methods have been added to the `Utility` class:

```
package javagames.util;

import java.awt.*;
import java.util.List;


public class Utility {

    // ... Other methods left out
    // ... New methods are below
    public static void fillPolygon( Graphics2D g, Vector2f[] polygon ) {
        Polygon p = new Polygon();
        for( Vector2f v : polygon ) {
            p.addPoint( (int)v.x, (int)v.y );
        }
        g.fill( p );
    }
    public static void fillPolygon( Graphics2D g, List<Vector2f> polygon ) {
        Polygon p = new Polygon();
        for( Vector2f v : polygon ) {
            p.addPoint( (int)v.x, (int)v.y );
        }
        g.fill( p );
    }

}
```

The `pointInPolygon()` method is the same method discussed previously. The `contains()` method takes a point and returns `true` if any of the polygons copied by the `PolygonWrapper` contain the point. Notice that there is no actual model code in the `PrototypeAsteroid`. That is the job of the editor and factory, shown next.

```
package javagames.prototype;

import java.awt.*;
import java.util.*;

import javagames.util.*;


public class PrototypeAsteroid {
    public enum Size {
        Large,
```

```
        Medium,
        Small;
    }

    private PolygonWrapper wrapper;
    private Size size;

    private float rotation;
    private float rotationDelta;

    private Vector2f[] polygon;
    private Vector2f position;
    private Vector2f velocity;
    private ArrayList<Vector2f[]> renderList;

    public PrototypeAsteroid( PolygonWrapper wrapper ) {
        this.wrapper = wrapper;
        renderList = new ArrayList<Vector2f[]>();
        velocity = getRandomVelocity();
        rotationDelta = getRandomRotationDelta();
    }

    private Vector2f getRandomVelocity() {
        float angle = getRandomRadians( 0, 360 );
        float radius = getRandomFloat( 0.06f, 0.3f );
        return Vector2f.polar( angle, radius );
    }

    private float getRandomRadians( int minDegree, int maxDegree ) {
        int rand = new Random().nextInt( maxDegree - minDegree + 1 );
        return (float)Math.toRadians( rand + minDegree );
    }

    private float getRandomRotationDelta() {
        float radians = getRandomRadians( 5, 45 );
        return new Random().nextBoolean() ? radians : -radians;
    }

    private float getRandomFloat( float min, float max ) {
        float rand = new Random().nextFloat();
        return rand * (max - min) + min;
    }

    public void setPolygon( Vector2f[] polygon ) {
        this.polygon = polygon;
    }

    public void setPosition( Vector2f position ) {
        this.position = position;
    }
```

```java
public Vector2f getPosition() {
    return position;
}

public void setSize( Size size ) {
    this.size = size;
}

public Size getSize() {
    return size;
}

public void update( float time ) {

    position = position.add( velocity.mul( time ) );
    position = wrapper.wrapPosition( position );

    rotation += rotationDelta * time;

    renderList.clear();
    Vector2f[] world = transformPolygon();
    renderList.add( world );
    wrapper.wrapPolygon( world, renderList );

}

private Vector2f[] transformPolygon() {
    Matrix3x3f mat = Matrix3x3f.rotate( rotation );
    mat = mat.mul( Matrix3x3f.translate( position ) );
    return transform( polygon, mat );
}

private Vector2f[] transform( Vector2f[] poly, Matrix3x3f mat ) {
    Vector2f[] copy = new Vector2f[ poly.length ];
    for( int i = 0; i < poly.length; ++i ) {
        copy[i] = mat.mul( poly[i] );
    }
    return copy;
}

public void draw( Graphics2D g, Matrix3x3f view ) {
    for( Vector2f[] poly : renderList ) {
        for( int i = 0; i < poly.length; ++i ) {
            poly[i] = view.mul( poly[i] );
        }
        g.setColor( Color.LIGHT_GRAY );
        Utility.fillPolygon( g, poly );
        g.setColor( Color.BLACK );
        Utility.drawPolygon( g, poly );
    }
}
```

```
public boolean contains( Vector2f point ) {
    for( Vector2f[] polygon : renderList ) {
        if( pointInPolygon( point, polygon ) ) {
            return true;
        }
    }
    return false;
}

private boolean pointInPolygon( Vector2f point, Vector2f[] polygon ) {
    boolean inside = false;
    Vector2f start = polygon[ polygon.length - 1 ];
    boolean startAbove = start.y >= point.y;
    for( int i = 0; i < polygon.length; ++i ) {
        Vector2f end = polygon[i];
        boolean endAbove = end.y >= point.y;
        if( startAbove != endAbove ) {
            float m = (end.y - start.y) / (end.x - start.x);
            float x = start.x + (point.y - start.y) / m;
            if( x >= point.x ) {
                inside = !inside;
            }
        }
        startAbove = endAbove;
        start = end;
    }
    return inside;
}
```

CREATING A PROTOTYPE EDITOR

It is time to make some polygons. Although it is possible to guess at each point, since there are nine asteroid shapes to create, it is a lot of work to do it by hand. Like most programmers, I'm lazy. Coding up an editor to create the polygons will be a lot easier. The PrototypeEditor, located in the javagames.prototype package, is shown in Figure 8.9.

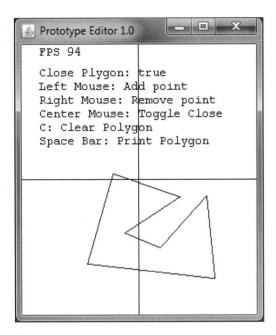

Figure 8.9
Prototype Editor.
© 2014 Timothy Wright.

If the models were stored as files, they could be loaded at runtime. However, none of the code necessary to do that has been covered, so the editor will cheat. When the spacebar is pressed, the editor will spit out the code that can be pasted into another source file. In the second section of the book, using actual files will be covered, so don't worry.

The polygon list holds the points for the model. The mousePos is the current position of the mouse, and the closed Boolean variable holds whether or not the polygon's last point is connected to the first point when drawn.

The processInput() method handles the interaction of the editor. When the left mouse button is pressed, a point is added to the polygon. The middle mouse button toggles the closed variable. The right mouse button removes points from the polygon. The C key clears the entire polygon, and the spacebar prints out the polygon code. The printPolygon() method prints the current polygon to the console so it can be pasted into a text file or copied into another code file. The output printed to the debug console is as follows:

```
Vector2f[] v = new Vector2f[] {
  new Vector2f(-0.2895149f, 0.3865415f),
  new Vector2f(-0.47104853f, -0.28012514f),
  new Vector2f(-0.14241004f, 0.15805948f),
```

```
        new Vector2f(-0.13615024f, -0.30516434f),
        new Vector2f(0.28012514f, -0.2832551f),
        new Vector2f(0.17370892f, 0.21752739f),
        new Vector2f(-0.19248825f, 0.40219092f),
        new Vector2f(-0.18622851f, 0.25195616f),
    };
```

The `render()` method displays the usual directions and draws the polygon as well as axis lines. The `drawAxisLines()` method draws two lines in the editor, representing the x- and y-axis lines.

The `drawPolygon()` method is responsible for rendering the current model. If the polygon is only one point, then a single point is drawn. Next, all the points, except the last one, are drawn if the polygon has more than one point. If the polygon is closed, then the last point is connected to the first point. If the polygon is not closed, then a line from the last point to the current mouse position is drawn. The `drawPoint()` and `drawLine()` methods are the standard versions.

```
package javagames.prototype;

import java.awt.*;
import java.awt.event.*;
import java.util.ArrayList;

import javagames.util.*;


public class PrototypeEditor extends SimpleFramework {
    private ArrayList<Vector2f> polygon;
    private Vector2f mousePos;
    private boolean closed;
    public PrototypeEditor() {
        appTitle = "Prototype Editor 1.0";
        appWidth = 640;
        appHeight = 640;
        appBackground = Color.WHITE;
        appFPSColor = Color.BLACK;
    }
    protected void initialize() {
        super.initialize();
        polygon = new ArrayList<Vector2f>();
    }
    protected void processInput( float delta ) {
        super.processInput( delta );
```

```
      mousePos = getWorldMousePosition();

   if( mouse.buttonDownOnce( MouseEvent.BUTTON1 ) ) {
      polygon.add( mousePos );
   }
   if( mouse.buttonDownOnce( MouseEvent.BUTTON2 ) ) {
      closed = !closed;
   }
   if( mouse.buttonDownOnce( MouseEvent.BUTTON3 ) ) {
      if( !polygon.isEmpty() ) {
         polygon.remove( polygon.size() - 1 );
      }
   }

   if( keyboard.keyDownOnce( KeyEvent.VK_C ) ) {
      polygon.clear();
   }
   if( keyboard.keyDownOnce( KeyEvent.VK_SPACE ) ) {
      printPolygon();
   }
}

private void printPolygon() {
   System.out.println( "Vector2f[] v = new Vector2f[] { " );
   for( Vector2f v : polygon ) {
      System.out.print( "    new Vector2f(" );
      System.out.print( v.x + "f, " );
      System.out.print( v.y + "f)" );
      System.out.println( "," );
   }
   System.out.println( "};" );
}

protected void render( Graphics g ) {
   super.render( g );

   g.drawString( "Close Polygon: " + closed, 20, 35 );
   g.drawString( "Left Mouse: Add point", 20, 50 );
   g.drawString( "Right Mouse: Remove point", 20, 65 );
   g.drawString( "Center Mouse: Toggle Close", 20, 80 );
   g.drawString( "C: Clear Polygon", 20, 95 );
   g.drawString( "Space Bar: Print Polygon", 20, 110 );


   drawAxisLines( g );
   drawPolygon( g );

}
```

```java
private void drawAxisLines( Graphics g ) {
    g.setColor( Color. BLUE );
    Vector2f left = new Vector2f( appWorldWidth / 2.0f, 0.0f );
    Vector2f right = new Vector2f( -left.x, 0.0f );
    drawLine( g, left, right );
    Vector2f top = new Vector2f( 0.0f, appWorldHeight / 2.0f );
    Vector2f bottom = new Vector2f( 0.0f, -top.y );
    drawLine( g, top, bottom );
}

private void drawPolygon( Graphics g ) {
    g.setColor( Color.BLACK );

    if( polygon.size() == 1 ) {
        drawPoint( g, polygon.get( 0 ) );
    }

    for( int i = 0; i < polygon.size() - 1; ++i ) {
        drawLine( g, polygon.get(i), polygon.get( i+1 ) );
    }

    if( closed && polygon.size() > 1 ) {
        Vector2f P = polygon.get( polygon.size() - 1 );
        Vector2f S = polygon.get( 0 );
        drawLine( g, S, P );
    }
    if( !(polygon.isEmpty() || closed) ) {
        Vector2f P = polygon.get( polygon.size() - 1 );
        Vector2f S = mousePos;
        drawLine( g, S, P );
    }
}

private void drawPoint( Graphics g, Vector2f v ) {
    Matrix3x3f view = getViewportTransform();
    Vector2f s = view.mul( v );
    g.drawRect( (int)s.x, (int)s.y, 1, 1 );
}

private void drawLine( Graphics g, Vector2f v0, Vector2f v1 ) {
    Matrix3x3f view = getViewportTransform();
    Vector2f S = view.mul( v0 );
    Vector2f P = view.mul( v1 );
     g.drawLine( (int)S.x, (int)S.y, (int)P.x, (int)P.y );
}
```

```
   public static void main( String[] args ) {
      launchApp( new PrototypeEditor() );
   }
}
```

MAKING ROCKS WITH A PROTOTYPE ASTEROID FACTORY

The PrototypeAsteroidFactory, located in the javagames.prototype package, contains three large, three medium, and three small asteroids designed with the editor and pasted into the code. Given a position, the three methods generate a random number to select the asteroid to return:

```
createLargeAsteroid( Vector2f position )
createMediumAsteroid( Vector2f position )
createSmallAsteroid( Vector2f position )
```

The one method, mirror(), is used to flip the model on the x- and y-axis so there are even more unique versions of the model.

```
// PrototypeAsteroidFactory.java
private Vector2f[] mirror( Vector2f[] polygon ) {
   Vector2f[] mirror = new Vector2f[ polygon.length ];
   float x = rand.nextBoolean() ? 1.0f : -1.0f;
   float y = rand.nextBoolean() ? 1.0f : -1.0f;
      Matrix3x3f mat = Matrix3x3f.scale( x, y );
      for( int i = 0; i < polygon.length; ++i ) {
      mirror[i] = mat.mul( polygon[i] );
   }
   return mirror;
}
```

Just like using the matrix to flip the y-axis when performing the viewport matrix multiplication, scaling the model by –1 will flip the x- or y-axis values.

```
package javagames.prototype;

import java.util.Random;

import javagames.prototype.PrototypeAsteroid.Size;
import javagames.util.Matrix3x3f;
import javagames.util.Vector2f;


public class PrototypeAsteroidFactory {

private static final Vector2f[][] LARGE = {
```

```
    { // Large 0
        new Vector2f(-0.029733956f, 0.283255100f),
        new Vector2f(-0.183098610f, 0.111111104f),
        new Vector2f(-0.230046930f,-0.057902932f),
        new Vector2f(-0.092331770f,-0.139280080f),
        new Vector2f( 0.117370844f,-0.142410040f),
        new Vector2f( 0.161189320f,-0.048513293f),
        new Vector2f( 0.151799680f, 0.067292630f),
        new Vector2f( 0.195618150f, 0.129890440f),
        new Vector2f( 0.017214417f, 0.158059480f),
    }, { // Large 1
        new Vector2f(-0.001763641f, 0.325800420f),
        new Vector2f(-0.082892360f, 0.220339000f),
        new Vector2f(-0.227513200f, 0.065913380f),
        new Vector2f(-0.206349200f,-0.141242860f),
        new Vector2f(-0.061728360f,-0.080979230f),
        new Vector2f( 0.061728418f,-0.167608260f),
        new Vector2f( 0.192239940f,-0.092278720f),
        new Vector2f( 0.167548480f, 0.126177010f),
        new Vector2f( 0.107583820f, 0.269303200f),
    }, { // Large 2
        new Vector2f( 0.176838760f,-0.107981205f),
        new Vector2f(-0.070422530f,-0.076682330f),
        new Vector2f(-0.220657290f,-0.123630640f),
        new Vector2f(-0.273865400f, 0.048513293f),
        new Vector2f(-0.186228510f, 0.086071970f),
        new Vector2f(-0.214397490f, 0.223787190f),
        new Vector2f(-0.026604056f, 0.148669780f),
        new Vector2f( 0.104851365f, 0.220657290f),
        new Vector2f( 0.211267590f, 0.032863855f),
    },
};

private static final Vector2f[][] MEDIUM = {
    { // Medium 0
        new Vector2f(-0.045383394f, 0.186228510f),
        new Vector2f(-0.167449180f, 0.123630700f),
        new Vector2f(-0.067292630f, 0.039123654f),
        new Vector2f(-0.107981205f,-0.073552370f),
        new Vector2f( 0.057902932f,-0.073552370f),
        new Vector2f( 0.133020280f, 0.098591566f),
    }, { // Medium 1
        new Vector2f(-0.023474216f, 0.189358350f),
        new Vector2f(-0.107981205f, 0.107981205f),
```

```java
        new Vector2f(-0.129890440f,-0.098591566f),
        new Vector2f( 0.020344257f,-0.120500800f),
        new Vector2f( 0.139280080f,-0.001564979f),
        new Vector2f( 0.076682330f, 0.092331770f),
        new Vector2f(-0.007824719f, 0.095461670f),
    }, { // Medium 2
        new Vector2f(-0.064162790f, 0.158059480f),
        new Vector2f(-0.173708920f, 0.126760600f),
        new Vector2f(-0.142410040f, 0.023474216f),
        new Vector2f(-0.039123654f, 0.029733956f),
        new Vector2f( 0.010954618f,-0.035993695f),
        new Vector2f( 0.117370844f, 0.023474216f),
        new Vector2f( 0.117370844f, 0.120500800f),
        new Vector2f(-0.001564979f, 0.092331770f),
    },
};
private static final Vector2f[][] SMALL = {
    { // Small 0
        new Vector2f(-0.048513293f, 0.057902990f),
        new Vector2f(-0.073552430f,-0.042253494f),
        new Vector2f( 0.004694819f,-0.035993695f),
        new Vector2f( 0.042253494f, 0.026604056f),
        new Vector2f(-0.001564979f, 0.082942130f),
    }, { // Small 1
        new Vector2f( 0.067292690f, 0.007824719f),
        new Vector2f(-0.029733956f,-0.076682330f),
        new Vector2f(-0.067292630f,-0.042253494f),
        new Vector2f(-0.061032890f, 0.082942130f),
        new Vector2f( 0.032863855f, 0.111111104f),
    }, { // Small 2
        new Vector2f(-0.007824719f, 0.089201870f),
        new Vector2f(-0.114241004f, 0.001564979f),
        new Vector2f(-0.004694819f,-0.067292690f),
        new Vector2f( 0.039123654f,-0.039123654f),
        new Vector2f(-0.014084518f, 0.020344317f),
    },
};
private PolygonWrapper wrapper;
private Random rand;
public PrototypeAsteroidFactory( PolygonWrapper wrapper ) {
    this.wrapper = wrapper;
    this.rand = new Random();
}
```

```java
public PrototypeAsteroid createLargeAsteroid( Vector2f position ) {
   PrototypeAsteroid asteroid = new PrototypeAsteroid( wrapper );
   asteroid.setPosition( position );
   asteroid.setPolygon( getRandomAsteroid( LARGE ) );
   asteroid.setSize( Size.Large );
   return asteroid;
}

public PrototypeAsteroid createMediumAsteroid( Vector2f position ) {
   PrototypeAsteroid asteroid = new PrototypeAsteroid( wrapper );
   asteroid.setPosition( position );
   asteroid.setPolygon( getRandomAsteroid( MEDIUM ) );
   asteroid.setSize( Size.Medium );
   return asteroid;
}

public PrototypeAsteroid createSmallAsteroid( Vector2f position ) {
   PrototypeAsteroid asteroid = new PrototypeAsteroid( wrapper );
   asteroid.setPosition( position );
   asteroid.setPolygon( getRandomAsteroid( SMALL ) );
   asteroid.setSize( Size.Small );
   return asteroid;
}

private Vector2f[] getRandomAsteroid( Vector2f[][] asteroids ) {
   return mirror( asteroids[ rand.nextInt( asteroids.length ) ] );
}

private Vector2f[] mirror( Vector2f[] polygon ) {
   Vector2f[] mirror = new Vector2f[ polygon.length ];
   float x = rand.nextBoolean() ? 1.0f : -1.0f;
   float y = rand.nextBoolean() ? 1.0f : -1.0f;
   Matrix3x3f mat = Matrix3x3f.scale( x, y );
   for( int i = 0; i < polygon.length; ++i ) {
      mirror[i] = mat.mul( polygon[i] );
   }
   return mirror;
 }

}
```

The RandomAsteroidExample, shown in Figure 8.10 and located in the javagames. prototype package, uses PolygonWrapper, PrototypeAsteroid, and PrototypeAsteroid Factory to generate random rocks flying around the screen.

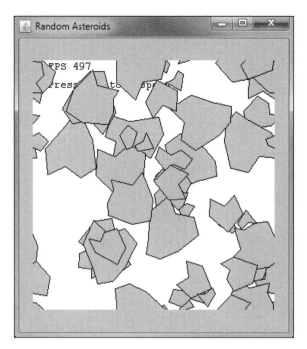

Figure 8.10
Random Asteroid Example.
© 2014 Timothy Wright.

The getRandomAsteroid() method creates a random position and then chooses a random size: small, medium, or large. Remember that each method of the factory chooses from one of the three different polygon models for each size and produces four mirrored versions of each model. With four mirrors per polygon, three shapes per size, and three sized, that's 36 different models.

Also notice that because the PrototypeAsteroid uses the new Utility.fillPolygon() method, the Graphics object is cast to a Graphics2D object.

```
// RandomAsteroidExample.java
protected void render( Graphics g ) {
    super.render( g );
    g.drawString( "Press ESC to respawn", 20, 35 );
    Matrix3x3f view = getViewportTransform();
    for( PrototypeAsteroid asteroid : asteroids ) {
        asteroid.draw( (Graphics2D)g, view );
    }
}
```

The `RandomAsteroidExample` code is as follows:

```java
package javagames.prototype;

import java.awt.*;
import java.awt.event.KeyEvent;
import java.util.*;

import javagames.prototype.PrototypeAsteroid.Size;
import javagames.util.*;


public class RandomAsteroidExample extends SimpleFramework {

    private PrototypeAsteroidFactory factory;
    private ArrayList<PrototypeAsteroid> asteroids;
    private Random rand;

    public RandomAsteroidExample() {
        appBorderScale = 0.9f;
        appWidth = 640;
        appHeight = 640;
        appMaintainRatio = true;
        appSleep = 1L;
        appTitle = "Random Asteroids";
        appBackground = Color.WHITE;
        appFPSColor = Color.BLACK;
    }

    @Override
    protected void initialize() {
        super.initialize();

        rand = new Random();
        asteroids = new ArrayList<PrototypeAsteroid>();
        PolygonWrapper wrapper =
            new PolygonWrapper( appWorldWidth, appWorldHeight );
        factory = new PrototypeAsteroidFactory( wrapper );

        createAsteroids();
    }

    private void createAsteroids() {
        asteroids.clear();
        for( int i = 0; i < 42; ++i ) {
            asteroids.add( getRandomAsteroid() );
        }
    }

    private PrototypeAsteroid getRandomAsteroid() {
        float x = rand.nextFloat() * 2.0f - 1.0f;
        float y = rand.nextFloat() * 2.0f - 1.0f;
```

```
        Vector2f position = new Vector2f( x, y );
        Size[] sizes = Size.values();
        Size randomSize = sizes[ rand.nextInt( sizes.length ) ];
        switch( randomSize ) {
            case Small: return factory.createSmallAsteroid( position );
            case Medium: return factory.createMediumAsteroid( position );
            case Large:
            default: return factory.createLargeAsteroid( position );
        }
    }

    @Override
    protected void processInput( float delta ) {
        super.processInput( delta );
        if( keyboard.keyDownOnce( KeyEvent.VK_ESCAPE ) ) {
            createAsteroids();
        }
    }

    @Override
    protected void updateObjects( float delta ) {
        super.updateObjects( delta );
        for( PrototypeAsteroid asteroid : asteroids ) {
            asteroid.update( delta );
        }
    }

    @Override
    protected void render( Graphics g ) {
        super.render( g );
        g.drawString( "Press ESC to respawn", 20, 35 );
        Matrix3x3f view = getViewportTransform();
        for( PrototypeAsteroid asteroid : asteroids ) {
            asteroid.draw( (Graphics2D)g, view );
        }
    }

    public static void main( String[] args ) {
        launchApp( new RandomAsteroidExample() );
    }
}
```

Prototype Bullet Class

The PrototypeBullet code, also located in the javagames.prototype package, is the simplest prototype game source code. Other than drawing the circle so that the screen can be resized, there isn't anything worth discussing.

```java
package javagames.prototype;

import java.awt.*;

import javagames.util.*;

public class PrototypeBullet {

    private Vector2f velocity;
    private Vector2f position;
    private Color color;
    private float radius;

    public PrototypeBullet( Vector2f position, float angle ) {
        this.position = position;
        velocity = Vector2f.polar( angle, 1.0f );
        radius = 0.006f;
        color = Color.GREEN;
    }

    public Vector2f getPosition() {
        return position;
    }

    public void draw( Graphics2D g, Matrix3x3f view ) {

        g.setColor( color );
        Vector2f topLeft = new Vector2f(
            position.x - radius, position.y + radius );
        topLeft = view.mul( topLeft );
        Vector2f bottomRight = new Vector2f(
            position.x + radius, position.y - radius );
        bottomRight = view.mul( bottomRight );

        int circleX = (int)topLeft.x;
        int circleY = (int)topLeft.y;
        int circleWidth = (int)(bottomRight.x - topLeft.x);
        int circleHeight = (int)(bottomRight.y - topLeft.y);
        g.fillOval(
            circleX, circleY, circleWidth, circleHeight
        );
    }

    public void update( float time ) {
        position = position.add( velocity.mul( time ) );
    }
}
```

PROTOTYPE SHIP CLASS

The PrototypeShip code, located in the javagames.prototype package, is mostly self-explanatory. The constructor sets some constants for moving the ship and hard-codes the model points. There are set*() and get*() methods for damage state, angle, thrusting, as well as methods to rotate the ship left or right.

The launchBullet() method returns a new PrototypeBullet object translated to the nose of the ship.

```java
// PrototypeShip.java
public PrototypeBullet launchBullet() {
    Vector2f bulletPos = position.add( Vector2f.polar( angle, 0.0325f ) );
    return new PrototypeBullet( bulletPos, angle );
}
```

The isTouching() method checks for collisions with every ship in the render list with the given asteroid object. The cool part is the updatePosition() method, which flies the ship around. First, the velocity is updated:

$$V_1 = V_0 + at$$

The acceleration is set inside the setThrusting() method. If the ship is not moving forward, then the acceleration is 0 and the velocity remains the same. Notice that the new acceleration vector uses the current angle, which slowly changes the direction the ship is traveling.

```java
Vector2f accel = Vector2f.polar(angle, curAcc);
```

Next, the new velocity is kept below the maximum value. If this wasn't performed, the ship would continue to gain speed and would eventually be moving faster than the bullet. Notice that the smallest value is used, so when the maximum velocity is not smaller than the actual velocity, the maximum speed is 1.0 and nothing changes. Only when the maximum velocity is smaller than the actual value is the speed constrained.

```java
float maxSpeed = Math.min( maxVelocity / velocity.len(), 1.0f );
velocity = velocity.mul( maxSpeed );
```

Next, friction is applied. Even though there isn't friction in space, I wanted to add it to the ship so it would slow down eventually. If the ship is not accelerating, the friction will keep slowing it down.

```java
float slowDown = 1.0f - friction * time;
velocity = velocity.mul( slowDown );
```

Finally, the position is updated and then wrapped.

```
position = position.add( velocity.mul( time ) );
position = wrapper.wrapPosition( position );
```

The `PrototypeShip` code is as follows:

```java
package javagames.prototype;

import java.awt.*;
import java.util.ArrayList;

import javagames.util.*;


public class PrototypeShip {
    private float angle;
    private float acceleration;
    private float friction;
    private float maxVelocity;
    private float rotationDelta;
    private float curAcc;

    private Vector2f position;
    private Vector2f velocity;

    private PolygonWrapper wrapper;

    private boolean damaged;

    private Vector2f[] polyman;
    private ArrayList<Vector2f[]> renderList;

    public PrototypeShip( PolygonWrapper wrapper ) {
        this.wrapper = wrapper;

        friction = 0.25f;
        rotationDelta = (float)Math.toRadians( 180.0 );
        acceleration = 1.0f;
        maxVelocity = 0.5f;
        velocity = new Vector2f();

        position = new Vector2f();
        polyman = new Vector2f[] {
            new Vector2f( 0.0325f, 0.0f ),
            new Vector2f( -0.0325f, -0.0325f ),
            new Vector2f( 0.0f, 0.0f ),
            new Vector2f( -0.0325f, 0.0325f ),
        };

        renderList = new ArrayList<Vector2f[]>();
    }
```

```java
public void setDamaged( boolean damaged ) {
    this.damaged = damaged;
}

public boolean isDamaged() {
    return damaged;
}

public void rotateLeft( float delta ) {
    angle += rotationDelta * delta;
}

public void rotateRight( float delta ) {
    angle -= rotationDelta * delta;
}

public void setThrusting( boolean thrusting ) {
    curAcc = thrusting ? acceleration : 0.0f;
}

public void setAngle( float angle ) {
    this.angle = angle;
}

public PrototypeBullet launchBullet() {
    Vector2f bulletPos = position.add( Vector2f.polar( angle, 0.0325f ) );
    return new PrototypeBullet( bulletPos, angle );
}

public void update( float time ) {

    updatePosition( time );

    renderList.clear();
    Vector2f[] world = transformPolygon();
    renderList.add( world );
    wrapper.wrapPolygon( world, renderList );

}

private Vector2f[] transformPolygon() {
    Matrix3x3f mat = Matrix3x3f.rotate( angle );
    mat = mat.mul( Matrix3x3f.translate( position ) );
    return transform( polyman, mat );
}

private void updatePosition( float time ) {
    Vector2f accel = Vector2f.polar( angle, curAcc );
    velocity = velocity.add( accel.mul( time ) );
    float maxSpeed = Math.min( maxVelocity / velocity.len(), 1.0f );
    velocity = velocity.mul( maxSpeed );
```

```
      float slowDown = 1.0f - friction * time;
      velocity = velocity.mul( slowDown );
      position = position.add( velocity.mul( time ) );
      position = wrapper.wrapPosition( position );
   }
   private Vector2f[] transform( Vector2f[] poly, Matrix3x3f mat ) {
      Vector2f[] copy = new Vector2f[ poly.length ];
      for( int i = 0; i < poly.length; ++i ) {
         copy[i] = mat.mul( poly[i] );
      }
      return copy;
   }
   public void draw( Graphics2D g, Matrix3x3f view ) {
      g.setColor( new Color( 50, 50, 50 ) );
      for( Vector2f[] poly : renderList ) {
         for( int i = 0; i < poly.length; ++i ) {
            poly[i] = view.mul( poly[i] );
         }
         g.setColor( Color.DARK_GRAY );
         Utility.fillPolygon( g, poly );
         g.setColor( isDamaged() ? Color.RED : Color.GREEN );
         Utility.drawPolygon( g, poly );
      }
   }
   public boolean isTouching( PrototypeAsteroid asteroid ) {
      for( Vector2f[] poly : renderList ) {
         for( Vector2f v : poly ) {
            if( asteroid.contains( v ) ) {
               return true;
            }
         }
      }
      return false;
   }
}
```

The FlyingShipExample, located in the javagames.prototype package and shown in Figure 8.11, uses the ship and bullet code to test flying the ship around the screen. The left arrow and right arrow spin the ship, the up arrow moves the ship forward, and the spacebar fires the bullets.

Figure 8.11
Flying Ship Example.
© 2014 Timothy Wright.

Notice the Java magic in the `updateObject()` method. If the collection of bullets tries to remove the bullet while iterating through it, then the list will throw a `ConcurrentModificationException`. By making a copy of the list and removing it from the original, the exception is not thrown.

```java
// FlyingShipExample.java
protected void updateObjects( float delta ) {
    super.updateObjects( delta );

    ship.update( delta );

    ArrayList<PrototypeBullet> copy =
        new ArrayList<PrototypeBullet>( bullets );
    for( PrototypeBullet bullet : copy ) {
        bullet.update( delta );
        if( wrapper.hasLeftWorld( bullet.getPosition() ) ) {
            bullets.remove( bullet );
        }
    }
}
```

The `FlyingShipExample` is as follows:

```java
package javagames.prototype;

import java.awt.*;
import java.awt.event.KeyEvent;
import java.util.ArrayList;

import javagames.util.*;


public class FlyingShipExample extends SimpleFramework {

    private PrototypeShip ship;
    private PolygonWrapper wrapper;
    private ArrayList<PrototypeBullet> bullets;

    public FlyingShipExample() {
        appBorderScale = 0.9f;
        appWidth = 640;
        appHeight = 640;
        appMaintainRatio = true;
        appSleep = 1L;
        appTitle = "Flying Ship Example";
    }

    @Override
    protected void initialize() {
        super.initialize();

        bullets = new ArrayList<PrototypeBullet>();
        wrapper = new PolygonWrapper( appWorldWidth, appWorldHeight );
        ship = new PrototypeShip( wrapper );

    }

    @Override
    protected void processInput( float delta ) {
        super.processInput( delta );

        if( keyboard.keyDown( KeyEvent.VK_LEFT ) ) {
            ship.rotateLeft( delta );
        }
        if( keyboard.keyDown( KeyEvent.VK_RIGHT ) ) {
            ship.rotateRight( delta );
        }
        if( keyboard.keyDownOnce( KeyEvent.VK_SPACE ) ) {
            bullets.add( ship.launchBullet() );
        }
        ship.setThrusting( keyboard.keyDown( KeyEvent.VK_UP ) );

    }
```

```java
    @Override
    protected void updateObjects( float delta ) {
        super.updateObjects( delta );

        ship.update( delta );

        ArrayList<PrototypeBullet> copy =
            new ArrayList<PrototypeBullet>( bullets );
        for( PrototypeBullet bullet : copy ) {
            bullet.update( delta );
            if( wrapper.hasLeftWorld( bullet.getPosition() ) ) {
                bullets.remove( bullet );
            }
        }
    }

    @Override
    protected void render( Graphics g ) {

        super.render( g );
        g.drawString( "Rotate: Left/Right Arrow", 20, 35 );
        g.drawString( "Thrust: Up Arrow", 20, 50 );
        g.drawString( "Fire: Space Bar", 20, 65 );

        Matrix3x3f view = getViewportTransform();
        ship.draw( (Graphics2D)g, view );
        for( PrototypeBullet b : bullets ) {
            b.draw( (Graphics2D)g, view );
        }

    }

    public static void main( String[] args ) {
        launchApp( new FlyingShipExample() );
    }
}
```

CODING THE PROTOTYPE GAME

The prototype game, shown in Figure 8.12 and located in the `javagames.prototype` package, uses everything you've seen so far. Although this is just a prototype and nowhere close to a complete game, I've presented enough tools to get something working. Waiting until the very end to finally make a game is too long to wait. :-)

Figure 8.12
Prototype Game.
© 2014 Timothy Wright.

This prototype game uses the following classes presented previously in the chapter:

- `PolygonWrapper`
- `PrototypeShip`
- `PrototypeAsteroid`
- `PrototypeAsteroidFactory`
- `PrototypeBullet`

Make sure that these classes are created before you try to compile and run the code at the end of the chapter.

The `initialize()` method creates all the objects for the prototype, including creating some stars for the background. The following code creates the stars and creates an array of colors. The `Color` class takes three values: red, blue, and green, between zero and one. Setting each color value to the same value produces shades of grey.

Color is covered in detail later in the book, but for now, just use the `java.awt.Color` class provided by the language.

```
// PrototypeGame.java
private void createStars() {
stars = new Vector2f[ STAR_COUNT ];
```

```
    colors = new Color[ STAR_COUNT ];
    for( int i = 0; i < stars.length; ++i ) {
        float x = rand.nextFloat() * 2.0f - 1.0f;
        float y = rand.nextFloat() * 2.0f - 1.0f;
        stars[i] = new Vector2f( x, y );
        float color = rand.nextFloat();
        colors[i] = new Color( color, color, color );
    }
}
```

Notice the getAsteroidStartPosition() method when the asteroids are created. Unlike the example that generated random asteroids of all sizes, this one creates only large random asteroids and uses the following code to place them in a circle so they are never generated over the ship.

```
// PrototypeGame.java
private Vector2f getAsteroidStartPosition() {
    float angle = (float)Math.toRadians( rand.nextInt( 360 ) );
    float minimum = appWorldWidth / 4.0f;
    float extra = rand.nextFloat() * minimum;
    float radius = minimum + extra;
    return Vector2f.polar( angle, radius );
}
```

The previous code places the new polygons in a circle that is one quarter of the screen, as shown in Figure 8.13.

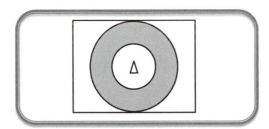

Figure 8.13
Random Asteroid Placement.
© 2014 Timothy Wright.

This keeps the newly generated rocks from appearing on top of the ship and blowing it up before the player has a chance to fire. This is a good example of the kind of challenges game programmers face. This problem didn't become apparent until the prototype was already working. No matter how simple the game, there will always be weird problems to solve.

The processInput() method uses the left and right arrow keys to rotate the ship, the up arrow key to activate the thrusters, the spacebar to fire the bullets, and the Escape key to respawn the asteroids.

When the bullets hit an asteroid, not only is the asteroid removed from the render list, but if the asteroid is not a small one, then it is split into two asteroids of a smaller size.

The updateShip() method checks for collisions. If the ship is hit, the damaged flag is set. Although the real game would restart when the ship is hit, there is no concept of player lives or a game-over state yet, so for now, when the ship is hit, it is drawn in red.

The render() method draws the stars, all the asteroids, the bullets, the ship, and the usual frame rate and instructions. There is some new code that turns on antialiasing so the lines are drawn smooth. Antialiasing is covered in detail in Chapter 10, "Images."

```
Graphics2D g2d = (Graphics2D)g;
    g2d.setRenderingHint(
        RenderingHints.KEY_ANTIALIASING,
        RenderingHints.VALUE_ANTIALIAS_ON
    );
```

The drawStars(), drawShip(), drawAsteroids(), and drawBullets() methods are responsible for drawing the various objects in the prototype. The PrototypeGame code is as follows:

```
package javagames.prototype;

import java.awt.*;
import java.awt.event.KeyEvent;
import java.util.*;

import javagames.prototype.PrototypeAsteroid.Size;
import javagames.util.*;


public class PrototypeGame extends SimpleFramework {
    private static final int STAR_COUNT = 1500;

    private PrototypeShip ship;
    private PolygonWrapper wrapper;
    private PrototypeAsteroidFactory factory;
```

```java
private ArrayList<PrototypeBullet> bullets;
private ArrayList<PrototypeAsteroid> asteroids;
private Random rand;
private Vector2f[] stars;
private Color[] colors;

public PrototypeGame() {
    appBorderScale = 0.9f;
    appWidth = 640;
    appHeight = 640;
    appMaintainRatio = true;
    appSleep = 1L;
    appTitle = "Prototype Game";
}

@Override
protected void initialize() {
    super.initialize();
    // create game objects
    rand = new Random();
    bullets = new ArrayList<PrototypeBullet>();
    asteroids = new ArrayList<PrototypeAsteroid>();
    wrapper = new PolygonWrapper( appWorldWidth, appWorldHeight );
    ship = new PrototypeShip( wrapper );
    factory = new PrototypeAsteroidFactory( wrapper );

    createStars();
    createAsteroids();
}
// this creates the random stars for the background
private void createStars() {
    stars = new Vector2f[ STAR_COUNT ];
    colors = new Color[ STAR_COUNT ];
    for( int i = 0; i < stars.length; ++i ) {
        float x = rand.nextFloat() * 2.0f - 1.0f;
        float y = rand.nextFloat() * 2.0f - 1.0f;
        stars[i] = new Vector2f( x, y );
        float color = rand.nextFloat();
        colors[i] = new Color( color, color, color );
    }
}
// create the random asteroids
private void createAsteroids() {
    asteroids.clear();
```

```java
        for( int i = 0; i < 4; ++i ) {
            Vector2f position = getAsteroidStartPosition();
            asteroids.add( factory.createLargeAsteroid( position ) );
        }
    }
    // create random position for an asteroid
    private Vector2f getAsteroidStartPosition() {
        float angle = (float)Math.toRadians( rand.nextInt( 360 ) );
        float minimum = appWorldWidth / 4.0f;
        float extra = rand.nextFloat() * minimum;
        float radius = minimum + extra;
        return Vector2f.polar( angle, radius );
    }

    @Override
    protected void processInput( float delta ) {
        super.processInput( delta );
        // fly the ship
        if( keyboard.keyDown( KeyEvent.VK_LEFT ) ) {
            ship.rotateLeft( delta );
        }
        if( keyboard.keyDown( KeyEvent.VK_RIGHT ) ) {
            ship.rotateRight( delta );
        }
        if( keyboard.keyDownOnce( KeyEvent.VK_SPACE ) ) {
            bullets.add( ship.launchBullet() );
        }
        if( keyboard.keyDownOnce( KeyEvent.VK_ESCAPE ) ) {
            createAsteroids();
        }
        ship.setThrusting( keyboard.keyDown( KeyEvent.VK_UP ) );

    }

    @Override
    protected void updateObjects( float delta ) {
        super.updateObjects( delta );
        updateAsteroids( delta );
        updateBullets( delta );
        updateShip( delta );
    }

    private void updateAsteroids( float delta ) {
        for( PrototypeAsteroid asteroid : asteroids ) {
```

```
            asteroid.update( delta );
        }
    }

    private void updateBullets( float delta ) {
        ArrayList<PrototypeBullet> copy =
            new ArrayList<PrototypeBullet>( bullets );
        for( PrototypeBullet bullet : copy ) {
            updateBullet( delta, bullet );
        }
    }
    // check for bullet collisions
    private void updateBullet( float delta, PrototypeBullet bullet ) {
        bullet.update( delta );
        if( wrapper.hasLeftWorld( bullet.getPosition() ) ) {
            bullets.remove( bullet );
        } else {
            ArrayList<PrototypeAsteroid> ast =
                new ArrayList<PrototypeAsteroid>( asteroids );
            for( PrototypeAsteroid asteroid : ast ) {
                if( asteroid.contains( bullet.getPosition() ) ) {
                    bullets.remove( bullet );
                    asteroids.remove( asteroid );
                    spawnBabies( asteroid );
                }
            }
        }
    }
    // create smaller asteroids when one is broken apart
    private void spawnBabies( PrototypeAsteroid asteroid ) {
        if( asteroid.getSize() == Size.Large ) {
            asteroids.add(
                factory.createMediumAsteroid( asteroid.getPosition() ) );
            asteroids.add(
                factory.createMediumAsteroid( asteroid.getPosition() ) );
        }
        if( asteroid.getSize() == Size.Medium ) {
            asteroids.add(
                factory.createSmallAsteroid( asteroid.getPosition() ) );
            asteroids.add(
                factory.createSmallAsteroid( asteroid.getPosition() ) );
        }
    }
    // update the ship object
    private void updateShip( float delta ) {
```

```java
        ship.update( delta );
        boolean isHit = false;
        for( PrototypeAsteroid asteroid : asteroids ) {
            if( ship.isTouching( asteroid ) ) {
                isHit = true;
            }
        }
        ship.setDamaged( isHit );
    }

    @Override
    protected void render( Graphics g ) {
        // render instructions
        super.render( g );
        g.drawString( "Rotate: Left/Right Arrow", 20, 35 );
        g.drawString( "Thrust: Up Arrow", 20, 50 );
        g.drawString( "Fire: Space Bar", 20, 65 );
        g.drawString( "Press ESC to respawn", 20, 80 );

        Graphics2D g2d = (Graphics2D)g;
         g2d.setRenderingHint(
            RenderingHints.KEY_ANTIALIASING,
            RenderingHints.VALUE_ANTIALIAS_ON
        );
        // draw game objects
        Matrix3x3f view = getViewportTransform();
        drawStars( g2d, view );
        drawAsteroids( g2d, view );
        drawBullets( g2d, view );
        drawShip( g2d, view );

    }

    private void drawStars( Graphics2D g, Matrix3x3f view ) {
        for( int i = 0; i < stars.length; ++i ) {
            g.setColor( colors[i] );
            Vector2f screen = view.mul( stars[i] );
            g.fillRect( (int)screen.x, (int)screen.y, 1, 1 );
        }
    }

    private void drawShip( Graphics2D g, Matrix3x3f view ) {
        ship.draw( g, view );
    }
```

```
    private void drawAsteroids( Graphics2D g, Matrix3x3f view ) {
        for( PrototypeAsteroid asteroid : asteroids ) {
            asteroid.draw( g, view );
        }
    }

    private void drawBullets( Graphics2D g, Matrix3x3f view ) {
        for( PrototypeBullet b : bullets ) {
            b.draw( g, view );
        }
    }

    public static void main( String[] args ) {
        launchApp( new PrototypeGame() );
    }
}
```

RESOURCES AND FURTHER READING

"How to Finish a Game," http://makegames.tumblr.com/post/1136623767/finishing-a-game.

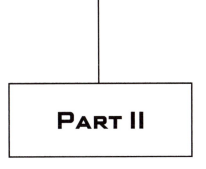

PART II

THE POLISH

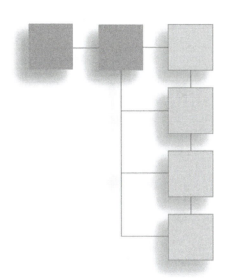

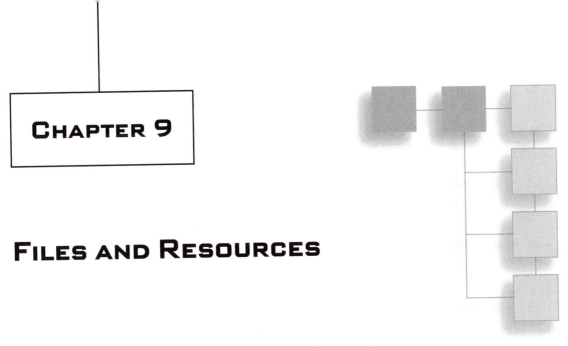

CHAPTER 9

FILES AND RESOURCES

There are many advantages to using files, but the most important are:

- The ability to create, read, update, and delete data without recompiling the software.
- The ability to save and restore information between software runs.

Understanding how files are read and written to is essential for game programming because audio, images, dialogue, 3D models, level data, and anything else needed by your game is stored in files.

This chapter explores reading and writing property files for simple tasks, and covers storing complex data with XML files. There is also a section on using resources (which is just a fancy way of saying "stuff in files") packaged inside a Java archive file (*.jar). Once you have audio and images files, it is important to understand where to put them, and how to access them from inside the game.

UNDERSTANDING HOW JAVA HANDLES FILES AND DIRECTORIES

Before the software reads and writes files, it is important to understand what Java does with files and directories. Experienced Java developers can skip this section, and then simply take a look at the later information about files and resources. There are some interesting problems to consider.

The `File` class can represent a file or a directory. There are many ways to create a file:

■ `File(URI uri)`

■ `File(String pathname)`

■ `File(String parent, String child)`

■ `File(File parent, String child)`

Most of the methods in the `File` class are self-explanatory, and since all you need to do at this point is introduce them, walking a file tree is a good example. See Figure 9.1.

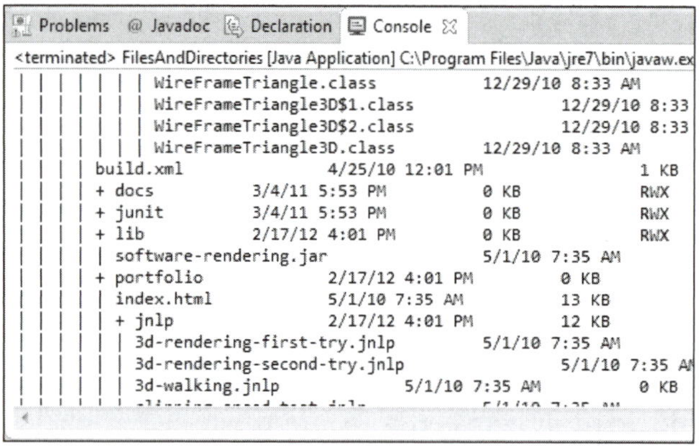

Figure 9.1
Directory Tree.
© 2014 Timothy Wright.

The `FilesAndDirectories` example, located in the `javagames.filesandres` package, walks a directory on the hard drive and displays information for each file and folder. The `main()` method invokes the `runTest()` method, which contains the code to walk the file tree. The `runTest()` method starts by creating a new file object for each folder on the hard drive and then calling the `displayInfo()` method, which prints the information about the file to the console, recursively walking the remaining files.

The following methods are used to gather the information about each file:

■ `canExecute()`—Whether the file is executable

■ `canRead()`—Whether the file is readable

■ `canWrite()`—Whether the file is writable

■ `isHidden()`—If it's a hidden file

■ `isDirectory()`—True if it's a directory, false if it's a file

- `lastModified()`—Date and time of last modification
- `length()`—The size of the file in bytes
- `getName()`—The filename

Other methods are available. See the Java Docs for more information.

The `StringBuilder` class is used to format the file information. The `lastModified` value is wrapped in a `Date()` class and formatted with a `SimpleDateFormat()`. The length is converted to kilobytes and formatted to include comas using the `DecimalFormat()` class. Finally, the read, write, and execute file attributes are appended to the end.

After the file information is printed to the screen, the `listFiles()` method is used to display all the information for any subfolders. The `FilesAndDirectories` code is as follows:

```
package javagames.filesandres;

import java.io.File;
import java.text.DecimalFormat;
import java.text.SimpleDateFormat;
import java.util.Date;


public class FilesAndDirectories {

    public FilesAndDirectories() {

    }

    public void runTest() {
        // list files and folders
        String dir = "C:\\temp";
        File file = new File( dir );
        displayInfo( 0, file );
    }

    private void displayInfo( int depth, File file ) {
        // Name, Date, Size, Attr
        boolean executable = file.canExecute();
        boolean readable = file.canRead();
        boolean writable = file.canWrite();
        boolean hidden = file.isHidden();
        boolean directory = file.isDirectory();
        long lastModified = file.lastModified();
        long length = file.length();
        String name = file.getName();
        // create ASCII file structure
```

```java
        StringBuilder buf = new StringBuilder();
        for( int i = 0; i < depth; ++i ) {
            buf.append( "|" );
        }
        if( directory ) {
            buf.append( "+ " );
        }
        if( name.isEmpty() ) {
            buf.append( "." );
        } else {
            buf.append( name );
        }
        // add modification date
        buf.append( "\t\t" );
        Date date = new Date( lastModified );
        buf.append( new SimpleDateFormat().format( date ) );
        buf.append( "\t\t" );
        // add file size in kilobytes
        long kb = length / 1024;
        DecimalFormat format = new DecimalFormat();
        format.setGroupingUsed( true );
        buf.append( format.format( kb ) );
        buf.append( " KB" );
        // add read, write, execute attribute flags
        buf.append( "\t\t" );
        if( hidden ) buf.append( "." );
        if( readable ) buf.append( "R" );
        if( writable ) buf.append( "W" );
        if( executable ) buf.append( "X" );
        // print everything to the command line
        System.out.println(buf.toString());
        File[] children = file.listFiles();
        if( children != null ) {
            for( File child : children ) {
                displayInfo( depth + 1, child );
            }
        }
    }

    public static void main( String[] args ) {
        new FilesAndDirectories().runTest();
    }

}
```

UNDERSTANDING INPUT/OUTPUT STREAMS

In the land of Java, the InputStream is the interface used to deal with many sources of data. The InputStream can be files, arrays, network sockets, and external devices. The following lists the different input sources that can be used to create different resources.

- Properties: InputStream, Reader
- Images: File, InputStream, ImageInputStream, URL
- Audio: InputStream
- XML: InputStream, Reader, File, InputSource

Although there are different kinds of classes available for reading and writing data, the InputStream is the only one available to everyone. Even using the Class and ClassLoader to access classpath resources uses an InputStream.

With all these classes depending on the InputStream, it should be easy to use. However, because of the exception-handling patterns associated with many early Java APIs, using the InputStream can be tedious and error prone.

Because the stream should always be closed after it is used, even if there is an error, the basic pattern is as follows:

```
InputStream in = null;
try {
    in = [make new stream]
    while( [has more data] ) {
        [process data]
    }
} catch( IOException ex ) {
    [handle error or rethrow]
} finally {
    try {
        in.close();
    } catch( Exception ex ) { }
}
```

Not only does creating and reading an InputStream have exceptions that must be caught, so does closing the stream.

The read() method returns an integer, so remember to cast it to the correct data type. When the read() method returns a −1, there is no more data available. Reading strings uses a Reader interface, which wraps an InputStream. The pattern is the same, except instead of returning a single byte, each readLine() method returns a single line of text.

The example code reads from the `lorem-ipsum.txt` file, which contains the following text:

```
Lorem ipsum dolor sit amet, consectetur adipisicing elit,
sed do eiusmod tempor incididunt ut labore et dolore magna
aliqua. Ut enim ad minim veniam, quis nostrud exercitation
ullamco laboris nisi ut aliquip ex ea commodo consequat.
Duis aute irure dolor in reprehenderit in voluptate velit
esse cillum dolore eu fugiat nulla pariatur. Excepteur sint
occaecat cupidatat non proident, sunt in culpa qui officia
deserunt mollit anim id est laborum.
```

The `ReadingDataFromFiles` code, located in the `javagames.filesandres` package, is a small example of reading bytes and strings from a file.

```java
package javagames.filesandres;

import java.io.*;

public class ReadingDataFromFiles {

    public void runTest() {

        String path = "./res/assets/text/lorem-ipsum.txt";
        File file = new File( path );

        readInBytes( file );
        readInStrings( file );

    }

    public void readInBytes( File file ) {
        System.out.println();
        System.out.println();
        System.out.println( "********************" );
        System.out.println( "Reading in bytes" );
        System.out.println();
        InputStream in = null;
        try {
            in = new FileInputStream( file );
            int next = -1;
            while( (next = in.read()) != -1 ) {
                System.out.print( (char)next );
            }
        } catch( IOException ex ) {
            ex.printStackTrace();
        } finally {
            try {
```

```
                in.close();
            } catch( IOException ex ) { }
        }
    }
    public void readInStrings( File file ) {
        System.out.println();
        System.out.println();
        System.out.println( "********************" );
        System.out.println( "Reading in strings" );
        System.out.println();
        Reader reader = null;
        try {
            reader = new FileReader( file );
            BufferedReader buf = new BufferedReader( reader );
            String line = null;
            while( (line = buf.readLine()) != null ) {
                System.out.println( line );
            }
        } catch( IOException ex ) {
            ex.printStackTrace();
        } finally {
            try {
                reader.close();
            } catch( IOException ex ) { }
        }
    }
    public static void main( String[] args ) {
        new ReadingDataFromFiles().runTest();
    }
}
```

Writing files using the OutputStream class is similar to using an InputStream. The pattern is as follows:

```
OutputStream out = null;
try {
    out = [open output stream]
    [write out data]
} catch( FileNotFoundException fex ) {
    [handle error]
} catch( IOException ioex ) {
    [handle error]
} finally {
```

```
   try {
      out.close()
   } catch( Exception ex ) { }
}
```

Writing out bytes is as simple as opening a `FileOutputStream` with a file and writing the bytes. Notice the extra catch with the `FileNotFoundException`. This is an optional catch because the `FileNotFoundException` is an `IOException`, but sometimes it is good to handle these two errors differently.

However, Java likes to make things difficult. Although strings can be read with a `BufferedReader`, a `BufferedWriter` cannot write out whole strings. To write out entire strings with a newline, the `PrintWriter` class is used. This class has lots of methods for writing out strings to a file. Just don't go looking for the `PrintReader` class. There isn't one.

The good news is that many have already fought these battles, so a quick Internet search will almost always be able to provide answers. The `WritingDataToFiles` example, located in the `javagames.filesandres` package, is an example of writing data to files.

```java
package javagames.filesandres;

import java.io.*;
import java.util.Random;


public class WritingDataToFiles {

   private Random rand = new Random();

   public void runTest() {
      writeOutBytes( "./res/assets/text/byte-file.bin" );
      writeOutStrings( "./res/assets/text/string-file.txt" );
   }

   public void writeOutBytes( String fileName ) {
      System.out.println();
      System.out.println();
      System.out.println("*********************");
      File file = new File( fileName );
      OutputStream out = null;
      try {
         out = new FileOutputStream( file );
         for( int i = 0; i < 1000; ++i ) {
            out.write( rand.nextInt( 256 ) );
         }
      } catch( FileNotFoundException fex ) {
         fex.printStackTrace();
```

```
       } catch( IOException ioex ) {
          ioex.printStackTrace();
       } finally {
          try {
             out.close();
             System.out.println("Wrote: " + file.getPath());
          } catch( Exception ex ) { }
       }
   }
}

public void writeOutStrings( String fileName ) {
   System.out.println();
   System.out.println();
   System.out.println("*********************");

   // We read with a BufferedReader, and write with
   // Expect a BufferedWriter, but no...
   // Damn Java, a PrintWriter.
   // Is there a PrintReader? No. Why? No idea.

   String[] strings = {
          "Lorem ipsum dolor sit amet, consectetur adipisicing elit,",
          "sed do eiusmod tempor incididunt ut labore et dolore magna",
          "aliqua. Ut enim ad minim veniam, quis nostrud exercitation",
          "ullamco laboris nisi ut aliquip ex ea commodo consequat.",
          "Duis aute irure dolor in reprehenderit in voluptate velit",
          "esse cillum dolore eu fugiat nulla pariatur. Excepteur sint",
          "occaecat cupidatat non proident, sunt in culpa qui officia",
          "deserunt mollit anim id est laborum.",
   };

   File file = new File( fileName );
   PrintWriter out = null;
   try {
      out = new PrintWriter( file );
      for( String string : strings ) {
         out.println( string );
      }
   } catch( FileNotFoundException fex ) {
      fex.printStackTrace();
   } finally {
      try {
         out.close();
         System.out.println("Wrote: " + file.getPath());
```

```
            } catch( Exception e ) { }
        }
    }

    public static void main( String[] args ) {
        new WritingDataToFiles().runTest();
    }
}
```

CREATING THE RESOURCES.JAR FILE FOR TESTING

Java archive files are *.zip files renamed to *.jar. These files can hold data, resources, code, other archive files, native libraries, or anything needed by your program. Because all operating systems that can run Java can also perform file operations on *.zip files, it is a convenient format to use. Later in the book, all the images and audio files will be stored in an archive file using the ANT build tool. However, once the files are stored in the archive, they need to be accessed in a special way. It is difficult enough to load images and sound without also worrying about the archive file, so this section explores the process of using resources inside *.jar files in detail.

In order to learn how to pull data from an archive file, you first need to create one. If you want more information about these files, see the resources section at the end of the chapter.

Java's jar command-line utility is used to create the test file that is added to the class-path in the following examples. This file will be needed to test using resources from inside JAR files.

Tip

Keep in mind that the jar.exe (Windows) or jar.sh (Linux) file needs to be in the system path to be used to archive files. This program is located in the same location as the javac program.

To create the Java archive file used in the following examples, create the following structure on the local hard drive:

```
+ javagames (folder)
  + filesandres (folder)
    Test1.txt
    Test2.txt
    Test3.txt
```

Inside each text file, add the title and the "Lorem ipsum" text.

```
Test1
--------------------
Lorem ipsum dolor sit amet, consectetur adipiscing elit.
Duis id ante quis justo ultricies euismod. Vestibulum ante
ipsum primis in faucibus orci luctus et ultrices posuere
cubilia Curae; Donec urna nibh, feugiat vitae facilisis ut,
iaculis id metus. Suspendisse eu enim vitae ligula auctor
dictum eu et orci. Pellentesque habitant morbi tristique senectus
et netus et malesuada fames ac turpis egestas. Phasellus
elementum rhoncus ante eu fringilla. Integer volutpat dolor
sed tellus pulvinar id laoreet metus sollicitudin.
Pellentesque vitae vehicula justo. Donec dolor mi,
mattis ut posuere eget, bibendum non velit. Etiam eget felis
diam, non venenatis neque. Integer nec libero quis libero
rhoncus volutpat. Duis volutpat ultricies erat, at tincidunt
lectus facilisis sit amet.
```

Navigate the command line to the folder that contains the top `javagames` folder, and run the following command:

```
jar -cf resources.jar.
```

The Java Archive tool can be used to package applications. Later in the book, you'll learn about the ANT build tool, which makes this kind of task easier. The `-cf` flag is really two flags: the c is a create flag, and the f is a filename flag. The `resources.jar` file is the name of the file to create, and the . (dot), which is the current directory, is the location of the files added to the archive file. The current directory is used because no directory information is specified.

In the following code example, the files located in the `resources.jar` file will be loaded from the classpath. Make sure that the `resources.jar` file is added to the classpath in the development environment used, or the files will not be found.

Refer to the development environment documentation to add the `resources.jar` file to the classpath. If it was running from the command line, it would look something like this:

```
java -cp resources.jar class.to.Run
```

PUTTING RESOURCES ON THE CLASSPATH

One problem with using files is that you must know the path to the file in order to locate it. Absolute file paths, such as the following:

```
C:\Users\Java\Game
```

don't work if the user doesn't have a C: drive or is using another operating system. Relative paths have a similar but less obvious problem.

```
./relative/path/to/file.txt
```

Using a relative file path works if the Java application is launched in the correct folder, but can break if the application is started from another location. For example, creating a script that launches the program from another directory will break the relative path. Although it is acceptable to allow the users to start the application only from the current directory, there is an easier way.

Most people who have used Java for a while are familiar with the classpath; that magical list of all the directories and JAR files needed to run the application. Not only can you add JAR files and folders to the classpath, but you can access JAR files and folders with resources. When you include resources in the classpath, it doesn't matter where the application is launched. Paths to the files are the same on any file system in any operating system.

Before you get too excited, it is important to understand some weird differences between the different methods of opening classpath resources. There are two different classes that can be used to load resources from the classpath.

- `ClassLoader.getSystemResourceAsStream()`
- `Class.getResourceAsStream()`

These two methods look very similar, so it is easy to confuse them. Because they are almost, but not quite, the same, you must be careful to ensure the correct resource is given to the correct method.

Here is where the confusing part comes into play. Both `ClassLoader` and `Class` can load resources with an absolute path, but only `Class` can load relative resources. See Figure 9.2.

	Absolute	Relative
ClassLoader	☑	
Class	☑	☑

Figure 9.2
Class Loader Resources.
© 2014 Timothy Wright.

If the full path to the resource is path/to/file.txt, then both ClassLoader and Class can load it. But because Class can also load files relative to itself, Class needs a / at the beginning of the path if the path is absolute.

```
ClassLoader - "path/to/file.txt"
Class - "/path/to/file.txt"
```

If the / is left off the beginning path for the Class, the resource will not be found because it will look relative to itself instead of at the root directory. There is another problem when Class is used. The normal way to get the class object is to use the getClass() method. This can work just fine:

```
getClass().getResourceAsStream( "resource" );
```

However, the problem with the getClass() method is that it will always return the deepest child class, even in the parent class. If the deepest subclass is created in a different package, then the resource loaded in the parent will no longer be found. To prevent this from happening, the static class should be used when relative resource loading is used. This will work no matter what subclasses are created.

```
ClassName.class.getResourceAsStream( "resource" );
```

The ClasspathResources example, located in the javagames.filesandres package, demonstrates the different ways to load a resource. Remember to create the resources.jar file and manually add it to the classpath so the resources are available at runtime.

```
package javagames.filesandres;

import java.io.*;


public class ClasspathResources {

    public ClasspathResources() {
    }

    public void runTest() {

        /*
         * ClassLoader uses absolute path. There is
         * NO '/' at the beginning of the path!
         */
        System.out.println();
        System.out.println("***************************");
        System.out.println("ClassLoader - Absolute Path");
        System.out.println();
```

```
InputStream in = ClassLoader.getSystemResourceAsStream(
    "javagames/filesandres/Test1.txt" );
printResource( in );

/*
 * getClass() instead of class loader.
 * Can be relative...
 */
System.out.println();
System.out.println("****************************");
System.out.println("getClass() - Relative path");
System.out.println();
in = getClass().getResourceAsStream( "Test2.txt" );
printResource( in );

/*
 * getClass() can also use the absolute path,
 * but it needs a '/' at the start of the path.
 */
System.out.println();
System.out.println("****************************");
System.out.println("getClass() - Absolute path");
System.out.println();
in = getClass().getResourceAsStream(
    "/javagames/filesandres/Test3.txt" );
printResource( in );

/*
 * Because getClass() always returns the subclass,
 * if a subclass is created in another package,
 * the relative path may not be correct.
 * However, using an absolute path doesn't allow
 * packages to be moved around. Use the static class,
 * which also works in static methods.
 */
System.out.println();
System.out.println("****************************");
System.out.println("getClass() - Absolute path");
System.out.println();
in = ClasspathResources.class.getResourceAsStream( "Test3.txt" );
printResource( in );

/*
 * Either ClassLoader or Class will return null
 * for unknown resources
 */
in = getClass().getResourceAsStream( "fat/finger/mistake" );
```

```
      if( in == null ) {
         System.out.println();
         System.out.println( "***************************" );
         System.out.println( "Got a null back!!!" );
      }
      in = ClassLoader.getSystemResourceAsStream( "fat/finger/mistake" );
      if( in == null ) {
         System.out.println( "Got another null back!!!" );
      }
   }

   private void printResource( InputStream in ) {
      try {
         InputStreamReader reader = new InputStreamReader( in );
         BufferedReader buf = new BufferedReader( reader );
         String line = null;
         while( (line = buf.readLine()) != null ) {
            System.out.println(line);
         }
      } catch( IOException e ) {
         e.printStackTrace();
      } finally {
         try {
            in.close();
         } catch( Exception e ) { }
      }
   }

   public static void main( String[] args ) {
      new ClasspathResources().runTest();
   }
}
```

MAKING A RESOURCE LOADER UTILITY

Although loading resources from inside JAR files is great for a deployed application, it is terrible during the development process. If every time there is a change in resource files, and a new JAR file must be created and added to the classpath before the change can be testing, development will be very slow. Luckily, there are many ways to deal with loading resources from the classpath during development:

- Add the JAR file to the classpath. Not only is it a pain to keep rebuilding and deploying a new JAR every time changes are made, any resources inside the JAR cannot be changed.

- Add the resources folder to the classpath. This is better, but the folder structure of the resource folder and the JAR file must match. Also, I have used this method but forgotten to add the folder when setting up a new project and had trouble figuring out the problem.

- Load resources from both the file system and the classpath. This requires extra code to try loading the resource from two different places, but there is no setup required in the project to make it work.

For the purposes of this book, the third option is used because it doesn't require any additional setup in the development environment.

The following ResourceLoader class, located in the javagames.util package, is used to load resources from both the classpath and the file system.

```
package javagames.util;

import java.io.FileInputStream;
import java.io.FileNotFoundException;
import java.io.InputStream;


public class ResourceLoader {
    public static InputStream load(
        Class<?> clazz, String filePath, String resPath ) {
        // try the resource first
        InputStream in = null;
        if( !( resPath == null || resPath.isEmpty() ) ) {
            in = clazz.getResourceAsStream( resPath );
        }

        if( in == null ) {
            // try the file path
            try {
                in = new FileInputStream( filePath );
            } catch( FileNotFoundException e ) {
                e.printStackTrace();
            }
        }

        return in;
    }
}
```

The ResourceLoaderExample code, located in the javagames.filesandres package, uses the ResourceLoader to load files from both the file system and the classpath. Make sure to adjust the file paths in the example to match the file system on your system.

```java
package javagames.filesandres;

import java.io.*;

import javagames.util.ResourceLoader;


public class ResourceLoaderExample {

    public ResourceLoaderExample() {

    }

    public void runTest() {

        Class<?> clazz = ResourceLoaderExample.class;

        // load absolute resource
        String filePath = "not/used";
        String resPath = "/javagames/filesandres/Test1.txt";
        InputStream in = ResourceLoader.load( clazz, filePath, resPath );
        printResource( in );

        // load relative resource
        filePath = "not/used";
        resPath = "Test2.txt";
        in = ResourceLoader.load( clazz, filePath, resPath );
        printResource( in );

        // load absolute file path
        filePath = "C:/Book/res/assets/lib/javagames/filesandres/Test3.txt";
        resPath = "/not/available";
        in = ResourceLoader.load( clazz, filePath, resPath );
        printResource( in );

        // load relative file path
        filePath = "res/assets/lib/javagames/filesandres/Test3.txt";
        resPath = "/not/available";
        in = ResourceLoader.load( clazz, filePath, resPath );
        printResource( in );

        // error with both is null
        filePath = "fat/finger";
        resPath = "fat/finger/too";
        in = ResourceLoader.load( clazz, filePath, resPath );
        printResource( in );
    }
```

```java
    private void printResource( InputStream in ) {
        try {
            InputStreamReader reader = new InputStreamReader( in );
            BufferedReader buf = new BufferedReader( reader );
            String line = null;
            while( (line = buf.readLine()) != null ) {
                System.out.println(line);
            }
        } catch( IOException e ) {
            e.printStackTrace();
        } finally {
            try {
                in.close();
            } catch( Exception e ) { }
        }
    }

    public static void main( String[] args ) {
        new ResourceLoaderExample().runTest();
    }
}
```

Exploring Java Properties

Java contains a very helpful class for dealing with simple name-value pair properties. The Properties class can read in a file containing lines with name-value pairs. The Properties class is available from the System object for system-wide properties, but any property class that has been created can be used.

```
name1=value1
name2=value2
```

The PrintSystemProperties example, located in the javagames.filesandres package, prints out all the system property values and then highlights some useful system properties.

```java
package javagames.filesandres;

import java.util.Properties;


public class PrintSystemProperties {
    public static void main( String[] args ) {
        Properties system = System.getProperties();
```

```
        for( Object key : system.keySet() ) {
            System.out.println(
                key + "=" + system.getProperty( key.toString() )
            );
        }

        System.out.println();
        System.out.println( "------- Some Cool Props ------------" );
        System.out.println( "java.version=" +
            System.getProperty( "java.version" ) );
        System.out.println( "os.name=" + System.getProperty( "os.name" ) );
        System.out.println( "user.country=" +
            System.getProperty( "user.country" ) );
        System.out.println( "user.language=" +
            System.getProperty( "user.language" ) );
        System.out.println(
            "user.home=" + System.getProperty( "user.home" ) );
        System.out.println( "user.dir=" + System.getProperty( "user.dir" ) );
        System.out.println(
            "user.name=" + System.getProperty( "user.name" ) );
    }
}
```

One of the reasons that the system properties are useful is because Java includes the -D command-line flag, which lets system properties be defined on the command line. The format for the flag is -Dname=value. To set a command-line property, simply include as many -D flags as necessary. As shown in the following code snippet, when passing the flags, they cannot be placed at the very end for the command, because any text after the classname with a JAR name is passed as a string value to the main() method.

```
C:\> java -Dname1=value1 -Dname2=value2 -jar CoolGame.jar
    "Don't put the -D stuff here. It won't work."
```

The properties can be easily retrieved because the System class is available from anywhere. There are two methods for retrieving the property values:

```
String prop = System.getProperty( "name" );
String default = System.getProperty( "name", "default" );
```

The first method passes in only a property name, and if the property is not available, null is returned. The second method includes a default value that is returned if the property is not found. There is a catch to using properties: once they are set, they can still be overwritten. You must be careful when loading multiple property files and system properties, because the last property defined will erase previous property values.

The SavingPropertyFiles example, located in the javagames.filesandres package, creates a simple file called testing.properties. There are three properties in this file:
prop1, prop2, and override. There are also comments, which begin with either the # or
! characters.

```java
package javagames.filesandres;
import java.io.*;


public class SavingPropertyFiles {
    public SavingPropertyFiles() {

    }
    public void saveFile() {
        File file = new File( "testing.properties" );
        PrintWriter out = null;
        try {
            out = new PrintWriter( file );

            out.println( "# This is a comment" );
            out.println( "prop1=fileValue1" );

            out.println( "# This is another comment" );
            out.println( "prop2=fileValue2" );

            out.println( "# This can be overriden from the" );
            out.println( "! command line, or not..." );
            out.println( "override=fileoverride" );

        } catch( FileNotFoundException fex ) {
            fex.printStackTrace();
        } finally {
            try {
                out.close();
                System.out.println("Wrote: " + file.getPath());
            } catch( Exception e ) { }
        }
    }
    public static void main( String[] args ) {
        new SavingPropertyFiles().saveFile();
    }
}
```

The `PropertyFileExample` uses the `testing.properties` file from the previous example. The code looks first for a property called `load.props.first`. This `System` property is retrieved as follows:

```
// PropertyFileExample.java
private boolean getLoadFirstProperty() {
    try {
      String value = System.getProperty( "load.props.first", "false" );
      return Boolean.parseBoolean( value );
    } catch( Exception e ) {
      return false;
    }
}
```

If the property is found, it is parsed into a Boolean value. If it is not found, it defaults to `false`. This property is used to determine if the `System` properties are loaded before or after the `testing.properties` file. Because the last loaded file determines the available properties, it will depend on the order in which the files are loaded as to which property will be available at runtime.

If `load.props.first` is `false`, then the `System` properties will not be loaded first and will overwrite the `testing.properties` file. If `load.props.first` is `true`, then the command-line override property will be overwritten by the loaded file.

Tip

Try running the example program by passing a command-line override and setting the `load.props.first` to both `true` and `false` to see what happens.

```
java -Dload.props.first=true -Doverride=command-line -classpath
C:\javagames\book\bin javagames.filesandres.PropertyFileExample
```

The command-line example should be similar on your machine.

```
package javagames.filesandres;

import java.io.*;

import java.util.Properties;

import javagames.util.ResourceLoader;


public class PropertyFileExample {

    private Properties props;
```

```java
public PropertyFileExample() {
   props = new Properties();
}

private void loadAndPrintProperties() {
   boolean loadPropsFirst = getLoadFirstProperty();
   if( loadPropsFirst ) {
      props.putAll( System.getProperties() );
   }

   loadProperties();

   if( !loadPropsFirst ) {
      props.putAll( System.getProperties() );
   }
   printProperties();
}

private void loadProperties() {
   InputStream in = null;
   try {
       in = ResourceLoader.load( PropertyFileExample.class,
          "./testing.properties", "/testing.properties" );
      props.load( in );
   } catch( IOException e ) {
      e.printStackTrace();
   } finally {
      try {
         in.close();
      } catch( Exception e ) { }
   }
}

private boolean getLoadFirstProperty() {
   try {
      String value = System.getProperty( "load.props.first", "false" );
      return Boolean.parseBoolean( value );
   } catch( Exception e ) {
      return false;
   }
}

private void printProperties() {
   System.out.println(
      "load.props.first=" + getLoadFirstProperty()
   );
```

```
    System.out.println(
        "user.home=" + props.getProperty( "user.home", "." )
    );
     System.out.println(
        "prop1=" + props.getProperty( "prop1", "default1" )
    );
     System.out.println(
        "prop2=" + props.getProperty( "prop2", "default2" )
    );
     System.out.println(
        "prop3=" + props.getProperty( "prop3", "default3" )
    );
     System.out.println(
          "override=" + props.getProperty( "override", "defaultOverride" )
    );
  }

  public static void main( String[] args ) {
     PropertyFileExample example = new PropertyFileExample();
     example.loadAndPrintProperties();
  }

}
```

AN OVERVIEW OF XML FILES

Using XML files is one way to store, save, and load information about a game. Although there are many different file formats, because XML is supported without any third-party libraries, it is the format used in this book.

There are numerous books, tutorials, and examples on the web, but if you are not familiar with XML, it is a good idea to review the basics. The following are the different kinds of XML tags.

The XML version is included at the top of each file:

```
<?xml version="1.0" encoding="UTF-8"?>
```

Every XML file can have only one root tag:

```
<root>
</root>
```

Every tag consists of a start and end tag. Each start tag must have an end tag with the same name:

```
<tag></tag>
```

If a tag has no content inside its tags, a shorthand version can be used:

```
<shorthand/>
```

Tags can contain text, other tags, or both, inside themselves:

```
<text>I'm some text</text>
<nested><child/></nested>
<nested-text>some text and <child/></nested-text>
```

A tag can also contain attributes inside the start tag as follows:

```
<attributes attr1="value1" attr2="values"/>
```

The following characters are not allowed inside XML: < > & ' and ". Each of these characters is represented by the following special character sequences:

```
< = &lt;
> = &gt;
& = &amp;
" = &quot;
' = &apos;
```

To include unparsed text, the CDATA character tags can be used:

```
Start tag = <![CDATA[
End tag = ]]>
```

Inside these tags, even special characters are captured without being parsed.

Finally, comments are written as follows:

```
<!-- comment -->
```

The only character sequence not allowed in a comment is two dashes --. Comments can span multiple lines.

SaveXMLExample, located in the javagames.filesandres package, creates an XML file by writing the file out using the PrintWriter class. The sample.xml file created with this code is used later as the test file for parsing XML.

```
package javagames.filesandres;

import java.io.File;
import java.io.FileNotFoundException;
import java.io.PrintWriter;


public class SaveXMLExample {

    public SaveXMLExample() {

    }
```

```java
public void createXMLFile() {
    File file = new File( "sample.xml" );
    PrintWriter out = null;
    try {
        out = new PrintWriter( file );
        writeXML( out );
    } catch( FileNotFoundException fex ) {
        fex.printStackTrace();
    } finally {
        try {
            out.close();
            System.out.println("Wrote: " + file.getPath());
        } catch( Exception e ) { }
    }
}

private void writeXML( PrintWriter out ) {
    out.println( "<?xml version=\"1.0\" encoding=\"UTF-8\" ?>" );
    // all XML must have a single root tag
    out.println( "<root>" );
    // a comment
    out.println( "  <!-- This is a comment -->" );
    // and empty tag
    out.println( "  <empty></empty>" );
    // shorthand for a tag with no children
    out.println( "  <shorthand/>" );
    // text element
    out.println( "  <text>I'm some text</text>" );
    // nested elements
    out.println( "  <nested><child/></nested>" );
    // nested text with child
    out.println( "  <nested-text>I'm some text <child/></nested-text>" );
    // attributes
    out.println( "  <attributes attr1=\"value1\" attr2=\"value2\" />" );
    // special characters
    out.println(
        " <special-chars> &lt; &gt; &amp; &apos;" +
        " &quot; </special-chars>" );
    // unparsed character data CDATA
    out.println( " <cdata>" ) ;
```

```
        // Starting CDATA tag
        out.println( "   <![CDATA[" );

        out.println( "<xml><attr=\"xml inside xml\"/></xml>" );

        // Ending CDATA tag
        out.println( "   ]]>" );

        out.println( "  </cdata>" );

        // ending root tag
        out.println( "</root>" );
    }
    public static void main( String[] args ) {
        new SaveXMLExample().createXMLFile();
    }
}
```

Writing out XML files is a lot easier than parsing them. Fortunately, none of the really complicated and confusing parts of the XML specification are needed for loading game data.

The XMLUtility class, which is added to the javagames.util package, contains some helper methods for parsing XML files. The parseDocument() method takes either an InputStream or a Reader and returns a Document object that contains the entire XML file in memory. The getElements() and getAllElements() methods return elements with the given tag name. The difference is that the getElements() method searches only one level deep for tags, whereas getAllElements() returns any tags that have the given name, no matter where they are in the document.

```
package javagames.util;

import java.io.*;
import java.util.*;

import javax.xml.parsers.*;

import org.w3c.dom.*;
import org.xml.sax.*;


public class XMLUtility {

    public static Document parseDocument( InputStream inputStream )
    throws ParserConfigurationException, SAXException, IOException {
        DocumentBuilderFactory factory = DocumentBuilderFactory.newInstance();
        DocumentBuilder builder = factory.newDocumentBuilder();
```

```
        Document document = builder.parse( new InputSource( inputStream ) );
        return document;
    }

    public static Document parseDocument( Reader reader )
    throws ParserConfigurationException, SAXException, IOException {
        DocumentBuilderFactory factory = DocumentBuilderFactory.newInstance();
        DocumentBuilder builder = factory.newDocumentBuilder();
        Document document = builder.parse( new InputSource( reader ) );
        return document;
    }

    public static List<Element> getAllElements(
        Element element, String tagName ) {
        ArrayList<Element> elements = new ArrayList<Element>();
        NodeList nodes = element.getElementsByTagName( tagName );
        for( int i = 0; i < nodes.getLength(); i++ ) {
            elements.add( (Element)nodes.item( i ) );
        }
        return elements;
    }

    public static List<Element> getElements(
        Element element, String tagName ) {
        ArrayList<Element> elements = new ArrayList<Element>();
        NodeList children = element.getChildNodes();
        for( int i = 0; i < children.getLength(); i++ ) {
            Node node = children.item( i );
            if( node.getNodeType() == Node.ELEMENT_NODE ) {
                String nodeName = node.getNodeName();
                if( nodeName != null && nodeName.equals( tagName ) ) {
                    elements.add( (Element)node );
                }
            }
        }
        return elements;
    }
}
```

The `LoadXMLExample` code, located in the `javagames.filesandres` package, parses the `sample.xml` file from the previous example.

```
<?xml version="1.0" encoding="UTF-8" ?>
<root>
  <!-- This is a comment -->
  <empty></empty>
```

```
<shorthand/>
<text>I'm some text</text>
<nested><child/></nested>
<nested-text>I'm some text <child/></nested-text>
<attributes attr1="value1" attr2="value2" />
<special-chars> &lt; &gt; &amp; &apos; &quot; </special-chars>
<cdata>
  <![CDATA[
<xml><attr="xml inside xml"/></xml>
  ]]>
</cdata>
</root>
```

You need to take a recursive approach for processing the document because XML tags can contain other tags. For inspecting documents without knowing their structure, you use the following pattern:

```java
// LoadXMLExample.java
private void inspectXML( Node node ) {
    printNode( node );
    if( node.hasAttributes() ) {
        NamedNodeMap nodeMap = node.getAttributes();
        for( int i = 0; i < nodeMap.getLength(); ++i ) {
            inspectXML( nodeMap.item( i ) );
        }
    }
    if( node.hasChildNodes() ) {
        NodeList nodeList = node.getChildNodes();
        for( int i = 0; i < nodeList.getLength(); ++i ) {
            inspectXML( nodeList.item( i ) );
        }
    }
}
```

Each node's type, name, and value are printed. Then any attributes are processed recursively using the same function. The same is done for any children elements. The method parseXML() uses the XMLUtility class to pull out each element using its tag name.

The following methods get the necessary information from each element:

■ Element.getNodeName()—Returns the name of the XML tag.

■ Element.getTextContent()—Returns the text value between the start and end tags.

■ Element.getAttribute(String name)—Given the attribute name, this method returns the attribute value, or null if the attribute is available.

Pay attention to the sections that attempt to get the "child" tags. There are two different elements with that tag name, but depending on which method is used to retrieve them, either none, one, or two tags will be returned. Sometimes you will want to retrieve all tags with a specific name, but sometimes all elements have a tag with the same name, such as <name>, and you only want the tags for the current element. Using both the getElements() and getAllElements() methods from the utility class makes this possible.

```java
package javagames.filesandres;


import java.io.*;
import java.util.List;
import org.w3c.dom.*;
import org.xml.sax.*;

import javagames.util.*;

import javax.xml.parsers.ParserConfigurationException;


public class LoadXMLExample {
    public LoadXMLExample() {

    }
    public void loadFile() {
        InputStream in = null;
        try {
            in = ResourceLoader.load( LoadXMLExample.class, "sample.xml",
                    "/sample/xml" );
            Document document = XMLUtility.parseDocument( in );

            System.out.println( "*********" );
            System.out.println( "* INSPECT" );
            inspectXML( document );
            System.out.println( "*********" );
            System.out.println( "* PARSE" );
            parseXML( document );
        } catch( ParserConfigurationException pex ) {
            System.out.println( "ParserConfigurationException" );
            pex.printStackTrace();
        } catch( SAXException ex ) {
            System.out.println( "SAXException" );
            ex.printStackTrace();
        } catch( IOException ex ) {
            System.out.println( "IOException" );
```

```
            ex.printStackTrace();
        } finally {
            try {
                in.close();
            } catch( IOException ex ) {
            }
        }
    }
}

private void inspectXML( Node node ) {
    printNode( node );
    if( node.hasAttributes() ) {
        NamedNodeMap nodeMap = node.getAttributes();
        for( int i = 0; i < nodeMap.getLength(); ++i ) {
            inspectXML( nodeMap.item( i ) );
        }
    }
    if( node.hasChildNodes() ) {
        NodeList nodeList = node.getChildNodes();
        for( int i = 0; i < nodeList.getLength(); ++i ) {
            inspectXML( nodeList.item( i ) );
        }
    }
}

private void printNode( Node node ) {
    System.out.print( "Type: " + getNodeType( node ) );
    System.out.print( ", Name: " + node.getNodeName() );
    String value = node.getNodeValue() == null ?
        "" : node.getNodeValue().trim();
    System.out.println( ", Value: '" + value + "'" );
}

private String getNodeType( Node node ) {
    switch( node.getNodeType() ) {
        case Node.ATTRIBUTE_NODE:
            return "ATTRIBUTE_NODE";
        case Node.CDATA_SECTION_NODE:
            return "CDATA_SECTION_NODE";
        case Node.COMMENT_NODE:
            return "COMMENT_NODE";
        case Node.DOCUMENT_NODE:
            return "DOCUMENT_NODE";
        case Node.ELEMENT_NODE:
            return "ELEMENT_NODE";
```

```java
                case Node.ENTITY_NODE:
                    return "ENTITY_NODE";
                case Node.TEXT_NODE:
                    return "TEXT_NODE";
                default:
                    return "Unknown";
        }
    }

    private void parseXML( Document document ) {

        Element element = document.getDocumentElement();

        List<Element> elements =
            XMLUtility.getAllElements( element, "empty" );
        System.out.println( "Element: " + elements.get( 0 ).getNodeName() );

        List<Element> shorthand =
            XMLUtility.getAllElements( element, "shorthand" );
        System.out.println( "Element: " + shorthand.get( 0 ).getNodeName() );

        List<Element> text = XMLUtility.getAllElements( element, "text" );
        System.out.println( "Text: " + text.get( 0 ).getTextContent() );

        List<Element> nested = XMLUtility.getAllElements( element, "nested" );
        System.out.println( "Element: " + nested.get( 0 ).getNodeName() );

        List<Element> elementChildren =
            XMLUtility.getElements( element, "child" );
        System.out.println( "Get-Child-Count: " + elementChildren.size() );

        List<Element> child =
            XMLUtility.getElements( nested.get( 0 ), "child" );
        System.out.println( "Get-Child-Count: " + child.size() );

        List<Element> allChildren =
            XMLUtility.getAllElements( element, "child" );
        System.out.println( "Get-AllChild-Count: " + allChildren.size() );

        List<Element> nestedText =
            XMLUtility.getElements( element, "nested-text" );
        System.out.println( "nested-text: " +
            nestedText.get( 0 ).getTextContent()
        );

        List<Element> nestedChild =
            XMLUtility.getElements( nestedText.get( 0 ), "child" );
        System.out.println( "nested-text: " +
            nestedChild.get( 0 ).getNodeName() );
```

```
        List<Element> attributes =
            XMLUtility.getElements( element, "attributes" );
        Element attrElement = attributes.get( 0 );
        System.out.println(
            "attr1: " + attrElement.getAttribute( "attr1" ) );
        System.out.println(
            "attr2: " + attrElement.getAttribute( "attr2" ) );

        List<Element> specialChars =
            XMLUtility.getElements( element, "special-chars" );
        System.out.println( "special-chars: " +
            specialChars.get( 0 ).getTextContent() );

        List<Element> cdata = XMLUtility.getElements( element, "cdata" );
        System.out.println( "cdata: " + cdata.get( 0 ).getTextContent() );
    }

    public static void main( String[] args ) {
        new LoadXMLExample().loadFile();
    }
}
```

There was a lot of information covered about using XML files, and if you don't feel like everything is solid, do not worry. In Chapters 16, "Tools," and 17, "Space Rocks," the complete game will create and load polygons using XML files pulled from archive files located on the classpath. So hang in there. If game programming was easy, everyone would do it. :-)

RESOURCES AND FURTHER READING

Roubtsov, Vladimir, "Smartly Load Your Properties," 2003, http://www.javaworld.com/javaqa/2003-08/01-qa-0808-property.html.

"Document Object Model," 1995, http://docs.oracle.com/javase/tutorial/jaxp/dom/index.html.

"How to Use JAR Files," 1995, http://docs.oracle.com/javase/tutorial/deployment/jar/basicsindex.html.

CHAPTER 10

IMAGES

Java has a variety of methods for creating images. Some of the more common are ImageIcon, BufferedImage, and VolatileImage. There are other formats and other classes, but for the purposes of this book, BufferedImage and VolatileImage are all that are covered. Also, because the language has been around a long time and works on multiple operating systems, some of the image formats are only available for backward compatibility, and should not be used for new development. Even though they are not all needed, it is good to be familiar with all the different options.

LEARNING ABOUT COLORS IN JAVA

Before understanding the different formats for images, it is important to understand how Java represents colors. Colors in Java consist of red, green, and blue components, with an optional alpha component that is used for transparency. Colors can be created using floating-point values from 0.0f to 1.0f, where 0.0f is no color component at all, and 1.0f is the brightest of that component. Each color, regardless of the method used to create it, consists of a single value, with red, green, blue, and alpha values represented as a certain number of bits. Together, the bits of each color are combined to form a single value of 32 bits. But this value is only the representation of the color before it is drawn to an image. Ultimately, it is the format of the destination image that determines the color. These different formats are covered later in the chapter.

```
Color( float r, float g, float b )
Color( float r, float g, float b, float a )
```

The previous methods construct a color with the given red, green, blue, and optional alpha value, which controls the transparency of the object. If the alpha value is not supplied, it is set to 1.0f, which represents a completely opaque value (no transparency).

There are also constructors using integer values from 0–255. The 0–255 values represent one of the four bytes available to represent the color. These methods construct a color the same as the floating-point versions.

```
Color( int r, int g, int b )
Color( int r, int g, int b, int a )
```

Another constructor takes a single integer. This single value contains the (r, g, b, a) components of each color component or-ed together into a single value.

```
Color( int rgba )
```

The alpha value is defaulted to 255 (0xFF in hexadecimal representation). The color is constructed by shifting each integer value into the correct position.

```
int rgba = 0xFF << 24 | r << 16 | g << 8 | b;
```

Another way to think of this value is the following:

```
0xAARRGGBB
```

where each pair of letters represents that color's corresponding byte.

```
Color( int rgba, boolean hasAlpha )
```

This constructor allows a different alpha value to be used to produce transparency.

EXPLORING DIFFERENT IMAGE TYPES

Understanding how Java represents color is only part of the puzzle. When a color is constructed, and is drawn onto an image with a Graphics object, it is the color format of the destination image that ultimately determines the color format written to the image.

The BufferedImage class supports a wide variety of image types. The following list briefly describes the different image formats supported by the BufferedImage class.

- TYPE_BYTE_BINARY—1-, 2-, or 4-bit image with an IndexColorModel used to select the appropriate color values.

- TYPE_BYTE_GRAY—Each color is represented as a single byte from 0 (black) to 255 (white).

- TYPE_BYTE_INDEXED—Each byte value is an index into a 256 value array of colors containing web-safe colors and gray values.

- TYPE_CUSTOM—Unknown types use this value for the image type.

- TYPE_3BYTE_BGR—Each three byte group represents a color, where index 0 is blue, index 1 is green, and index 2 is red.

- TYPE_4BYTE_ABGR—Each four byte group represents a color, where index 0 is alpha, index 1 is blue, index 2 is green, and index 3 is red.

- TYPE_4BYTE_ABGR_PRE—This is the same as the previous type, but all the colors have been pre-multiplied by the alpha value before being stored.

- TYPE_USHORT_555_RGB—Represents an image with five bits for each color, packed into a 16-bit value, with no alpha value. See Figure 10.1.

- TYPE_USHORT_565_RGB—Five bits for each red and blue component, and 6 bits for green, with no alpha component. See Figure 10.2.

- TYPE_USHORT_GRAY—Same as an 8-bit gray-scale image, with the upper eight bits unused.

- TYPE_INT_BGR—Integer with the format 0x00BBGGRR with no alpha value.

- TYPE_INT_RGB—Integer with the format 0x00RRGGBB with no alpha value.

- TYPE_INT_ARGB—Integer with the format 0xAARRGGBB where the alpha value has not been pre-multiplied with the RGB color values.

- TYPE_INT_ARGB_PRE—Integer with the format 0xAARRGGBB where the alpha value has been pre-multiplied with the RGB color values.

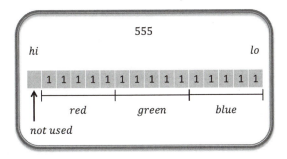

Figure 10.1
555 Unsigned Short Color.
© 2014 Timothy Wright.

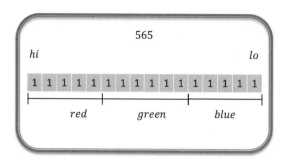

Figure 10.2
565 Unsigned Short Color.
© 2014 Timothy Wright.

When it comes to saving and loading images, Java has some very helpful methods in
the ImageIO class:

```
BufferedImage read( File input )
BufferedImage read( InputStream input )
BufferedImage read( ImageInputStream input )
BufferedImage read( URL input )
boolean write( RenderedImage img, String formatName, File output )
boolean write( RenderedImage img, String formatName,
                    ImageOutputStream output )
boolean write( RenderedImage img, String formatName, OutputStream output )
```

The ImageIO class supports JPG, GIF, BMP, and PNG files. For example, to save a JPG
file, you use the following code:

```
ImageIO.write( image, "jpg", file );
```

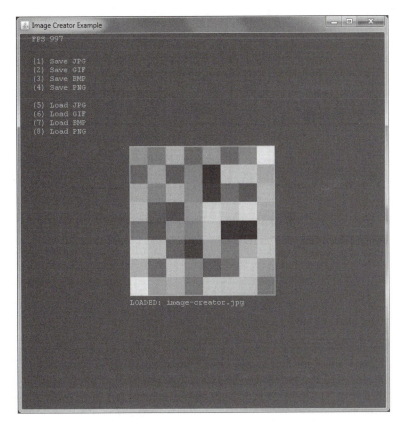

Figure 10.3
Image Creator Example.
© 2014 Timothy Wright.

The ImageCreator example, shown in Figure 10.3 and located in the javagames.images package, creates a buffered image and then saves and loads the file in *.gif, *.bmp, *.jpg, and *.png formats. The createCustomImage() method creates a BufferedImage from scratch. Notice that the image format used is BufferedImage.TYPE_INT_RGB, and does not support transparency, because not all of the file formats support transparency. Also, always remember to dispose of the BufferedImage's graphics object once you are finished using it for drawing.

```
BufferedImage img = new BufferedImage( imgWidth, imgHeight, imgFormat );
Graphics2D g = img.createGraphics();
// draw stuff here
g.dispose(); // clean up memory
```

Tip

Most of the time, you never have to worry about cleaning up memory in Java, but the Graphics2D object created from a BufferedImage.createGraphics() method is the exception. Make sure to always call dispose() when you are finished or memory can quickly disappear.

The render() method draws the usual help text and draws the created image. The file information is displayed when the file has been loaded. The createFile() method generates a new image with random colors and saves it to the hard drive in the given format. The loadFile() method attempts to load an already saved file from the hard drive. If the file isn't available, the loaded file is set to null. The processInput() method uses the 1–4 number keys to save files and the 5–8 number keys to load files from the hard drive.

```
package javagames.images;


import java.awt.*;
import java.awt.event.KeyEvent;
import java.awt.image.BufferedImage;
import java.io.*;
import java.util.Random;

import javagames.util.SimpleFramework;

import javax.imageio.ImageIO;


public class ImageCreator extends SimpleFramework {

    private static final int IMG_WIDTH = 256;
    private static final int IMG_HEIGHT = 256;
    private static final int SQUARES = 8;

    private Random rand = new Random();
    private BufferedImage sprite;
    private String loadedFile;

    public ImageCreator() {
        appWidth = 640;
        appHeight = 640;
        appSleep = 1L;
        appTitle = "Image Creator Example";
        appBackground = Color.DARK_GRAY;
    }
```

```java
@Override
protected void processInput( float delta ) {
    super.processInput( delta );
    if( keyboard.keyDownOnce( KeyEvent.VK_1 ) ) {
        createFile( "jpg", "image-creator.jpg" );
    }
    if( keyboard.keyDownOnce( KeyEvent.VK_2 ) ) {
        createFile( "bmp", "image-creator.bmp" );
    }
    if( keyboard.keyDownOnce( KeyEvent.VK_3 ) ) {
        createFile( "gif", "image-creator.gif" );
    }
    if( keyboard.keyDownOnce( KeyEvent.VK_4 ) ) {
        createFile( "png", "image-creator.png" );
    }
    if( keyboard.keyDownOnce( KeyEvent.VK_5 ) ) {
        loadFile( "image-creator.jpg" );
    }
    if( keyboard.keyDownOnce( KeyEvent.VK_6 ) ) {
        loadFile( "image-creator.bmp" );
    }
    if( keyboard.keyDownOnce( KeyEvent.VK_7 ) ) {
        loadFile( "image-creator.gif" );
    }
    if( keyboard.keyDownOnce( KeyEvent.VK_8 ) ) {
        loadFile( "image-creator.png" );
    }
}

private void createFile( String type, String fileName ) {
    try {
        sprite = createCustomImage();
        File file = new File( fileName );
        if( !ImageIO.write( sprite, type, file ) ) {
            throw new IOException( "No '" + type + "' image writer found" );
        }
        loadedFile = "SAVED: " + fileName;
    } catch( IOException ex ) {
        ex.printStackTrace();
    }
}
```

```
private void loadFile( String fileName ) {
    try {
        sprite = ImageIO.read( new File( fileName ) );
        loadedFile = "LOADED: " + fileName;
    } catch( IOException e ) {
        e.printStackTrace();
        sprite = null;
    }
}

private BufferedImage createCustomImage() {

    BufferedImage image = new BufferedImage( IMG_WIDTH, IMG_HEIGHT,
                          BufferedImage.TYPE_INT_RGB );

    Graphics2D g2d = image.createGraphics();

    int dx = image.getWidth() / SQUARES;
    int dy = image.getHeight() / SQUARES;

    for( int i = 0; i < SQUARES; ++i ) {
        for( int j = 0; j < SQUARES; ++j ) {
            g2d.setColor( new Color( rand.nextInt() ) );
            g2d.fillRect( i*dx, j*dy, dx, dy );
        }
    }
    g2d.setColor( Color.GREEN );
    g2d.drawRect( 0, 0, image.getWidth()-1, image.getHeight()-1 );
    g2d.dispose();

    return image;
}

@Override
protected void render( Graphics g ) {
    super.render( g );

    // draw help
    g.drawString( "", 20, 35 );
    g.drawString( "(1) Save JPG", 20, 50 );
    g.drawString( "(2) Save GIF", 20, 65 );
    g.drawString( "(3) Save BMP", 20, 80 );
    g.drawString( "(4) Save PNG", 20, 95 );
    g.drawString( "", 20, 110 );
    g.drawString( "(5) Load JPG", 20, 125 );
    g.drawString( "(6) Load GIF", 20, 140 );
    g.drawString( "(7) Load BMP", 20, 155 );
    g.drawString( "(8) Load PNG", 20, 170 );

    if( sprite != null ) {
```

```
        int x = (canvas.getWidth() - sprite.getWidth()) / 2;
        int y = (canvas.getHeight() - sprite.getHeight()) / 2;
        g.drawImage( sprite, x, y, null );
        g.drawString( loadedFile, x, y + sprite.getHeight() + 15 );
    } else {
        g.drawString(
    "ERROR - File Not Found!",
    canvas.getWidth() / 3,
    canvas.getHeight() / 3
);
    }

}

public static void main( String[] args ) {
    launchApp( new ImageCreator() );
}

}
```

PERFORMING COLOR INTERPOLATION

Color interpolation is blending from one color to another. The first part of the process is linear interpolation, and because the equation is a straight line, the math is not complicated. This example involves many interesting concepts. You can apply the math behind the color blending to any values that need to be interpolated over a distance. The techniques used to capture the individual pixel values enable you to perform custom image manipulation. Plus, it is always fun to learn how to perform an image effect by hand instead of relying on hidden algorithms.

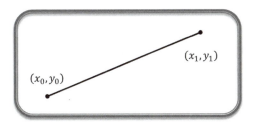

Figure 10.4
Line Segment.
© 2014 Timothy Wright.

Given any two points, such as Figure 10.4, any x value on the line corresponds to a y value, as shown in Figure 10.5.

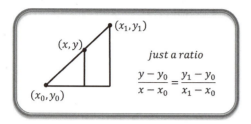

Figure 10.5
Just a Ratio.
© 2014 Timothy Wright.

Solving for y using this ratio produces the following:

$$\frac{y - y_0}{x - x_0} = \frac{y_1 - y_0}{x_1 - x_0}$$

$$y = y_0 + (x - x_0)\frac{y_1 - y_0}{x_1 - x_0}$$

If you make $x_0 = 0$ and $x_1 = 1$:

$$y = y_0 + (x - 0)(y_1 - y_0/1 - 0)$$
$$y = y_0 + x(y_1 - y_0/1)$$
$$y = y_0 + x(y_1 - y_0)$$

This is also known as the *Parametric Line* equation:

$$P = P_0 + t(P_1 - P_0)$$

This makes sense, because this equation interpolates the point along a line from P_0 to P_1.

It is more complicated to blend colors, however. Given a starting and ending color, along with the distance in pixels between the two points, the colors can be blended, but each color component must be blended separately and combined at each stage to create that specific color. For example, blending from red to green, each component must be interpolated.

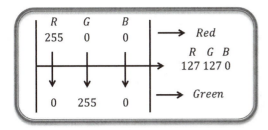

Figure 10.6
Color Interpolation.
© 2014 Timothy Wright.

As seen in Figure 10.6, the red color is blended from 255 to 0, but green goes the other way, and nothing happens to blue.

When blending colors using the interpolation equation, the unknown value y is the color at any specific spot. To blend a single color component, such as red from 255 to 0 over the span of 20 pixels, the code would be:

```
int y0 = 255; int y1 = 0;
int x0 = 0; int x1 = 20;
for( int x = x0; x < x1; ++x ) {
    int y = y0 + (x - x0) * (y1 - y0) / (x1 - x0);
    System.out.println(y);
}
```

Once individual colors can be created and blended between colors, it would be helpful to be able to just set the individual pixel values in a BufferedImage. The following code is used to gain access to the pixel data of a BufferedImage.

```
BufferedImage img = new BufferedImage( 400, 400,
    BufferedImage.TYPE_INT_ARGB );
WritableRaster raster = img.getRaster();
DataBuffer dataBuffer = raster.getDataBuffer();
DataBufferInt data = (DataBufferInt)dataBuffer;
int[] pixels = data.getData();
```

Notice the cast to a DataBufferInt. If the image format was bytes or shorts, the appropriate type must be used when casting to the correct buffer in order to get the pixel data.

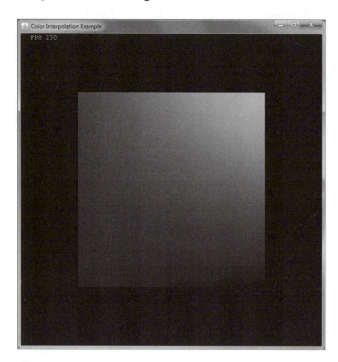

Figure 10.7
Color Interpolation Example.
© 2014 Timothy Wright.

The ColorInterpolationExample, as seen in Figure 10.7 and located in the javagames.images package, blends colors in a square.

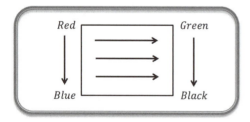

Figure 10.8
Color Interpolation Square.
© 2014 Timothy Wright.

The left color is blended from red to blue and the right color from green to black. The horizontal colors are also blended from red to green on top and blue to black on the bottom. See Figure 10.8. The BufferedImage is created every frame by clearing all the pixels using the clear[] array, which just contains pixels set to 0. The initialize()

method creates the buffered image, gets the raw pixel values as an array, and then creates a copy array full of zero values used to clear the pixels every frame.

Each frame, the updateObjects() method sets each pixel value in the image by interpolating from the starting to ending colors. The following code is used to clear the pixel array:

```
System.arraycopy( clear, 0, pixels, 0, pixels.length );
```

Although the image is a square with a width and height, the pixel array is only a single dimension. The following code is used to iterate over the single array with a width and height.

```
for( int row = 0; row < height; ++row ) {
    for( int col = 0; col < width; ++col ) {
        pixels[ row * width + col ] = 0;
    }
}
```

The ColorInterpolationExample code is as follows:

```
package javagames.images;

import java.awt.Graphics;
import java.awt.image.*;

import javagames.util.SimpleFramework;


public class ColorInterpolationExample extends SimpleFramework {
    private BufferedImage img;
    private int[] pixels;
    private int[] clear;

    public ColorInterpolationExample() {
        appWidth = 640;
        appHeight = 640;
        appSleep = 0L;
        appTitle = "Color Interpolation Example";
    }

    @Override
    protected void initialize() {
        super.initialize();

        img = new BufferedImage( 400, 400, BufferedImage.TYPE_INT_ARGB );

        // get pixels
        WritableRaster raster = img.getRaster();
```

```
        DataBuffer dataBuffer = raster.getDataBuffer();
        DataBufferInt data = (DataBufferInt)dataBuffer;
        pixels = data.getData();
        clear = new int[ pixels.length ];
    }

    @Override
    protected void updateObjects( float delta ) {
        super.updateObjects( delta );

        createColorSquare();
    }

    private void createColorSquare() {
        int w = img.getWidth();
        float w0 = 0.0f;
        float w1 = w - 1.0f;

        int h = img.getHeight();
        float h0 = 0.0f;
        float h1 = h - 1.0f;

        System.arraycopy( clear, 0, pixels, 0, pixels.length );

        // Top-Left
        float tlr = 255.0f;
        float tlg = 0.0f;
        float tlb = 0.0f;

        // Bottom-Left
        float blr = 0.0f;
        float blg = 0.0f;
        float blb = 255.0f;

        // Top-Right
        float trr = 0.0f;
        float trg = 255.0f;
        float trb = 0.0f;

        // Bottom-Right
        float brr = 0.0f;
        float brg = 0.0f;
        float brb = 0.0f;

        float h1h0 = h1 - h0;
        float w1w0 = w1 - w0;

        for( int row = 0; row < h; ++row ) {
            // left pixel
            int lr = (int)(tlr + (row - h0) * (blr - tlr) / h1h0);
```

```
        int lg = (int)(tlg + (row - h0) * (blg - tlg) / h1h0);
        int lb = (int)(tlb + (row - h0) * (blb - tlb) / h1h0);

        // right pixel
        int rr = (int)(trr + (row - h0) * (brr - trr) / h1h0);
        int rg = (int)(trg + (row - h0) * (brg - trg) / h1h0);
        int rb = (int)(trb + (row - h0) * (brb - trb) / h1h0);

        for( int col = 0; col < w; ++col ) {
            int r = (int)(lr + (col - w0) * (rr - lr) / w1w0);
            int g = (int)(lg + (col - w0) * (rg - lg) / w1w0);
            int b = (int)(lb + (col - w0) * (rb - lb) / w1w0);
            int index = row * w + col;
            pixels[ index ] = 0xFF << 24 | r << 16 | g << 8 | b;

        }
    }
}

@Override
protected void render( Graphics g ) {
    super.render( g );

    int xPos = (canvas.getWidth() - img.getWidth()) / 2;
    int yPos = (canvas.getHeight() - img.getHeight()) / 2;
    g.drawImage( img, xPos, yPos, null );
}

public static void main( String[] args ) {
    launchApp( new ColorInterpolationExample() );
}

}
```

Using Volatile Images for Speed

BufferedImage is not the only kind of image available. VolatileImage is another image type that can be much faster than using a BufferedImage. Because the contents of a VolatileImage can be lost at any time (hence the name), using it is more difficult; but depending on the speed requirements for your application, it can be an option.

When an image is located in the memory of the graphics card, that memory is global to any programs in the operating system. For example, on Windows, a user can use Ctrl+Alt+Delete to view running programs, or press Alt+Tab to switch from a full screen application back to the desktop. When either of these operations happen, any volatile images can be lost. Switching back to the game but not reloading the lost images would put garbage data on the screen.

The first difference with a `VolatileImage` is that it can't be created with a constructor. The following code is used to create a `VolatileImage`.

```
GraphicsEnvironment ge =
    GraphicsEnvironment.getLocalGraphicsEnvironment();
GraphicsDevice gd = ge.getDefaultScreenDevice();
GraphicsConfiguration gc = gd.getDefaultConfiguration();
VolatileImage vi = gc.createCompatibleVolatileImage( width, height );
```

Once an image is available, the following pattern is used for rendering:

```
GraphicsConfiguration gc;
VolatileImage vi;
Graphics g;

do {
    int returnCode = vi.validate( gc );
    if( returnCode == VolatileImage.IMAGE_RESTORED ) {
    // Contents need to be restored
    renderVolatileImage();

    } else if( returnCode == VolatileImage.IMAGE_INCOMPATIBLE ) {
    // incompatible GraphicsConfig
      createVolatileImage();
      renderVolatileImage();
    }

    g.drawImage( vi, 0, 0, null );
    } while( vi.contentsLost() );
```

All the extra work can be worth it because the `VolatileImage` can be hardware accelerated. One downside is that the individual pixels are not available as an array like the `BufferedImage`.

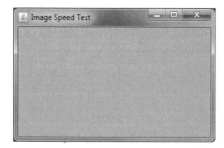

Figure 10.9
Image Speed Test.
© 2014 Timothy Wright.

The `ImageSpeedTest`, as seen in Figure 10.9 and located in the `javagames.images` package, explores four different methods of drawing an image to the screen. Both a `BufferedImage` and `VolatileImage` are drawn, with one state only creating the image once and drawing that every frame, and the other state creating the image every frame and then drawing it to the scene. There isn't a real difference between the two image types when the image is created only once. The reason is that the `BufferStrategy` uses a `VolatileImage` behind the scenes, hiding the complexity and allowing for hardware acceleration. The big speed difference comes from creating the image every frame. The `VolatileImage` can be created much faster, so if redrawing the image every frame is something the game needs to do, a `VolatileImage` is the way to go. Loading images only at startup, it is easier to use a `BufferedImage` that will stay in memory until the program terminates.

The `initialize()` method creates both a `BufferedImage` and a `VolatileImage`. Both the `renderToBufferedImage()` and `renderToVolatileImage()` use the same code to render the images. The `processInput()` method toggles between the `BufferedImage` and `VolatileImage` with the B key, and toggles between rendering only once and rendering each frame with the R key. The `render()` method uses the `realtime` and `bufferedImage` variables to determine if the `VolatileImage` or `BufferedImage` should be used as well as whether or not to render to the image before drawing it to the screen.

The `renderToVolatileImage()` method draws the already rendered image. The `renderToVolatileImageEveryFrame()` also redraws the image before drawing it to the screen. As you will see, rendering the `VolatileImage` every frame can be faster than using a `BufferedImage`.

```
package javagames.images;


import java.awt.*;
import java.awt.event.KeyEvent;
import java.awt.image.*;
import java.util.Random;

import javagames.util.SimpleFramework;


public class ImageSpeedTest extends SimpleFramework {
    private Random rand = new Random();
    private GraphicsConfiguration gc;

    private BufferedImage bi;
    private VolatileImage vi;
```

```java
    private boolean realtime = true;
    private boolean bufferedImage = true;

    public ImageSpeedTest() {
        appWidth = 640;
        appHeight = 640;
        appSleep = 0L;
        appTitle = "Image Speed Test";
    }

    @Override
    protected void initialize() {
        super.initialize();

        GraphicsEnvironment ge = GraphicsEnvironment
                .getLocalGraphicsEnvironment();
        GraphicsDevice gd = ge.getDefaultScreenDevice();
        gc = gd.getDefaultConfiguration();
        bi = gc.createCompatibleImage( appWidth, appHeight );

        createVolatileImage();
        renderToBufferedImage();
    }

    @Override
    protected void processInput( float delta ) {
        super.processInput( delta );
        if( keyboard.keyDownOnce( KeyEvent.VK_B ) ) {
            bufferedImage = !bufferedImage;
        }
        if( keyboard.keyDownOnce( KeyEvent.VK_R ) ) {
            realtime = !realtime;
        }
    }

    private void createVolatileImage() {
        if( vi != null ) {
            vi.flush();
            vi = null;
        }
        vi = gc.createCompatibleVolatileImage(getWidth(), getHeight());
    }

    @Override
    protected void render( Graphics g ) {

        if( bufferedImage ) {
            renderToBufferedImage( g );
        } else if( realtime ) {
            renderToVolatileImageEveryFrame( g );
```

```
      } else {
         renderToVolatileImage( g );
      }

      super.render( g );

      // spit out help
      g.drawString( "(B)uffered Image: " + bufferedImage, 20, 35 );
      g.drawString( "(R)eal Time Rendering: " + realtime, 20, 65 );
   }
   private void renderToVolatileImage( Graphics g ) {
      do {
         int returnCode = vi.validate( gc );
         if( returnCode == VolatileImage.IMAGE_RESTORED ) {
            // Contents need to be restored
            renderVolatileImage();

         } else if( returnCode == VolatileImage.IMAGE_INCOMPATIBLE ) {
            // incompatible GraphicsConfig
            createVolatileImage();
            renderVolatileImage();
         }

         g.drawImage( vi, 0, 0, null );
      } while( vi.contentsLost() );
   }

   private void renderToVolatileImageEveryFrame( Graphics g ) {
      do {
         int returnCode = vi.validate( gc );
         if( returnCode == VolatileImage.IMAGE_INCOMPATIBLE ) {
            // incompatible GraphicsConfig
            createVolatileImage();
         }

         renderVolatileImage();
         g.drawImage( vi, 0, 0, null );
      } while( vi.contentsLost() );
   }

   protected void renderVolatileImage() {
      Graphics2D g2d = vi.createGraphics();
      g2d.setColor( new Color( rand.nextInt() ) );
      g2d.fillRect( 0, 0, getWidth(), getHeight() );
      g2d.dispose();
   }
```

```
private void renderToBufferedImage( Graphics g ) {
    if( realtime ) {
        renderToBufferedImage();
    }
    g.drawImage( bi, 0, 0, null );
}

private void renderToBufferedImage() {
    Graphics2D g2d = bi.createGraphics();
    g2d.setColor( new Color( rand.nextInt() ) );
    g2d.fillRect( 0, 0, getWidth(), getHeight() );
    g2d.dispose();
}

public static void main( String[] args ) {
    launchApp( new ImageSpeedTest() );
}
}
```

CREATING TRANSPARENT IMAGES

The TransparentImageExample, as seen in Figure 10.10 and located in the javagames.images package, creates an image with transparent pixels. Up until now, none of the images had any transparent pixels. For any kind of game sprite (*sprite* is used as a generic term for any image file drawn to the screen) that isn't a square, transparent pixels around the edges are necessary so that there are no borders around all the game objects.

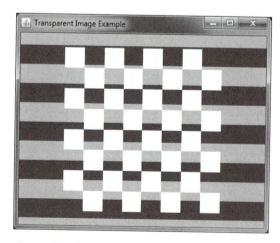

Figure 10.10
Transparent Image Example.
© 2014 Timothy Wright.

If all that is required is to create an image with a transparent background, it is very easy. A newly created `BufferedImage` with a type supporting transparency is by default full of zeros, which means the whole image is transparent.

```
BufferedImage img =
    new BufferedImage( 256, 256, BufferedImage.TYPE_INT_ARGB );
```

The image created in the previous code snippet, which includes alpha values, defaults to a transparent background. The `TransparentImageExample` code creates a new `BufferedImage` in the `initialize()` method. Every even square is drawn white, leaving the other squares as transparent.

The `updateObjects()` method divides the drawing area into five parts. Each of the five bars is shaded by covering half of each bar with a light gray bar. These bars are shifted using the delta value so that the bars move toward the bottom of the screen. The shift value is reset once it is larger than the ribbon height.

The `render()` method divides the height into pieces and renders each strip, starting one strip before the top of the screen so the strips enter from the top. Finally, the transparent image is drawn over the top of the shifting bars. Because the background of the checkerboard image was transparent, the background can be seen underneath the image.

```
package javagames.images;

import java.awt.*;
import java.awt.image.BufferedImage;

import javagames.util.SimpleFramework;


public class TransparentImageExample extends SimpleFramework {

    private BufferedImage img;
    private float shift;

    public TransparentImageExample() {
        appWidth = 400;
        appHeight = 300;
        appSleep = 10L;
        appTitle = "Transparent Image Example";
        appBackground = Color.DARK_GRAY;
    }

    @Override
    protected void initialize() {
        super.initialize();

        img = new BufferedImage( 256, 256, BufferedImage.TYPE_INT_ARGB );
```

```java
        Graphics2D g2d = img.createGraphics();

        int w = 8;
        int h = 8;
        int dx = img.getWidth() / w;
        int dy = img.getHeight() / h;
        for( int i = 0; i < w; ++i ) {
            for( int j = 0; j < h; ++j ) {
                if( (i+j) % 2 == 0 ) {
                    g2d.setColor( Color.WHITE );
                    g2d.fillRect( i*dx, j*dy, dx, dy );
                }
            }
        }

        g2d.dispose();
    }

    @Override
    protected void updateObjects( float delta ) {
        super.updateObjects( delta );
        int ribbonHeight = canvas.getHeight() / 5;
        shift += delta * ribbonHeight;
        if( shift > ribbonHeight ) {
            shift -= ribbonHeight;
        }
    }

    @Override
    protected void render( Graphics g ) {

        super.render( g );

        // draw shifting background
        int hx = canvas.getHeight() / 5;
        g.setColor( Color.LIGHT_GRAY );
        for( int i = -1; i < 5; ++i ) {
            g.fillRect( 0, (int)shift + hx * i, canvas.getWidth(), hx / 2 );
        }

        int x = ( canvas.getWidth() - img.getWidth() ) / 2;
        int y = ( canvas.getHeight() - img.getHeight() ) / 2;
        g.drawImage( img, x, y, null );

    }

    public static void main( String[] args ) {
        launchApp( new TransparentImageExample() );
    }

}
```

Using the Alpha Composite Rules

In the previous example, the transparent image was drawn on top and the background was visible underneath. But that is not the only option. When the pixels in the source image and destination image have some transparency, there are many ways to blend them. The `AlphaComposite` contains many rules.

TIP

The Java Docs (see Class AlphaComposite, 2013 at http://docs.oracle.com/javase/7/docs/api/java/awt/ AlphaComposite.html) do a great job of explaining the math involved.

The "Compositing Digital Images" paper goes into even greater detail (see T. Porter and T. Duff, "Compositing Digital Images," SIGGRAPH, 1984, pp. 253–259; http://keithp.com/~keithp/porterduff /p253-porter.pdf).

The different blending operations are as follows:

- `SRC`—Source is copied to the destination.
- `DEST`—The destination is unchanged.
- `SRC_IN`—Only the source inside the destination is copied.
- `DEST_IN`—Only the destination inside the source is copied.
- `SRC_OUT`—The destination is replaced only by the outside source.
- `DEST_OUT`—Only the outside portion of the destination is copied.
- `SRC_OVER`—The source is copied over the destination.
- `DEST_OVER`—The destination is copied over the source.
- `SRC_ATOP`—The source inside the destination is copied onto the destination.
- `DEST_ATOP`—The destination inside the source is copied over the source.
- `XOR`—The parts of the source and destination that are outside each other are copied.
- `CLEAR`—The color and alpha of the destination are cleared.

Not only do each source and destination image have an alpha value, Java adds an extra alpha composite that is applied to the source alpha.

One of the tricky things is understanding that applying an `AlphaComposite` rule to a shape drawn with a graphics objects is not the same as drawing an entire image. When shapes are used, only the pixels inside the shape follow the composite rule, while images use the entire area.

Note

When first trying to get alpha composite results that matched the Porter and Duff paper, I couldn't get the same results because I was using a triangle shape instead of complete images copied onto each other. As an exercise, change the example to use various shapes and note the difference.

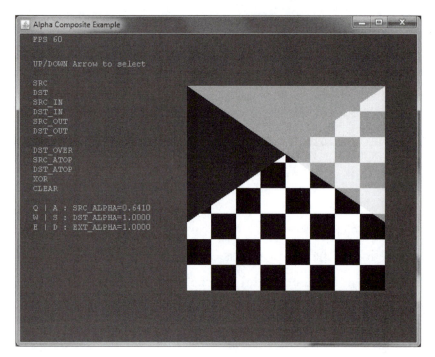

Figure 10.11
Alpha Composite Example.
© 2014 Timothy Wright.

The best way to understand how all the different options work is to play with them and see the results. Although reading the equations is great from a theoretical point of view, once you see the results, it becomes a lot more intuitive. Most of the code in the AlphaCompositeExample, shown in Figure 10.11 and located in the javagames.images package, has to do with displaying and changing all the different options. The code that uses the AlphaComposite is located in the createImages() method.

The first step is to use the AlphaComposite.CLEAR rule to clear the pixels from the source image, so that the entire image has only transparent pixels. Although it would work to create a brand new image every frame, clearing the pixels is quicker.

```
Graphics2D g2d = sourceImage.createGraphics();
g2d.setComposite( AlphaComposite.getInstance( AlphaComposite.CLEAR ) );
g2d.fillRect( 0, 0, sourceImage.getWidth(), sourceImage.getHeight() );
```

Next, the default composite rule, `AlphaComposite.SRC_OVER` is used to draw the yellow triangle. Notice that the color uses the `srcAlpha` variable for the alpha value.

```
g2d.setComposite(
    AlphaComposite.getInstance( AlphaComposite.SRC_OVER ) );
Polygon p = new Polygon();
p.addPoint( 0, 0 );
p.addPoint( sourceImage.getWidth(), 0 );
p.addPoint(
    sourceImage.getWidth(), (int)(sourceImage.getHeight() / 1.5 ));
g2d.setColor( new Color( 1.0f, 1.0f, 0.0f, srcAlpha ) );
g2d.fill( p );
```

Next, you use the same process to clear the destination image.

```
g2d = destinationImage.createGraphics();
g2d.setComposite( AlphaComposite.getInstance( AlphaComposite.CLEAR ) );
g2d.fillRect(
    0, 0, destinationImage.getWidth(), destinationImage.getHeight() );
```

Next, the blue triangle is drawn on the opposite side. Notice that the color uses the `dstAlpha` value.

```
g2d.setComposite(
    AlphaComposite.getInstance( AlphaComposite.SRC_OVER ) );
p = new Polygon();
p.addPoint( 0, 0 );
p.addPoint( destinationImage.getWidth(), 0 );
p.addPoint( 0, (int)(destinationImage.getHeight() / 1.5 ));
g2d.setColor( new Color( 0.0f, 0.0f, 1.0f, dstAlpha ) );
g2d.fill( p );
```

Next the source image is drawn on top of the destination image. This is where the `AlphaComposite` rule chosen by the user is applied to both images.

```
int rule = compositeRule[ compositeIndex ];
g2d.setComposite( AlphaComposite.getInstance( rule, extAlpha ) );
g2d.drawImage( sourceImage, 0, 0, null );
```

The last step is to redraw the background image with a checkerboard, clearing the results of the last frame, and then drawing the alpha composite image over the top. Using the checkerboard is helpful to see the blending effects.

```
g2d = sprite.createGraphics();

int dx = (sprite.getWidth()) / 8;
int dy = (sprite.getHeight()) / 8;
```

```
for( int i = 0; i < 8; ++i ) {
    for( int j = 0; j < 8; ++j ) {
        g2d.setColor( (i+j) % 2 == 0 ? Color.BLACK : Color.WHITE );
        g2d.fillRect( i*dx, j*dy, dx, dy );
    }
}
g2d.drawImage( destinationImage, 0, 0, null );
```

The processInput() method uses the arrow keys to select the different composite rules. The A and Q keys control the source alpha value, the S and W keys control the destination alpha values, and the D and E keys control the extra alpha value.

The render() method draws the different composition rules and colors the currently selected rule red. The source, destination, and extra alpha values are drawn with their key values used to increment and decrement them. Finally, the sprite image is rendered to show the results of the alpha composite.

```
package javagames.images;

import java.awt.*;
import java.awt.event.KeyEvent;
import java.awt.image.BufferedImage;

import javagames.util.SimpleFramework;


public class AlphaCompositeExample extends SimpleFramework {
    private String[] compositeName = {
            "SRC",
            "DST",
            "SRC_IN",
            "DST_IN",
            "SRC_OUT",
            "DST_OUT",
            "SRC_OVER",
            "DST_OVER",
            "SRC_ATOP",
            "DST_ATOP",
            "XOR",
            "CLEAR",
    };

    private int[] compositeRule = {
            AlphaComposite.SRC,
            AlphaComposite.DST,
            AlphaComposite.SRC_IN,
            AlphaComposite.DST_IN,
```

```java
            AlphaComposite.SRC_OUT,
            AlphaComposite.DST_OUT,
            AlphaComposite.SRC_OVER,
            AlphaComposite.DST_OVER,
            AlphaComposite.SRC_ATOP,
            AlphaComposite.DST_ATOP,
            AlphaComposite.XOR,
            AlphaComposite.CLEAR,
    };

    private int compositeIndex;
    private float srcAlpha;
    private float dstAlpha;
    private float extAlpha;

    private BufferedImage sprite;
    private BufferedImage sourceImage;
    private BufferedImage destinationImage;

    public AlphaCompositeExample() {
        appBackground = Color.DARK_GRAY;
        appWidth = 640;
        appHeight = 480;
        appSleep = 10L;
        appTitle = "Alpha Composite Example";
    }

    @Override
    protected void initialize() {
        super.initialize();

        srcAlpha = 1.0f;
        dstAlpha = 1.0f;
        extAlpha = 1.0f;

        destinationImage =
            new BufferedImage( 320, 320, BufferedImage.TYPE_INT_ARGB );
        sourceImage =
            new BufferedImage( 320, 320, BufferedImage.TYPE_INT_ARGB );
        sprite = new BufferedImage( 320, 320, BufferedImage.TYPE_INT_ARGB );

        createImages();
    }

    private void createImages() {
        // source image
        Graphics2D g2d = sourceImage.createGraphics();
        g2d.setComposite( AlphaComposite.getInstance( AlphaComposite.CLEAR ) );
        g2d.fillRect( 0, 0, sourceImage.getWidth(), sourceImage.getHeight() );
```

```
g2d.setComposite(
   AlphaComposite.getInstance( AlphaComposite.SRC_OVER ) );
Polygon p = new Polygon();
p.addPoint( 0, 0 );
p.addPoint( sourceImage.getWidth(), 0 );
p.addPoint(
   sourceImage.getWidth(), (int)(sourceImage.getHeight() / 1.5 ));
g2d.setColor( new Color( 1.0f, 1.0f, 0.0f, srcAlpha ) );
g2d.fill( p );

g2d.dispose();

// destination image
g2d = destinationImage.createGraphics();
g2d.setComposite( AlphaComposite.getInstance( AlphaComposite.CLEAR ) );
g2d.fillRect(
   0, 0, destinationImage.getWidth(), destinationImage.getHeight() );

g2d.setComposite(
   AlphaComposite.getInstance( AlphaComposite.SRC_OVER ) );
p = new Polygon();
p.addPoint( 0, 0 );
p.addPoint( destinationImage.getWidth(), 0 );
p.addPoint( 0, (int)(destinationImage.getHeight() / 1.5 ));
g2d.setColor( new Color( 0.0f, 0.0f, 1.0f, dstAlpha ) );
g2d.fill( p );

int rule = compositeRule[ compositeIndex ];
g2d.setComposite( AlphaComposite.getInstance( rule, extAlpha ) );
g2d.drawImage( sourceImage, 0, 0, null );

g2d.dispose();

// checkerboard background
g2d = sprite.createGraphics();

int dx = (sprite.getWidth()) / 8;
int dy = (sprite.getHeight()) / 8;

for( int i = 0; i < 8; ++i ) {
   for( int j = 0; j < 8; ++j ) {
      g2d.setColor( (i+j) % 2 == 0 ? Color.BLACK : Color.WHITE );
      g2d.fillRect( i*dx, j*dy, dx, dy );
   }
}

g2d.drawImage( destinationImage, 0, 0, null );
g2d.dispose();
}
```

```java
@Override
protected void processInput( float delta ) {
    super.processInput( delta );

    if( keyboard.keyDownOnce( KeyEvent.VK_UP ) ) {
        compositeIndex--;
        if( compositeIndex < 0 ) {
            compositeIndex = compositeRule.length - 1;
        }
    }
    if( keyboard.keyDownOnce( KeyEvent.VK_DOWN ) ) {
        compositeIndex++;
        if( compositeIndex > compositeRule.length - 1 ) {
            compositeIndex = 0;
        }
    }
    if( keyboard.keyDown( KeyEvent.VK_A ) ) {
        srcAlpha = dec( srcAlpha, delta );
    }
    if( keyboard.keyDown( KeyEvent.VK_Q ) ) {
        srcAlpha = inc( srcAlpha, delta );
    }
    if( keyboard.keyDown( KeyEvent.VK_S ) ) {
      dstAlpha = dec( dstAlpha, delta );
    }
    if( keyboard.keyDown( KeyEvent.VK_W ) ) {
        dstAlpha = inc( dstAlpha, delta );
    }
    if( keyboard.keyDown( KeyEvent.VK_D ) ) {
        extAlpha = dec( extAlpha, delta );
    }
    if( keyboard.keyDown( KeyEvent.VK_E ) ) {
        extAlpha = inc( extAlpha, delta );
    }

    createImages();
}

private float inc( float val, float delta ) {
    val += 0.5f * delta;
    if( val > 1.0f ) {
        val = 1.0f;
    }
    return val;
}
```

```java
private float dec( float val, float delta ) {
    val -= 0.5f * delta;
    if( val < 0.0f ) {
        val = 0.0f;
    }
    return val;
}

@Override
protected void render( Graphics g ) {
    super.render( g );

    Graphics2D g2d = (Graphics2D)g;

    int xPos = 20;
    int yPos = 35;
    g2d.drawString( "", xPos, yPos );
    yPos += 15;
    g2d.drawString( "UP/DOWN Arrow to select", xPos, yPos );
    yPos += 15;
    g2d.drawString( "", xPos, yPos );
    yPos += 15;

    for( int i = 0; i < compositeName.length; ++i ) {
        if( i == compositeIndex ) {
            g2d.setColor( Color.RED );
        } else {
            g2d.setColor( Color.GREEN );
        }
        g2d.drawString( compositeName[i], xPos, yPos );
        yPos += 15;
    }

    g2d.drawString( "", xPos, yPos );
    yPos += 15;

    g2d.setColor( Color.GREEN );
    g2d.drawString(
        String.format( "Q | A : SRC_ALPHA=%.4f", srcAlpha ), xPos, yPos );
    yPos += 15;
    g2d.drawString(
        String.format( "W | S : DST_ALPHA=%.4f", dstAlpha ), xPos, yPos );
    yPos += 15;
    g2d.drawString(
        String.format( "E | D : EXT_ALPHA=%.4f", extAlpha ), xPos, yPos );
    yPos += 15;
```

```
      int x = (canvas.getWidth() - destinationImage.getWidth() - 50);
      int y = (canvas.getHeight() - destinationImage.getHeight()) / 2;

      g2d.drawImage( sprite, x, y, null );
  }

  public static void main( String[] args ) {
      launchApp( new AlphaCompositeExample() );
  }

}
```

DRAWING SPRITES

Up until this point, the chapter has been concerned with loading, saving, creating, and using buffered images. Although it is important to understand how BufferedImage can be used to create images from scratch, the most used method for making games is loading and drawing sprites that have been created with a paint program and saved as a file.

For testing the concepts, instead of actually creating sprites and making them available for loading, the same checkerboard used in the previous example will be used. This image is not only easy to create, it will highlight some of the problems with drawing rotated images.

Like most of the previous examples, the example code at the end of this section allows you to explore all the different combinations of settings. When drawing sprites on the screen, there is always a balance between speed and quality. The better the image looks, the better the experience; but if the frame rate drops too low, it doesn't matter how good the game looks. In the search for a balance, you need to examine all the different properties and methods of drawing sprites.

The first property that can affect the speed and quality of an image is the antialiasing rendering hint. Aliasing of an image occurs when straight lines that are rotated look blocky, and the pixel shapes are visible. Antialiasing is a process of blending the pixels with the background to make them smooth. But this process takes time and reduces rendering speed.

```
Key: RenderingHints.KEY_ANTIALIASING
Antialiasing On: RenderingHints.VALUE_ANTIALIAS_ON
Antialiasing Off: RenderingHints.VALUE_ANTIALIAS_OFF
```

The next property that can affect the rendered image is the interpolation algorithm. These algorithms control how the image's colors are interpolated when the image is rotated or scaled. There are three main interpolation methods used by Java:

- *Nearest neighbor*—Finds the closest value and uses it, without considering any of the other surrounding values.

- *Bilinear*—Similar to the interpolation used in the color interpolation code example.

- *Bicubic*—Similar to the bilinear example, but uses 16 neighbor values instead of the four used in the bilinear method.

The nearest neighbor method is the fastest, while the bicubic produces the best quality.

```
Key: RenderingHints.KEY_INTERPOLATION
Nearest Neighbor: RenderingHints.VALUE_INTERPOLATION_NEAREST_NEIGHBOR
Bilinear: RenderingHints.VALUE_INTERPOLATION_BILINEAR
Bicubic: RenderingHints.VALUE_INTERPOLATION_BICUBIC
```

These properties, combined with the different methods of rendering the image to the screen, produce results from really good to really bad, and really fast to really slow.

Three methods for rendering the image are examined: Affine Transform, Affine Transform Op, and Texture Paint. Regardless of the method used, they all use an `AffineTransform` as a starting point.

Note

Remember that the `AffineTransform` is a column major matrix representation, so the matrix concatenation is from right to left. Review the section on row major versus column major matrices in Chapter 3, "Transformations," for a refresher.

Final = $4^{th} * 3^{rd} * 2^{nd} * 1^{st}$

Given an `AffineTransform`, the first method uses the `drawImage` method of the `Graphics2D` object.

```
AffineTransform transform = ...;
g2d.drawImage( sourceImage, transform, null );
```

The second method uses the `AffineTransformOp` class. First, create the `AffineTransformOp` using the `AffineTransform` and the interpolation algorithm type. The filter method is then used to transform the image.

```
AffineTransform transform = ...;
AffineTransformOp op =
```

```
      new AffineTransformOp( transform, AffineTransformOp.TYPE_BILINEAR );
BufferedImage transformedImage = op.filter( sourceImage, null );
g2d.drawImage( transformedImage, 0, 0, null );
```

The third method uses the TexturePaint class to draw the sprite. Because this method actually sets the transform directly to the graphics object, it must be cleared when finished rendering.

```
AffineTransform transform = ...;
g2d.setTransform( transform );
Rectangle2D anchor = new Rectangle2D.Float(
      0, 0, sprite.getWidth(), sprite.getHeight() );
TexturePaint paint = new TexturePaint( sprite, anchor );
g2d.setPaint( paint );
g2d.fillRect( 0, 0, sprite.getWidth(), sprite.getHight() );
// reset!!!
g2d.setTransform( new AffineTransform() );
```

Although some methods are better than others, the AffineTransform and TexturePaint methods both have trouble rendering the edges of the image. The AffineTransform with a bilinear interpolation value renders the inside of the image correctly but fails to blend the edges. The TexturePaint method interpolates the edges by wrapping the texture, which can cause issues like wrapping the image from one side around to the other side.

A solution to fix both the TexturePaint and AffineTransform is to leave a border of transparent pixels around the outside of the image. The AffineTransform blends the clear pixels, so no jagged edges are visible, and the TexturePaint wraps the invisible pixels, which does not cause visible problems.

Using the example program, you can test all the different properties and rendering methods to determine which produce the best quality at the fastest speed. The two best methods on my test machine are:

- Antialiasing off, Bicubic Interpolation, Texture Paint rendering with a transparent border.

- Antialiasing on, Bilinear Interpolation, Affine Transform rendering with transparent border.

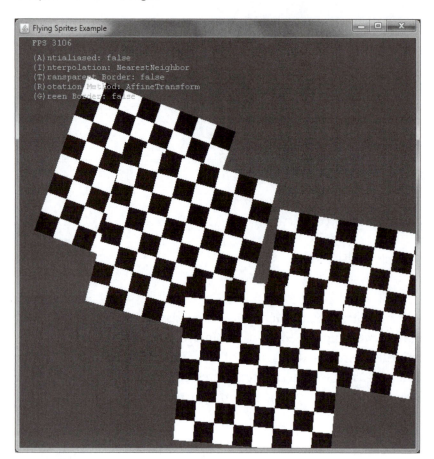

Figure 10.12
Flying Sprites Example.
© 2014 Timothy Wright.

The FlyingSpritesExample, as shown in Figure 10.12 and located in the javagames.images package, allows the different properties and rendering methods to be examined for speed and quality. The initialize() method creates positions, velocities, angles, and rotations for the four images, as well as sets the default properties and creates the test image.

The createSprite() method is used to recreate the checkerboard image anytime rendering properties change. The image is created in the createCheckerboard() method; the addTransparentBorder() method puts a border of four pixels around the image; and the drawGreenBorder() method adds a green border so the edge of the image is visible.

The processInput() method switches all the different properties and render methods. The A key toggles the antialiased property. The I key cycles through the different interpolation algorithms. The T key toggles the transparent border around the image on and off. The R key cycles between the three different render methods, and the G key toggles the green border on and off. The sprite is recreated as needed.

The updateObject() method updates the positions and rotations of each of the four objects. The render() method displays the usual information along with the current state of each property. The antialiasing and interpolation rendering hints are set and the four images are drawn using the selected rendering method.

The setAntialiasing() and setInterpolation() methods configure the rendering hints. The createTransform() rotates each object around its center before translating it across the screen. The createTransformOp() generates the transform operation based on the selected interpolation value.

The doAffineTransform(), doAffineTransformOp(), and doTexturePaint() methods render the images using the different methods described in the previous section.

```java
package javagames.images;

import java.awt.*;
import java.awt.event.KeyEvent;
import java.awt.geom.*;
import java.awt.image.*;

import javagames.util.*;


public class FlyingSpritesExample extends SimpleFramework {
    private static final int IMG_WIDTH = 256;
    private static final int IMG_HEIGHT = 256;
    private enum Interpolation {
        NearestNeighbor,
        BiLinear,
        BiCubic;
    }

    private enum RotationMethod {
        AffineTransform,
        AffineTransformOp,
        TexturePaint;
    }

    private boolean antialiased;
    private boolean transparent;
    private boolean greenBorder;
    private Interpolation interpolation;
```

```java
    private RotationMethod rotationMethod;

    private BufferedImage sprite;
    private Vector2f[] positions;
    private float[] angles;
    private Vector2f[] velocities;
    private float[] rotations;

    public FlyingSpritesExample() {
        appWidth = 640;
        appHeight = 640;
        appSleep = 0L;
        appTitle = "Flying Sprites Example";
        appBackground = Color.DARK_GRAY;
    }

    @Override
    protected void initialize() {
        super.initialize();

        positions = new Vector2f[] {
                new Vector2f( -0.15f,  0.3f ),
                new Vector2f(  0.15f,  0.0f ),
                new Vector2f(  0.25f, -0.3f ),
                new Vector2f( -0.25f, -0.6f ),
        };
        velocities = new Vector2f[] {
                new Vector2f( -0.04f,  0.0f ),
                new Vector2f( -0.05f,  0.0f ),
                new Vector2f(  0.06f,  0.0f ),
                new Vector2f(  0.07f, -0.0f ),
        };
        angles = new float[] {
                (float)Math.toRadians( 0 ),
                (float)Math.toRadians( 0 ),
                (float)Math.toRadians( 0 ),
                (float)Math.toRadians( 0 ),
        };
        rotations = new float[] {
                1.0f, 0.75f, 0.5f, 0.25f
        };

        antialiased = false;
        transparent = false;
        greenBorder = false;
        interpolation = Interpolation.NearestNeighbor;
```

```
      rotationMethod = RotationMethod.AffineTransform;

      createSprite();


   }
   @Override
   protected void processInput( float delta ) {
      super.processInput( delta );

      if( keyboard.keyDownOnce( KeyEvent.VK_A ) ) {
         antialiased = !antialiased;
      }
      if( keyboard.keyDownOnce( KeyEvent.VK_I ) ) {
         Interpolation[] values = Interpolation.values();
         int index = (interpolation.ordinal() + 1) % values.length;
         interpolation = values[ index ];
      }
      if( keyboard.keyDownOnce( KeyEvent.VK_T ) ) {
         transparent = !transparent;
         createSprite();
      }
      if( keyboard.keyDownOnce( KeyEvent.VK_R ) ) {
         RotationMethod[] methods = RotationMethod.values();
         int index = (rotationMethod.ordinal() + 1) % methods.length;
         rotationMethod = methods[ index ];
      }
      if( keyboard.keyDownOnce( KeyEvent.VK_G ) ) {
         greenBorder = !greenBorder;
         createSprite();
      }
   }

   private void createSprite() {
      createCheckerboard();
      if( transparent ) {
         addTransparentBorder();
      }
      if( greenBorder ) {
         drawGreenBorder();
      }
   }

   private void createCheckerboard() {
      sprite =
         new BufferedImage( IMG_WIDTH, IMG_HEIGHT,
```

```
            BufferedImage.TYPE_INT_ARGB );
        Graphics2D g2d = sprite.createGraphics();
        int dx = IMG_WIDTH / 8;
        int dy = IMG_HEIGHT / 8;
        for( int i = 0; i < 8; ++i ) {
            for( int j = 0; j < 8; ++j ) {
                if( (i+j) % 2 == 0 ) {
                    g2d.setColor( Color.WHITE );
                } else {
                    g2d.setColor( Color.BLACK );
                }
                g2d.fillRect( i*dx, j*dy, dx, dy );
            }
        }
        g2d.dispose();
    }

    private void addTransparentBorder() {
        int borderWidth = IMG_WIDTH + 8;
        int borderHeight = IMG_HEIGHT + 8;
        BufferedImage newSprite =
            new BufferedImage( borderWidth, borderHeight,
                BufferedImage.TYPE_INT_ARGB );
        Graphics2D g2d = newSprite.createGraphics();
        g2d.drawImage( sprite, 4, 4, null );
        g2d.dispose();
        sprite = newSprite;
    }

    private void drawGreenBorder() {
        Graphics2D g2d = sprite.createGraphics();
        g2d.setColor( Color.GREEN );
        g2d.drawRect( 0, 0, sprite.getWidth() - 1, sprite.getHeight() - 1 );
        g2d.dispose();
    }

    @Override
    protected void updateObjects( float delta ) {
        super.updateObjects( delta );

        for( int i = 0; i < positions.length; ++i ) {
            positions[i] = positions[i].add( velocities[i].mul( delta ) );
            if( positions[i].x >= 1.0f ) {
                positions[i].x = -1.0f;
            } else if( positions[i].x <= -1.0f ) {
                positions[i].x = 1.0f;
            }
```

```java
         if( positions[i].y <= -1.0f ) {
            positions[i].y = 1.0f;
         } else if( positions[i].y >= 1.0f ) {
            positions[i].y = -1.0f;
         }
         angles[i] += rotations[i] * delta;
      }
   }

   @Override
   protected void render( Graphics g ) {
      Graphics2D g2d = (Graphics2D)g;
      setAntialasing( g2d );
      setInterpolation( g2d );

      switch( rotationMethod ) {
         case AffineTransform: doAffineTransform( g2d ); break;
         case AffineTransformOp: doAffineTransformOp( g2d ); break;
         case TexturePaint: doTexturePaint( g2d ); break;
      }

      super.render( g );
      g.drawString( "(A)ntialiased: " + antialiased, 20, 35 );
      g.drawString( "(I)nterpolation: " + interpolation, 20, 50 );
      g.drawString( "(T)ransparent Border: " + transparent, 20, 65 );
      g.drawString( "(R)otation Method: " + rotationMethod, 20, 80 );
      g.drawString( "(G)reen Border: " + greenBorder, 20, 95 );
   }

   private void setAntialasing( Graphics2D g2d ) {
      if( antialiased ) {
         g2d.setRenderingHint(
            RenderingHints.KEY_ANTIALIASING,
            RenderingHints.VALUE_ANTIALIAS_ON
         );
      } else {
         g2d.setRenderingHint(
            RenderingHints.KEY_ANTIALIASING,
            RenderingHints.VALUE_ANTIALIAS_OFF
         );
      }
   }

   private void setInterpolation( Graphics2D g2d ) {
      if( interpolation == Interpolation.NearestNeighbor ) {
         g2d.setRenderingHint(
```

```
                    RenderingHints.KEY_INTERPOLATION,
                    RenderingHints.VALUE_INTERPOLATION_NEAREST_NEIGHBOR
                );
            } else if( interpolation == Interpolation.BiLinear ) {
                g2d.setRenderingHint(
                    RenderingHints.KEY_INTERPOLATION,
                    RenderingHints.VALUE_INTERPOLATION_BILINEAR
                );
            } else if( interpolation == Interpolation.BiCubic ) {
                g2d.setRenderingHint(
                    RenderingHints.KEY_INTERPOLATION,
                    RenderingHints.VALUE_INTERPOLATION_BICUBIC
                );
            }
        }

        private AffineTransform createTransform( Vector2f position, float angle ) {
            Vector2f screen = getViewportTransform().mul( position );
            AffineTransform transform =
                AffineTransform.getTranslateInstance( screen.x, screen.y );
            transform.rotate( angle );
            transform.translate( -sprite.getWidth() / 2, -sprite.getHeight() / 2 );
            return transform;
        }

        private void doAffineTransform( Graphics2D g2d ) {
            for( int i = 0; i < positions.length; ++i ) {
                AffineTransform tranform =
                    createTransform( positions[i], angles[i] );
                g2d.drawImage( sprite, tranform, null );
            }
        }

        private AffineTransformOp createTransformOp(
            Vector2f position, float angle ) {

            AffineTransform transform = createTransform( position, angle );
            if( interpolation == Interpolation.NearestNeighbor ) {
                return new AffineTransformOp(
                    transform, AffineTransformOp.TYPE_NEAREST_NEIGHBOR );
            } else if( interpolation == Interpolation.BiLinear ) {
                return new AffineTransformOp(
                    transform, AffineTransformOp.TYPE_BILINEAR );
            } else { // interpolation == Interpolation.BiCubic
```

```
        return new AffineTransformOp(
            transform, AffineTransformOp.TYPE_BICUBIC );
    }
}

private void doAffineTransformOp( Graphics2D g2d ) {
    for( int i = 0; i < positions.length; ++i )   {
        AffineTransformOp op = createTransformOp( positions[i], angles[i] );
        g2d.drawImage( op.filter( sprite, null ), 0, 0, null );
    }
}

private void doTexturePaint( Graphics2D g2d ) {
    for( int i = 0; i < positions.length; ++i ) {
        Rectangle2D anchor =
            new Rectangle2D.Float(
                0, 0, sprite.getWidth(), sprite.getHeight() );
        TexturePaint paint = new TexturePaint( sprite, anchor );
        g2d.setPaint( paint );
        AffineTransform transform =
            createTransform( positions[i], angles[i] );
        g2d.setTransform( transform );
        g2d.fillRect( 0, 0, sprite.getWidth(), sprite.getHeight() );
    }
    // very important!!!
    g2d.setTransform( new AffineTransform() );
}

public static void main( String[] args ) {
    launchApp( new FlyingSpritesExample() );
}
}
```

EXPLORING DIFFERENT SCALING ALGORITHMS

Rotating images is not the only place where you need to balance speed and quality. Scaling images up or down from their original size can also cause problems if it's not done correctly. Because there are many different ways to scale images, it can be difficult to figure out which method to use that is still fast enough for games.

The first way to scale images is using the following code:

```
BufferedImage imgToScale;
Image scaledImg = imgToScale.getScaledInstance(
    200, 200, Image.SCALE_AREA_AVERAGING
);
```

There are only two rendering hints available with the method:

```
Image.SCALE_AREA_AVERAGING
Image.SCALE_REPLICATE
```

The second method to scale images is by using the Graphics object:

```
BufferedImage toScale;
BufferedImage destImg;

Graphics2D g2d = destImg.createGraphics();
g2d.setRenderingHint( key, value );
g2d.drawImage(
    toScale, 0, 0, destImg.getWidth(), destImg.getHeight(), null );
g2d.dispose();
```

There are problems with both approaches that are not obvious when first scaling images. The first method, using getScaledInstance(), is slow, and only returns an Image, not a BufferedImage. The second method produces very poor results when scaling images down to more than half their size, regardless of which interpolation method is used.

A third option is to scale the image down gradually using the second method, repeating the scale by only half the image size each time until the image is scaled down to the requested size. Although this method is slower, it is usually faster than the getScaledInstance() method, with only a slight loss in quality.

```
BufferedImage ret = sprite;
int targetWidth = sprite.getWidth() / 4;
int targetHeight = sprite.getHeight() / 4;

int w = sprite.getWidth();
int h = sprite.getHeight();

do {
    w = w / 2;
    if( w < targetWidth ) {
       w = targetWidth;
    }
    h = h / 2;
    if( h < targetHeight ) {
    h = targetHeight;
    }

    BufferedImage tmp =
        new BufferedImage( w, h, BufferedImage.TYPE_INT_ARGB );
    Graphics2D g2d = tmp.createGraphics();
    g2d.setRenderingHint( RenderingHints.KEY_INTERPOLATION, hintValue );
```

```
        g2d.drawImage( ret, 0, 0, w, h, null );
        g2d.dispose();
        ret = tmp;
} while( w != targetWidth || h != targetHeight );
```

One of the problems encountered when trying to measure the time required to scale the images was that the getScaledInstance() times were really fast, but when tested by scaling the image in the game framework code, the frames-per-second time did not match based on the measured rendering times. The reason that the measured time did not match the frame rate time was that the image returned from the getScaledInstance() method is loaded asynchronously. This is another reason to avoid this method. In order to force the returned image object to complete the rendering, an ImageConsumer is used as follows:

```
private void generateAveragedInstance() {
        averaged = sprite.getScaledInstance(
            sprite.getWidth() / 4, sprite.getHeight() / 4,
            Image.SCALE_AREA_AVERAGING
        );
        averaged.getSource().startProduction( getConsumer() );
    }

private ImageConsumer getConsumer() {
        return new ImageConsumer() {
        public void setProperties( Hashtable<?, ?> props ) { }
        public void setPixels( int x, int y, int w, int h, ColorModel model,
                int[] pixels, int off, int scansize ) { }
        public void setPixels( int x, int y, int w, int h, ColorModel model,
                byte[] pixels, int off, int scansize ) { }
        public void setHints( int hintflags ) { }
        public void setDimensions( int width, int height ) { }
        public void setColorModel( ColorModel model ) { }
        public void imageComplete( int status ) { }
        };
    }
```

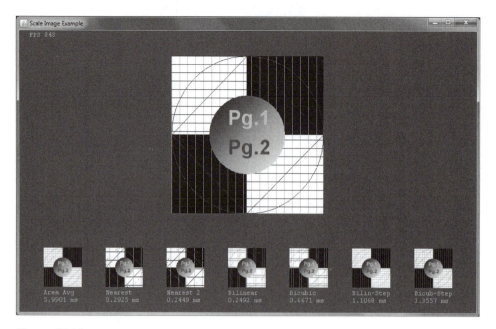

Figure 10.13
Scale Image Example.
© 2014 Timothy Wright.

The ScaleImageExample, as shown in Figure 10.13 and located in the javagames.images package, contains a lot of setup code for measuring the rendering times for six different methods of image scaling and creating the test image. It is good to see the difference in quality and speed produced by the different methods of scaling an image to a smaller size. Thanks to Chris Campbell for his excellent article and example image ideas.

Note

For more information, see Campbell, Chris, "The Perils of Image.getScaledInstance()," 2007. https://today .java.net/pub/a/today/2007/04/03/perils-of-image-getscaledinstance.html.

The initialize() method creates 100 copies of each image, measuring the time it takes to render them and then dividing that time by 100 to obtain an average rendering time. These times are not exactly accurate and will vary each time the program is run, but it is close enough to determine which methods are faster or slower than the others.

```
long start = System.nanoTime();
for( int i = 0; i < 100; ++i ) {
    generateAveragedInstance();
}
```

```
long end = System.nanoTime();
averagedSpeed = (end - start) / 1.0E6; // convert to milliseconds
averagedSpeed /= 100;
```

The createTestImage() method is responsible for creating the test image used in the examples. The line spacing is specifically chosen to highlight the problems with some of the scaling methods. This is evident in the scaled results, where some of the vertical and horizontal lines are missing.

The render() method draws the original image and all the scaled versions, along with a label describing the rendering hint and the time in milliseconds to scale the image. The generateAveragedInstance() and generateNearestNeighbor() methods scale the image using the getScaledInstance() method from the Image class. The scaleWithGraphics() method takes a rendering hint and scales the image using the Graphics object. Finally, the scaleDownImage() method steps down the scaled result gradually.

Note

The scaledDownImage() method is not a generic method for scaling an image. The scale-down size is hard-coded to one-forth (¼) the size and the do/while loop will not work if the image is scaled to a larger size. That is covered in the next section.

```java
package javagames.images;

import java.awt.*;
import java.awt.image.*;
import java.util.Hashtable;

import javagames.util.SimpleFramework;


public class ScaleImageExample extends SimpleFramework {
    private static final int IMG_WIDTH = 320;
    private static final int IMG_HEIGHT = 320;

    private BufferedImage sprite;

    private Image averaged;
    private double averagedSpeed;
    private Image nearestNeighbor;
    private double nearestSpeed;
    private BufferedImage nearest2;
    private double nearest2Speed;
    private BufferedImage bilinear;
    private double bilinearSpeed;
    private BufferedImage bicubic;
```

```java
private double bicubicSpeed;
private BufferedImage stepDownBilinear;
private double stepDownBilinearSpeed;
private BufferedImage stepDownBicubic;
private double stepDownBicubicSpeed;

public ScaleImageExample() {
    appWidth = 960;
    appHeight = 570;
    appBackground = Color.DARK_GRAY;
    appSleep = 1L;
    appTitle = "Scale Image Example";
}

@Override
protected void initialize() {
    super.initialize();

    System.out.println( "Creating test image..." );
    createTestImage();

    System.out.println( "Generating Averaged Image" );
    long start = System.nanoTime();
    for( int i = 0; i < 100; ++i ) {
        generateAveragedInstance();
    }
    long end = System.nanoTime();
    averagedSpeed = (end - start) / 1.0E6;
    averagedSpeed /= 100;

    System.out.println( "Generating Nearest Neighbor Image" );
    start = System.nanoTime();
    for( int i = 0; i < 100; ++i ) {
        generateNearestNeighbor();
    }
    end = System.nanoTime();
    nearestSpeed = (end - start) / 1.0E6;
    nearestSpeed /= 100;

    System.out.println( "Generating Nearest Neighbor 2" );
    start = System.nanoTime();
    for( int i = 0; i < 100; ++i ) {
        nearest2 = scaleWithGraphics(
            RenderingHints.VALUE_INTERPOLATION_NEAREST_NEIGHBOR );
    }
    end = System.nanoTime();
    nearest2Speed = (end - start) / 1.0E6;
```

```
    nearest2Speed /= 100;

    System.out.println( "Generating Bilinear" );
    start = System.nanoTime();
    for( int i = 0; i < 100; ++i ) {
        bilinear = scaleWithGraphics(
            RenderingHints.VALUE_INTERPOLATION_BILINEAR );
    }
    end = System.nanoTime();

    bilinearSpeed = (end - start) / 1.0E6;
    bilinearSpeed /= 100;

    System.out.println( "Generating Bicubic" );
    start = System.nanoTime();
    for( int i = 0; i < 100; ++i ) {
        bicubic = scaleWithGraphics(
            RenderingHints.VALUE_INTERPOLATION_BICUBIC );
    }
    end = System.nanoTime();
    bicubicSpeed = (end - start) / 1.0E6;
    bicubicSpeed /= 100;

    System.out.println( "Generating Step Down Bilinear" );
    start = System.nanoTime();
    for( int i = 0; i < 100; ++i ) {
        stepDownBilinear = scaleDownImage(
            RenderingHints.VALUE_INTERPOLATION_BILINEAR );
    }
    end = System.nanoTime();
    stepDownBilinearSpeed = (end - start) / 1.0E6;
    stepDownBilinearSpeed /= 100;

    System.out.println( "Generating Step Down Bicubic" );
    start = System.nanoTime();
    for( int i = 0; i < 100; ++i ) {
        stepDownBicubic = scaleDownImage(
            RenderingHints.VALUE_INTERPOLATION_BICUBIC );
    }
    end = System.nanoTime();
    stepDownBicubicSpeed = (end - start) / 1.0E6;
    stepDownBicubicSpeed /= 100;
}

private void createTestImage() {

    sprite = new BufferedImage(
```

```java
                IMG_WIDTH, IMG_HEIGHT, BufferedImage.TYPE_INT_ARGB );
Graphics2D g2d = sprite.createGraphics();

// draw checker board
g2d.setColor( Color.WHITE );
g2d.fillRect( 0, 0, IMG_WIDTH / 2, IMG_HEIGHT / 2 );
g2d.fillRect( IMG_WIDTH / 2, IMG_HEIGHT / 2, IMG_WIDTH, IMG_HEIGHT );
g2d.setColor( Color.BLACK );
g2d.fillRect( IMG_WIDTH / 2, 0, IMG_WIDTH , IMG_HEIGHT / 2 );
g2d.fillRect( 0, IMG_HEIGHT / 2, IMG_WIDTH / 2, IMG_HEIGHT );

// draw red diamond
g2d.setColor( Color.RED );
g2d.drawLine( 0, sprite.getHeight() / 2, sprite.getWidth() / 2, 0 );
g2d.drawLine(
    sprite.getWidth() / 2, 0, sprite.getWidth(), sprite.getHeight() / 2
);
g2d.drawLine(
    sprite.getWidth(), sprite.getHeight() / 2, sprite.getWidth() / 2,
    sprite.getHeight()
);
g2d.drawLine(
    sprite.getWidth() / 2, sprite.getHeight(), 0, sprite.getHeight() / 2
);

// draw circle
g2d.drawOval( 0, 0, sprite.getWidth(), sprite.getHeight() );

// draw hash lines
g2d.setColor( Color.GREEN );
int dx = sprite.getWidth() / 18;
for( int i = 0; i < sprite.getWidth(); i += dx ) {
    g2d.drawLine( i, 0, i, sprite.getHeight() );
}

g2d.setColor( Color.BLUE );
dx = sprite.getHeight() / 18;

for( int i = 0; i < sprite.getHeight(); i += dx ) {
    g2d.drawLine( 0, i, sprite.getWidth(), i );
}

// gradient circle
float x1 = sprite.getWidth() / 4;
float x2 = sprite.getWidth() * 3 / 4;
float y1 = sprite.getHeight() / 4;
float y2 = sprite.getHeight() * 3 / 4;
```

```java
GradientPaint gp =
    new GradientPaint( x1, y1, Color.BLACK, x2, y2, Color.WHITE );
g2d.setPaint( gp );
g2d.fillOval(
    sprite.getWidth() / 4, sprite.getHeight() / 4,
    sprite.getWidth() / 2, sprite.getHeight() / 2
);

g2d.setFont( new Font( "Arial", Font.BOLD, 42 ) );
g2d.setRenderingHint(
    RenderingHints.KEY_ANTIALIASING, RenderingHints.VALUE_ANTIALIAS_ON
);
g2d.setColor( Color.LIGHT_GRAY );
g2d.drawString(
    "Pg.1", sprite.getWidth()/2-40, sprite.getHeight()/2-20 );
g2d.setColor( Color.DARK_GRAY );
g2d.drawString(
    "Pg.2", sprite.getWidth()/2-40, sprite.getHeight()/2+40 );
g2d.dispose();
}

@Override
protected void processInput( float delta ) {
    super.processInput( delta );
}

@Override
protected void updateObjects( float delta ) {
    super.updateObjects( delta );
}

@Override
protected void render( Graphics g ) {
    super.render( g );

    // Test Image
    g.drawImage(
        sprite, (canvas.getWidth() - sprite.getWidth())/2, 50, null );

    int sw = averaged.getWidth( null );
    int sh = averaged.getHeight( null );
    int pos = canvas.getHeight() - sh - 50;
    int textPos = pos + sh;

    // Averaged Image
    int imgPos = (sw + 50) * 0 + 50;
    g.drawImage( averaged, imgPos, pos, null );
```

```java
    String time = String.format( "%.4f ms", averagedSpeed );
    g.drawString( "Area Avg", 50, textPos + 15 );
    g.drawString( time, 50, textPos + 30 );

    // Nearest Image
    imgPos = (sw + 50) * 1 + 50;
    g.drawImage( nearestNeighbor, imgPos, pos, null );
    time = String.format( "%.4f ms", nearestSpeed );
    g.drawString( "Nearest", imgPos, textPos + 15 );
    g.drawString( time, imgPos, textPos + 30 );

    // Nearest2 Image
    imgPos = (sw + 50) * 2 + 50;
    g.drawImage( nearest2, imgPos, pos, null );
    time = String.format( "%.4f ms", nearest2Speed );
    g.drawString( "Nearest 2", imgPos, textPos + 15 );
    g.drawString( time, imgPos, textPos + 30 );

    // Bilinear Image
    imgPos = (sw + 50) * 3 + 50;
    g.drawImage( bilinear, imgPos, pos, null );
    time = String.format( "%.4f ms", bilinearSpeed );
    g.drawString( "Bilinear", imgPos, textPos + 15 );
    g.drawString( time, imgPos, textPos + 30 );

    // Bicubic Image
    imgPos = (sw + 50) * 4 + 50;
    g.drawImage( bicubic, imgPos, pos, null );
    time = String.format( "%.4f ms", bicubicSpeed );
    g.drawString( "Bicubic", imgPos, textPos + 15 );
    g.drawString( time, imgPos, textPos + 30 );

    // Step Down Bilinear Image
    imgPos = (sw + 50) * 5 + 50;
    g.drawImage( stepDownBilinear, imgPos, pos, null );
    time = String.format( "%.4f ms", stepDownBilinearSpeed );
    g.drawString( "Bilin-Step", imgPos, textPos + 15 );
    g.drawString( time, imgPos, textPos + 30 );

    // Step Down Bicubic Image
    imgPos = (sw + 50) * 6 + 50;
    g.drawImage( stepDownBicubic, imgPos, pos, null );
    time = String.format( "%.4f ms", stepDownBicubicSpeed );
    g.drawString( "Bicub-Step", imgPos, textPos + 15 );
    g.drawString( time, imgPos, textPos + 30 );

}
```

```java
private void generateAveragedInstance() {
    averaged = sprite.getScaledInstance(
        sprite.getWidth() / 4, sprite.getHeight() / 4,
        Image.SCALE_AREA_AVERAGING
    );
    averaged.getSource().startProduction( getConsumer() );
}

private void generateNearestNeighbor() {
    nearestNeighbor = sprite.getScaledInstance(
        sprite.getWidth() / 4, sprite.getHeight() / 4, Image.SCALE_REPLICATE
    );
    nearestNeighbor.getSource().startProduction( getConsumer() );
}

private BufferedImage scaleWithGraphics( Object hintValue ) {
    BufferedImage image = new BufferedImage(
        sprite.getWidth() / 4, sprite.getHeight() / 4,
        BufferedImage.TYPE_INT_ARGB
    );
    Graphics2D g2d = image.createGraphics();
    g2d.setRenderingHint( RenderingHints.KEY_INTERPOLATION, hintValue );
    g2d.drawImage(
        sprite, 0, 0, image.getWidth(), image.getHeight(), null );
    g2d.dispose();
    return image;
}

private BufferedImage scaleDownImage( Object hintValue ) {

    BufferedImage ret = sprite;
    int targetWidth = sprite.getWidth() / 4;
    int targetHeight = sprite.getHeight() / 4;

    int w = sprite.getWidth();
    int h = sprite.getHeight();

    do {
        w = w / 2;
        if( w < targetWidth ) {
            w = targetWidth;
        }
        h = h / 2;
        if( h < targetHeight ) {
            h = targetHeight;
        }
```

```
            BufferedImage tmp =
                new BufferedImage( w, h, BufferedImage.TYPE_INT_ARGB );
            Graphics2D g2d = tmp.createGraphics();
            g2d.setRenderingHint( RenderingHints.KEY_INTERPOLATION, hintValue );
            g2d.drawImage( ret, 0, 0, w, h, null );
            g2d.dispose();
            ret = tmp;
        } while( w != targetWidth || h != targetHeight );

        return ret;
    }

    private ImageConsumer getConsumer() {
        return new ImageConsumer() {
            public void setProperties( Hashtable<?, ?> props ) { }
            public void setPixels( int x, int y, int w, int h, ColorModel model,
                    int[] pixels, int off, int scansize ) { }
            public void setPixels( int x, int y, int w, int h, ColorModel model,
                    byte[] pixels, int off, int scansize ) { }
            public void setHints( int hintflags ) { }
            public void setDimensions( int width, int height ) { }
            public void setColorModel( ColorModel model ) { }
            public void imageComplete( int status ) { }
        };
    }

    public static void main( String[] args ) {
        launchApp( new ScaleImageExample() );
    }
}
```

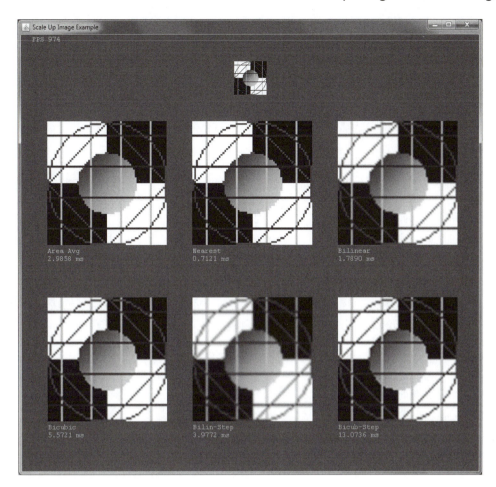

Figure 10.14
Scale Up Image Example.
© 2014 Timothy Wright.

The `ScaleUpImageExample`, as seen in Figure 10.14 and located in the `javagames.images` package, is just like the previous example, except that a small image is generated and it is scaled up to a much larger size. Notice that some of the methods that produce the best looking images when shrinking them do not perform the same when the image grows.

The Bilinear step-down method is good for scaling the images down, and the regular Bilinear approach for up-scaling would be my choice. But it all depends on the situation and the images. If the slower methods are performed only at startup and never again, it may be worth it to take the speed hit when loading the resource.

```
package javagames.images;

import java.awt.*;
```

```java
import java.awt.image.*;
import java.util.Hashtable;

import javagames.util.SimpleFramework;


public class ScaleUpImageExample extends SimpleFramework {

    private static final int IMG_WIDTH = 64;
    private static final int IMG_HEIGHT = 64;

    private BufferedImage sprite;

    private Image averaged;
    private double averagedSpeed;
    private BufferedImage nearestNeighbor;
    private double nearestNeighborSpeed;
    private BufferedImage bilinear;
    private double bilinearSpeed;
    private BufferedImage bicubic;
    private double bicubicSpeed;
    private BufferedImage stepDownBilinear;
    private double stepDownBilinearSpeed;
    private BufferedImage stepDownBicubic;
    private double stepDownBicubicSpeed;

    public ScaleUpImageExample() {
        appWidth = 900;
        appHeight = 830;
        appBackground = Color.DARK_GRAY;
        appSleep = 1L;
        appTitle = "Scale Up Image Example";
    }

    @Override
    protected void initialize() {
        super.initialize();

        System.out.println( "Creating test image..." );
        createTestImage();

        System.out.println( "Generating Averaged Image" );
        long start = System.nanoTime();
        for( int i = 0; i < 100; ++i ) {
            generateAveragedInstance();
        }
        long end = System.nanoTime();
        averagedSpeed = (end - start) / 1.0E6;
        averagedSpeed /= 100;
```

```java
System.out.println( "Generating Nearest Neighbor" );
start = System.nanoTime();
for( int i = 0; i < 100; ++i ) {
   nearestNeighbor =
      scaleWithGraphics(
         RenderingHints.VALUE_INTERPOLATION_NEAREST_NEIGHBOR );
}
end = System.nanoTime();
nearestNeighborSpeed = (end - start) / 1.0E6;
nearestNeighborSpeed /= 100;

System.out.println( "Generating Bilinear" );
start = System.nanoTime();
for( int i = 0; i < 100; ++i ) {
   bilinear = scaleWithGraphics(
      RenderingHints.VALUE_INTERPOLATION_BILINEAR );
}
end = System.nanoTime();

bilinearSpeed = (end - start) / 1.0E6;
bilinearSpeed /= 100;

System.out.println( "Generating Bicubic" );
start = System.nanoTime();
for( int i = 0; i < 100; ++i ) {
   bicubic = scaleWithGraphics(
      RenderingHints.VALUE_INTERPOLATION_BICUBIC );
}
end = System.nanoTime();
bicubicSpeed = (end - start) / 1.0E6;
bicubicSpeed /= 100;

System.out.println( "Generating Step Down Bilinear" );
start = System.nanoTime();
for( int i = 0; i < 100; ++i ) {
   stepDownBilinear = scaleUpImage(
      RenderingHints.VALUE_INTERPOLATION_BILINEAR );
}
end = System.nanoTime();
stepDownBilinearSpeed = (end - start) / 1.0E6;
stepDownBilinearSpeed /= 100;

System.out.println( "Generating Step Down Bicubic" );
start = System.nanoTime();
for( int i = 0; i < 100; ++i ) {
   stepDownBicubic = scaleUpImage(
      RenderingHints.VALUE_INTERPOLATION_BICUBIC );
}
```

```
        end = System.nanoTime();
        stepDownBicubicSpeed = (end - start) / 1.0E6;
        stepDownBicubicSpeed /= 100;

    }

    private void createTestImage() {
        sprite = new BufferedImage(
            IMG_WIDTH, IMG_HEIGHT, BufferedImage.TYPE_INT_ARGB );
        Graphics2D g2d = sprite.createGraphics();

        // draw checker board
        g2d.setColor( Color.WHITE );
        g2d.fillRect( 0, 0, IMG_WIDTH / 2, IMG_HEIGHT / 2 );
        g2d.fillRect( IMG_WIDTH / 2, IMG_HEIGHT / 2, IMG_WIDTH, IMG_HEIGHT );
        g2d.setColor( Color.BLACK );
        g2d.fillRect( IMG_WIDTH / 2, 0, IMG_WIDTH , IMG_HEIGHT / 2 );
        g2d.fillRect( 0, IMG_HEIGHT / 2, IMG_WIDTH / 2, IMG_HEIGHT );

        // gradient circle
        float x1 = sprite.getWidth() / 4;
        float x2 = sprite.getWidth() * 3 / 4;
        float y1 = sprite.getHeight() / 4;
        float y2 = sprite.getHeight() * 3 / 4;
        GradientPaint gp =
            new GradientPaint( x1, y1, Color.BLACK, x2, y2, Color.WHITE );
        g2d.setPaint( gp );
        g2d.fillOval(
            sprite.getWidth() / 4, sprite.getHeight() / 4,
            sprite.getWidth() / 2, sprite.getHeight() / 2
        );

        // draw hash lines
        g2d.setColor( Color.GREEN );
        int dx = sprite.getWidth() / 4;
        for( int i = 0; i < sprite.getWidth(); i += dx ) {
            g2d.drawLine( i + 7, 0, i + 7, sprite.getHeight() );
        }

        g2d.setColor( Color.BLUE );
        dx = sprite.getHeight() / 4;

        for( int i = 0; i < sprite.getHeight(); i += dx ) {
            g2d.drawLine( 0, i + 7, sprite.getWidth(), i + 7 );
        }

        // draw red diamond
        g2d.setColor( Color.RED );
        g2d.drawLine( 0, sprite.getHeight() / 2, sprite.getWidth() / 2, 0 );
```

```java
        g2d.drawLine( sprite.getWidth() / 2, 0,
            sprite.getWidth(), sprite.getHeight() / 2 );
        g2d.drawLine( sprite.getWidth(), sprite.getHeight() / 2,
            sprite.getWidth() / 2, sprite.getHeight() );
        g2d.drawLine( sprite.getWidth() / 2, sprite.getHeight(), 0,
            sprite.getHeight() / 2 );

        // draw circle
        g2d.drawOval( 0, 0, sprite.getWidth(), sprite.getHeight() );

        g2d.dispose();
    }

    @Override
    protected void render( Graphics g ) {
        super.render( g );

        // Test Image
        g.drawImage( sprite,
            (canvas.getWidth() - sprite.getWidth())/2, 50, null );

        int sw = averaged.getWidth( null );
        int sh = averaged.getHeight( null );
        int pos = sprite.getHeight() + 100;
        int textPos = pos + sh;

        // Averaged Image
        int imgPos = (sw + 50) * 0 + 50;
        g.drawImage( averaged, imgPos, pos, null );
        String time = String.format( "%.4f ms", averagedSpeed );
        g.drawString( "Area Avg", 50, textPos + 15 );
        g.drawString( time, 50, textPos + 30 );

        // Nearest Image
        imgPos = (sw + 50) * 1 + 50;
        g.drawImage( nearestNeighbor, imgPos, pos, null );
        time = String.format( "%.4f ms", nearestNeighborSpeed );
        g.drawString( "Nearest", imgPos, textPos + 15 );
        g.drawString( time, imgPos, textPos + 30 );

        // Bilinear Image
        imgPos = (sw + 50) * 2 + 50;
        g.drawImage( bilinear, imgPos, pos, null );
        time = String.format( "%.4f ms", bilinearSpeed );
        g.drawString( "Bilinear", imgPos, textPos + 15 );
        g.drawString( time, imgPos, textPos + 30 );

        pos += nearestNeighbor.getHeight() + 100;
        textPos = pos + nearestNeighbor.getHeight();
```

```
      // Bicubic Image
      imgPos = (sw + 50) * 0 + 50;
      g.drawImage( bicubic, imgPos, pos, null );
      time = String.format( "%.4f ms", bicubicSpeed );
      g.drawString( "Bicubic", imgPos, textPos + 15 );
      g.drawString( time, imgPos, textPos + 30 );

      // Step Down Bilinear Image
      imgPos = (sw + 50) * 1 + 50;
      g.drawImage( stepDownBilinear, imgPos, pos, null );
      time = String.format( "%.4f ms", stepDownBilinearSpeed );
      g.drawString( "Bilin-Step", imgPos, textPos + 15 );
      g.drawString( time, imgPos, textPos + 30 );

      // Step Down Bicubic Image
      imgPos = (sw + 50) * 2 + 50;
      g.drawImage( stepDownBicubic, imgPos, pos, null );
      time = String.format( "%.4f ms", stepDownBicubicSpeed );
      g.drawString( "Bicub-Step", imgPos, textPos + 15 );
      g.drawString( time, imgPos, textPos + 30 );
   }

   private void generateAveragedInstance() {
      averaged = sprite.getScaledInstance( (int)(sprite.getWidth() * 3.7),
         (int)(sprite.getHeight() * 3.7), Image.SCALE_AREA_AVERAGING );
      averaged.getSource().startProduction( getConsumer() );
   }

   private BufferedImage scaleWithGraphics( Object hintValue ) {
      BufferedImage image = new BufferedImage(
         (int)(sprite.getWidth() * 3.7),
         (int)(sprite.getHeight() * 3.7), BufferedImage.TYPE_INT_ARGB );
      Graphics2D g2d = image.createGraphics();
      g2d.setRenderingHint( RenderingHints.KEY_INTERPOLATION, hintValue );
      g2d.drawImage(
         sprite, 0, 0, image.getWidth(), image.getHeight(), null );
      g2d.dispose();
      return image;
   }

   private BufferedImage scaleUpImage( Object hintValue ) {

      BufferedImage ret = sprite;
      int targetWidth = (int)(sprite.getWidth() * 3.7);
      int targetHeight = (int)(sprite.getHeight() * 3.7);

      int w = sprite.getWidth();
      int h = sprite.getHeight();
```

```
        do {
            w = (int)(w * 1.5);
            if( w > targetWidth ) {
                w = targetWidth;
            }
            h = (int)(h * 1.5);
            if( h > targetHeight ) {
                h = targetHeight;
            }

            BufferedImage tmp =
                new BufferedImage( w, h, BufferedImage.TYPE_INT_ARGB );
            Graphics2D g2d = tmp.createGraphics();
            g2d.setRenderingHint( RenderingHints.KEY_INTERPOLATION, hintValue );
            g2d.drawImage( ret, 0, 0, w, h, null );
            g2d.dispose();
            ret = tmp;
        } while( w != targetWidth || h != targetHeight );

        return ret;
    }
    private ImageConsumer getConsumer() {
        return new ImageConsumer() {
            public void setProperties( Hashtable<?, ?> props ) { }
            public void setPixels( int x, int y, int w, int h, ColorModel model,
                    int[] pixels, int off, int scansize ) { }
            public void setPixels( int x, int y, int w, int h, ColorModel model,
                    byte[] pixels, int off, int scansize ) { }
            public void setHints( int hintflags ) { }
            public void setDimensions( int width, int height ) { }
            public void setColorModel( ColorModel model ) { }
            public void imageComplete( int status ) { }
        };
    }
    public static void main( String[] args ) {
        launchApp( new ScaleUpImageExample() );
    }
}
```

RESOURCES AND FURTHER READING

Campbell, Chris, "Java 2D Trickery: Antialiased Image Transforms," 2007, https://weblogs.java.net/blog/campbell/archive/2007/03/java_2d_tricker.html.

Haase, Chet, "BufferedImage as Good as Butter," 2003, https://weblogs.java.net/blog/chet/archive/2003/08/bufferedimage_a.html.

Haase, Chet, "BufferedImage as Good as Butter, Part II," 2003, https://weblogs.java.net/blog/chet/archive/2003/08/bufferedimage_a_1.html.

Haase, Chet, "VolatileImage: Now You See it, Now You Don't," 2003, https://weblogs.java.net/blog/chet/archive/2003/09/volatileimage_n.html.

Haase, Chet, "VolatileImage Q&A," 2003, https://weblogs.java.net/blog/chet/archive/2003/09/volatileimage_q.html.

Haase, Chet, "ImageIO: Just Another Example of Better Living by Doing it Yourself," 2004, https://weblogs.java.net/blog/chet/archive/2004/07/imageio_just_an.html.

Haase, Chet, "ToolkitBufferedVolatileManagedImage Strategies," 2004, https://weblogs.java.net/blog/chet/archive/2004/08/toolkitbuffered.html.

CHAPTER 11

TEXT

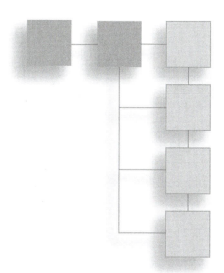

The first time I tried to draw some text on the screen for the frame-per-second, it was easy. But for those of you who have noticed, all of the text drawing has hard-coded values, such as the following code:

```
// draw directions on top of bouncing balls
super.render( g );
g.drawString( "Ball Count: " + ballCount, 20, 35 );
g.drawString( "Press [SPACE] to launch.", 20, 50 );
g.drawString( "Press Up arrow to increase ball count", 20, 65 );
g.drawString( "Press Down arrow to decrease ball count", 20, 80 );
```

If the font size changes, the hard-coded numbers for the height no longer work. But placing text in a specific position is harder than it seems.

UNDERSTANDING JAVA FONTS

To create a new font in Java, three parameters are passed to the constructor: the font name, style, and size.

```
Font( String name, int style, int size )
```

The font name is a string with the name of the font, such as Courier New. You can obtain a list of all available fonts from the `GraphicsEnvironment` object.

```
public static void main( String[] args ) {
    GraphicsEnvironment ge =
      GraphicsEnvironment.getLocalGraphicsEnvironment();
    String[] fontFamilies = ge.getAvailableFontFamilyNames();
```

```
    for( String fontFamily : fontFamilies ) {
        System.out.println( fontFamily );
    }
}
```

The size of the font is the point size, such as 12 for a twelve-point font. The style can be plain, bold, italic, or bold and italic, which is obtained by combining the bold and italic with the OR | operator.

```
Font plain = new Font("Name", Font.PLAIN, 12 );
Font bold = new Font( "Name", Font.BOLD, 12 );
Font italic = new Font( "Name", Font.ITALIC, 12 );
Font boldItalic = new Font( "Name", Font.BOLD | Font.ITALIC, 12 );
```

Remember, before you get the width and height of the current font, you must create the font object and set it in the Graphics object.

The BoxedTextProblem example code, shown in Figure 11.1 and located in the javagames.text package, shows the differences between drawing text and images to the screen by trying to draw a rectangle around some text.

```
package javagames.text;


import java.awt.Color;
import java.awt.Font;
import java.awt.Graphics;

import javagames.util.SimpleFramework;


public class BoxedTextProblem extends SimpleFramework {
    public BoxedTextProblem() {
        appWidth = 640;
        appHeight = 640;
        appSleep = 10L;
        appTitle = "Boxed Text Problem";
        appBackground = Color.WHITE;
        appFPSColor = Color.BLACK;
    }

    @Override
    protected void initialize() {
        super.initialize();
    }
```

```java
@Override
protected void render( Graphics g ) {
    super.render( g );

    // Box this text...
    g.setColor( Color.BLACK );
    String box = "great Java, now what?";
    Font font = new Font( "Arial", Font.PLAIN, 24 );
    g.setFont( font );
    g.drawString( box, 20, 50 );
    g.setColor( Color.RED );
    g.drawRect( 20, 50, 200, 20 );

}

public static void main( String[] args ) {
    launchApp( new BoxedTextProblem() );
}
}
```

Ignore that the width of the rectangle is just a guess. Even though both the rectangle and text are drawn with their upper-left position at (20, 50), the results are not similar. See Figure 11.1.

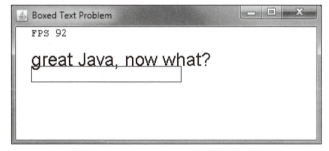

Figure 11.1
Boxed Text Problem.
© 2014 Timothy Wright.

The problem is that text is not treated the same as images. Although images are drawn from the upper-left corner, text is drawn from the baseline, and the height and width of the rendered string depends on the selected font type, style, and size.

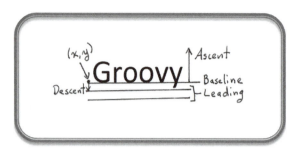

Figure 11.2
Text Metrics.
© 2014 Timothy Wright.

The baseline runs across the bottom of the font. However, some letters will drop below the baseline. The ascent value rises from the baseline to the top of the font. The descent value is the distance letters drop below the baseline, and the leading value is the space between lines so that the letters do not touch. Together, these three values form the total height of the font. See Figure 11.2.

```
Height = ascent + descent + leading
```

As with most problems in Java, there are multiple ways to solve this problem.

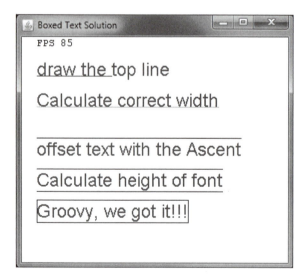

Figure 11.3
Boxed Text Solution.
© 2014 Timothy Wright.

The BoxedTextSolution code, as shown in Figure 11.3 and located in the javagames.text package, demonstrates the necessary steps to place a border around some text without guessing at the values. The first step is to get the FontMetrics from the Graphics object.

```
FontMetrics fm = g.getFontMetrics();
```

Because some fonts have a different width for each letter, you need the string value to determine the width.

```
int width = fm.stringWidth( str );
```

Now that the width of the string is available, the next step is to draw the text so that the upper-left corner is not placed at the baseline, but remains the upper-left corner. Because the starting point is drawn at the baseline, adding the ascent, which is the distance the text rises from the y coordinate, places the text in the correct position.

```
g.drawString( str, x, y + fm.getAscent() );
```

A line can now be drawn using the upper-left position because the text is shifted by the ascent value. All that is left is to calculate the height of the font.

```
int height = fm.getAscent() + fm.getDescent() + fm.getLeading();
```

With the upper-left position, the height, the width, and the text drawn in the correct spot, placing a box around the text is easy. The BoxedTextSolution steps through the necessary method calls to place a box around some text. Correctly boxing text is essential to placing game text exactly where it is needed.

```
package javagames.text;

import java.awt.*;
import javagames.util.SimpleFramework;

public class BoxedTextSolution extends SimpleFramework {

    public BoxedTextSolution() {
        appWidth = 640;
        appHeight = 640;
        appSleep = 10L;
        appTitle = "Boxed Text Solution";
        appBackground = Color.WHITE;
        appFPSColor = Color.BLACK;
    }

    @Override
    protected void initialize() {
        super.initialize();
    }

    @Override
    protected void render( Graphics g ) {
        super.render( g );

        // Set the font...
        Font font = new Font( "Arial", Font.PLAIN, 24 );
```

```
g.setFont( font );
FontMetrics fm = g.getFontMetrics();
int x = 20;
int y = 50;

// Draw the top...
String str = "draw the top line";
g.setColor( Color.DARK_GRAY );
g.drawString( str, x, y );

int width = 100;
g.setColor( Color.RED );
g.drawLine( x, y, x + width, y );

// Calculate the string width...
y += 40;
str = "Calculate correct width";
g.setColor( Color.DARK_GRAY );
g.drawString( str, x, y );

width = fm.stringWidth( str );
g.setColor( Color.GREEN );
g.drawLine( x, y, x + width, y );

// Use Ascent to offset y
y += 40;
g.setColor( Color.DARK_GRAY );
str = "offset text with the Ascent";
g.drawString( str, x, y + fm.getAscent() );

width = fm.stringWidth( str );
g.setColor( Color.BLUE );
g.drawLine( x, y, x + width, y );

// Ascent+Decent+Leading=Height
y += 40;
g.setColor( Color.DARK_GRAY );
str = "Calculate height of font";
g.drawString( str, x, y + fm.getAscent() );

width = fm.stringWidth( str );
g.setColor( Color.BLUE );
g.drawLine( x, y, x + width, y );
int height = fm.getAscent() + fm.getDescent() + fm.getLeading();
g.drawLine( x, y + height, x + width, y + height );

// Box the text
y += 40;
g.setColor( Color.DARK_GRAY );
str = "Groovy, we got it!!!";
g.drawString( str, x, y + fm.getAscent() );
```

```
        width = fm.stringWidth( str );
        g.setColor( Color.BLUE );
        height = fm.getAscent() + fm.getDescent() + fm.getLeading();
        g.drawRect( x, y, width, height );
    }
    public static void main( String[] args ) {
        launchApp( new BoxedTextSolution() );
    }
}
```

MAKING A DRAW STRING UTILITY

Now that you can determine the placement of text based on the font size, you can add some utility methods to the Utility class, located in the javagames.util package. Given a starting position and an array of strings, the utility methods draw the text to the screen with the correct spacing, keeping the starting position in the upper-left corner.

```
public class Utility {
    // previous code here
    public static int drawString( Graphics g, int x, int y, String str ) {
        return drawString( g, x, y, new String[]{ str } );
    }
    public static int drawString(
        Graphics g, int x, int y, List<String> str ) {
        return drawString( g, x, y, str.toArray( new String[0] ) );
    }
    public static int drawString(
        Graphics g, int x, int y, String... str ) {
        FontMetrics fm = g.getFontMetrics();
        int height = fm.getAscent() + fm.getDescent() + fm.getLeading();
        for( String s : str ) {
            g.drawString( s, x, y + fm.getAscent() );
            y += height;
        }
        return y;
    }
}
```

Notice that the new methods return the new y position once the text is drawn. This allows more text to be appended to the previously drawn text. Using the new utility methods, the following code can be added to the SimpleFramework, located in the javagames.util package.

```
public class SimpleFramework extends JFrame implements Runnable {
    // attributes
    protected int textPos = 0; // this is new!
    public SimpleFramework() {

    }
    protected void render( Graphics g ) {
        g.setFont( appFont );
        g.setColor( appFPSColor );
        frameRate.calculate();
        textPos =
            Utility.drawString( g, 20, 0, frameRate.getFrameRate() );
                                //new
    }
    // rest of the code
}
```

Now that you're using the Utility method to draw the text, the y position of the frame rate can be the upper-left corner no matter how big the font. Previously, large fonts would cause the frame rate to leave the screen.

Figure 11.4
Utility Draw String Example.
© 2014 Timothy Wright.

The UtilityDrawStringExample, shown in Figure 11.4 and located in the javagames.text package, uses the new updates to the SimpleFramework and the Utility class to demonstrate using the new methods to draw text. The processInput() method handles up and down arrow presses, adjusting the font size larger or smaller to test the new methods.

Note

Java has two different antialiasing methods, one for images, and a separate one for text. Make sure you turn on the text-based antialiasing rendering hint when drawing text.

The render() method first enables text antialiasing. Then it uses the textPos variable to draw text many different ways: one with a single value, another with an array of strings, another with a list of strings, and another with multiple string values. Because the new method calculates the height of the font, the strings are always spaced correctly.

```java
package javagames.text;

import java.awt.*;
import java.awt.event.KeyEvent;
import java.util.Vector;

import javagames.util.*;


public class UtilityDrawStringExample extends SimpleFramework {

    public UtilityDrawStringExample() {
        appFont = new Font( "Courier New", Font.BOLD, 48 );
        appWidth = 640;
        appHeight = 640;
        appSleep = 10L;
        appTitle = "Utility Draw String Example";
        appBackground = Color.WHITE;
        appFPSColor = Color.BLACK;
    }

    @Override
    protected void processInput( float delta ) {
        super.processInput( delta );

        if( keyboard.keyDownOnce( KeyEvent.VK_UP ) ) {
            int fontSize = appFont.getSize();
            appFont = new Font(
                appFont.getFamily(), appFont.getStyle(), fontSize + 2 );
        }
        if( keyboard.keyDownOnce( KeyEvent.VK_DOWN ) ) {
            int fontSize = appFont.getSize();
```

```java
        appFont = new Font(
            appFont.getFamily(), appFont.getStyle(), fontSize - 2 );
    }
}

@Override
protected void render( Graphics g ) {
    super.render( g );
    Graphics2D g2d = (Graphics2D)g;
    g2d.setRenderingHint(
        RenderingHints.KEY_ANTIALIASING,
        RenderingHints.VALUE_ANTIALIAS_ON
    );

    textPos = Utility.drawString( g2d, 20, textPos,
        "Font Size: " + g2d.getFont().getSize()
    );
    textPos = Utility.drawString( g2d, 20, textPos,
        "Use the arrow keys",
        "to tweak the font size",
        ""
    );

    g2d.setColor( Color.WHITE );
    textPos = Utility.drawString( g2d, 20, textPos, "Single String" );
    g2d.setColor( Color.BLUE );
    textPos = Utility.drawString( g2d, 20, textPos,
        "Strings ",
        "With",
        "Commas"
    );

    g2d.setColor( Color.DARK_GRAY );
    String[] array = new String[] {
        "Strings",
        "With",
        "Arrays",
    };
    textPos = Utility.drawString( g2d, 20, textPos, array );

    g2d.setColor( Color.RED );
    Vector<String> list = new Vector<String>();
    list.add( "Strings" );
    list.add( "With" );
    list.add( "Lists" );
    textPos = Utility.drawString( g2d, 20, textPos, list );
}
```

```
public static void main( String[] args ) {
    launchApp( new UtilityDrawStringExample() );
}

}
```

USING TEXT METRICS FOR LAYOUT

The FontMetrics class is not the only way to get information about a font. Java has some other classes and methods available to provide all the available information about a font object.

The FontMetrics object provides a LineMetrics objects, which has additional information, such as the center baseline of a font.

```
float dy = fm.getLineMetrics(
    str, graphics).getBaselineOffsets()[ Font.CENTER_BASELINE ];
```

Even more useful is the TextLayout object. This object can be constructed using a Font, a FontRenderContext, and a String.

```
Graphics2D g2d;
Font font;
String str;
FontRenderContext frc = g2d.getFontRenderContext();
TextLayout tl = new TextLayout( str, font, frc );
```

The text layout object is useful because it provides a lot of information as floating point values, not integers, so more exact placement is possible. The following values are available from the TextLayout object:

- Ascent
- Descent
- Leading
- Baseline
- Roman baseline
- Center baseline
- Hanging baseline
- Advance
- Bounds
- Visible bounds

The TextMetricsExample, shown in Figure 11.5 and located in the javagames.text package, demonstrates using all the different information available for fonts.

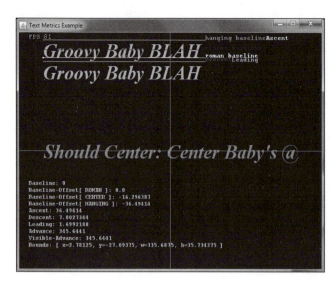

Figure 11.5
Text Metrics Example.
© 2014 Timothy Wright.

The example displays a lot of information about the font. These values are also listed at the bottom of the application. Notice that some of the font values are negative. The negative values are added to the baseline, not subtracted.

```java
package javagames.text;


import java.awt.*;
import java.awt.font.*;
import java.awt.geom.Rectangle2D;
import java.util.ArrayList;

import javagames.util.*;


public class TextMetricsExample extends SimpleFramework {
    public TextMetricsExample() {
        appWidth = 640;
        appHeight = 480;
        appSleep = 10L;
        appTitle = "Text Metrics Example";
    }

    @Override
    protected void initialize() {
        super.initialize();
    }
```

```java
@Override
protected void render( Graphics g ) {
    super.render( g );

    Graphics2D g2d = (Graphics2D)g;
    g2d.setRenderingHint( RenderingHints.KEY_ANTIALIASING,
            RenderingHints.VALUE_ANTIALIAS_ON );

    Font font = new Font( "Times New Roman", Font.BOLD | Font.ITALIC, 40 );
    g2d.setFont( font );
    g2d.setColor( Color.GREEN );
    String str = "Groovy Baby BLAH";
    int x = 50;
    int y = 50;
    g2d.drawString( str, x, y );

    // Text Layout gives floating point values
    FontRenderContext frc = g2d.getFontRenderContext();
    TextLayout tl = new TextLayout( str, font, frc );

    // draw another line, should be at
    // y + ascent + decent + leading
    int newY =
        y + (int)( tl.getAscent() + tl.getDescent() + tl.getLeading() );
    g2d.drawString( str, x, newY );

    // draw centered Text
    // first lets draw the center of the window...
    g2d.setColor( Color.GRAY );
    int sw = canvas.getWidth();
    int sh = canvas.getHeight();
    int cx = sw / 2;
    int cy = sh / 2;
    g2d.drawLine( 0, cy, sw, cy );
    g2d.drawLine( cx, 0, cx, sh );

    String center = "Should Center: Center Baby's @";
    // to calculate the x, need the width...
    int stringWidth = g2d.getFontMetrics().stringWidth( center );
    float dy = g2d.getFontMetrics().getLineMetrics( center, g2d )
            .getBaselineOffsets()[ Font.CENTER_BASELINE ];
    g2d.drawString( center, cx - stringWidth / 2, cy - dy );

    // draw the pixel where we are drawing the text...
    g2d.setColor( Color.WHITE );
    g2d.fillRect( x - 1, y - 1, 3, 3 );
```

```
ArrayList<String> console = new ArrayList<String>();
console.add( "Baseline: " + tl.getBaseline() );
float[] baselineOffsets = tl.getBaselineOffsets();
console.add( "Baseline-Offset[ ROMAN ]: "
        + baselineOffsets[ Font.ROMAN_BASELINE ] );
console.add( "Baseline-Offset[ CENTER ]: "
        + baselineOffsets[ Font.CENTER_BASELINE ] );
console.add( "Baseline-Offset[ HANGING ]: "
        + baselineOffsets[ Font.HANGING_BASELINE ] );
console.add( "Ascent: " + tl.getAscent() );
console.add( "Descent: " + tl.getDescent() );
console.add( "Leading: " + tl.getLeading() );
console.add( "Advance: " + tl.getAdvance() );
console.add( "Visible-Advance: " + tl.getVisibleAdvance() );
console.add( "Bounds: " + toString( tl.getBounds() ) );

Font propFont = new Font( "Courier New", Font.BOLD, 14 );
g2d.setFont( propFont );

int xLeft = x;
int xRight = xLeft + (int)tl.getVisibleAdvance();

// draw baseline
g2d.setColor( Color.WHITE );
int baselineY = y + (int)baselineOffsets[ Font.ROMAN_BASELINE ];
g2d.drawLine( xLeft, baselineY, xRight, baselineY );
g2d.drawString( "roman baseline", xRight, baselineY );

// draw center
g2d.setColor( Color.BLUE );
int centerY = y + (int)baselineOffsets[ Font.CENTER_BASELINE ];
g2d.drawLine( xLeft, centerY, xRight, centerY );
g2d.drawString( "center baseline", xRight, centerY );

// draw hanging
g2d.setColor( Color.GRAY );
int hangingY = y + (int)baselineOffsets[ Font.HANGING_BASELINE ];
g2d.drawLine( xLeft, hangingY, xRight, hangingY );
g2d.drawString( "hanging baseline", xRight, hangingY );

// draw Ascent
g2d.setColor( Color.YELLOW );
int propY = y - (int)tl.getAscent();
g2d.drawLine( xLeft, propY, xRight, propY );
TextLayout temp = new TextLayout( "hanging baseline", propFont,
        g2d.getFontRenderContext() );
g2d.drawString( "Ascent", xRight + temp.getVisibleAdvance(), propY );
```

```java
        // draw Descent
        g2d.setColor( Color.RED );
        propY = y + (int)tl.getDescent();
        g2d.drawLine( xLeft, propY, xRight, propY );
        g2d.drawString( "Descent", xRight, propY );

        // draw Leading
        g2d.setColor( Color.GREEN );
        propY = y + (int)tl.getDescent() + (int)tl.getLeading();
        g2d.drawLine( xLeft, propY, xRight, propY );
        temp = new TextLayout(
            "Descent", propFont, g2d.getFontRenderContext() );
        g2d.drawString( "Leading", xRight + temp.getVisibleAdvance(), propY );

        // draw console output...
        g2d.setColor( Color.LIGHT_GRAY );
        g2d.setFont( new Font( "Courier New", Font.BOLD, 12 ) );
        Utility.drawString( g2d, 20, 300, console );
    }

    private String toString( Rectangle2D r ) {
        return "[ x=" + r.getX() + ", y=" + r.getY() + ", w=" + r.getWidth()
            + ", h=" + r.getHeight() + " ]";
    }

    public static void main( String[] args ) {
        launchApp( new TextMetricsExample() );
    }
}
```

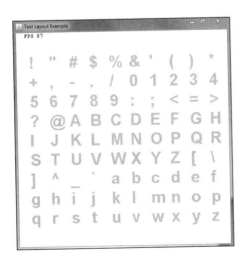

Figure 11.6
Text Layout Example.
© 2014 Timothy Wright.

The TextLayoutExample, as shown in Figure 11.6 and located in the javagames.text package, uses the font information to draw a retro-style high score input screen. The initialize() method is responsible for calculating the width of each letter to determine the maximum width. A problem arises because the graphics object is not yet available in the initialize() method. There are two ways to handle this problem. One way is to get the font metrics object from the JFrame class:

```
Font font = new Font(...);
FontMetrics fm = this.getFontMetrics(font);
```

The second way is to have the JFrame create a FontMetrics object by giving it a Font object. However, both of these solutions require access to a JFrame object. If the current class does not have access to a JFrame, another way to acquire the FontMetrics object needed for font calculations is to create an image and use its Graphics object.

```
BufferedImage img = new
    BufferedImage( 1, 1, BufferedImage.TYPE_INT_ARGB );
Graphics2D g = img.createGraphics();
FontMetrics fontMetrics = g.getFontMetrics( font );
g.dispose();
```

Although it takes some code to create a new image from scratch, it is an option if the JFrame class is not available.

```
package javagames.text;


import java.awt.*;
import java.awt.RenderingHints;
import java.awt.image.BufferedImage;

import javagames.util.SimpleFramework;


public class TextLayoutExample extends SimpleFramework {
    private Font font;
    private int maxWidth;

    public TextLayoutExample() {
        appWidth = 640;
        appHeight = 640;
        appSleep = 10L;
        appTitle = "Text Layout Example";
        appBackground = Color.WHITE;
        appFPSColor = Color.BLACK;
    }
```

```java
@Override
protected void initialize() {
   super.initialize();

   font = new Font( "Arial", Font.BOLD, 40 );
   FontMetrics fm = getFontMetrics( font );
   maxWidth = Integer.MIN_VALUE;
   for( int i = (int)'!'; i < (int)'z'; ++i ) {
      String letter = " " + (char)i;
      maxWidth = Math.max( maxWidth, fm.stringWidth( letter ) );
   }

   // another way
   BufferedImage img =
      new BufferedImage( 1, 1, BufferedImage.TYPE_INT_ARGB );
   Graphics2D g = img.createGraphics();
   FontMetrics fontMetrics = g.getFontMetrics( font );
   g.dispose();
}

@Override
protected void render( Graphics g ) {
   super.render( g );

   Graphics2D g2d = (Graphics2D)g;

   g2d.setRenderingHint( RenderingHints.KEY_ANTIALIASING,
         RenderingHints.VALUE_ANTIALIAS_ON );
   g2d.setColor( Color.GREEN );

   g2d.setFont( font );

   FontMetrics fm = g2d.getFontMetrics();
   int height = fm.getAscent() + fm.getDescent() + fm.getLeading();
   int x = 20;
   int y = 50;

   y += fm.getAscent();
   int count = 0;
   for( int i = (int)'!'; i <= (int)'z'; ++i ) {
      String letter = " " + (char)i;
      g2d.drawString( letter, x, y );
      x += maxWidth;
      count++;
      if( count % 10 == 0 ) {
         y += height;
         x = 20;
      }
   }
}
```

```
public static void main( String[] args ) {
    launchApp( new TextLayoutExample() );
}

}
```

Figure 11.7
Console Overlay Example.
© 2014 Timothy Wright.

The `ConsoleOverlayExample`, as shown in Figure 11.7 and located in the `javagames.text` package, combines text placement and transparency to create a text console that scrolls and hides itself. The `initialize()` method creates the `Font` and calculates the font height. The scrolling text is created in a `Vector` object. The first line of text is copied to the bottom for scrolling. The console is set to be the height of the text plus an extra line, but because the top line is copied, there are actually two extra lines.

The `processInput()` method is responsible for two things. First, it monitors the mouse and updates the transparency when the mouse is inside the bounds of the console. Second, it kicks off scrolling text whenever the spacebar is pressed, toggles the scrolling text boxes with the B key, and shows or hides the console with the H key.

The `updateObjects()` method is responsible for processing the console state. The console is first filled with a gray background, and then the text is drawn onto the background. The scrolling boxes are then drawn on top of the text, or the green rectangles are drawn showing the positions of the boxes.

The hidden value variable is a floating-point number from zero to one, where one is completely hidden, and zero is completely visible. Depending on whether the console is being shown or hidden, the hidden value is updated using the delta time value to slowly show or hide the console. If the hidden value is not yet zero percent, then a portion of each side of the console is cleared using the AlphaComposite object. This allows the console to become visible over any background.

Note

The AlphaComposite class and transparency are covered in Chapter 10, "Images." Review that chapter if any of the code in the ConsoleOverlayExample doesn't make sense.

The render() method creates the checkerboard background, sets the AlphaComposite, and overlays the text console on the background image.

```
package javagames.text;

import java.awt.*;
import java.awt.event.KeyEvent;
import java.awt.image.BufferedImage;
import java.util.Vector;

import javagames.util.*;


public class ConsoleOverlayExample extends SimpleFramework {

    private BufferedImage console;
    private int xConsole;
    private int yConsole;
    private float alpha;
    private Font consoleFont;
    private int fontHeight;
    private Vector<String> text;
    private float currY;
    private boolean boxes;
    private boolean hide;
    private float hidden;

    public ConsoleOverlayExample() {
        appWidth = 640;
        appHeight = 640;
        appSleep = 10L;
        appTitle = "Console Overlay Example";
    }

    @Override
    protected void initialize() {
        super.initialize();
```

```java
consoleFont = new Font( "Courier New", Font.BOLD, 20 );
FontMetrics fm = getFontMetrics( consoleFont );
fontHeight = fm.getAscent() + fm.getDescent() + fm.getLeading();

currY = 0;

text = new Vector<String>();
text.add( "Press the 'H' key to" );
text.add( "show and hide the console." );
text.add( "Hover the mouse over the" );
text.add( "text to change transparency." );
text.add( "Press Space Bar to move text." );
text.add( "Press 'B' to toggle hidden boxes." );

text.add( 0, text.lastElement() );

int consoleHeight = fontHeight * (text.size() + 1);

console = new BufferedImage(
    canvas.getWidth() - 40,
    consoleHeight,
    BufferedImage.TYPE_INT_ARGB
);
xConsole = 20;
yConsole = 50;

hide = false;
hidden = 1.0f;

}

@Override
protected void processInput( float delta ) {
    super.processInput( delta );

    Point pos = mouse.getPosition();
    int minX = xConsole;
    int minY = yConsole;
    int maxX = minX + console.getWidth();
    int maxY = minY + console.getHeight();

    if( pos.x > minX && pos.x < maxX &&
        pos.y > minY && pos.y < maxY ) {

        alpha = 1.0f;
    } else {
        alpha = 0.75f;
    }

    if( keyboard.keyDownOnce( KeyEvent.VK_SPACE ) ) {
        text.remove( 0 );
        text.add( text.get( 0 ) );
        currY = fontHeight;
```

```
        }
        if( keyboard.keyDownOnce( KeyEvent.VK_B ) ) {
            boxes = !boxes;
        }
        if( keyboard.keyDownOnce( KeyEvent.VK_H ) ) {
            hide = !hide;
        }
    }

    @Override
    protected void updateObjects( float delta ) {
        super.updateObjects( delta );

        if( hide && hidden == 1.0f ) {
            return; // don't bother
        }

        if( currY > 0 ) {
            currY -= delta* fontHeight;
        }

        Graphics2D g = console.createGraphics();
        g.setRenderingHint(
            RenderingHints.KEY_TEXT_ANTIALIASING,
            RenderingHints.VALUE_TEXT_ANTIALIAS_ON
        );

        g.setColor( Color.DARK_GRAY );
        g.fillRect( 0, 0, console.getWidth(), console.getHeight() );

        g.setColor( Color.LIGHT_GRAY );
        g.setFont( consoleFont );
        int x = 20;
        int y = (int)currY;
        Utility.drawString( g, x, y, text );

        if( boxes ) {
            g.setColor( Color.DARK_GRAY );
            g.fillRect( 0, 0, console.getWidth(), fontHeight );
            g.fillRect(
                0, fontHeight * text.size(), console.getWidth(), fontHeight );
        } else {
            g.setColor( Color.GREEN );
            g.drawRect( 0, 0, console.getWidth() - 1, fontHeight - 1 );
            g.drawRect(
                0, fontHeight * text.size(),
                console.getWidth() - 1, fontHeight - 1
            );
        }
```

```
        if( hide && hidden < 1.0f ) {
           hidden += delta ;
           if( hidden > 1.0f ) hidden = 1.0f;
        } else if( !hide && hidden > 0.0f ) {
           hidden -= delta;
           if( hidden <0.0f ) hidden = 0.0f;
        }

        if( hidden > 0.0f ) {
           g.setComposite(
              AlphaComposite.getInstance( AlphaComposite.CLEAR ) );
           // clear left
           int xHide = (int)(console.getWidth() * hidden * 0.5f);
           g.fillRect( 0, 0, xHide, console.getHeight() );
           // clear right
           g.fillRect(
              console.getWidth() - xHide, 0,
              console.getWidth(), console.getHeight()
           );
           // clear top
           int yHide = (int)(console.getHeight() * hidden * 0.5f);
           g.fillRect( 0, 0, console.getWidth(), yHide );
           // clear bottom
           g.fillRect(
              0, console.getHeight() - yHide,
              console.getWidth(), console.getHeight()
           );
        }
        g.dispose();
     }

     @Override
     protected void render( Graphics g ) {
        super.render( g );

        Graphics2D g2d = (Graphics2D)g;

        int dx = (canvas.getWidth()) / 8;
        int dy = (canvas.getHeight()) / 8;

        for( int i = 0; i < 8; ++i ) {
           for( int j = 0; j < 8; ++j ) {
              g2d.setColor( (i+j) % 2 == 0 ? Color.BLACK : Color.WHITE );
              g2d.fillRect( i*dx, j*dy, dx, dy );
           }
        }
```

```
    g2d.setComposite(
        AlphaComposite.getInstance( AlphaComposite.SRC_OVER, alpha ) );
    g2d.drawImage( console, xConsole, yConsole, null );
  }

  public static void main( String[] args ) {
    launchApp( new ConsoleOverlayExample() );
  }

}
```

ENABLING THREAD-SAFE KEYBOARD INPUT

At this point, it would be nice to type some text and have it be available. However, there are two problems with the KeyboardInput class that need to be fixed. The first is that the KeyListener interface doesn't do anything with typed key events. That is an easy problem to solve. What is not easy to solve is that the polling method of examining input can miss some keypresses if the frame rate is low enough.

For example, if the frame rate is polling only once every five seconds, repeated keypresses will be missed. You may have noticed in some of the previous examples when the frame rate drops low enough some keypresses are missed. This is not acceptable when typing text. If even a single key is missed, it will be obvious and frustrating to the user.

The solution is to capture all the events and iterate over them in the game loop so that no events are missed, regardless of the frame rate. The SafeKeyboardInput class contains an inner class Event and an EventType enum with the following types:

- EventType.PRESSED
- EventType.RELEASED
- EventType.TYPED

The EventType object is combined with the keyboard event object and saved into the Event class. The two lists of events, gameThread and eventThread, are used to capture and iterate over these keyboard events. Inside each of the key listener methods, the events are added to the event thread list. This ensures that no events are missed.

The poll() method is also simplified. The eventThread and gameThread lists are swapped, passing any events to the game loop and continuing to process events while the game loop handles the previous keyboard events. Because the event thread collection is used in the event thread and the game loop, all methods that access the eventThread collection are synchronized.

The processInput() method is called until all the events in the list have been processed and the method returns false. After each event is processed, the state of the keys are examined for keypresses.

There is one issue that arises using this method. If five keys are pressed between polling, then the next time the state is polled, there will be five events. If the first event is a pressed spacebar, then that key will be set as down once. Since there are no more spacebar events, the spacebar state will stay the same for all five events, appearing to have been down once five times. This is not the desired result. The keyDown and keyDownOnce methods are updated to check the current event key code so that extra events are not processed. Finally, the getKeyTyped() method is added to return typed keys that can be used to display typed text on the screen.

```java
package javagames.util;

import java.awt.event.KeyEvent;
import java.awt.event.KeyListener;
import java.util.LinkedList;

public class SafeKeyboardInput implements KeyListener {

    enum EventType {
        PRESSED,
        RELEASED,
        TYPED;
    }

    class Event {

        KeyEvent event;
        EventType type;

        public Event( KeyEvent event, EventType type ) {
            this.event = event;
            this.type = type;
        }

    }

    private LinkedList<Event> eventThread = new LinkedList<Event>();
    private LinkedList<Event> gameThread = new LinkedList<Event>();

    private Event event = null;
    private int[] polled;


    public SafeKeyboardInput() {
        polled = new int[ 256 ];
    }
```

```java
public boolean keyDown( int keyCode ) {
    return keyCode == event.event.getKeyCode() && polled[ keyCode ] > 0;
}

public boolean keyDownOnce( int keyCode ) {
    return keyCode == event.event.getKeyCode() && polled[ keyCode ] == 1;
}

public boolean processEvent() {
    event = gameThread.poll();
    if( event != null ) {
        int keyCode = event.event.getKeyCode();
        if( keyCode >= 0 && keyCode < polled.length ) {
            if( event.type == EventType.PRESSED ) {
                polled[keyCode]++;
            } else if( event.type == EventType.RELEASED ) {
                polled[keyCode] = 0;
            }
        }
    }
    return event != null;
}

public Character getKeyTyped() {
    if( event.type != EventType.TYPED ) {
        return null;
    } else {
        return event.event.getKeyChar();
    }
}

public synchronized void poll() {
    LinkedList<Event> swap = eventThread;
    eventThread = gameThread;
    gameThread = swap;
}

public synchronized void keyPressed( KeyEvent e ) {
    eventThread.add( new Event( e, EventType.PRESSED ) );
}

public synchronized void keyReleased( KeyEvent e ) {
    eventThread.add( new Event( e, EventType.RELEASED ) );
}

public synchronized void keyTyped( KeyEvent e ) {
    eventThread.add( new Event( e, EventType.TYPED ) );
}
}
```

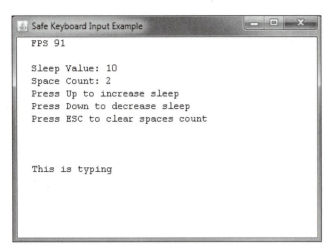

Figure 11.8
Safe Keyboard Input.
© 2014 Timothy Wright.

The SafeKeyboardInputExample, as shown in Figure 11.8 and located in the javagames. text package, uses the new input class to type text to the screen. To simplify testing, a new framework class, SafeKeyboardFramework, has been added to the javagames.util package using the new SafeKeyboardInput class. Because the new keyboard input processing is different, simply replacing the input class in the other framework would require refactoring all the previous examples.

The SafeKeyboardFramework framework is exactly the same as the SimpleFramework, replacing the keyboard input framework with the new class.

```
public class SafeKeyboardFramework extends JFrame implements Runnable {

    private BufferStrategy bs;
    private volatile boolean running;
    private Thread gameThread;

    protected FrameRate frameRate;
    protected Canvas canvas;
    protected RelativeMouseInput mouse;
    protected SafeKeyboardInput keyboard;

//... rest of the class
}
```

The processInput() method for any classes using the new framework needs to be updated to use the new method for handling input. Make sure you update any code using the new input handling by wrapping the event processing inside a while loop so that no events are missed.

```
@Override
    protected void processInput( float delta ) {
        super.processInput( delta );
        while( keyboard.processEvent() ) {
            if( keyboard.keyDownOnce( KeyEvent.VK_UP ) ) {
                appSleep += Math.min( appSleep * 2, 1000L );
            }
            if( keyboard.keyDownOnce( KeyEvent.VK_DOWN ) ) {
                appSleep -= Math.min( appSleep / 2, 1000L );
            }
            if( keyboard.keyDownOnce( KeyEvent.VK_ESCAPE ) ) {
                spacesCount = 0;
            }
            if( keyboard.keyDownOnce( KeyEvent.VK_SPACE ) ) {
                spacesCount++;
            }
            processTypedChar();
        }
    }
```

The up and down arrows adjust the frame rate to test that keypresses are not missed. The number of spacebar presses is counted, and the Escape key resets the spacebar count. The processTypedChar() method handles the typed keys. Because all typed characters are processed in this method, including keys that do not need to be displayed, such as Backspace and Enter, it is necessary to handle them. The addCharater() and removeCharacter() methods are responsible for updating the text that is typed to the screen. The updateObject() method is responsible for controlling the blinking cursor at the end of the text. Notice, at the end of the processTypedChar() method, that the cursor blinking is reset. This keeps the cursor from blinking while text is being typed.

```
drawCursor = true;
blink = 0.0f;
```

The render() method draws the usual directions, along with a count of the spacebar presses. This count can be used to verify that no keyboard presses are missed. The typed text is drawn below the instructions using the Utility class. Finally, the blinking cursor is drawn.

```
package javagames.text;

import java.awt.*;
import java.awt.event.KeyEvent;
import java.util.ArrayList;
```

```java
import javagames.util.*;


public class SafeKeyboardInputExample extends SafeKeyboardFramework {

    private int spacesCount;
    private float blink;
    private boolean drawCursor;

    private ArrayList<String> strings = new ArrayList<String>();

    public SafeKeyboardInputExample() {
        appSleep = 10L;
        appTitle = "Safe Keyboard Input Example";

        strings.add( "" );
    }

    @Override
    protected void processInput( float delta ) {
        super.processInput( delta );

        while( keyboard.processEvent() ) {

            if( keyboard.keyDownOnce( KeyEvent.VK_UP ) ) {
                appSleep += Math.min( appSleep * 2, 1000L );
            }
            if( keyboard.keyDownOnce( KeyEvent.VK_DOWN ) ) {
                appSleep -= Math.min( appSleep / 2, 1000L );
            }
            if( keyboard.keyDownOnce( KeyEvent.VK_ESCAPE ) ) {
                spacesCount = 0;
            }
            if( keyboard.keyDownOnce( KeyEvent.VK_SPACE ) ) {
                spacesCount++;
            }

            processTypedChar();
        }

    }

    private void processTypedChar() {

        Character typedChar = keyboard.getKeyTyped();
        if( typedChar != null ) {
            if( Character.isISOControl( typedChar ) ) {
                if( KeyEvent.VK_BACK_SPACE == typedChar ) {
                    removeCharacter();
                }
```

```
               if( KeyEvent.VK_ENTER == typedChar ) {
                  strings.add( "" );
               }
         } else {
            addCharacter( typedChar );
         }

         drawCursor = true;
         blink = 0.0f;
      }
   }
}

private void addCharacter( Character c ) {
   strings.add( strings.remove( strings.size() - 1 ) + c );
}

private void removeCharacter() {
   String line = strings.remove( strings.size() - 1 );
   if( !line.isEmpty() ) {
      strings.add( line.substring( 0, line.length() - 1 ) );
   }

   if( strings.isEmpty() ) {
      strings.add( "" );
   }
}

@Override
protected void updateObjects( float delta ) {
   super.updateObjects( delta );

   blink += delta;
   if( blink > 0.5f ) {
      blink -= 0.5f;
      drawCursor = !drawCursor;
   }
}

@Override
protected void render( Graphics g ) {
   super.render( g );

   textPos = Utility.drawString( g, 20, textPos,
         "",
         "Sleep Value: " + appSleep,
         "Space Count: " + spacesCount,
         "Press Up to increase sleep",
         "Press Down to decrease sleep",
```

```
                        "Press ESC to clear spaces count",
                        "",
                        "",
                        ""
            );

            textPos = Utility.drawString( g, 20, textPos, strings );

            if( drawCursor ) {
                FontMetrics fm = g.getFontMetrics();
                int height = fm.getAscent() + fm.getDescent() + fm.getLeading();
                int y = textPos - height;
                int x = 20 + fm.stringWidth( strings.get( strings.size() - 1 ) );
                g.drawString( "_", x, y + fm.getAscent() );
            }
        }

        public static void main( String[] args ) {
            launchApp( new SafeKeyboardInputExample() );
        }
    }
```

RESOURCES AND FURTHER READING

"Working with Text APIs," 1995, http://docs.oracle.com/javase/tutorial/2d/text/index.html.

"Fonts and Text Layout," 2011, http://docs.oracle.com/javase/6/docs/technotes/guides/2d/spec/j2d-fonts.html#wp73059.

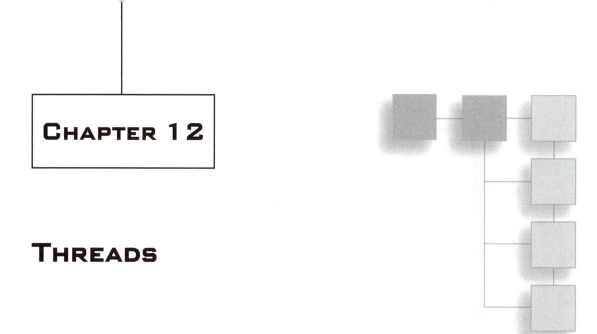

CHAPTER 12

THREADS

Threads can add complexity to software. They are very complicated and easy to get wrong. Bugs, deadlocks, and race conditions can be difficult to find, and the simple act of logging or stepping through the code can change the timing enough so the bugs no longer happen. It has been said that threads can solve any problem except too many threads. Although I would prefer to never need them, because they are so complex, there are some situations where threads are the best solution.

Tip

Deadlocks can occur when two parts of the program are waiting for the other to finish. For example, if thread A is waiting for thread B to finish a task, but thread B is waiting for thread A to finish a task, both threads will wait forever.

A *race* condition occurs when two threads are both updating a resource at the same time. If that resource is not protected so that only one thread can have access at a time, both threads will try to update the variable simultaneously. These two threads are *racing* to update the data, and depending on which one gets there first, the results can produce bugs that are very hard to find.

There is no way to teach everything you need to understand threads in a single chapter. Entire books exist on the subject and some of these don't even cover everything. So, if you have never done any thread programming, check out the resources at the end of the chapter.

Since the very first chapter, you have been using threads to create a custom game loop that runs apart from Swing's event dispatch thread. However, there are many more classes available in the language, which makes multithreaded programming easier.

Using the Callable Task with Threads

There exists an `ExecutorService` interface that can process `Callable` tasks and return `Future` objects. Two really cool features that make `Callable` objects different from `Runnable` objects are that `Callable` objects can return a result, and they can capture and rethrow exceptions inside other threads. This is possible by using a `Future` object. The `Callable` interface is as follows:

```
public interface Callable<V> {
    V call() throws Exception;
}
```

The `ExecutorService` contains a submit method, which executes a `Callable` task and returns a `Future` object.

```
public interface ExecutorService extends Executor {
    <T> Future<T> submit( Callable<T> task );
}
```

The `Future` object returned from the executor has a `get()` method that will block until the `Callable` task has finished. It will return the result that was returned from the `Callable` method. If the `call()` method threw an exception, that exception will be rethrown so the software can handle the error in the current thread.

The `CallableTaskExample`, located in the `javagames.threads` package, is a simple program to demonstrate using the `ExecutorService` to execute `Callable` tasks. It also demonstrates using the `Future` objects to get the results and exceptions from the tasks. The `CallalbleTaskExample` implements the `Callable<Boolean>` interface. Notice that the `call()` method returns a `Boolean` result. The task sleeps for a few milliseconds, returns `true` or `false`, and even throws an exception when the random sleep time is zero. The `main()` method uses the `Executors` class to create a new cached thread pool:

```
ExecutorService exec = Executors.newCachedThreadPool();
```

The cached thread pool creates a new thread for each task, but keeps those threads around for a little while before destroying them. If other tasks are submitted, the cached threads are reused. Notice how the `get()` method from the `Future` object will not return until the `Callable` task is finished; it rethrows any exceptions thrown by the `Callable` task.

The thread pool is shut down with the `shutdown()` method. It uses the `awaitTermination()` method to block until all the threads in the thread pool have finished.

```java
package javagames.threads;

import java.util.Random;
import java.util.concurrent.*;


public class CallableTaskExample implements Callable<Boolean> {
    @Override
    public Boolean call() throws Exception {
        // simulate some stupid long task and maybe fail...
        Random rand = new Random();
        int seconds = rand.nextInt( 6 );
        if( seconds == 0 ) {
            // pretend there was an error
            throw new RuntimeException( "I love the new thread stuff!!! :)" );
        }

        try {
            Thread.sleep( seconds * 100 );
        } catch( InterruptedException e ) { }

        // even = true, odd = false
        return seconds % 2 == 0;
    }

    public static void main( String[] args ) {

        ExecutorService exec = Executors.newCachedThreadPool();
        try {
            for( int i = 0; i < 50; ++i ) {
                try {
                    Future<Boolean> result =
                        exec.submit( new CallableTaskExample() );
                    Boolean success = result.get();
                    System.out.println( "Result: " + success );
                } catch( ExecutionException ex ) {
                    Throwable throwable = ex.getCause();
                    System.out.println( "Error: " + throwable.getMessage() );
                } catch( InterruptedException e ) {
                    System.out.println( "Awesome! Thread was canceled" );
                    e.printStackTrace();
                }
            }
        } finally {
            try {
                exec.shutdown();
                exec.awaitTermination( 10, TimeUnit.SECONDS );
```

```
                    System.out.println( "Threadpool Shutdown :)" );
                } catch( InterruptedException e ) {
                    // at this point, just give up...
                    e.printStackTrace();
                    System.exit( -1 );
                }
            }
        }
    }
}
```

Using Threads to Load Files

The FileLoadingExample, as shown in Figure 12.1 and located in the javagames.threads package, uses the Callable, Future, and ExecutorService objects to simulate loading a bunch of files. There are three different thread pools that can be used to simulate loading the 100 files. One is a single threaded executor, another has a maximum of 32 threads, and the last is an unlimited cached thread pool.

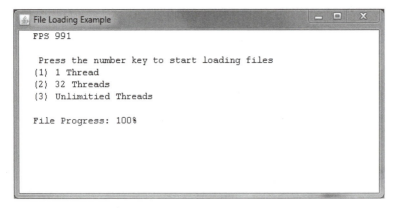

Figure 12.1
File Loading Example.
© 2014 Timothy Wright.

The initialize() method creates all three thread pools and creates 100 callable tasks that simulate loading 100 files. The processInput() method submits each task to the different thread pools. If you press 1, the single threaded pool is used. The 2 key uses the thread pool with a maximum of 32 threads. The 3 key uses the unlimited cached thread pool.

The updateObject() method loops through the list of Future tasks and removes any completed tasks. The render() method displays the usual directions and the percentage of tasks complete. The terminate() method shuts down each thread pool before the application shuts down.

Although threads can make some tasks more complicated, this is an example of a task that is suited for threads.

```java
package javagames.threads;

import java.awt.Graphics;
import java.awt.event.KeyEvent;
import java.util.*;
import java.util.concurrent.*;

import javagames.util.*;


public class FileLoadingExample extends SimpleFramework {

    private static final int NUMBER_OF_FILES = 100;

    private ExecutorService singleThread;
    private ExecutorService thirtyTwoThreads;
    private ExecutorService unlimitedThreads;

    private boolean loading = false;
    private List<Callable<Boolean>> fileTasks;
    private List<Future<Boolean>> fileResults;

    public FileLoadingExample() {
        appWidth = 640;
        appHeight = 640;
        appSleep = 1L;
        appTitle = "File Loading Example";
        appBackground = Color.WHITE;
        appFPSColor = Color.BLACK;
    }

    @Override
    protected void initialize() {
        super.initialize();

        singleThread = Executors.newSingleThreadExecutor();
        thirtyTwoThreads = Executors.newFixedThreadPool( 32 );
        unlimitedThreads = Executors.newCachedThreadPool();

        fileTasks = new ArrayList<Callable<Boolean>>();
        for( int i = 0; i < NUMBER_OF_FILES; ++i ) {
            final int taskNumber = i;
            fileTasks.add( new Callable<Boolean>() {
                @Override
                public Boolean call() throws Exception {
                    try {
                        // pretend to load a file
```

```
                            // just sleep a little
                            Thread.sleep( new Random().nextInt(750) );
                            System.out.println( "Task: " + taskNumber );
                        } catch( InterruptedException ex ) { }
                        return Boolean.TRUE;
                    }
                });
        }
        fileResults = new ArrayList<Future<Boolean>>();
    }

    @Override
    protected void processInput( float delta ) {
        super.processInput( delta );

        if( keyboard.keyDownOnce( KeyEvent.VK_1 ) ) {
            if( !loading ) {
                for( Callable<Boolean> task : fileTasks ) {
                    fileResults.add( singleThread.submit( task ) );
                }
            }
        }
        if( keyboard.keyDownOnce( KeyEvent.VK_2 ) ) {
            if( !loading ) {
                for( Callable<Boolean> task : fileTasks ) {
                    fileResults.add( thirtyTwoThreads.submit( task ) );
                }
            }
        }
        if( keyboard.keyDownOnce( KeyEvent.VK_3 ) ) {
            if( !loading ) {
                for( Callable<Boolean> task : fileTasks ) {
                    fileResults.add( unlimitedThreads.submit( task ) );
                }
            }
        }
    }

    @Override
    protected void updateObjects( float delta ) {
        super.updateObjects( delta );
        Iterator<Future<Boolean>> it = fileResults.iterator();
        while( it.hasNext() ) {
            Future<Boolean> next = it.next();
            if( next.isDone() ) {
```

```
        try {
            if( next.get() ) {
                it.remove();
            }
        } catch( ExecutionException ex ) {
            ex.printStackTrace();
        } catch( InterruptedException ex ) {
            ex.printStackTrace();
        }
    }
}
loading = !fileResults.isEmpty();
}

@Override
protected void render( Graphics g ) {
    super.render( g );

    textPos = Utility.drawString( g, 20, textPos,
        "",
        " Press the number key to start loading files",
        "(1) 1 Thread",
        "(2) 32 Threads",
        "(3) Unlimitied Threads",
        ""
    );

    double percentComplete =
        (NUMBER_OF_FILES - fileResults.size()) / (double)NUMBER_OF_FILES;
    String fileProgress =
        String.format( "File Progress: %.0f%%", 100.0 * percentComplete );
    textPos = Utility.drawString( g, 20, textPos, fileProgress );
}

@Override
protected void terminate() {
    super.terminate();
    shutdownExecutor( singleThread );
    shutdownExecutor( thirtyTwoThreads );
    shutdownExecutor( unlimitedThreads );
}

private void shutdownExecutor( ExecutorService exec ) {
    try {
        exec.shutdown();
        exec.awaitTermination( 10, TimeUnit.SECONDS );
        System.out.println( "Executor Shutdown!!!" );
```

```
        } catch( InterruptedException e ) { }
    }
    public static void main( String[] args ) {
        launchApp( new FileLoadingExample() );
    }
}
```

USING THE FAKEHARDWARE CLASS FOR TESTING

Next, you are going to create a FakeHardware class, located in the javagames.threads
package, to pretend to use some hardware. Do not be confused by the name. Any
task that takes a long time to complete—such as really long file loading, complicated
artificial intelligence calculations, or network communication—can benefit from this
kind of non-blocking class design. In the next chapter, this same idea is needed to
make the sound classes work, so hang in there. If these examples do not make sense,
there are many more in the next chapter.

The FakeHardware class is a non-blocking class. Each of the following methods returns
immediately, performing the task later in another thread:

- turnOn()
- turnoff()
- start()
- stop()

The FakeHardwareListener callback is used to notify interested objects when the
non-blocking methods have completed.

```
package javagames.threads;

import javagames.threads.FakeHardware.FakeHardwareEvent;

public interface FakeHardwareListener {

    public void event( FakeHardware source, FakeHardwareEvent event );

}
```

The FakeHardwareEvent is an enum with four events:

```
public enum FakeHardwareEvent {
    START,
    STOP,
    ON,
    OFF;
}
```

The FakeHardware class contains listeners created with the Collections.synchronized List() method. The listener list is thread-safe for adding and removing items. As long as the list iteration is protected in a synchronized block, it is also safe for use in multiple threads.

The fireEvent() method notifies all the listeners of completed events:

```java
private void fireEvent( FakeHardwareEvent event ) {
    synchronized( listeners ) {
        for( FakeHardwareListener listener : listeners ) {
            listener.event( this, event );
        }
    }
}
```

There is a problem with the setStart() method. Once the event is sent, it calls the runTask() method. This method cannot be completely synchronized, or none of the other synchronized blocks could be called while the task is running. However, because of the way the method is coded, it isn't thread-safe. If the hardware is stopped after the synchronized block but before the next Boolean check, the task will never run and the STOP event will never be sent. This is intentional, and simulates a similar bug with the sound class in the next chapter. Instead of fixing the code, you have to use the class in a thread-safe way even when the class is not thread-safe.

Notice how all of the non-blocking methods spawn a new thread to complete the task and then return immediately. The task actually happens in another thread and then fires the listeners to notify observers that the task has finished.

```java
package javagames.threads;

import java.util.*;


/*
 * This will simulate some fake hardware.
 */
public class FakeHardware {

    private static final int SLEEP_MIN = 100;
    private static final int SLEEP_MAX = 500;

    public enum FakeHardwareEvent {
        START,
        STOP,
        ON,
        OFF;
    }
```

```java
    private volatile boolean on = false;
    private volatile boolean running = false;
    private String name;

    private List<FakeHardwareListener> listeners =
        Collections.synchronizedList( new ArrayList<FakeHardwareListener>() );

    public FakeHardware( String name ) {
        this.name = name;
    }

    public boolean addListener( FakeHardwareListener listener ) {
        return listeners.add( listener );
    }

    public boolean isOn() {
        return on;
    }

    public boolean isRunning() {
        return running;
    }

    private void sleep() {
        int rand = new Random().nextInt( SLEEP_MAX - SLEEP_MIN + 1 );
        sleep( rand + SLEEP_MIN );
    }

    private void sleep( int ms ) {
        try {
            Thread.sleep( ms );
        } catch( InterruptedException ex ) { }
    }

    public void turnOn() {
        new Thread( new Runnable() {
            public void run() {
                sleep();
                setOn();
            }
        }).start();
    }

    public void turnOff() {
        new Thread( new Runnable() {
            public void run() {
                sleep();
                setOff();
            }
        }).start();
    }
```

```java
public void start( final int timeMS, final int slices ) {
    new Thread( new Runnable() {
        public void run() {
            sleep();
            setStart( timeMS, slices);
        }
    }).start();
}
public void stop() {
    new Thread( new Runnable() {
        public void run() {
            sleep();
            setStop();
        }
    }).start();
}
private synchronized void setOn() {
    if( !on ) {
        on = true;
        fireEvent( FakeHardwareEvent.ON );
    }
}
private synchronized void setOff() {
    if( on ) {
        setStop();
        on = false;
        fireEvent( FakeHardwareEvent.OFF );
    }
}

/*
 * There is a problem with this method.
 * If the lock running is set to false after the lock
 * is released but before the next if statement,
 * the task will never run...
 *
 * Let's pretend this Hardware driver doesn't work well,
 * even though that NEVER happens :)
 */
private void setStart( int timeMS, int slices ) {
    synchronized( this ) {
        if( on && !running ) {
```

```
                running = true;
                fireEvent( FakeHardwareEvent.START );
            }
        }
        if( running ) {
            runTask( timeMS, slices );
            running = false;
            fireEvent( FakeHardwareEvent.STOP );
        }
    }

    private synchronized void setStop() {
        if( running ) {
            running = false;
            // don't send the event
            // not actually done yet :)
        }
    }

    private void runTask( int timeMS, int slices ) {
        int sleep = timeMS / slices;
        for( int i = 0; i < slices; ++i ) {
            if( !running ) {
                return;
            }
            System.out.println( name + "[" + (i+1) + "/" + slices + "]" );
            sleep( sleep );
        }
    }

    private void fireEvent( FakeHardwareEvent event ) {
        synchronized( listeners ) {
            for( FakeHardwareListener listener : listeners ) {
                listener.event( this, event );
            }
        }
    }
}
```

USING THE WAIT/NOTIFY METHODS

The FakeHardware class is a great example of creating a non-blocking class using threads and callback listeners to notify event completion. But sometimes it is necessary to create a blocking version of a non-blocking class. The wait() and notify() methods work perfectly for this situation.

Every object has a wait() method which, as long as a synchronized lock is held on that object, will block until it is notified to wake up.

```
synchronized( object ) {
    while( conditionNotTrue() ) {
        object.wait();
    }
}
```

The wait() method will block until another thread obtains the object lock and notifies all threads waiting on that object. It is necessary to use a while loop to check the condition, because the wait() method may, under certain circumstances, wake up from the wait() method without any classes waking up the waiting threads. Just because the wait() method returned, that doesn't mean that the condition is guaranteed to be true. To wake up waiting threads, the notifyAll() method is used:

```
synchronized( object) {
    object.notifyAll();
}
```

This all works because when the wait() method is called, the lock is released, only then allowing other interested classes to obtain the lock. By requesting a non-blocking class to perform some action and waiting until the callback has been fired, it is possible to wrap a non-blocking class with a blocking version. The WaitNotifyExample, located in the javagames.threads package, is a simple program that uses the FakeHardware class, combined with the wait() and notifyAll() methods, to block until each operation is complete.

```
package javagames.threads;

import javagames.threads.FakeHardware.FakeHardwareEvent;


public class WaitNotifyExample implements FakeHardwareListener {

    public WaitNotifyExample() {

    }

    public void runTest() throws Exception {
        FakeHardware hardware = new FakeHardware( "name" );
        hardware.addListener( this );

        synchronized( this ) {
            hardware.turnOn();
```

```
            while( !hardware.isOn() ) {
                wait();
            }
        }

        System.out.println( "Hardware is on!" );

        synchronized( this ) {
            hardware.start( 1000, 4 );
            while( !hardware.isRunning() ) {
                wait();
            }
        }

        System.out.println( "Hardware is running" );

        synchronized( this ) {
            while( hardware.isRunning() ) {
                wait();
            }
        }

        System.out.println( "Hardware has stopped!" );

        synchronized( this ) {
            hardware.turnOff();
            while( hardware.isOn() ) {
                wait();
            }
        }
    }

    @Override
    public synchronized void event(
        FakeHardware source, FakeHardwareEvent event ) {
        System.out.println( "Got Event: " + event );
        notifyAll();
    }

    public static void main( String[] args ) throws Exception {
        new WaitNotifyExample().runTest();
    }

}
```

USING THREADS IN THE GAME LOOP

The BlockingHardware class, located in the javagames.threads package, is a class that wraps the FakeHardware class with a blocking version. However, instead of using the wait/notify methods, it uses the Lock and Condition classes, which are part of the concurrency library. It is good to learn about these classes, because they provide some functionality not available with the wait/notify methods. Notice that the lock object provides the condition object used for notification. The objects are created as follows:

```
Lock lock = new ReentrantLock();
Condition cond = lock.newCondition();
```

To wait for an object, you call the condition await() method. The Lock class has both lock() and unlock() methods that are used to acquire and release the lock. A try/finally block is used to ensure that the lock is always released.

```
lock.lock();
try {
    while( conditionNotTure() ) {
        cond.await();
    }
} finally {
    lock.unlock();
}
```

To notify waiting threads, use the signalAll() method:

```
lock.lock();
try {
    cond.signalAll();
} finally {
    lock.unlock();
}
```

At this point, you might be wondering why anyone would use these classes instead of the simpler wait/notify methods available to all objects. The reason is that the Lock /Condition objects have many methods that allow for greater flexibility. For example, the wait/notify pattern uses a synchronized block.

```
synchronized( object ) {
    // do stuff here
}
```

That code will block until the lock is acquired, even if it waits forever. However, the Lock object has other methods that can be used to acquire a lock, as follows:

- tryLock()—This method will try to acquire the lock and return true if it is acquired. It will not block, however; returning false if the lock was not acquired.

- tryLock(long, TimeUnit)—This method can take a timeout value, and gives up trying to acquire the lock after a set amount of time.

- `lockInterruptibly()`—The `synchronized` block in the `wait/notify` method does not respond to thread interruption. This method blocks until the lock is acquired, but will return with an exception if the `Lock` object is interrupted.

In addition, the `Condition` object has timeout values available for the `await()` methods as well as this method:

- `awaitUninterruptibly()`—This method will wait for notification and not respond to thread interruption.

Another feature is multiple lock types. `ReentrantLock` can be created with a fairness policy so the lock acquisition is granted to the thread that has been waiting the longest. There is also a `ReadWriteLock` that maintains two different locks so that while only one thread can write to the object at a time, many threads can read.

The `BlockingHardwareListener` interface, located in the `javagames.threads` package, is used for event notification when the hardware task is finished.

```
package javagames.threads;


public interface BlockingHardwareListener {
    public void taskFinished();

}
```

The `BlockingHardware` class maintains a list of listeners and notifies the listeners when the hardware task is complete. The `BlockingHardware` also maintains its own state variables in case the `FakeHardware` class state doesn't match reality.

The `turnOn()`, `turnoff()`, `start()`, and `stop()` methods all block using the `Lock/Condition` objects. This makes the `FakeHardware` class easier to use in a single threaded loop, like a game loop, and keeps the chance of race conditions and deadlock bugs to a minimum.

```
package javagames.threads;
import java.util.*;
import java.util.concurrent.locks.*;

import javagames.threads.FakeHardware.FakeHardwareEvent;


public class BlockingHardware {
    private final Lock lock = new ReentrantLock();
    private final Condition cond = lock.newCondition();
```

```java
private volatile boolean on = false;
private volatile boolean started = false;

private FakeHardware hardware;

private List<BlockingHardwareListener> listeners =
    Collections.synchronizedList(
        new ArrayList<BlockingHardwareListener>() );
public BlockingHardware( String name ) {
    hardware = new FakeHardware( name );
    hardware.addListener( new FakeHardwareListener() {
        @Override
        public void event( FakeHardware source, FakeHardwareEvent event ) {
            handleHardwareEvent( source, event );
        }
    });
}
public boolean addListener( BlockingHardwareListener listener ) {
    return listeners.add( listener );
}
public void start( int ms, int slices ) {
    lock.lock();
    try {
        hardware.start( ms, slices );
        while( !started ) {
            cond.await();
        }
        System.out.println( "It's Started" );
    } catch( InterruptedException e ) {
        e.printStackTrace();
    } finally {
        lock.unlock();
    }

}
public void stop() {
    lock.lock();
    try {
        hardware.stop();
        while( started ) {
            cond.await();
        }
    } catch( InterruptedException ex ) {
        ex.printStackTrace();
```

```
         } finally {
            lock.unlock();
         }
      }

   public void turnOn() {
      lock.lock();
      try {
         hardware.turnOn();
         while( !on ) {
            cond.await();
         }
         System.out.println( "Turned on" );
      } catch( InterruptedException ex ) {
         ex.printStackTrace();
      } finally {
         lock.unlock();
      }
   }

   public void turnOff() {
      lock.lock();
      try {
         hardware.turnOff();
         while( on ) {
            cond.await();
         }
         System.out.println( "Turned off" );
      } catch( InterruptedException ex ) {
         ex.printStackTrace();
      } finally {
         lock.unlock();
      }
   }

   protected void handleHardwareEvent(
      FakeHardware source, FakeHardwareEvent event ) {

      boolean wasStarted = started;
      lock.lock();
      try {
         if( event == FakeHardwareEvent.ON ) {
            on = true;
         } else if( event == FakeHardwareEvent.OFF ) {
            on = false;
         } else if( event == FakeHardwareEvent.START ) {
```

```
            started = true;
        } else if( event == FakeHardwareEvent.STOP ) {
            started = false;
        }
        cond.signalAll();
    } finally {
        lock.unlock();
    }

    if( wasStarted && !started ) {
        fireTaskFinished();
    }
}

private void fireTaskFinished() {
    synchronized( listeners ) {
        for( BlockingHardwareListener listener : listeners ) {
            listener.taskFinished();
        }
    }
}
}


}
```

You have looked at creating a class that has non-blocking methods that notify listeners on completion, and you have looked at using the wait/notify mechanism to wrap a non-blocking class with a blocking version. But while this blocking class waits until the code has finished, the methods can take half a second. This class can't be used in the main game loop because it takes too long. This idea can be applied to any code that takes a long time to run. For example, maybe the AI component needs seconds to compute the next move, or the army of wizards needs time to calculate a strategy. Whatever the code is doing, these long tasks cannot be called on the main game loop without a serious pause in the game. A simple way to get the long task into another thread, but still keep the code easy to use in the game loop, is to use a BlockingQueue.

A BlockingQueue is a thread-safe class providing methods to get items from the queue and put items into the queue. Although there are many different types, with many different features, all you need is a simple LinkedBlockingQueue that stores the items as a linked list. The two important methods for the queue are:

- void BlockingQueue<E>.put(E e)
- E BlockingQueue<E>.get()

These two methods allow the BlockingQueue to pass messages between threads. Items passed to the put() method are added to the queue, and as long as the queue size has not been reached, the method returns immediately. It does not wait for some other thread to take the value. The get() method will block until there is something available. It is easy to imagine how this code uses the same wait/notify method to wait for something to be placed into the queue before the method returns.

There is another interesting aspect to using the queue to pass messages. The BlockingQueue example uses the following messages:

```
enum Message {
    MESSAGE_ONE,
    MESSAGE_TWO,
    MESSAGE_THREE,
    POISON_PILL; // Quit :)
}
```

Because the get() method will block until there is a message waiting, one way to shut down the thread is to pass a special POISON_PILL message that the consumer recognizes as the queue (pun intended) to shut down the thread.

The BlockingQueueExample creates a Producer and Consumer, which both implement a Callable interface. Notice that the Producer uses a Void object for the return type.

```
class Producer implements Callable<Void> {

    public Void call() throws Exception {
        return null;
    }
}
```

The Void type is used for callable objects that do not return anything. This way, the Future.get() can still be called to wait for the callable to finish and throw an exception if there is a problem.

The runTest() method creates both the Producer and Consumer tasks and submits them to the thread pool. The method then calls the get() method of the consumer, which doesn't return until the Producer has finished, sends the POISION_PILL message, and shuts down the thread. It finally stops the thread pool and returns.

The Producer is given a message count and a sleep time. It randomly generates messages (not including the POISION_PILL) and sends the messages until the given count has been reached, sleeping between each message. Once it is finished, it puts the POISION_PILL message into the queue and exits.

```java
package javagames.threads;

import java.util.Random;
import java.util.concurrent.*;


public class BlockingQueueExample {

    class Producer implements Callable<Void> {

        private Random rand = new Random();
        private int numberOfMessages;
        private int sleep;

        private Producer( int numberOfMessages, int sleep ) {
            this.numberOfMessages = numberOfMessages;
            this.sleep = sleep;
        }

        @Override
        public Void call() throws Exception {
            Message[] messages = Message.values();
            for( int i = 0; i < numberOfMessages; ++i ) {
                try {
                    // don't include last message (POISON)
                    int index = rand.nextInt( messages.length - 2 ); // 0 - 2

                    queue.put( messages[ index ] );
                    System.out.println(
                        "PUT(" + (i+1) + ") " + messages[ index ]
                    );
                    sleep( sleep );
                } catch( InterruptedException ex ) { }
            }
            // All done. Shut her down...
            queue.put( messages[ messages.length - 1 ] );
            return null;
        }

    }

    class Consumer implements Callable<Integer> {

        private int messageCount = 0;

        @Override
        public Integer call() throws Exception {
            while( true ) {
                // take will block forever unless we do something
                Message msg = queue.take();
```

```
                messageCount++;
                System.out.println( "Received: " + msg );
                if( msg == Message.POISON_PILL ) {
                    break;
                }
            }
            return new Integer( messageCount );
        }

    }

    enum Message {
        MESSAGE_ONE,
        MESSAGE_TWO,
        MESSAGE_THREE,
        POISON_PILL; // Quit :)
    }

    private ExecutorService exec;
    private BlockingQueue<Message> queue;

    public BlockingQueueExample() {
        exec = Executors.newCachedThreadPool();
        queue = new LinkedBlockingQueue<BlockingQueueExample.Message>();
    }

    public void runTest() {

        int numberOfMessages = 100;
        int sleep = 100;

        System.out.println( "Messages Sent: " + numberOfMessages );

        exec.submit( new Producer( numberOfMessages, sleep ) );
        // sleep a little
        sleep( 2000 ); // two seconds..

        try {
            // Start the consumer much later, but that's ok!
            Future<Integer> consumer = exec.submit( new Consumer() );
            try {
                System.out.println( "Messages Processed: " + consumer.get() );
            } catch( ExecutionException ex ) {
            } catch( InterruptedException ex ) { }
        } finally {
            try {
                exec.shutdown();
                exec.awaitTermination( 10, TimeUnit.SECONDS );
```

```
            System.out.println( "Threadpool Shutdown :)" );
        } catch( InterruptedException e ) {
            // at this point, just give up...
            e.printStackTrace();
            System.exit( -1 );
        }
    }
}

protected void sleep( int ms ) {
    try {
        Thread.sleep( ms );
    } catch( InterruptedException ex ) { }
}

public static void main( String[] args ) {
    new BlockingQueueExample().runTest();
}
```
}

USING A STATE MACHINE

One way to use the new BlockingHardware class in a game loop is with a state machine. This state machine idea will also be used in Chapter 13, "Sound," so if it doesn't make sense, there are more examples coming. A state machine is a simple way to perform certain actions based on received events. A classic state machine example is a door, with open, closed, and locked states. The unlocked state is the same as closed, so it is excluded. Events could be (for example) a key event and a hand event. If a hand event is used on a closed door, it would transition to open. A hand event on an open door would close it. A key event on a closed door would lock it. A key event on a locked door would return it to the closed state. A hand event on a locked door or a key event on an open door would do nothing. See Figure 12.2.

	Hand	Key
Open(0)	(1)	X
Closed(1)	(0)	(2)
Locked(2)	X	(1)

Figure 12.2
Door State Machine.
© 2014 Timothy Wright.

A first attempt at modeling a state machine for the FakeHardware class might look something like Figure 12.3.

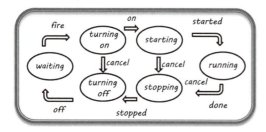

Figure 12.3
Complicated State.
© 2014 Timothy Wright.

But this is not only complicated, it seems backward. On and Off should be states, not events. But if you try to model the state machine after the events sent to the FakeHardwareListener, it can become really complicated. Since you have wrapped the FakeHardware with the BlockingHardware class, the transitions can perform tasks in order, such as turning the hardware on and starting the task, as shown in Figure 12.4.

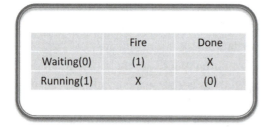

	Fire	Done
Waiting(0)	(1)	X
Running(1)	X	(0)

Figure 12.4
Simple State.
© 2014 Timothy Wright.

If the state is waiting and a fire event is received, the task starts running. When the task is done, either because it has completed or was canceled, the state returns to waiting. If this seems unclear, an example should help.

THE ONESHOTEVENT CLASS

The OneShotEvent, as shown in Figure 12.5 and located in the javagames.threads package, is your first state machine. It fires an event that runs once and then waits for another fire event. If the event is canceled while running, it stops. The initialize() method creates a blocking queue for passing events to the consumer thread, which processes the events and transitions the state machine. The `run()` method processes events from the queue one at a time. The `shutdown()` method stops the consumer thread by passing the DONE event.

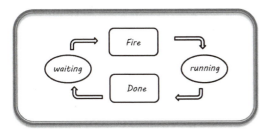

Figure 12.5
One Shot Event.
© 2014 Timothy Wright.

A `BlockingHardwareListener` is added to listen for the finished task and sends a DONE event. The `processEvent()` method transitions the state based on the received events, turning the hardware on or off as requested.

```
package javagames.threads;

import java.util.concurrent.BlockingQueue;
import java.util.concurrent.LinkedBlockingQueue;


public class OneShotEvent implements Runnable {

    private enum State {
        WAITING,
        RUNNING;
    };

    private enum Event {
        FIRE,
        DONE;
    }

    private BlockingQueue<Event> queue;
    private BlockingHardware hardware;
    private State currentState;

    private Thread consumer;
    private int ms;
    private int slices;

    public OneShotEvent( int ms, int slices ) {
```

```java
            this.ms = ms;
            this.slices = slices;
        }
        public void initialize() {
            hardware = new BlockingHardware( "oneshot" );
            hardware.addListener( getListener() );

            queue = new LinkedBlockingQueue<Event>();

            currentState = State.WAITING; // default state

            // startup the consumer thread
            consumer = new Thread( this );
            consumer.start();

        }
        public void fire() {
            try {
                queue.put( Event.FIRE );
            } catch( InterruptedException e ) { }
        }
        public void done() {
            try {
                queue.put( Event.DONE );
            } catch( InterruptedException e ) { }
        }
        public void shutDown() {
            Thread temp = consumer;
            consumer = null;
            try {
                // send event to wake up consumer
                // and/or stop.
                queue.put( Event.DONE );
                temp.join( 10000L );
                System.out.println( "OneShot shutdown!!!" );
            } catch( InterruptedException ex ) { }
        }
        @Override
        public void run() {
            while( Thread.currentThread() == consumer ) {
                try {
                    processEvent( queue.take() );
                } catch( InterruptedException e ) { }
            }
        }
```

```
private void processEvent( Event event ) throws InterruptedException {
    System.out.println( "Got " + event + " event" );
    if( currentState == State.WAITING ) {
        if( event == Event.FIRE ) {
            hardware.turnOn();
            hardware.start( ms, slices );
            currentState = State.RUNNING;
        }
    } else if( currentState == State.RUNNING ) {
        if( event == Event.DONE ) {
            hardware.turnOff();
            currentState = State.WAITING;
        }
    }
}

private BlockingHardwareListener getListener() {
    return new BlockingHardwareListener() {
        @Override
        public void taskFinished() {
            try {
                queue.put( Event.DONE );
            } catch( InterruptedException e ) {}
        }
    };
}

}
```

THE LOOPEVENT CLASS

The LoopEvent, as shown in Figure 12.6 and located in the javagames.threads package, is almost the same as the OneShotEvent. However, when the loop event finishes, it restarts and continues to loop until a DONE event is received.

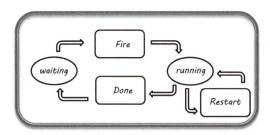

Figure 12.6
Loop Event.
© 2014 Timothy Wright.

If multiple fire() events are sent to the event task while it is already running, they are simply ignored.

```java
package javagames.threads;

import java.util.concurrent.BlockingQueue;
import java.util.concurrent.LinkedBlockingQueue;

public class LoopEvent implements Runnable {

    private enum State {
        WAITING,
        RUNNING;
    };

    private enum Event {
        FIRE,
        RESTART,
        DONE;
    }

    private BlockingQueue<Event> queue;
    private BlockingHardware hardware;
    private State currentState;

    private Thread consumer;
    private int ms;
    private int slices;

    public LoopEvent( int ms, int slices ) {
        this.ms = ms;
        this.slices = slices;
    }

    public void initialize() {

        hardware = new BlockingHardware( "looper" );
        hardware.addListener( getListener() );

        queue = new LinkedBlockingQueue<Event>();

        currentState = State.WAITING; // default state

        // startup the consumer thread
        consumer = new Thread( this );
        consumer.start();

    }

    public void fire() {
        try {
            queue.put( Event.FIRE );
```

```java
        } catch( InterruptedException e ) { }
    }
    public void done() {
        try {
            queue.put( Event.DONE );
        } catch( InterruptedException e ) { }
    }
    public void shutDown() {
        Thread temp = consumer;
        consumer = null;
        try {
            // send event to wake up consumer
            // and/or stop.
            queue.put( Event.DONE );
            temp.join( 10000L );
            System.out.println( "Loop shutdown!!!" );
        } catch( InterruptedException ex ) { }
    }

    @Override
    public void run() {
        while( Thread.currentThread() == consumer ) {
            try {
                processEvent( queue.take() );
            } catch( InterruptedException e ) { }
        }
    }
    private void processEvent( Event event ) throws InterruptedException {
        System.out.println( "Got " + event + " event" );
        if( currentState == State.WAITING ) {
            if( event == Event.FIRE ) {
                hardware.turnOn();
                hardware.start( ms, slices );
                currentState = State.RUNNING;
            }
        } else if( currentState == State.RUNNING ) {
            if( event == Event.RESTART ) {
                hardware.start( ms, slices );
                currentState = State.RUNNING;
            }
            if( event == Event.DONE ) {
                hardware.stop();
```

```
                    hardware.turnOff();
                    currentState = State.WAITING;
                }
            }
        }

    private BlockingHardwareListener getListener() {
        return new BlockingHardwareListener() {
            @Override
            public void taskFinished() {
                try {
                    queue.put( Event.RESTART );
                } catch( InterruptedException e ) {}
            }
        };
    }

}
```

THE RESTARTEVENT CLASS

The RestartEvent, as shown in Figure 12.7 and located in the javagames.threads package, is a little more complicated. If the RestartEvent is in the waiting state, a FIRE event starts the task.

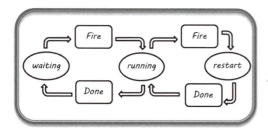

Figure 12.7
Restart Event.
© 2014 Timothy Wright.

When the RestartEvent is finished, it stops. If another FIRE event is sent to the RestartEvent while it is running, the RestartEvent will restart (hence the name). The restart state is necessary so that when the task is finished the state machine will know to restart the task. If the task is done and the state is running, the state is transitioned to WAITING. If the task finished and the state is RESTART, instead of stopping the task, it is restarted, and the state is set back to RUNNING.

```
package javagames.threads;

import java.util.concurrent.BlockingQueue;
import java.util.concurrent.LinkedBlockingQueue;
```

```java
public class RestartEvent implements Runnable {
    private enum State {
        WAITING,
        RESTART,
        RUNNING;
    };
    private enum Event {
        FIRE,
        DONE;
    }
    private BlockingQueue<Event> queue;
    private BlockingHardware hardware;
    private State currentState;

    private Thread consumer;
    private int ms;
    private int slices;
    public RestartEvent( int ms, int slices ) {
        this.ms = ms;
        this.slices = slices;
    }
    public void initialize() {

        hardware = new BlockingHardware( "restart" );
        hardware.addListener( getListener() );

        queue = new LinkedBlockingQueue<Event>();

        currentState = State.WAITING; // default state

        // start up the consumer thread
        consumer = new Thread( this );
        consumer.start();

    }
    public void fire() {
        try {
            queue.put( Event.FIRE );
        } catch( InterruptedException e ) { }
    }
    public void shutDown() {
        Thread temp = consumer;
        consumer = null;
        try {
            // send event to wake up consumer
```

```java
            // and/or stop.
            queue.put( Event.DONE );
            temp.join( 10000L );
            System.out.println( "Restart shutdown!!!" );
        } catch( InterruptedException ex ) { }
    }

    @Override
    public void run() {
        while( Thread.currentThread() == consumer ) {
            try {
                processEvent( queue.take() );
            } catch( InterruptedException e ) { }
        }
    }

    private void processEvent( Event event ) throws InterruptedException {
        System.out.println( "Got " + event + " event" );
        if( currentState == State.WAITING ) {
            if( event == Event.FIRE ) {
                hardware.turnOn();
                hardware.start( ms, slices );
                currentState = State.RUNNING;
            }
        } else if( currentState == State.RUNNING ) {
            if( event == Event.FIRE ) {
                hardware.stop();
                currentState = State.RESTART;
            }
            if( event == Event.DONE ) {
                hardware.turnOff();
                currentState = State.WAITING;
            }
        } else if( currentState == State.RESTART ) {
            if( event == Event.DONE ) {
                hardware.start( ms, slices );
                currentState = State.RUNNING;
            }
        }
    }

    private BlockingHardwareListener getListener() {
        return new BlockingHardwareListener() {
            @Override
            public void taskFinished() {
                try {
```

```
                queue.put( Event.DONE );
            } catch( InterruptedException e ) {}
        }
    };
    }
}
```

THE MULTI-THREAD EVENT EXAMPLE

The MultiThreadEventExample, as shown in Figure 12.8 and located in the javagames.threads package, is a simple game loop that uses the three different state classes.

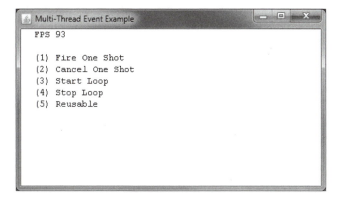

Figure 12.8
Multi-Thread Event Example.
© 2014 Timothy Wright.

Each state machine is running in its own thread, using the blocking queue to communicate events from the game thread. Each event contains a BlockingHardware class that wraps the FakeHardware class and waits for those tasks that run in even more threads. While the game loop code is simple, there is a lot going on here. Time spent understanding the tools in this example is well spent.

```
package javagames.threads;

import java.awt.Graphics;
import java.awt.event.KeyEvent;

import javagames.util.SimpleFramework;
import javagames.util.Utility;


public class MultiThreadEventExample extends SimpleFramework {
```

```java
    private OneShotEvent oneShot;
    private LoopEvent loop;
    private RestartEvent restart;

    public MultiThreadEventExample() {
        appWidth = 640;
        appHeight = 640;
        appSleep = 10L;
        appTitle = "Multi-Thread Event Example";
        appBackground = Color.WHITE;
        appFPSColor = Color.BLACK;
    }

    @Override
    protected void initialize() {
        super.initialize();

        oneShot = new OneShotEvent( 5000, 10 );
        oneShot.initialize();

        loop = new LoopEvent( 1000, 4 );
        loop.initialize();

        restart = new RestartEvent( 5000, 10 );
        restart.initialize();

    }

    @Override
    protected void processInput( float delta ) {
        super.processInput( delta );

        if( keyboard.keyDownOnce( KeyEvent.VK_1 ) ) {
            oneShot.fire();
        }
        if( keyboard.keyDownOnce( KeyEvent.VK_2 ) ) {
            oneShot.done();
        }
        if( keyboard.keyDownOnce( KeyEvent.VK_3 ) ) {
            loop.fire();
        }
        if( keyboard.keyDownOnce( KeyEvent.VK_4 ) ) {
            loop.done();
        }
        if( keyboard.keyDownOnce( KeyEvent.VK_5 ) ) {
            restart.fire();
        }
    }
```

```
@Override
protected void render( Graphics g ) {
   super.render( g );

   textPos = Utility.drawString( g, 20, textPos,
      "",
      "(1) Fire One Shot",
      "(2) Cancel One Shot",
      "(3) Start Loop",
      "(4) Stop Loop",
      "(5) Reusable"
   );
}

@Override
protected void terminate() {
   super.terminate();

   oneShot.shutDown();
   loop.shutDown();
   restart.shutDown();
}

public static void main( String[] args ) {
   launchApp( new MultiThreadEventExample() );
}
```
}

This chapter covered a lot of ground. In Chapter 13, "Sound," all of these concepts are used to create a wrapper API for the Java sound library. All of the ideas presented here—including spawning threads to process logic and then wrapping those calls in a blocking library so that they can be used in the single-threaded game loop—are shown in detail in Chapter 13 too. It can take a long time to feel comfortable with multithreaded programming, so don't worry if you're not getting it. The next chapter should help (and don't forget to check out the resources).

RESOURCES AND FURTHER READING

Goetz, Brian, *Java Concurrency in Practice*, Addison-Wesley, Upper Saddle River, 2006.

Oaks, Scott, Henry Wong, *Java Threads,* 3rd Edition, O'Reilly, Sebastopol, CA, 2004.

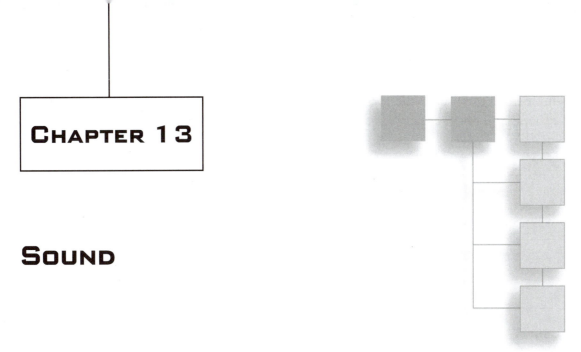

Chapter 13

Sound

The Java Sound API is a low-level library for playing and recording sound and MIDI files. Although there are many aspects of the sound library, this chapter focuses only on playing *.wav files. The portion of the library that you are going to use is organized as shown in Figure 13.1.

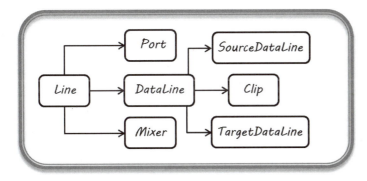

Figure 13.1
Sound API.
© 2014 Timothy Wright.

All classes inherit from the base class `Line`. This abstract class splits into three different subclasses. A `Port` object represents the physical sound inputs and output, such as speakers, headset jack, and microphones. `Mixer` objects have input and output lines and can mix input data and create new output data. This class is modeled after a sound mixer in a recording studio. Finally, there is the `DataLine`, which represents the bits of audio data passed around to the other classes.

The DataLine consists of three subclasses. This is where the API gets confusing, so hang in there. There is a SourceDataLine, a TargetDataLine, and a Clip. Normally, a source is the input and the target is the output, but because the data lines are mixer-centric, the names seem backward. See Figure 13.2.

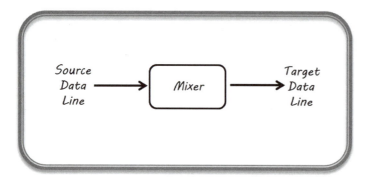

Figure 13.2
Input/Output Issue.
© 2014 Timothy Wright.

To write data to the mixer, data is written out to the source, and read in from the target. Read that again. I have no idea why it is this way, but it makes it confusing.

- SourceDataLine = OutputStream
- TargetDataLine = InputStream

The good news is that the SourceDataLine has only a write() method and the TargetDataLine has only a read() method, so it isn't possible to use them incorrectly. Just be aware that the names don't make sense. The Clip class also seems out of place. While both data lines stream data to or from other lines, a Clip class is really a wrapper around a SourceDataLine (output) for small sound files that fit completely into memory. So, while a Clip object should wrap a SourceDataLine, not *be* one, that is the way the API is organized.

The API is also designed to be a non-blocking API by using the LineListener interface. Most of the sound API calls return immediately, sending an update event on another thread when the task is complete.

```
public void LineListener.update( LineEvent )
```

The LineEvent.Type has the following event types:

- OPEN
- CLOSE

- START

- STOP

The actual causes of these events being generated depend on the context. For example, a STOP event is sent when a SourceDataLine stops streaming data, or when the stop() method is called. The code to add a listener is as follows:

```
Clip clip = magicalJavaCode();
clip.addLineListener( new LineListener() {
   @Override
   public void update( LineEvent event ) {
      // TODO handle line event
   }
});
```

Don't worry about the code to create a Clip just yet. That will be covered shortly.

The following methods are used to play sounds:

- open()—Used to open a data line. Because there is a maximum of 32 lines available, each line must be opened before it can be used.

- start()—Calling start on a line allows the data sent to the line to be processed by the other end. For example, writing data to a line will not play the data unless the line has been started.

- stop()—Data lines have two internal buffers: the data frames currently being played and a buffer waiting to be played. When the line is stopped, the data currently being played is finished, and no new data is played. However, any data left in the intermediate buffer is still there. Calling start again will continue playing the data from where it was stopped.

- drain()—This method blocks until all the buffered data available to be played has been played and there is no data left. This method is used to play all the sound data before stopping the sound. Calling the stop() method without using drain() first will cut the sound off immediately and leave data in the buffer.

- flush()—This method removes any remaining data from the sound buffer. If the sound has been stopped but data remains, the flush() method will clear the buffer. If this method isn't used after stopping a sound with remaining data, the last bit of sound will still play when the sound is restarted.

- close()—This method releases the line and makes it available to be reused.

WORKING WITH SOUND FILES

The sound API only handles a few file formats: *.wav, *.aiff, and *.au. Other more popular formats are not supported without third-party software.

A sound file has a number of attributes that are important. Each file contains a number of samples. Each sample, or frame, is the sound at that specific point in time. Sound files have a frame rate, or sample rate, measured in hertz. For example, a sample rate of 44,100Hz has 44,100 samples per second. Another important attribute is bits-per-sample. An 8-bit sound file stores the frame as eight bits of data, or one byte, whereas a 16-bit sound files stores the sound as two bytes. The number of channels is also important. There is one sample of data for each channel in every frame. That means that a 16-bit sound with two channels (stereo) has 16 bits + 16 bits, or 32 bits of data per frame.

$$frame\ size\ in\ bytes = \frac{bits\ per\ frame}{8} * number\ of\ channels$$

The format of the sound data and calculating the number of bytes for each frame is important later, when buffer sizes for streaming data need to be created. For now, just be aware that all these attributes will change for every different type of sound file.

To play an audio file, you need an `AudioInputStream`. The problem with these stream objects is, like most `InputStream` objects, they can be used only once. In order to use sounds over and over for a game, the raw sound bytes need to be extracted from the file. They can then be wrapped in a `ByteArrayInputStream` and used to create an `AudioInputStream` without streaming the data from an `InputStream` each time the sound is played.

```
InputStream soundFile =
    ResourceLoader.load( Object.class, "filepath", "respath" );
byte[] rawBytes = null;
try {
    BufferedInputStream buf = new BufferedInputStream( soundFile );
    ByteArrayOutputStream out = new ByteArrayOutputStream();
    int read;
    while( (read = buf.read()) != -1 ) {
        out.write( read );
    }
    soundFile.close();
    rawBytes = out.toByteArray();
} catch( IOException ex ) {
    ex.printStackTrace();
}
```

```
ByteArrayInputStream audioStream =
    new ByteArrayInputStream( rawBytes );
AudioInputStream audioInputStream
    = AudioSystem.getAudioInputStream( audioStream );
```

As you saw in the previous code sample, the AudioSystem is a helper class provided by the sound API. Once an AudioInputStream is available, a clip can be opened and will be ready to play the sound.

```
InputStream soundFile = loadSoundFile();
byte[] rawBytes = readBytes( soundFile );

ByteArrayInputStream in = new ByteArrayInputStream( rawBytes );
AudioInputStream audioInputStream =
    AudioSystem.getAudioInputStream( in );

Clip clip = AudioSystem.getClip();
clip.open( audioInputStream );
```

Some sounds are too big to fit into the Clip buffer. Very large sounds, like ambient noise or music, need to use a SourceDataLine output line. Because this line doesn't open the audio file, it needs the audio format to open the line.

```
InputStream soundFile = loadSoundFile();
byte[] rawBytes = readBytes( soundFile );

ByteArrayInputStream in = new ByteArrayInputStream( rawBytes );
AudioInputStream audioInputStream =
    AudioSystem.getAudioInputStream( in );

AudioFormat audioFormat = audioInputStream.getFormat();
DataLine.Info info = new DataLine.Info(
    SourceDataLine.class,
    audioFormat,
    AudioSystem.NOT_SPECIFIED
);
SourceDataLine dataLine = (SourceDataLine)AudioSystem.getLine( info );
dataLine.open( audioFormat );
```

Notice that the SourceDataLine is opened using the AudioFormat object, not the audio file. If the line is opened without passing in the format, then the line will be opened with whatever the default line is for the user's system, and that format may not be compatible with the sound file.

PROBLEMS WITH THE SOUND LIBRARY

Now before you go running off to create the next great music game, the sound library needs to be integrated with the game loop, and that is where the trouble begins. Some of the methods in the sound library send notification events in another thread but take some time to actually complete, so it is easy to use the library incorrectly. Let's examine a simple loop, which starts and stops a clip sound.

```
for( int i = 0; i < 10; ++i ) {
    clip.start();
    while( !clip.isActive() ) {
        Thread.sleep(100);
    }
    clip.stop();
    clip.flush();
    clip.setFramePosition(0);
    clip.start();
    clip.drain();
}
```

This code starts the clip and then sleeps while waiting for the clip to become active. At that point, the clip is restarted. First it is stopped, the remaining data in the buffer is flushed out, the frame position is set back to the beginning, and the clip is started. Finally, the clip is drained so the entire sound will play before the next loop iteration.

On my computer, this loop locks up after a couple of iterations when using the latest Java 6.0 SDK. It is not clear why it locks up, but is has something to do with the drain() method blocking before the clip is restarted. Regardless, there are no errors thrown, and no indication that anything is wrong.

Another problem with the sound library is the difference between Java 6.0 and 7.0. While the previous example locked up with 6.0, there has been a replacement of the software mixer with 7.0 and the behavior has changed. Pay attention to the differences between 6.0 and 7.0 when testing the examples.

Experimenting with the library revealed that the events sent to the LineListener interface, such as START and STOP, must be received before any other actions are taken with the library. So although many of the methods return immediately, the software must block, or poll, waiting for the event before continuing. This makes the library very easy to use in a muliti-threaded Swing application, but it makes is very difficult to use in a single-threaded game loop. The wait/notify thread signals covered in the thread chapter solve this problem by blocking the non-blocking API so that the sound library doesn't lock up.

The PlayingClipsExample, located in the javagames.sound package, demonstrates playing sounds without waiting, locking up the sound API, and playing sound while blocking for the response using the wait/notify mechanism covered in Chapter 12,

"Threads." The example code implements the LineListener interface so that when the events are received, the state is stored in the open and started variables and waiting threads are notified to wake.

The readBytes() method reads the raw sound file bytes into an array for easy reuse. The runTestWithoutWaiting() method (which can lock up) demonstrates the wrong way to use the sound API. Because it doesn't wait for the LineListener events before continuing, it can lock up, draining a sound that will never play. The runWithWaiting() demonstrates using the wait/notify mechanism to wait for LineListener events before proceeding.

Finally, the main() method runs both tests. Even if you are able to run both tests without a lockup, someone may have a machine that is too fast or too slow (like me), and no one likes it when the sound stops playing.

```java
package javagames.sound;

import java.io.*;

import javagames.util.ResourceLoader;

import javax.sound.sampled.*;


public class PlayingClipsExample implements LineListener {
    private volatile boolean open = false;
    private volatile boolean started = false;
    public byte[] readBytes( InputStream in ) {
        try {
            BufferedInputStream buf = new BufferedInputStream( in );
            ByteArrayOutputStream out = new ByteArrayOutputStream();
            int read;
            while( (read = buf.read()) != -1 ) {
                out.write( read );
            }
            in.close();
            return out.toByteArray();
        } catch( IOException ex ) {
            ex.printStackTrace();
            return null;
        }
    }
}
```

```java
public void runTestWithoutWaiting() throws Exception {
    System.out.println( "runTestWithoutWaiting()" );

    Clip clip = AudioSystem.getClip();
    clip.addLineListener( this );

    InputStream resource = ResourceLoader.load(
        PlayingClipsExample.class,
        "res/assets/sound/WEAPON_scifi_fire_02.wav",
        "notneeded"
    );
    byte[] rawBytes = readBytes( resource );
    ByteArrayInputStream in = new ByteArrayInputStream( rawBytes );
    AudioInputStream audioInputStream =
        AudioSystem.getAudioInputStream( in );
    clip.open( audioInputStream );

    for( int i = 0; i < 10; ++i ) {
        clip.start();
        while( !clip.isActive() ) {
            Thread.sleep(100);
        }
        clip.stop();
        clip.flush();
        clip.setFramePosition(0);
        clip.start();
        clip.drain();
    }
    clip.close();
}

public void runTestWithWaiting() throws Exception {
    System.out.println( "runTestWithWaiting()" );

    Clip clip = AudioSystem.getClip();
    clip.addLineListener( this );

    InputStream resource = ResourceLoader.load(
        PlayingClipsExample.class,
        "res/assets/sound/WEAPON_scifi_fire_02.wav",
        "notneeded"
    );
    byte[] rawBytes = readBytes( resource );
    ByteArrayInputStream in = new ByteArrayInputStream( rawBytes );
    in = new ByteArrayInputStream( rawBytes );
    AudioInputStream audioInputStream =
        AudioSystem.getAudioInputStream( in );
```

```
    synchronized( this ) {
        clip.open( audioInputStream );
        while( !open ) {
            wait();
        }
    }

    for( int i = 0; i < 10; ++i ) {

        clip.setFramePosition( 0 );

        synchronized( this ) {
            clip.start();
            while( !started ) {
                wait();
            }
        }

        clip.drain();

        synchronized( this ) {
            clip.stop();
            while( started ) {
                wait();
            }
        }
    }

    synchronized( this ) {
        clip.close();
        while( open ) {
            wait();
        }
    }

}

@Override
public synchronized void update( LineEvent lineEvent ) {
    System.out.println( "Got Event: " + lineEvent.getType() );
    LineEvent.Type type = lineEvent.getType();
    if( type == LineEvent.Type.OPEN ) {
        open = true;
    } else if( type == LineEvent.Type.START ) {
        started = true;
    } else if( type == LineEvent.Type.STOP ) {
        started = false;
```

```
        } else if( type == LineEvent.Type.CLOSE ) {
            open = false;
        }
        notifyAll();
    }
    public static void main( String[] args ) throws Exception {
        PlayingClipsExample lineListenerExample = new PlayingClipsExample();
        lineListenerExample.runTestWithWaiting();
        lineListenerExample.runTestWithoutWaiting();
    }
}
```

DEVELOPING BLOCKING AUDIO CLASSES

You are going to develop a simple set of classes that can be used to add sound to the game loop. The first issue is creating blocking classes that will wait for the sound library events before returning. This technique of wrapping a non-blocking class with a blocking class using the wait/notify methods is discussed in Chapter 12, "Threads."

The BlockingAudioListener interface, located in the javagames.sound package, is used to notify listeners when a sound has finished playing.

```
package javagames.sound;

public interface BlockingAudioListener {
    public void audioFinished();
}
```

The SoundException class, located in the same package, is used as a custom exception that extends RuntimeException so the sound API exceptions do not need to be specifically caught (there are lots of them).

```
package javagames.sound;

public class SoundException extends RuntimeException {
    public SoundException( String message ) {
        super( message );
    }
    public SoundException( String message, Throwable cause ) {
        super( message, cause );
    }
}
```

The AudioStream is a base class for blocking audio streams that wrap a Clip and SourceDataLine. Instead of using the wait/notify, it uses the Lock and Condition variables to monitor the LineListener. It also manages the listeners for the BlockingAudioListener interface and provides methods to start, stop, open, close, restart, and loop the sound. The LineListener contains code that fires events when the sound is finished, as well as signals all threads waiting on the condition variable.

```java
package javagames.sound;


import java.util.*;
import java.util.concurrent.locks.*;

import javax.sound.sampled.*;
import javax.sound.sampled.LineEvent.*;


public abstract class AudioStream implements LineListener {

    public static final int LOOP_CONTINUOUSLY = -1;

    protected final Lock lock = new ReentrantLock();
    protected final Condition cond = lock.newCondition();

    protected volatile boolean open = false;
    protected volatile boolean started = false;

    protected byte[] soundData;

    private List<BlockingAudioListener> listeners = Collections
            .synchronizedList( new ArrayList<BlockingAudioListener>() );

    public AudioStream( byte[] soundData ) {
        this.soundData = soundData;
    }

    public abstract void open();
    public abstract void close();
    public abstract void start();
    public abstract void loop( int count );
    public abstract void restart();
    public abstract void stop();

    public boolean addListener( BlockingAudioListener listener ) {
        return listeners.add( listener );
    }

    protected void fireTaskFinished() {
        synchronized( listeners ) {
            for( BlockingAudioListener listener : listeners ) {
                listener.audioFinished();
            }
        }
    }
}
```

```
@Override
public void update( LineEvent event ) {

    boolean wasStarted = started;
    lock.lock();
    try {
        if( event.getType() == Type.OPEN ) {
            open = true;
        } else if( event.getType() == Type.CLOSE ) {
            open = false;
        } else if( event.getType() == Type.START ) {
            started = true;
        } else if( event.getType() == Type.STOP ) {
            started = false;
        }
        cond.signalAll();
    } finally {
        lock.unlock();
    }

    if( wasStarted && !started ) {
        fireTaskFinished();
    }

  }

}
```

USING THE BLOCKING CLIP CLASS

The BlockingClip class extends the AudioStream base class and provides implementations for the following abstract methods:

- open

- close

- start

- stop

- restart

- loop

Each of these methods that has to block when the Clip object performs the task has the following signature:

```
lock.lock();
try {
```

```
    // use clip
    while( not finished ) {
        cond.await();
    }
} finally {
    lock.unlock();
}
```

As explained in Chapter 12, the lock is acquired before requesting that the clip perform some action, and then waits for a response, always unlocking in a try/finally block. This ensures that the lock is released no matter what happens in the method.

The open() method creates the AudioInputStream, obtains a Clip from the AudioSystem, adds itself as a LineListener, opens the clip, and blocks until the LineListener interface receives the LineEvent.OPEN event. Notice all the exceptions— UnsupportedAudioFileException, LineUnavailableExcetion, and IOException—that are wrapped with the custom sound exception. This makes the class a lot easier to use.

The start() method clears the clip of any remaining data with flush(), sets the frame position to zero, starts the Clip, and waits for the LineEvent.START event before returning.

The loop() method is similar to start, but uses the Clip.loop() method to pass in a loop count. Using the AudioStream.LOOP_CONTINUOUSLY flag will allow the sound to loop forever.

The stop() method stops the Clip and waits for the LineEvent.STOP event. It does not need to drain the line first. The Clip class will play until the sound is finished and then call the BlockingAudio.audioFinished() method.

The restart() method is tricky. It overrides the fireTaskFinished() method, suppressing the event so that when the sound is stopped and started again, and the LineEvent.STOP event is received, the fireTaskFinished() will not incorrectly notify listeners that the task has stopped when it was only restarted.

The close() method closes the Clip and waits for the LineEvent.CLOSE event before returning.

```
package javagames.sound;

import java.io.*;
import javax.sound.sampled.*;

public class BlockingClip extends AudioStream {

    private Clip clip;
    private boolean restart;
```

```java
public BlockingClip( byte[] soundData ) {
    super( soundData );
}

/*
 * This guy could throw a bunch of exceptions.
 * We're going to wrap them all in a custom exception
 * handler that is a RuntimeException so we don't
 * have to catch and throw all these exceptions.
 */
@Override
public void open() {
    lock.lock();
    try {
        ByteArrayInputStream in = new ByteArrayInputStream( soundData );
        AudioInputStream ais = AudioSystem.getAudioInputStream( in );
        clip = AudioSystem.getClip();
        clip.addLineListener( this );
        clip.open( ais );
        while( !open ) {
            cond.await();
        }
        System.out.println( "open" );
    } catch( UnsupportedAudioFileException ex ) {
        throw new SoundException( ex.getMessage(), ex );
    } catch( LineUnavailableException ex ) {
        throw new SoundException( ex.getMessage(), ex );
    } catch( IOException ex ) {
        throw new SoundException( ex.getMessage(), ex );
    } catch( InterruptedException ex ) {
        ex.printStackTrace();
    } finally {
        lock.unlock();
    }
}

@Override
public void start() {
    lock.lock();
    try {
        clip.flush();
        clip.setFramePosition( 0 );
        clip.start();
```

```
        while( !started ) {
            cond.await();
        }
        System.out.println( "It's Started" );
    } catch( InterruptedException e ) {
        e.printStackTrace();
    } finally {
        lock.unlock();
    }
}

@Override
public void loop( int count ) {
    lock.lock();
    try {
        clip.flush();
        clip.setFramePosition( 0 );
        clip.loop( count );
        while( !started ) {
            cond.await();
        }
        System.out.println( "It's Started" );
    } catch( InterruptedException e ) {
        e.printStackTrace();
    } finally {
        lock.unlock();
    }
}

@Override
public void restart() {
    restart = true;
    stop();
    restart = false;
    start();
}

@Override
protected void fireTaskFinished() {
    if( !restart ) {
        super.fireTaskFinished();
    }
}
```

```java
@Override
public void stop() {
    lock.lock();
    try {
        clip.stop();
        while( started ) {
            cond.await();
        }
    } catch( InterruptedException ex ) {
        ex.printStackTrace();
    } finally {
        lock.unlock();
    }
}

@Override
public void close() {
    lock.lock();
    try {
        clip.close();
        while( open ) {
            cond.await();
        }
        clip = null;
        System.out.println( "Turned off" );
    } catch( InterruptedException ex ) {
        ex.printStackTrace();
    } finally {
        lock.unlock();
    }
}

}
```

USING THE AUDIODATALINE CLASS

The next thing you need to do for the sound library is to create a BlockingDataLine class so sounds can be streamed by hand. Keep in mind that there are behavior differences between the 6.0 SDK and the 7.0 SDK. While the Clip class cannot load large files in 6.0, they can be loaded and played with 7.0. However, while smaller clips work better in 6.0, using them in 7.0 can cause the short sounds to stop working. So regardless of which version you support, the ability to stream sounds by hand is necessary.

The AudioDataLine class, located in the javagames.sound package, is similar to the Clip class but it can stream large sound files. One of the issues with playing sounds this way is that the sound data needs to be written to the SourceDataLine in byte chunks. To do this, the actual audio data must be extracted from the AudioInputStream. The raw sound file cannot be played or the file header information will be interpreted as sound data. I tried it and it doesn't sound good. There is a lot of cracking and popping.

The sound data can be extracted from the AudioInputStream in frames. It is not possible to read the data one byte at a time unless each frame is only one byte in length.

```
InputStream soundFile = loadSoundFile();
byte[] rawBytes = readBytes( soundFile );

ByteArrayInputStream in = new ByteArrayInputStream( rawBytes );
AudioInputStream audioInputStream =
    AudioSystem.getAudioInputStream( in );
AudioFormat audioFormat = audioInputStream.getFormat();

ByteArrayOutputStream out = new ByteArrayOutputStream();
int chunk = (int)audioFormat.getFrameSize();
byte[] buf = new byte[ chunk ];
while( audioInputStream.read( buf ) != -1 ) {
    out.write( buf );
}
audioInputStream.close();
byte[] soundBytes = out.toByteArray();
```

Another issue with streaming data to a SourceDataLine from scratch is the buffer size. Unlike a Clip, the data written to the SourceDataLine should be drained before the sound is stopped. In order to have quick response, the buffer must be small; a 50-millisecond buffer seems to work well. Because sounds have different sample sizes, channels, and bit sample sizes, calculating a 50-millisecond buffer in bytes requires some work.

The computeBufferSize() method uses the buffer length in milliseconds, the sample size, number of sample bits, and number of channels to create a buffer of the correct size in bytes.

$$frame\ size = \frac{sample\ rate\ Hz}{1000} * milliseconds$$

The number of frames for a 50-millisecond sample is computed by converting the sample rate into milliseconds. You do this by dividing it by 1,000 and then multiplying by the desired number of milliseconds.

$$bytes\ per\ frame = \frac{sample\ bits}{1000} * channels$$

The byte size of each frame is calculated by converting the sample bits into bytes. You do this by dividing the sample bits by 8, and then multiplying that byte count by the number of channels.

$$buffer\ size = frame\ size * bytes\ per\ frame$$

The `initialize()` method creates the `AudioInputStream`, gets the `AudioFormat` needed to open the `SourceDataLine`, computes the 50-millisecond buffer size, and extracts the sound data from the `AudioInputStream`. The `readSoundData()` method is responsible for extracting the audio data. The `computeBufferSize()` method calculates a correct buffer size for a 50-millisecond sample. Also notice the buffer is checked to make sure it is divisible by 1,000 and is adjusted if the sample size does not divide evenly.

```
double temp = milliseconds;
double frames = sampleRate * temp / 1000.0;
while( frames != Math.floor( frames ) ) {
    temp++;
    frames = sampleRate * temp / 1000.0;
}
```

The `open()` method acquires a `SoundDataLine`. Notice that the computed buffer size is passed to the `open()` method, overriding the default size. This class also maintains a list of `LineListener` objects. Because the listeners need to be added after a line is acquired, the `LineListener` objects are added after the line is opened.

The `start()` and `loop()` methods flush the data line of any old data, start the line, and then fire off another thread that will loop through the extracted audio data and write it to the data line one buffer at a time.

The `stop()` method stops the writer thread by setting the reference to `null`. Notice that this method does not call `stop()` on the data line. Stopping the data line would prevent the currently buffered data from playing, causing a pop or crackle sound on occasion. Whatever sound data has been written needs to be drained before the line is stopped, which is why a small buffer size is needed. Otherwise, the sound would play for a long time after the stop event, which may cause a lag.

The `reset()` method simply sets a flag to tell the `write` thread to restart streaming the data from the start.

The `run()` method is the most complicated—it streams small chunks of data, supports loops and restarts, all the while continuously making sure the loop hasn't been stopped. The run() method continues to write the data until the loop value is zero. When the loop value is set to -1 it loops forever. If the loop is stopped or the loop count reaches zero, the line is drained, stopped, and the thread exits. If the sound is restarted, the loop count is incremented so that the loop count stays the same when the sound is restarted.

```java
package javagames.sound;

import java.io.*;
import java.util.*;

import javax.sound.sampled.*;


public class AudioDataLine implements Runnable {
    private static final int BUFFER_SIZE_MS = 50;

    private List<LineListener> listeners =
        Collections.synchronizedList( new ArrayList<LineListener>() );

    private Thread writer;
    private AudioFormat audioFormat;
    private SourceDataLine dataLine;
    private byte[] rawData;
    private byte[] soundData;
    private int bufferSize;
    private int loopCount;

    private volatile boolean restart = false;

    public AudioDataLine( byte[] rawData ) {
        this.rawData = rawData;
    }

    public void initialize() {
        try {
            ByteArrayInputStream in = new ByteArrayInputStream( rawData );
            AudioInputStream ais = AudioSystem.getAudioInputStream( in );
            audioFormat = ais.getFormat();
            bufferSize = computeBufferSize( BUFFER_SIZE_MS );
            soundData = readSoundData( ais );
        } catch( UnsupportedAudioFileException ex ) {
            throw new SoundException( ex.getMessage(), ex );
        } catch( IOException ex ) {
            throw new SoundException( ex.getMessage(), ex );
        }
    }
}
```

```java
private byte[] readSoundData( AudioInputStream ais ) {
    try {
        ByteArrayOutputStream out = new ByteArrayOutputStream();
        long chunk = audioFormat.getFrameSize();
        byte[] buf = new byte[ (int)chunk ];
        while( ais.read( buf ) != -1 ) {
            out.write( buf );
        }
        ais.close();
        return out.toByteArray();
    } catch( IOException ex ) {
        ex.printStackTrace();
        return null;
    }
}

public void addLineListener( LineListener listener ) {
    listeners.add( listener );
}

public void open() {
    try {
        DataLine.Info info =
            new DataLine.Info( SourceDataLine.class, audioFormat,
                AudioSystem.NOT_SPECIFIED );
        dataLine = (SourceDataLine)AudioSystem.getLine( info );
        synchronized( listeners ) {
            for( LineListener listener : listeners ) {
                dataLine.addLineListener( listener );
            }
        }
        dataLine.open( audioFormat, bufferSize );
    } catch( LineUnavailableException ex ) {
        throw new SoundException( ex.getMessage(), ex );
    }
}

private int computeBufferSize( int milliseconds ) {
    double sampleRate = audioFormat.getSampleRate();
    double bitSize = audioFormat.getSampleSizeInBits();
    double channels = audioFormat.getChannels();

    System.out.println( "Sample Rate: " + sampleRate );
    System.out.println( "Bit Size: " + bitSize );
    System.out.println( "Channels: " + channels );
    System.out.println( "Milliseconds: " + milliseconds );
```

```
    if( bitSize == AudioSystem.NOT_SPECIFIED ||
        sampleRate == AudioSystem.NOT_SPECIFIED ||
        channels == AudioSystem.NOT_SPECIFIED ) {
        System.out.println( "BufferSize: " + -1 );
        return -1;
    } else {
        double temp = milliseconds;
        double frames = sampleRate * temp / 1000.0;
        while( frames != Math.floor( frames ) ) {
            temp++;
            frames = sampleRate * temp / 1000.0;
        }
        double bytesPerFrame = bitSize / 8.0;
        double size = (int)(frames * bytesPerFrame * channels);
        System.out.println( "BufferSize: " + size );
        return (int)size;
    }
}

public void close() {
    dataLine.close();
}

public void start() {
    loopCount = 0;
    dataLine.flush();
    dataLine.start();
    writer = new Thread( this );
    writer.start();
}

public void reset() {
    restart = true;
}

public void loop( int count ) {
    loopCount = count;
    dataLine.flush();
    dataLine.start();
    writer = new Thread( this );
    writer.start();
}

public void stop() {
    if( writer != null ) {
        Thread temp = writer;
        writer = null;
```

```java
        try {
            temp.join( 10000 );
        } catch( InterruptedException ex ) { }
    }
}

public Line getLine() {
    return dataLine;
}

@Override
public void run() {
    System.out.println( "write stream" );
    try {
        while( true ) {

            int written = 0;
            int length =
                bufferSize == -1 ? dataLine.getBufferSize() : bufferSize;

            while( written < soundData.length ) {

                if( Thread.currentThread() != writer ) {
                    System.out.println( "Stream canceled" );
                    loopCount = 0;
                    break; // stop writing data
                } else if( restart ) {
                    restart = false;
                    System.out.println( "Stream canceled" );
                    if( loopCount != AudioStream.LOOP_CONTINUOUSLY ) {
                        loopCount++;
                    }
                    break; // stop writing data
                }

                int bytesLeft = soundData.length - written;
                int toWrite = bytesLeft > length * 2 ? length : bytesLeft;
                written += dataLine.write( soundData, written, toWrite );
            }

            if( loopCount == 0 ) {
                break;
            } else if( loopCount != AudioStream.LOOP_CONTINUOUSLY ) {
                loopCount--;
            }
        }
    } catch( Exception e ) {
        e.printStackTrace();
```

```
    } finally {
        System.out.println( "Stream finished" );
        dataLine.drain();
        dataLine.stop();
    }
  }
}
```

CREATING THE BLOCKINGDATALINE CLASS

Now that the AudioDataStream wraps a SourceDataLine and provides a similar class as the Clip class, a BlockingDataLine can be created that waits for the sound events before returning. This creates blocking classes for small and large sound files.

The BlockingDataLine uses the same structure as the BlockClip.

```
lock.lock();
try {
    // use clip
    while( not finished ) {
        cond.await();
    }
} finally {
    Lock.unlock();
}
```

The open() method creates a new AudioDataLine, adds a LineListener, opens the stream, and blocks until it is complete. The start() method starts the stream and waits until data has begun streaming before returning. The loop() method does the same.

The restart() method forwards the request to the AudioDataLine. The stop() method stops the stream and waits for the stop() event before returning. The close() method closes the stream.

```
package javagames.sound;


public class BlockingDataLine extends AudioStream {
    private AudioDataLine stream;
    public BlockingDataLine( byte[] soundData ) {
        super( soundData );
    }
```

```java
@Override
public void open() {
    lock.lock();
    try {
        stream = new AudioDataLine( soundData );
        stream.initialize();
        stream.addLineListener( this );
        stream.open();
        while( !open ) {
            cond.await();
        }
        System.out.println( "open" );
    } catch( InterruptedException ex ) {
        ex.printStackTrace();
    } finally {
        lock.unlock();
    }
}

@Override
public void start() {
    lock.lock();
    try {
        stream.start();
        while( !started ) {
            cond.await();
        }
        System.out.println( "started" );
    } catch( InterruptedException ex ) {
        ex.printStackTrace();
    } finally {
        lock.unlock();
    }
}

@Override
public void loop( int count ) {
    lock.lock();
    try {
        stream.loop( count );
        while( !started ) {
            cond.await();
        }
        System.out.println( "started" );
```

```
        } catch( InterruptedException ex ) {
            ex.printStackTrace();
        } finally {
            lock.unlock();
        }
    }

    @Override
    public void restart() {
        stream.reset();
    }

    @Override
    public void stop() {
        lock.lock();
        try {
            stream.stop();
            while( started ) {
                cond.await();
            }
            System.out.println( "stopped" );
        } catch( InterruptedException ex ) {
            ex.printStackTrace();
        } finally {
            lock.unlock();
        }
    }

    @Override
    public void close() {
        lock.lock();
        try {
            stream.close();
            while( open ) {
                cond.await();
            }
            System.out.println( "closed" );
        } catch( InterruptedException ex ) {
            ex.printStackTrace();
        } finally {
            lock.unlock();
        }
    }
}
```

CREATING A SOUNDEVENT CLASS

Luckily, perhaps by design, this issue was also covered in Chapter 12. By using the blocking queue method, you can create a `SoundEvent` class that runs in another thread off the game loop and processes sound events in a single threaded queue. Refer to the `BlockingQueueExample` in Chapter 12 for a detailed explanation of using the blocking queue to communicate between threads.

```java
package javagames.sound;

import java.util.concurrent.BlockingQueue;
import java.util.concurrent.LinkedBlockingQueue;


public class SoundEvent implements Runnable {

    public static final String SHUT_DOWN = "shutdown";

    protected AudioStream audio;

    protected BlockingQueue<String> queue;
    private Thread consumer;

    public SoundEvent( AudioStream audio ) {
        this.audio = audio;
    }

    public void initialize() {
        audio.addListener( getListener() );
        queue = new LinkedBlockingQueue<String>();
        consumer = new Thread( this );
        consumer.start();
    }

    public void put( String event ) {
        try {
            queue.put( event );
        } catch( InterruptedException e ) { }
    }

    public void shutDown() {
        Thread temp = consumer;
        consumer = null;
        try {
            // send event to wake up consumer
            // and/or stop.
            queue.put( SHUT_DOWN );
            temp.join( 10000L );
            System.out.println( "Event shutdown!!!" );
        } catch( InterruptedException ex ) { }
    }
```

```
@Override
public void run() {
    while( Thread.currentThread() == consumer ) {
        try {
            processEvent( queue.take() );
        } catch( InterruptedException e ) { }
    }
}

protected void processEvent( String event )
throws InterruptedException { }

protected void onAudioFinished() { }

private BlockingAudioListener getListener() {
    return new BlockingAudioListener() {
        @Override
        public void audioFinished() {
            onAudioFinished();
        }
    };
}

}
```

USING THE ONESHOTEVENT CLASS

The OneShotEvent, as shown in Figure 13.3 and located in the javagames.sound package, has two states—WAITING and RUNNING—and two events—FIRE and DONE.

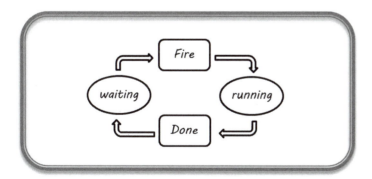

Figure 13.3
One Shot Event.
© 2014 Timothy Wright.

If the OneShotEvent is waiting, the fire event starts playing the sound. The fire event does nothing while the sound is playing. The DONE event will stop the sound, or the sound will stop when it is finished playing. This state machine concept is explored in detail in Chapter 12.

```java
package javagames.sound;


public class OneShotEvent extends SoundEvent {

    public static final String STATE_WAITING = "waiting";
    public static final String STATE_RUNNING = "running";

    public static final String EVENT_FIRE = "fire";
    public static final String EVENT_DONE = "done";

    private String currentState;

    public OneShotEvent( AudioStream audio ) {
        super( audio );
        currentState = STATE_WAITING;
    }

    public void fire() {
        put( EVENT_FIRE );
    }

    public void done() {
        put( EVENT_DONE );
    }

    protected void processEvent( String event ) throws InterruptedException {
        System.out.println( "Got " + event + " event" );
        if( currentState == STATE_WAITING ) {
            if( event == EVENT_FIRE ) {
                audio.open();
                audio.start();
                currentState = STATE_RUNNING;
            }
        } else if( currentState == STATE_RUNNING ) {
            if( event == EVENT_DONE ) {
                audio.stop();
                audio.close();
                currentState = STATE_WAITING;
            }
        }
    }
}
```

```
    @Override
    protected void onAudioFinished() {
        put( EVENT_DONE );
    }
}
```

USING THE LOOPEVENT CLASS

The LoopEvent, as shown in Figure 13.4 and located in the same package, is very similar to the OneShotEvent.

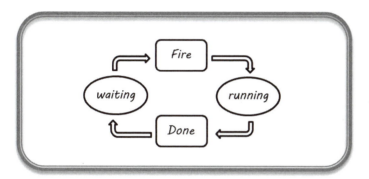

Figure 13.4
Loop Event.
© 2014 Timothy Wright.

The only difference is that the sound keeps repeating until the DONE method is called. This event does not stop by itself.

```
package javagames.sound;


public class LoopEvent extends SoundEvent {
    public static final String STATE_WAITING = "waiting";
    public static final String STATE_RUNNING = "running";

    public static final String EVENT_FIRE = "fire";
    public static final String EVENT_DONE = "done";

    private String currentState;

    public LoopEvent( AudioStream audio ) {
        super( audio );
        currentState = STATE_WAITING;
    }
```

```
   public void fire() {
      put( EVENT_FIRE );
   }

   public void done() {
      put( EVENT_DONE );
   }

   protected void processEvent( String event ) throws InterruptedException {
      System.out.println( "Got " + event + " event" );
      if( currentState == STATE_WAITING ) {
         if( event == EVENT_FIRE ) {
            audio.open();
            audio.loop( AudioStream.LOOP_CONTINUOUSLY );
            currentState = STATE_RUNNING;
         }
      } else if( currentState == STATE_RUNNING ) {
         if( event == EVENT_DONE ) {
            audio.stop();
            audio.close();
            currentState = STATE_WAITING;
         }
      }
   }
}
```

Using the RestartEvent Class

The RestartEvent, as shown in Figure 13.5, plays the sound only once, but another fire event issued while the sound is playing will restart the sound.

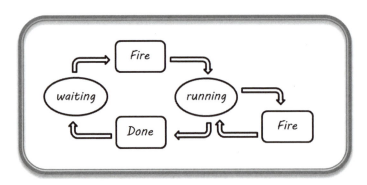

Figure 13.5
Restart Event.
© 2014 Timothy Wright.

```java
package javagames.sound;

public class RestartEvent extends SoundEvent {
    public static final String STATE_WAITING = "waiting";
    public static final String STATE_RUNNING = "running";

    public static final String EVENT_FIRE = "fire";
    public static final String EVENT_DONE = "done";

    private String currentState;

    public RestartEvent( AudioStream stream ) {
        super( stream );
        currentState = STATE_WAITING;
    }

    public void fire() {
        put( EVENT_FIRE );
    }

    protected void processEvent( String event ) throws InterruptedException {
        System.out.println( "Got " + event + " event" );
        if( currentState == STATE_WAITING ) {
            if( event == EVENT_FIRE ) {
                currentState = STATE_RUNNING;
                audio.open();
                audio.start();
            }
        } else if( currentState == STATE_RUNNING ) {
            if( event == EVENT_FIRE ) {
                audio.restart();
            }
            if( event == EVENT_DONE ) {
                currentState = STATE_WAITING;
                audio.close();
            }
        }
    }

    @Override
    protected void onAudioFinished() {
        put( EVENT_DONE );
    }
}
```

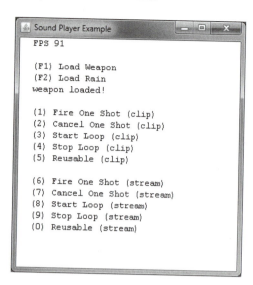

Figure 13.6
Sound Player Example.
© 2014 Timothy Wright.

These three events—one-shot, loop, and restart—for both small and large data files, provide many sound needs for computer games. The `SoundPlayerExample` code, seen in Figure 13.6 and located in the `javagames.sound` package, demonstrates using the new sound classes to add sound to the game loop.

The `initialize()` method loads two sounds: a weapon blast and a rain sound. The `readBytes()` method extracts the raw sound bytes from the file. The `loadWaveFile()` method creates all of the event objects. For short clips, the events use a `BlockingClip`. For large data, a `BlockingDataLine` can be used. This example uses a small sound with both types of sound types for testing. The `shutDownClips()` method stops each sound event thread before returning.

The `processInput()` method handles the keypresses as always. The F1 and F2 keys load the two different sounds. The number 1 key starts the one-shot clip and the 2 key stops the one-shot clip. The 3 key starts the clip loop, and 4 stops it. The 5 key fires the restart clip. The 6, 7, 8, 9, and 0 keys do the same things with a data line stream. The `render()` method displays the usual instructions.

And now…making a limited appearance, it's the `terminate()` method (I was beginning to think this method would never be needed). This method shuts down all the event threads when the program is shut down.

```
package javagames.sound;

import java.awt.Graphics;
```

```java
import java.awt.event.KeyEvent;
import java.io.*;

import javagames.util.*;


public class SoundPlayerExample extends SimpleFramework {
    private OneShotEvent oneShotClip;
    private LoopEvent loopClip;
    private RestartEvent restartClip;

    private OneShotEvent oneShotStream;
    private LoopEvent loopStream;
    private RestartEvent restartStream;

    private byte[] weaponBytes;
    private byte[] rainBytes;
    private String loaded;

    public SoundPlayerExample() {
        appWidth = 340;
        appHeight = 340;
        appSleep = 10L;
        appTitle = "Sound Player Example";
        appBackground = Color.WHITE;
        appFPSColor = Color.BLACK;
    }

    @Override
    protected void initialize() {
        super.initialize();
        InputStream in = ResourceLoader.load(
            SoundPlayerExample.class,
            "./res/assets/sound/WEAPON_scifi_fire_02.wav",
            "asdf"
        );
        weaponBytes = readBytes( in );

        in = ResourceLoader.load(
            SoundPlayerExample.class,
            "./res/assets/sound/WEATHER_rain_medium_5k.wav",
            "asdf"
        );
        rainBytes = readBytes( in );

        loadWaveFile( weaponBytes );
        loaded = "weapon";
    }
```

```java
    private byte[] readBytes( InputStream in ) {
        try {
            BufferedInputStream buf = new BufferedInputStream( in );
            ByteArrayOutputStream out = new ByteArrayOutputStream();
            int read;
            while( (read = buf.read()) != -1 ) {
                out.write( read );
            }
            in.close();
            return out.toByteArray();
        } catch( IOException ex ) {
            ex.printStackTrace();
            return null;
        }
    }

    private void loadWaveFile( byte[] rawData ) {
        shutDownClips();
        oneShotClip = new OneShotEvent( new BlockingClip( rawData ) );
        oneShotClip.initialize();
        loopClip = new LoopEvent( new BlockingClip( rawData ) );
        loopClip.initialize();
        restartClip = new RestartEvent( new BlockingClip( rawData ) );
        restartClip.initialize();
        oneShotStream = new OneShotEvent( new BlockingDataLine( rawData ) );
        oneShotStream.initialize();
        loopStream = new LoopEvent( new BlockingDataLine( rawData ) );
        loopStream.initialize();
        restartStream = new RestartEvent( new BlockingDataLine( rawData ) );
        restartStream.initialize();
    }

    private void shutDownClips() {
        if( oneShotClip != null ) oneShotClip.shutDown();
        if( loopClip != null ) loopClip.shutDown();
        if( restartClip != null ) restartClip.shutDown();
        if( oneShotStream != null ) oneShotStream.shutDown();
        if( loopStream != null ) loopStream.shutDown();
        if( restartStream != null ) restartStream.shutDown();
    }

    @Override
    protected void processInput( float delta ) {
        super.processInput( delta );
```

```java
if( keyboard.keyDownOnce( KeyEvent.VK_F1 ) ) {
   loadWaveFile( weaponBytes );
   loaded = "weapon";
}
if( keyboard.keyDownOnce( KeyEvent.VK_F2 ) ) {
   loadWaveFile( rainBytes );
   loaded = "rain";
}
if( keyboard.keyDownOnce( KeyEvent.VK_1 ) ) {
   oneShotClip.fire();
}
if( keyboard.keyDownOnce( KeyEvent.VK_2 ) ) {
   oneShotClip.done();
}
if( keyboard.keyDownOnce( KeyEvent.VK_3 ) ) {
   loopClip.fire();
}
if( keyboard.keyDownOnce( KeyEvent.VK_4 ) ) {
   loopClip.done();
}
if( keyboard.keyDownOnce( KeyEvent.VK_5 ) ) {
   restartClip.fire();
}
if( keyboard.keyDownOnce( KeyEvent.VK_6 ) ) {
   oneShotStream.fire();
}
if( keyboard.keyDownOnce( KeyEvent.VK_7 ) ) {
   oneShotStream.done();
}
if( keyboard.keyDownOnce( KeyEvent.VK_8 ) ) {
   loopStream.fire();
}
if( keyboard.keyDownOnce( KeyEvent.VK_9 ) ) {
   loopStream.done();
}
if( keyboard.keyDownOnce( KeyEvent.VK_0 ) ) {
   restartStream.fire();
}
}
@Override
protected void updateObjects( float delta ) {
   super.updateObjects( delta );
}
```

```
    @Override
    protected void render( Graphics g ) {
        super.render( g );

        textPos = Utility.drawString( g, 20, textPos,
            "",
            "(F1) Load Weapon",
            "(F2) Load Rain",
            loaded + " loaded!",
            "",
            "(1) Fire One Shot (clip)",
            "(2) Cancel One Shot (clip)",
            "(3) Start Loop (clip)",
            "(4) Stop Loop (clip)",
            "(5) Reusable (clip)",
            "",
            "(6) Fire One Shot (stream)",
            "(7) Cancel One Shot (stream)",
            "(8) Start Loop (stream)",
            "(9) Stop Loop (stream)",
            "(0) Reusable (stream)"
        );
    }

    @Override
    protected void terminate() {
        super.terminate();
        shutDownClips();
    }

    public static void main( String[] args ) {
        launchApp( new SoundPlayerExample() );
    }
}
```

ADDING SOUND CONTROLS

You're almost done. The only thing left to add are the sound controls. The following
controls are available:

```
Boolean:   MUTE
           APPLY_REVERB

Enum:   REVERB

Float: AUX_RETURN
       AUX_SEND
```

```
BALANCE
MASTER_GAIN
PAN
REVERB_RETURN
REVERB_SEND
SAMPLE_RATE
VOLUME
```

Not all lines support all controls, so it is important to check if the control is available before getting access. The following code checks for a MASTER_GAIN control and acquires the control if it is available:

```
if( line.isControlSupported( FloatControl.Type.MASTER_GAIN ) ) {
    FloatControl gainControl =
      (FloatControl)line.getControl( FloatControl.Type.MASTER_GAIN );
}
```

The MASTER_GAIN control will adjust the sound volume and the PAN control will determine from which speaker the sound is heard. If the sound is not a mono sound, but a stereo sound, use the BALANCE control. The updated AudioStream code adds support for GAIN and PAN controls.

```
package javagames.sound;


import java.util.*;
import java.util.concurrent.locks.*;

import javax.sound.sampled.*;
import javax.sound.sampled.LineEvent.*;


public abstract class AudioStream implements LineListener {
    public static final int LOOP_CONTINUOUSLY = -1;

    protected final Lock lock = new ReentrantLock();
    protected final Condition cond = lock.newCondition();

    protected volatile boolean open = false;
    protected volatile boolean started = false;

    // UPDATES
    protected FloatControl gainControl;
    protected FloatControl panControl;
    // UPDATES

    protected byte[] soundData;
```

```java
    private List<BlockingAudioListener> listeners =
        Collections.synchronizedList(
            new ArrayList<BlockingAudioListener>() );
    public AudioStream( byte[] soundData ) {
        this.soundData = soundData;
    }

    public abstract void open();
    public abstract void close();
    public abstract void start();
    public abstract void loop( int count );
    public abstract void restart();
    public abstract void stop();

    public boolean addListener( BlockingAudioListener listener ) {
        return listeners.add( listener );
    }

    protected void fireTaskFinished() {
        synchronized( listeners ) {
            for( BlockingAudioListener listener : listeners ) {
                listener.audioFinished();
            }
        }
    }
}

@Override
public void update( LineEvent event ) {
    boolean wasStarted = started;
    lock.lock();
    try {
        if( event.getType() == Type.OPEN ) {
            open = true;
        } else if( event.getType() == Type.CLOSE ) {
            open = false;
        } else if( event.getType() == Type.START ) {
            started = true;
        } else if( event.getType() == Type.STOP ) {
            started = false;
        }
        cond.signalAll();
    } finally {
        lock.unlock();
    }
```

```java
      if( wasStarted && !started ) {
         fireTaskFinished();
      }
   }
//UPDATES
public void clearControls() {
      gainControl = null;
      panControl = null;
}
public void createControls( Line line ) {
      if( line.isControlSupported( FloatControl.Type.MASTER_GAIN ) ) {
         gainControl =
            (FloatControl)line.getControl( FloatControl.Type.MASTER_GAIN );
      }
      if( line.isControlSupported( FloatControl.Type.PAN ) ) {
         panControl =
            (FloatControl)line.getControl( FloatControl.Type.PAN );
      }
}
public boolean hasGainControl() {
      return gainControl != null;
}
public void setGain( float fGain ) {
      if( hasGainControl() ) {
         gainControl.setValue( fGain );
      }
}
public float getGain() {
      return hasGainControl() ? gainControl.getValue() : 0.0f;
}
public float getMaximum() {
      return hasGainControl() ? gainControl.getMaximum() : 0.0f;
}
public float getMinimum() {
      return hasGainControl() ? gainControl.getMinimum() : 0.0f;
}
public boolean hasPanControl() {
      return panControl != null;
}
```

```
    public float getPrecision() {
       return hasPanControl() ? panControl.getPrecision() : 0.0f;
    }

    public float getPan() {
       return hasPanControl() ? panControl.getValue() : 0.0f;
    }

    public void setPan( float pan ) {
       if( hasPanControl() ) {
          panControl.setValue( pan );
       }
    }
 }
//UPDATES

}
```

There are also updates to the open() and close() methods of the BlockingClip and BlockingDataLine class:

```
// add to both open() methods
while( !open ) {
    cond.await();
}
//UPDATE
createControls( clip );
//UPDATE
System.out.println( "open" );

// add to both close() methods
clip.close();
while( open ) {
    cond.await();
}
clip = null;
//UPDATE
clearControls();
//UPDATE
System.out.println( "Turned off" );
```

Although there are lots of different controls, most are mixer-centric, and some don't even work. So while it would be nice to add them all, it is easier to edit the sounds with professional sound editing software and use the sound API just for playback. See the reference section at the end of this chapter for information about sound editing software.

The SoundControlsExample, shown in Figure 13.7 and located in the javagames.sound package, uses a computer beep sound and a loop event with a Clip and a SourceDataLine. The number keys enable and disable the loop, and the letter keys adjust the volume and the pan of the sound while the sound is playing.

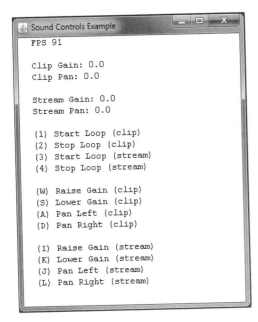

Figure 13.7
Sound Controls Example.
© 2014 Timothy Wright.

Another issue with the sound controls example is that the PAN control is available only when using the Java 6.0 SDK. The new implementation for the mixer replaced with Java 7.0 no longer supports the PAN control. If you are using the 7.0 version, the pan feature of the example will not work.

Notice that the pan has a value range of (-1, 1), where -1 is the left speaker, 1 is the right speaker, and zero is both speakers. The precision determines the number of decimal places supported by the PAN control.

```
package javagames.sound;

import java.awt.Graphics;
import java.awt.event.KeyEvent;
import java.io.*;

import javagames.util.*;
```

```java
public class SoundControlsExample extends SimpleFramework {

    private BlockingClip clip;
    private LoopEvent loopClip;

    private BlockingDataLine dataLine;
    private LoopEvent loopStream;

    private byte[] rawSound;

    public SoundControlsExample() {
        appWidth = 340;
        appHeight = 400;
        appSleep = 10L;
        appTitle = "Sound Controls Example";
        appBackground = Color.WHITE;
        appFPSColor = Color.BLACK;
    }

    @Override
    protected void initialize() {
        super.initialize();

        InputStream in = ResourceLoader.load(
            SoundControlsExample.class,
            "./res/assets/sound/ELECTRONIC_computer_beep_09.wav",
            "asdf"
        );
        rawSound = readBytes( in );

        clip = new BlockingClip( rawSound );
        loopClip = new LoopEvent( clip );
        loopClip.initialize();

        dataLine = new BlockingDataLine( rawSound );
        loopStream = new LoopEvent( dataLine );
        loopStream.initialize();

    }

    private byte[] readBytes( InputStream in ) {
        try {
            BufferedInputStream buf = new BufferedInputStream( in );
            ByteArrayOutputStream out = new ByteArrayOutputStream();
            int read;
            while( (read = buf.read()) != -1 ) {
                out.write( read );
            }
            in.close();
            return out.toByteArray();
```

```
      } catch( IOException ex ) {
         ex.printStackTrace();
         return null;
      }
   }

   private void shutDownClips() {
      if( loopClip != null ) loopClip.shutDown();
      if( loopStream != null ) loopStream.shutDown();
   }

   @Override
   protected void processInput( float delta ) {
      super.processInput( delta );

      if( keyboard.keyDownOnce( KeyEvent.VK_1 ) ) {
         loopClip.fire();
      }
      if( keyboard.keyDownOnce( KeyEvent.VK_2 ) ) {
         loopClip.done();
      }
      if( keyboard.keyDownOnce( KeyEvent.VK_3 ) ) {
         loopStream.fire();
      }
      if( keyboard.keyDownOnce( KeyEvent.VK_4 ) ) {
         loopStream.done();
      }
      if( keyboard.keyDownOnce( KeyEvent.VK_W ) ) {
         increaseGain( clip );
      }
      if( keyboard.keyDownOnce( KeyEvent.VK_S ) ) {
         decreaseGain( clip );
      }
      if( keyboard.keyDownOnce( KeyEvent.VK_A ) ) {
         panLeft( clip );
      }
      if( keyboard.keyDownOnce( KeyEvent.VK_D ) ) {
         panRight( clip );
      }
      if( keyboard.keyDownOnce( KeyEvent.VK_I ) ) {
         increaseGain( dataLine );
      }
      if( keyboard.keyDownOnce( KeyEvent.VK_K ) ) {
         decreaseGain( dataLine );
      }
```

```java
        if( keyboard.keyDownOnce( KeyEvent.VK_J ) ) {
            panLeft( dataLine );
        }
        if( keyboard.keyDownOnce( KeyEvent.VK_L ) ) {
            panRight( dataLine );
        }
    }

    private void increaseGain( AudioStream audio ) {
        float current = audio.getGain();
        if( current < 10.0f ) {
            audio.setGain( current + 3.0f );
        }
    }

    private void decreaseGain( AudioStream audio ) {
        float current = audio.getGain();
        if( current > -20.0f ) {
            audio.setGain( current - 3.0f );
        }
    }

    private void panLeft( AudioStream audio ) {
        float current = audio.getPan();
        float precision = audio.getPrecision();
        audio.setPan( current - precision * 10.0f );
    }

    private void panRight( AudioStream audio ) {
        float current = audio.getPan();
        float precision = audio.getPrecision();
        audio.setPan( current + precision * 10.0f );
    }

    @Override
    protected void updateObjects( float delta ) {
        super.updateObjects( delta );
    }

    @Override
    protected void render( Graphics g ) {
        super.render( g );

        textPos = Utility.drawString( g, 20, textPos,
            "",
            "Clip Gain: " + clip.getGain(),
            "Clip Pan: " + clip.getPan(),
            "",
```

```
        "Stream Gain: " + dataLine.getGain(),
        "Stream Pan: " + dataLine.getPan(),
        "",
        "(1) Start Loop (clip)",
        "(2) Stop Loop (clip)",
        "(3) Start Loop (stream)",
        "(4) Stop Loop (stream)",
        "",
        "(W) Raise Gain (clip)",
        "(S) Lower Gain (clip)",
        "(A) Pan Left (clip)",
        "(D) Pan Right (clip)",
        "",
        "(I) Raise Gain (stream)",
        "(K) Lower Gain (stream)",
        "(J) Pan Left (stream)",
        "(L) Pan Right (stream)"
      );
  }

  @Override
  protected void terminate() {
      super.terminate();
      shutDownClips();
  }

  public static void main( String[] args ) {
      launchApp( new SoundControlsExample() );
  }

}
```

Tip

There are many differences between 6.0 and 7.0 when it comes to sound. The playing clips example demonstrates different behavior between Java 7.0 and Java 6.0. Although large clips can be loaded in Java 7.0, and playing small clips has less latency, sometimes the Java 7.0 small clips stop working. I have not found a solution to this. As a workaround, if you're using Java 6.0, all large files need to be an AudioDataLine class, and smaller sounds work better as Clips. If you're using 7.0, small clips are better as AudioDataline objects and larger files should be loaded as Clips.

Unfortunately, there is no guarantee for consistent behavior between versions and operating systems without using a third-party library. If sound reliability is required and the behaviors of the current sound library are not sufficient, check out the OpenAL with the JOAL library wrappers listed in the resources section. Although

OpenAL is more difficult to set up and get working, it can provide the necessary functionality missing from the current sound implementation.

RESOURCES AND FURTHER READING

"Sound," 1995, http://docs.oracle.com/javase/tutorial/sound/.

Pfisterer, Matthias, Florian Bomers, "jsresources.org - Java Sound Resources," 2005, http://www.jsresources.org/.

Audacity, which is a free, open source, cross-platform software for recording and editing sounds; see http://audacity.sourceforge.net/.

OpenAL, which is a cross-platform 3D audio API appropriate for use with gaming; see http://connect.creativelabs.com/openal/default.aspx.

JOAL, which is a reference implementation of the Java bindings for the OpenAL API; see http://jogamp.org/joal/www/.

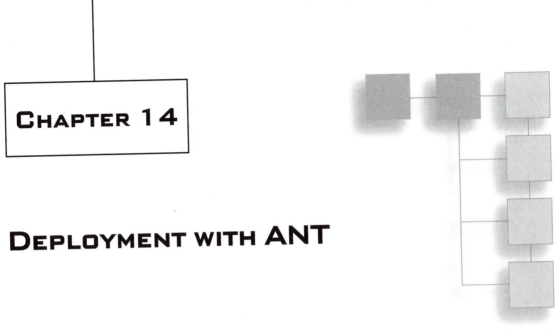

CHAPTER 14

DEPLOYMENT WITH ANT

Although the goal of this book is to provide the tools to make games from scratch without any third-party libraries, using the command line to build and deploy your game is just nuts. It would be nice to be able to do these things from scratch, but I'm not going to expect anyone to do that.

ANT stands for *Another Neat Tool,* and is used to provide platform-independent build script processing. The build scripts are written in XML, and while ANT is easily extendable, most of the tasks you'll need are already provided.

Using a build script is important, because it is very time consuming to package a game into an easy-to-run format. As a game increases in size, it becomes hard to remember all the steps necessary to package it. Build scripts not only document all the steps necessary to package software, but they enable the game to build on any platform.

INSTALLING THE ANT SOFTWARE

Regardless of the operating system, there are a few things to keep in mind when installing ANT. Downloading the required files from http://ant.apache.org/ is easy, and the downloaded files do not require any installation program to run. The files can be placed anywhere. However, it is necessary to set the following environment variables:

```
ANT_HOME=FOLDER_THAT_CONTAINS_BIN_AND_LIB
JAVA_HOME=JDK_HOME_FOLDER
Path=%Path%;ANT_HOME\bin
```

These variables are what I use on my Windows 7 machine. If you are running a flavor of Linux, it will depend on the flavor as to how these variables are set. Adding the

`ANT_HOME\bin` folder to the system path allows the ANT tool to be run from the command line. The ANT tool should also be integrated with most common IDEs, so feel free to use that version.

The `JAVA_HOME` environment variable should point to the JDK so that ANT has access to the Java tools needed to compile source code. The online documentation for installing ANT will be the most correct and up-to-date, so it is recommended that you use that documentation as an installation guide. See the resources at the end of the chapter for more information.

UNDERSTANDING THE FORMAT OF A BUILD SCRIPT

The build script has several tags. There's the `project` tag, which is the root tag for any build script. This tag has a name and optional `basedir` and `default` target attributes.

```
<project name="name" basedir="." default="default">
</project>
```

There are also `target` tags. A build script contains one or more targets, which is one step in the build process. Targets contain a `name`, a `description`, and an optional `depends` attribute, which is a comma-separated list of all the targets this target depends on. Before a target is run, all of its dependencies are run. Dependent targets run only once, regardless of the number of times they are referenced.

```
<target name="target-name" description="target description"
    depends="list,separated,with,commas">
</target>
```

ANT scripts also contain properties. Properties have a `name` and either a `value` or `location`. If the `location` attribute is used, the location is converted to a valid file path. Properties, once defined, cannot be overridden. No matter how many times a property is defined, it will only ever have the first value it is set to. This is the cause of many issues when importing multiple build scripts.

```
<property name="name1" value="value1"/>
<property name="name2" location="location/one"/>
```

Properties are useful because they can be referenced by surrounding the property name with a dollar sign and curly braces. `${property.name}` is expanded at runtime to the value of the property with the name `property.name`. This expansion can even happen inside `xml` attributes. ANT provides access to all the Java system properties with the same dollar sign syntax. `${os.name}` expands to the same value as `System.getProperty("os.name")`.

Additionally, ANT has some built-in properties:

- `basedir`—The absolute path of the build script project `basedir` attribute set in the `<project>` tag.
- `ant.file`—The absolute path of the build file.
- `ant.project.name`—The name attribute of the project tag.

See the documentation on the ANT website for more information about the built-in properties.

The following is a simple ANT script with a single target that prints `Hello World!` with the `echo` tag:

```xml
<?xml version="1.0" encoding="UTF-8"?>

<project name="hello-world" default="default">

    <description>
    This is a simple Hello World script
    </description>
    <target name="default" description="target description">
        <echo>Hello World!</echo>
    </target>

</project>
```

To run this script, you have two options. If the script is saved with the name `build.xml`, then simply pointing the command prompt to the same directory and typing `ant` will cause ANT to scan the current directory, load any file called `build.xml`, and execute the default target.

```
C:\Ant Tests>ant
Buildfile: C:\Ant Tests\build.xml

default:
     [echo] Hello World!

BUILD SUCCESSFUL
Total time: 0 seconds
```

If the script is not named `build.xml`, the `-f` command-line flag can be used to run any script by passing the filename:

```
C:\Ant Tests>ant -f hello-world.xml
Buildfile: C:\Ant Tests\hello-world.xml
```

```
default:
     [echo] Hello World!
BUILD SUCCESSFUL
Total time: 0 seconds
```

The -version flag is a good way to make sure the current version of ANT is in the system path:

```
C:\Ant Tests>ant -version
Apache Ant(TM) version 1.8.2 compiled on December 20 2010

C:\Ant Tests>
```

The -help flag is used to list all the available commands.

```
C:\Ant Tests>ant -help
ant [options] [target [target2 [target3] ...]]
Options:
   -help, -h               print this message
   -projecthelp, -p        print project help information
   -version                print the version information and exit
   -diagnostics            print information that might be helpful to
                           diagnose or report problems.
   -quiet, -q              be extra quiet
   -verbose, -v            be extra verbose
   ... lots more flags ...
```

The -p flag lists the project help, which shows all the information about a build script. The HelloWorld.xml script only has one target, but the output from the project help flag is still useful, showing all the tag documentation as well as the default target.

```
C:\Ant Tests>ant -p
Buildfile: C:\Ant Tests\build.xml

        This is a simple Hello World script

Main targets:

default target description
Default target: default
```

Finally, to run specific targets, the target name can be passed in at the end of the command. Passing in a target, or multiple targets separated by spaces, only runs those targets and not the default target. This is an easy way to run only specific build steps.

```
C:\Ant Tests>ant -f hello-world.xml default
Buildfile: C:\Ant Tests\hello-world.xml
```

```
default:
    [echo] Hello World!
BUILD SUCCESSFUL
Total time: 0 seconds
```

LEARNING COMMON ANT TASKS

ANT has many built-in tags that you can use to perform most of the tasks needed to build and package an application.

The `<echo>` tag prints out information to the console.

```
<echo>This prints out to the console</echo>
```

To create directories, you use the `<mkdir>` tag. The `<delete>` tag will remove directories. Notice how the `${basedir}` syntax can be used inside attribute values.

```
<delete dir="${basedir}/lib"/>
<mkdir dir="${basedir}/lib"/>
<delete dir="${basedir}/bin"/>
<mkdir dir="${basedir}/bin"/>
```

The `<copy>` tag can be used to copy and rename files, and copy entire directories. A single file copy and rename is as follows:

```
<copy file="./res/myfile.txt" tofile="./lib/mycopy.txt"/>
```

The following tag copies a file to a different directory:

```
<copy file="res/myfile.txt" todir="lib/some/other/dir"/>
```

To copy an entire directory, use the following:

```
<copy todir="lib/new/dir">
  <fileset dir="res"/>
</copy>
```

To exclude some files from the copy, use the following:

```
<copy todir="lib/new/dir">
  <fileset dir="res">
    <exclude name="**/*.java"/>
  </fileset>
</copy>
```

Notice the `**/*.java` syntax. The two stars `**` tell ANT to search all directories and sub-directories.

You can use the following to allow ANT to compile Java code from a build script:

```
<path id="common.classpath">
    <pathelement location="${basedir}/bin"/>
</path>

<javac
    srcdir="${basedir}/src"
    destdir="${basedir}/bin"
    classpathref="common.classpath"
    debug="on"
/>
```

The classpath reference is used so that many different libraries and code files can be defined elsewhere.

The following tag is used to create a JAR file:

```
<fileset id="jar.fileset" dir="bin">
    <exclude name="**/*Tests.class"/>
</fileset>


<jar destfile="lib/${ant.project.name}.jar">
    <fileset refid="jar.fileset"/>
    <manifest>
       <attribute name="Main-Class" value="javagames.ant.HelloWorld"/>
       <attribute name="Class-Path"
          value="jar1-name jar2-name directory-name/jar3-name"/>
    </manifest>
</jar>
```

Notice that you can include the `<manifest>` tag to specify the main class and dependent libraries. The `<fileset>` tag specifies which file will be placed in the JAR file. The destfile attribute is the name and location of the JAR file created by the `<jar>` tag.

The following can be used to sign a JAR file:

```
<delete file="signjar.keystore"/>

<genkey alias="${ant.project.name}"
      validity="999999"
      storepass="storepass"
      keystore="signjar.keystore">
   <dname>
      <param name="CN" value="Tim Wright"/>
      <param name="OU" value="Groovy Inc."/>
      <param name="O" value="Planet Earth"/>
```

```
    <param name="C" value="Milkyway"/>
    </dname>
</genkey>

<signjar jar="lib/${ant.project.name}.jar"
        keystore="signjar.keystore"
        alias="${ant.project.name}"
        storepass="storepass"/>

<delete file="signjar.keystore"/>
```

The `signjar.keystore` is deleted both at the beginning and end of the task to make sure that it is removed even if there were errors running the sign JAR task. The `<genkey>` tag creates the `keystore` and the `<signjar>` tag uses the `keystore` to sign the JAR file. These tags run the command-line tools that come with the JDK.

Finally, the following tag can be used to add files, folders, and other ZIP files, such as other Java libraries, to an already created JAR file.

```
<jar update="true" destfile="lib/${ant.project.name}.jar">
    <fileset dir="src"/>
    <fileset dir="res"/>
    <zipfileset src="res/gamelib.jar"/>
</jar>
```

This tag is handy when creating default scripts and then extending them to add additional resources to JAR files.

BUILDING AN EXTENDABLE BUILD SCRIPT

Creating an extendable script that can be used as a starting point is a lengthy process, but it can be worth the effort. The `<import>` tag is used to include other scripts in a build script.

```
<import file="toInclude.xml"/>
```

Any properties defined at the top level of the included script cannot be overridden, so be sure to set any properties before another script is included.

It can be helpful to define third-party libraries as properties in the common build script.

```
<property name="junit.lib"
    location="${common.home}/../3rd/JUnit/junit-4.5.jar"/>
```

Each default target in the common script is split into two targets. For example, the `clean` target is defined as follows:

```
<target name="clean" depends="project-clean">

    <echo>Deleting project directory structure...</echo>

    <delete dir="${common.bin}"/>
    <delete dir="${common.lib}"/>
    <delete dir="${common.docs}"/>
    <delete dir="${common.junit}"/>

</target>

<target name="project-clean"/>
```

Notice that the `clean` target depends on the empty `project-clean` target. This structure allows for the default target to be replaced, or executed before and after a custom target.

Unlike properties, targets can be overridden. The last target defined with the same name will be used, unlike properties, which use the first value given. If three different files all define the same target, the last defined target is used. To call a previously defined target, you can use the project name to reference the overridden target. For example, if the project named `common` defines a target named `clean`, you can always access that target with the name `common.clean`.

To override the default `clean` target, define a new target with the same name.

```
<project name="build">

    <import file="common.xml"/>

    <target name="clean">
    </target>

</project>
```

The previous example overrides the `clean` target, completely replacing it. If you need to define a custom tag that runs before the default `clean` target, but does not replace it, then override the `<project-clean>` tag that the default `clean` tag depends on.

```
<project name="custom" default="clean">

    <include file="common.xml"/>

    <target name="project-clean">
        <echo>Runs before default</echo>
    </target>

</project>
```

The previous example overrides the `project-clean` tag, which will be executed before the common `clean` tag.

The project name syntax explained previously can be used to reference the default clean tag. This feature can be used to define the default tag as a dependency to an overridden tag, so that the custom tag runs after the common one.

```
<project name="custom">

    <import file="common.xml"/>

    <target name="clean" depends="common.clean">
       <echo>Runs after default</echo>
    </target>

</project>
```

This example overrides the `clean` target, but since it depends on the `common.clean` target, the custom clean will run after the default target.

These three options make it possible to extend a script any number of ways.

- Replace a target—Create a new target with the same name.
- Custom after default—Use the `depends="projectname.target"` syntax.
- Custom before default—Override the `project-target` tag.

Overriding properties is not possible with ANT, so a simple trick is to define default properties in the target instead of at the top of the build script. As long as the properties are set before the target is called, the default properties can be overridden.

```
<target name="compile" depends="project-compile">

    <property name="compile.srcdir" value="${basedir}/src;${basedir}/test"/>
    <property name="compile.destdir" value="${basedir}/bin"/>
    <property name="compile.debug" value="on"/>
    <property name="compile.classpath" value="${common.classpath}"/>


    <echo>Compiling source code...</echo>

    <javac
    srcdir="${compile.srcdir}"
    destdir="${compile.destdir}"
    classpathref="${compile.classpath}"
    debug="${compile.debug}"
    />

</target>
```

All of the properties used in the target—compile.srdir, compile.destdir, compile.debug, and compile.classpath—are not set until the target runs. If the build script including the common script was to define one of these properties before the task is called, that property would already exist when the target property is set.

This following is an example of an extendable build script that you can use as the starting point for building future game projects.

```xml
<?xml version="1.0" encoding="UTF-8"?>

<!--
    This is the base script used for creating
    custom build scripts.
-->
<project name="common" basedir=".">

<dirname property="common.home" file="${ant.file.common}"/>

<property name="junit.lib"
        location="${common.home}/../3rd/JUnit/junit-4.5.jar"/>

<property name="common.bin" value="${basedir}/bin"/>
<property name="common.lib" value="${basedir}/lib"/>
<property name="common.docs" value="${basedir}/docs"/>
<property name="common.test" value="${basedir}/test"/>
<property name="common.junit" value="${basedir}/junit"/>
<property name="common.classpath" value="common.classpath"/>

<path id="common.classpath">
    <pathelement location="${common.bin}"/>
</path>


<!-- ================================
                BUILD
     ================================ -->
<target name="build" description="--> Builds the project"
        depends="project-build, clean, init, compile, jar"/>

<target name="project-build"/>


<!-- ================================
                INIT
     ================================ -->
<target name="init" depends="project-init">

    <echo>Creating project directory structure...</echo>

    <mkdir dir="${common.bin}"/>
```

```xml
    <mkdir dir="${common.lib}"/>
    <mkdir dir="${common.docs}"/>
    <mkdir dir="${common.test}"/>
    <mkdir dir="${common.junit}"/>

</target>

<target name="project-init"/>


<!-- ================================
            CLEAN
     ================================ -->
<target name="clean" depends="project-clean">

    <echo>Deleting project directory structure...</echo>

    <delete dir="${common.bin}"/>
    <delete dir="${common.lib}"/>
    <delete dir="${common.docs}"/>
    <delete dir="${common.junit}"/>

</target>

<target name="project-clean"/>


<!-- ================================
            COMPILE
     ================================ -->
<target name="compile" depends="project-compile">

    <property name="compile.srcdir" value="${basedir}/src;${basedir}/test"/>
    <property name="compile.destdir" value="${basedir}/bin"/>
    <property name="compile.debug" value="on"/>
    <property name="compile.classpath" value="${common.classpath}"/>


        <echo>Compiling source code...</echo>

      <javac
         srcdir="${compile.srcdir}"
         destdir="${compile.destdir}"
         classpathref="${compile.classpath}"
         debug="${compile.debug}"
      />

</target>

<target name="project-compile"/>
```

```xml
<!-- ================================
            JAR
     ================================ -->
<target name="jar" depends="project-jar">

    <property name="jar.name" value="${ant.project.name}"/>
    <property name="jar.mainclass" value=""/>
    <property name="jar.classpath" value=""/>
    <property name="jar.fileset" value="jar.fileset"/>
    <property name="jar.destfile" value="${common.lib}/${jar.name}.jar"/>

    <fileset id="jar.fileset" dir="${common.bin}">
       <exclude name="**/Test*.class"/>
       <exclude name="**/*Tests.class"/>
       <exclude name="**/*TestCase.class"/>
    </fileset>

    <echo>Creating ${common.lib}${file.separator}${jar.name}.jar...</echo>

    <jar destfile="${jar.destfile}">
       <fileset refid="${jar.fileset}"/>
     <manifest>
       <attribute name="Main-Class" value="${jar.mainclass}"/>
       <attribute name="Class-Path" value="${jar.classpath}"/>
     </manifest>
    </jar>

</target>
<target name="project-jar"/>


<!-- ================================
            SIGNJAR
     ================================ -->
<target name="signjar" depends="project-signjar">
    <property name="signjar.keystore"
              value="${basedir}/${ant.project.name}.keystore"/>
    <property name="signjar.alias" value="${ant.project.name}"/>
    <property name="signjar.storepass" value="storepass"/>
    <property name="signjar.validity" value="999999"/>
    <property name="signjar.jar" value="${common.lib}/${jar.name}.jar"/>

    <echo>Signing Jar File</echo>

    <delete file="${signjar.keystore}"/>

    <genkey alias="${signjar.alias}"
            validity="${signjar.validity}"
            storepass="${signjar.storepass}"
```

```
            keystore="${signjar.keystore}">
        <dname>
         <param name="CN" value="Tim Wright"/>
         <param name="OU" value="Groovy Inc."/>
         <param name="O" value="Rio Rancho"/>
         <param name="C" value="US"/>
        </dname>
      </genkey>

      <signjar jar="${signjar.jar}"
          keystore="${signjar.keystore}"
            alias="${signjar.alias}"
          storepass="${signjar.storepass}"/>

      <delete file="${signjar.keystore}"/>

</target>
<target name="project-signjar"/>

</project>
```

Using the common.xml build script is easy. The CustomBuild.xml file default target is set to the custom default target. The default target depends on the build and signjar tags, which are defined in the common build script. Notice that the common.classpath property is defined before the common build script is imported. Because the common.classpath is defined at the top of the common build script, it must be set before the common script is included.

Even though the common.classpath property is set before the import, the classpath can be defined after the import, as long as it is defined before it is used. The custom build example script is a good starting point for a custom build script. This will be used in the final game example at the end of the book to build, package, and deploy the game in its final configuration.

```
<?xml version="1.0" encoding="UTF-8"?>

<project name="custom-build" default="default">

   <description>
      Extending the common.xml
   </description>

   <property name="common.classpath" value="custom.classpath"/>
   <import file="common.xml"/>

   <path id="custom.classpath">
      <pathelement location="${basedir}/bin"/>
      <pathelement location="${junit.lib}"/>
   </path>
```

```
<target name="default" depends="build, signjar"
      description="--> This builds my first real game"/>

</project>
```

RESOURCES AND FURTHER READING

"Apache ANT Manual," 2013, http://ant.apache.org/manual/index.html.

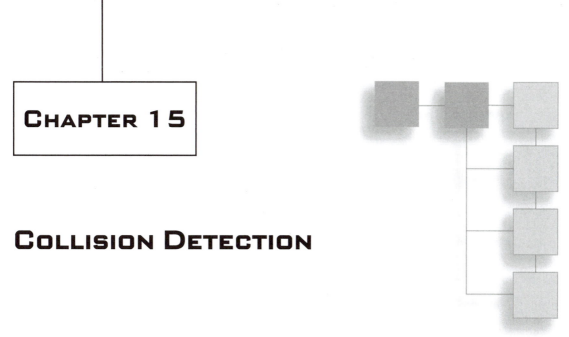

CHAPTER 15

COLLISION DETECTION

Collision detection can be an important part of many games. Although the algorithms presented in Chapter 7, "Intersection Testing," are important, they all lack one very important thing. None of them actually returns the point of collision. For creating games where objects hit each other and react correctly (or at least correctly enough), it is necessary to not only determine the exact point of the collision, but handle the collision with a response, such as bouncing in another directions, or blowing up.

The following sections discuss:

- Simple collision response
- Rectangle-line intersection
- Circle-line intersection
- Line segment intersection
- Collision response

Even though some of the math is more involved than in previous chapters, none of the algorithms covered is really hard, and effort has been made to explain them thoroughly.

BOUNCING BALLS WITH COLLISION DETECTION

The simplest collision response is to bounce objects off vertical and horizontal lines. In order to simulate the collision response of an object against an x- or y-axis, each component of the velocity vector is checked independently. See Figure 15.1.

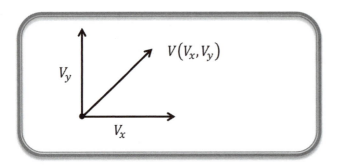

Figure 15.1
Bounce Vector.
© 2014 Timothy Wright.

Each X and Y component is checked for collision, and if it needs to bounce, the velocity is negated. The other component does not change unless it also hits something. The result is an object that appears to bounce. See Figure 15.2.

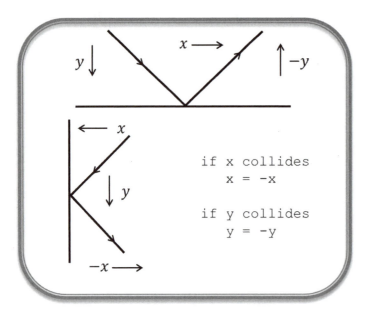

Figure 15.2
Bouncing Ball Collision.
© 2014 Timothy Wright.

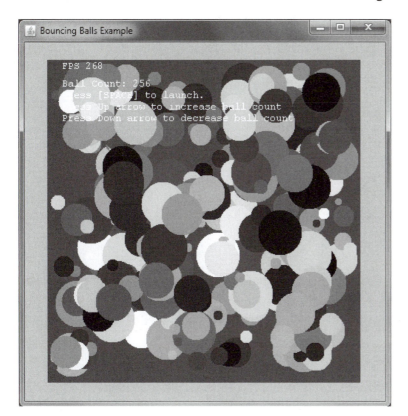

Figure 15.3
Bouncing Balls Example.
© 2014 Timothy Wright.

The BouncingBallsExample, as seen in Figure 15.3 and located in the javagames.collision package, creates random balls that bounce around the screen. The initial ball count is set to 64. Each ball is created to start at the upper-left corner of the game area, and has a random color, radius, and velocity. The initial array size is set to zero to wait for user interaction before launching the balls for the first time. These values are stored in the inner class shown here:

```
class Ball {
    Vector2f position;
    Vector2f velocity;
    float radius;
    Color color;
}
```

The processInput() method creates new random balls. When the spacebar is pressed, all the balls are randomly created again and launched from the upper-left corner. The ball count is increased or decreased when the arrow keys are pressed.

The `updateObjects()` method updates the position of each ball by adding its velocity multiplied by the time delta. Then each ball is checked for collision with the edges, taking the size of each ball into account. To simulate bouncing, each X and Y velocity component is inverted whenever the ball collides with the screen edge.

```
// simple collision response
if( x out of bounds )
    x = -x
if( y out of bounds )
    y = -y
```

The `render()` method draws each ball. Notice that the `super.render()` method is placed after the balls so that the frame rate and instructions are always drawn over the top of the balls.

The `drawOval()` method for drawing the balls that was presented in Chapter 7 is used to draw the balls. Because this application is maintaining the aspect ratio, using this code to stretch each ball to a different width and height is not needed unless the application size is not square.

```
package javagames.collision;

import java.awt.*;
import java.awt.event.KeyEvent;
import java.util.Random;

import javagames.util.*;


public class BouncingBallsExample extends SimpleFramework {
    private static final float WORLD_LEFT   = -1.0f;
    private static final float WORLD_RIGHT  =  1.0f;
    private static final float WORLD_TOP    =  1.0f;
    private static final float WORLD_BOTTOM = -1.0f;

    private static final int MAX_BALLS = 4096;
    private static final int MIN_BALLS = 5;
    private static final int MULTIPLE = 2;

    class Ball {
        Vector2f position;
        Vector2f velocity;
        float radius;
        Color color;
    }

    private Ball[] balls;
    private int ballCount;
```

```java
public BouncingBallsExample() {
    appTitle = "Bouncing Balls Example";
    appHeight = 640;
    appWidth = 640;
    appFPSColor = Color.WHITE;
    appBorder = Color.ORANGE;
    appBackground = Color.DARK_GRAY;
    appWorldWidth = 2.0f;
    appWorldHeight = 2.0f;
    appSleep = 1;
    appMaintainRatio = true;
    appBorderScale = .9f;
}

@Override
protected void initialize() {
    super.initialize();
    balls = new Ball[0];
    ballCount = 64;
}

private void createBalls() {
    Random rand = new Random();
    balls = new Ball[ ballCount ];
    for( int i = 0; i < balls.length; ++i ) {
        balls[i] = new Ball();
        balls[i].velocity =
            new Vector2f( rand.nextFloat(), rand.nextFloat() );
        float r = 0.025f + rand.nextFloat() / 8.0f;
        balls[i].position = new Vector2f( WORLD_LEFT - r, WORLD_TOP - r );
        balls[i].radius = r;
        float color = rand.nextFloat();
        balls[i].color = new Color( color, color, color );
    }
}

@Override
protected void processInput( float delta ) {
    super.processInput( delta );

    if( keyboard.keyDownOnce( KeyEvent.VK_SPACE ) ) {
        createBalls();
    }
    if( keyboard.keyDownOnce( KeyEvent.VK_UP ) ) {
        ballCount *= MULTIPLE;
```

```
            if( ballCount > MAX_BALLS ) {
                ballCount = MAX_BALLS;
            }
            createBalls();
        }
        if( keyboard.keyDownOnce( KeyEvent.VK_DOWN ) ) {
            ballCount /= MULTIPLE;
            if( ballCount < MIN_BALLS ) {
                ballCount = MIN_BALLS;
            }
            createBalls();
        }
    }

    @Override
    protected void updateObjects( float delta ) {
        super.updateObjects( delta );

        for( Ball ball : balls ) {

            ball.position = ball.position.add( ball.velocity.mul( delta ) );

            if( ball.position.x - ball.radius < WORLD_LEFT ) {
                ball.position.x = WORLD_LEFT + ball.radius;
                ball.velocity.x = -ball.velocity.x;
            } else if( ball.position.x + ball.radius > WORLD_RIGHT ) {
                ball.position.x = WORLD_RIGHT - ball.radius;
                ball.velocity.x = -ball.velocity.x;
            }

            if( ball.position.y + ball.radius > WORLD_TOP ) {
                ball.position.y = WORLD_TOP - ball.radius;
                ball.velocity.y = -ball.velocity.y;
            } else if( ball.position.y - ball.radius < WORLD_BOTTOM ) {
                ball.position.y = WORLD_BOTTOM + ball.radius;
                ball.velocity.y = -ball.velocity.y;
            }
        }
    }

    @Override
    protected void render( Graphics g ) {

        for( Ball ball : balls ) {
            g.setColor( ball.color );
            drawOval( g, ball );
        }

        // draw directions on top of bouncing balls
```

```
      super.render( g );
      g.drawString( "Ball Count: " + ballCount, 20, 35 );
      g.drawString( "Press [SPACE] to launch.", 20, 50 );
      g.drawString( "Press Up arrow to increase ball count", 20, 65 );
      g.drawString( "Press Down arrow to decrease ball count", 20, 80 );
   }

   private void drawOval( Graphics g, Ball ball ) {
      Matrix3x3f view = getViewportTransform();
      Vector2f center = ball.position;
      float radius = ball.radius;

      Vector2f topLeft =
         new Vector2f( center.x - radius, center.y + radius );
      topLeft = view.mul( topLeft );

      Vector2f bottomRight =
         new Vector2f( center.x + radius, center.y - radius );
      bottomRight = view.mul( bottomRight );

      int circleX = (int)topLeft.x;
      int circleY = (int)topLeft.y;
      int circleWidth = (int)(bottomRight.x - topLeft.x);
      int circleHeight = (int)(bottomRight.y - topLeft.y);

      g.fillOval( circleX, circleY, circleWidth, circleHeight );
   }

   public static void main( String[] args ) {
      launchApp( new BouncingBallsExample() );
   }
}
```

USING THE PARAMETRIC LINE EQUATION

The parametric line equation is a method of representing different points on a line by changing only a scalar value. The equation is as follows:

$$P = O + sd$$

P is the resulting point, O is the line origin, d is a directions vector, and s is a scalar value. By changing the scalar value, you can represent different points on a line, as shown in Figure 15.4.

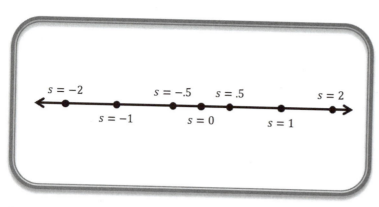

Figure 15.4
Parametric Values.
© 2014 Timothy Wright.

The following collision detection algorithms use the parametric line equation, solving for the scalar value. In the case of an intersection with a circle, the algorithm returns two scalar values.

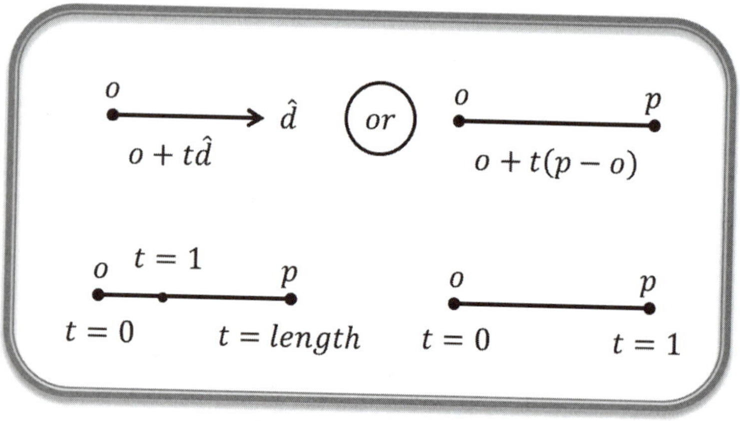

Figure 15.5
Parametric Segment Values.
© 2014 Timothy Wright.

If the direction vector for the parametric line equation is normalized, as shown in Figure 15.5, then the distance from the point 0 to the point P occurs when the t value is equal to the length from 0 to P. If, however, the vector used is not normalized, and instead is formed by just subtracting the two line end points, as shown on the right, the line will go from point 0 to point P when the t value is equal to 1.0.

When using the parametric values returned from the following intersections tests, it is important to know whether the direction vector was normalized. If it was normalized, then only values between zero and the length are on the line segment. If it was not normalized, only values between zero and one are on the line segment.

FINDING A LINE-RECTANGLE INTERSECTION

Determining whether a line has intersected a rectangle and knowing exactly where it intersects can be broken into two steps. The first step is to compute the intersections with the lines that form the rectangle. Keep in mind, there can be two or four intersections, and none of them may actually intersect the rectangle. See Figure 15.6.

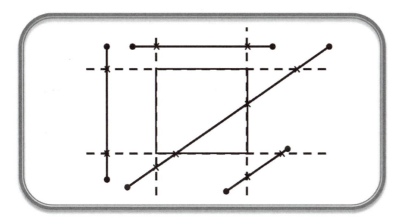

Figure 15.6
Rectangle Intersection.
© 2014 Timothy Wright.

Once these intersections are computed, then you can find the closest intersection that is actually on the rectangle. To simplify the test, the line being tested can be expressed as a parametric line. If an intersection is found, that point can then be tested to see if it is within the line segment bounds. The components of the rectangle are computed as shown in Figure 15.7.

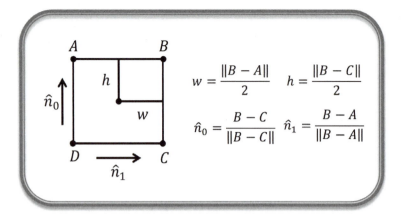

Figure 15.7
Rectangle Components.
© 2014 Timothy Wright.

To find the intersection of the ray with each of the four sides, the equation shown in Figure 15.8 is used, solving for the t value in the parametric line equation. Refer to Chapter 6, "Vector2f Updates," for a review of the dot product and its properties.

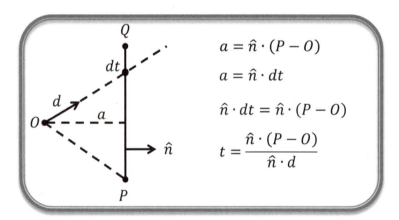

Figure 15.8
Rectangle Intersection Equation.
© 2014 Timothy Wright.

The initial algorithm is as follows:

```
public Float lineRectIntersection(
    Vector2f O, Vector2f d, Vector2f[] rect ) {
```

```
1:      for( int i = 0; i < 2; ++i ) {
2:          Vector2f n = rect[i].sub( rect[i+1] );
3:          n = n.norm();
4:          float e0 = n.dot( rect[i].sub( 0 ) );
5:          float e1 = n.dot( rect[i+1].sub( 0 ) );
6:          float f = n.dot( d );
7:          if( Math.abs(f) > EPSILON ) {
                // calculate intersection
8:          } else if( e0*e1 > 0 ) {
9:              return null;
            }
        }
10:     return intersection; // TODO
    }
```

1. Loop through the rectangle and test each pair of parallel sides.

2. Compute the perpendicular normal to the two sides being tested.

3. Normalize the vector, because this vector is used with the dot product (see Chapter 6 for more information).

4. Compute the numerator for the intersection equation of the first side.

5. Compute the numerator for the intersection equation of the second side.

6. Compute the denominator for the intersection equation.

7. Check if the denominator is zero, which means the ray is parallel to the sides.

8. Test if the parallel line is between the two sides. If it isn't, there can be no intersection.

9. Since the parallel line is outside the rectangle, no intersection is possible.

10. Return the intersection here, but that can't happen yet.

The test in line 8 can be confusing. The $e0$ and $e1$ values are the signed distances from the origin to the side. The only way for the parallel line to be between the sides is if one distance is negative and the other is positive. If they are both positive or both negative, then they cannot be between the sides. The product of two positive or two negative values is always positive, so only if the product is negative can they be between the two sides.

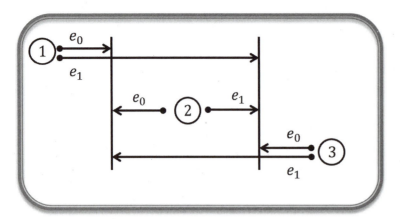

Figure 15.9
Rectangle Inside Test.
© 2014 Timothy Wright.

As shown in Figure 15.9, only the second case, where the e values have different signs, can be between the two sides. Even if there are intersections, the rays could miss the rectangle. By comparing the distances to see if they overlap, the closest intersection can be found. See Figure 15.10.

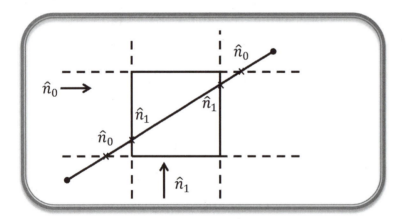

Figure 15.10
Rectangle Intersection Values.
© 2014 Timothy Wright.

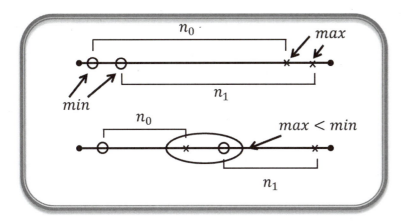

Figure 15.11
Min/Max Intersection Values.
© 2014 Timothy Wright.

The smallest maximum value is compared to the largest minimum value. If the largest minimum is greater than the smallest maximum, then the ray has missed the rectangle, as seen in Figure 15.11. It is similar to the overlap test for AABB objects shown in Figure 15.12.

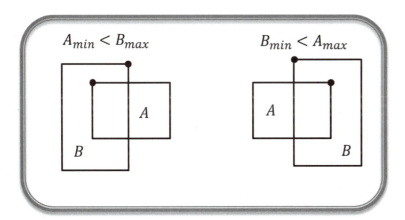

Figure 15.12
AABB Overlap.
© 2014 Timothy Wright.

The complete algorithm is as follows:

```
private Float lineRectIntersection(
    Vector2f O, Vector2f d, Vector2f[] rect ) {
```

```
1:        float largestMin = -Float.MAX_VALUE;
2:        float smallestMax = Float.MAX_VALUE;
          float swap;
          for( int i = 0; i < 2; ++i ) {
              Vector2f n = rect[i].sub( rect[i+1] );
              n = n.norm();
              float e0 = n.dot( rect[i].sub( 0 ) );
              float e1 = n.dot( rect[i+1].sub( 0 ) );
              float f = n.dot( d );
              if( Math.abs( f ) > EPSILON ) {
3:                float t0 = e0 / f;
4:                float t1 = e1 / f;
5:                if( t0 > t1 ) {
                      swap = t0;
                      t0 = t1;
                      t1 = swap;
                  }
6:                largestMin = Math.max( largestMin, t0 );
7:                smallestMax = Math.min( smallestMax, t1 );
8:                if( largestMin > smallestMax ) return null;
9:                if( smallestMax < 0 ) return null;
              } else if( e0*e1 > 0 ) {
                  return null;
              }
          }
10:       return largestMin > 0 ? largestMin : smallestMax;
      }
```

1. Initialize the largest minimum with the smallest possible number.

2. Initialize the smallest maximum with the largest possible number.

3. Calculate the t value of the parametric line equation for the first side.

4. Calculate the t value of the parametric line equation for the second side.

5. Swap the values to ensure that t0 is smaller than t1.

6. Update the largest minimum value.

7. Update the smallest maximum value.

8. If the minimum is larger than the maximum, there can be no intersection. Since the largest minimum will only get larger and the smallest maximum will only get smaller, if the minimum is larger than the maximum now, it will never be smaller and the method can exit.

9. If the smallest maximum value is less than zero, then all intersections occur behind the ray and the method can exit.

10. The first intersection is either the largest minimum value, or the smallest maximum value. Return the largest minimum unless it is less than zero, which means it is behind the ray.

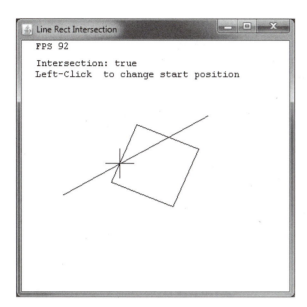

Figure 15.13
Line-Rectangle Intersection Example.
© 2014 Timothy Wright.

The LineRectIntersectionExample, as seen in Figure 15.13 and located in the javagames.collision package, places a spinning rectangle in the middle of the screen and computes the intersection of the rectangle and the line. The rect and rectCpy arrays hold the rectangle object. The angle holds the current rotation angle of the rectangle. The rot variable is the rotation to be added to the angle every frame. The start and end variables form the endpoints of the line. The intersection variable holds the results of the intersection test if an intersection is found.

The initialize() method creates the rectangle and initializes all the variables. The processInput() method adjusts the endpoint of the line to the mouse position and updates the start position when the left mouse button is clicked. The updateObjects() method adds the rotation to the angle so the rectangle spins. Then the rectangle is rotated and the results are stored in the rectCpy variable, which is used to test for an intersection with the line formed from the start and end points. Notice that the direction vector is calculated and passed to the intersection test.

```
Vector2f d = end.sub( start );
float len = d.len();
d = d.norm();

Float t = lineRectIntersection( start, d, rectCpy );
if( t != null && t > 0.0f && t < len ) {
    // intersect
}
```

Because the (d) direction vector is normalized, the range of 0 < t < length is used to verify that the intersection falls between the start and end points. The parametric line equation is used to find the actual intersection point.

```
// P = O + td
intersection = start.add( d.mul( t ) );
```

The lineRectIntersection() method takes the following inputs:

- O: The ray origin
- d: The ray direction
- rect[]: The rectangle to test

The method returns null if no intersection is found or a t value if an intersection occurs. Because this method tests a ray against the rectangle, the intersections may still be outside the line segment.

The render() method draws the rectangle and line, and draws crosshairs if there is an intersection.

```
package javagames.collision;

import java.awt.*;
import java.awt.event.MouseEvent;

import javagames.util.*;


public class LineRectIntersectionExample extends SimpleFramework {
    private static final float EPSILON = 0.00001f;

    private Vector2f[] rect;
    private Vector2f[] rectCpy;

    private Vector2f start;
    private Vector2f end;

    private Vector2f intersection;

    private float angle;
```

```java
private float rot;

public LineRectIntersectionExample() {
    appWidth = 640;
    appHeight = 640;
    appSleep = 10L;
    appTitle = "Line Rect Intersection";
    appBackground = Color.WHITE;
    appFPSColor = Color.BLACK;
}

@Override
protected void initialize() {
    super.initialize();

    angle = 0.0f;
    rot = (float)(Math.PI / 6.0);
    rect = new Vector2f[] {
        new Vector2f( -0.25f,  0.25f ),
        new Vector2f(  0.25f,  0.25f ),
        new Vector2f(  0.25f, -0.25f ),
        new Vector2f( -0.25f, -0.25f ),
    };
    rectCpy = new Vector2f[ rect.length ];
    start = new Vector2f();
    end = new Vector2f();
}

@Override
protected void processInput( float delta ) {
    super.processInput( delta );

    end = getWorldMousePosition();

    if( mouse.buttonDownOnce( MouseEvent.BUTTON1 ) ) {
        start = new Vector2f( end );
    }
}

@Override
protected void updateObjects( float delta ) {
    super.updateObjects( delta );
    angle += delta * rot;

    Matrix3x3f mat = Matrix3x3f.rotate( angle );
    for( int i = 0; i < rect.length; ++i ) {
        rectCpy[i] = mat.mul( rect[i] );
    }

    Vector2f d = end.sub( start );
```

```
        float len = d.len();
        d = d.norm();

        Float t = lineRectIntersection( start, d, rectCpy );
        if( t != null && t > 0.0f && t < len ) {
            intersection = start.add( d.mul( t ) );
        } else {
            intersection = null;
        }

    }

    private Float lineRectIntersection(
        Vector2f 0, Vector2f d, Vector2f[] rect ) {

        float largestMin = -Float.MAX_VALUE;
        float smallestMax = Float.MAX_VALUE;
        float swap;
        for( int i = 0; i < 2; ++i ) {
            Vector2f n = rect[i].sub( rect[i+1] );
            n = n.norm();
            float e0 = n.dot( rect[i].sub( 0 ) );
            float e1 = n.dot( rect[i+1].sub( 0 ) );
            float f = n.dot( d );
            if( Math.abs( f ) > EPSILON ) {
                float t0 = e0 / f;
                float t1 = e1 / f;
                if( t0 > t1 ) {
                    swap = t0;
                    t0 = t1;
                    t1 = swap;
                }
                largestMin = Math.max( largestMin, t0 );
                smallestMax = Math.min( smallestMax, t1 );
                if( largestMin > smallestMax ) return null;
                if( smallestMax < 0 ) return null;
            } else if( e0*e1 > 0 ) {
                return null;
            }
        }
        return largestMin > 0 ? largestMin : smallestMax;
    }

    @Override
    protected void render( Graphics g ) {
        super.render( g );
        boolean hasIntersection = intersection != null;
```

```
            g.drawString( "Intersection: " + hasIntersection, 20, 35 );
            g.drawString( "Left-Click to change start position", 20, 50 );

            Matrix3x3f view = getViewportTransform();
            for( int i = 0; i < rectCpy.length; ++i ) {
                rectCpy[i] = view.mul( rectCpy[i] );
            }

            Utility.drawPolygon( g, rectCpy );

            Vector2f startCpy = view.mul( start );
            Vector2f endCpy = view.mul( end );

            g.drawLine(
                (int)startCpy.x, (int)startCpy.y,
                (int)endCpy.x, (int)endCpy.y
            );

            if( hasIntersection ) {
                g.setColor( Color.BLUE );
                Vector2f temp = view.mul( intersection );
                g.drawLine(
                    (int)temp.x-20, (int)temp.y,
                    (int)temp.x+20, (int)temp.y
                );
                g.drawLine(
                    (int)temp.x, (int)temp.y-20,
                    (int)temp.x, (int)temp.y+20
                );
            }
        }

    public static void main( String[] args ) {
        launchApp( new LineRectIntersectionExample() );
    }

}
```

FINDING A CIRCLE-LINE INTERSECTION

To find the intersection with a line and a circle, you can use the same principle that you used in the rectangle-line intersection test. The line is treated as a ray. If there is an intersection with the circle, and the t value returned is between zero and the line length, then there is an intersection. Circles can have zero, one, or two intersection points. See Figure 15.14.

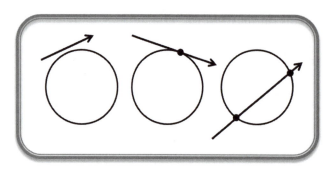

Figure 15.14
Circle Intersections.
© 2014 Timothy Wright.

The equation for the t value of the parametric line equation can be found in two steps. First, the parametric line equation can be substituted into the equation for a circle and simplified. The simplified equation can then be solved using the quadratic formula.

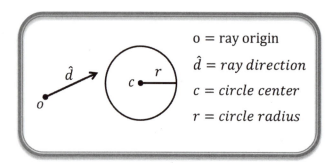

Figure 15.15
Circle-Line Variables.
© 2014 Timothy Wright.

The equation for a circle is easy to understand. Given any point on the circle, the distance from the point P to the center C, minus the radius r (which is the same distance), must equal zero.

$$circle = ||P - C|| - r = 0$$

Remembering that two lines $||x||$ represent the length, the parametric line equation:

$$P = O + td$$

Can be substituted into the circle equation, and simplified, as follows:

$$||O + td - C|| - r = 0$$

$$||O + td - C|| = r$$

$$\sqrt{(O + td - C)^2} = r$$

$$(O + td - C)^2 - r^2 = 0$$

$$[td + (O - C)] * [td + (O - C)] - r^2 = 0$$

$$t^2(d * d) + 2t[d * (O - C)] + (O - C) * (O - C) - r^2 = 0$$

If the d vector is normalized, the dot product of d with itself is one (d × d is 1). Because this equals 1,

$$t^2(d * d) + 2t[d * (O - C)] + (O - C) * (O - C) - r^2 = 0$$

$$t^2(1) + 2t[d * (O - C)] + (O - C) * (O - C) - r^2 = 0$$

$$t^2 + 2t[d * (O - C)] + (O - C) * (O - C) - r^2 = 0$$

$$\text{let } a = 1,\ b = d * (O - C),\ \text{and } c = (O - C) * (O - C) - r^2$$

This formula can be rewritten as:

$$(a)t^2 = (2b)t + (c) = 0$$

Using the quadratic formula, the solution is:

$$t = \frac{-(2b) \pm \sqrt{(2b)^2 - 4(a)(c)}}{2a}$$

$$t = \frac{-2b \pm \sqrt{4b^2 - 4c}}{2}$$

$$t = \frac{-2b \pm \sqrt{4(b^2 - c)}}{2}$$

$$t = \frac{-2b \pm 2\sqrt{b^2 - c}}{2}$$

$$t = -b \pm \sqrt{b^2 - c}$$

Where $b = d * (O - C)$ and $c = (O - C) * (O - C) - r^2$.

The intersection test is coded as follows:

```
private float[] lineCircleIntersection(
    Vector2f O, Vector2f d, Vector2f C, float r ) {
```

```
1:        Vector2f V = O.sub( C );
2:        float b = d.dot( V );
3:        float bb = b*b;
4:        float rr = r*r;
5:        float VV = V.dot( V );
6:        float c = VV - rr;
7:        if( bb < c ) return null;
8:        float root = (float)Math.sqrt( bb - c );
9:        return new float[]{ -b - root, -b + root };
      }
```

$$V = O - C$$
$$b = d * (O - C)$$
$$bb = b^2$$
$$rr = r^2$$
$$VV = V * V$$
$$c = (O - C) * (O - C) - r^2 = V * V - r^2 = VV - rr$$

If $b^2 < c$, then the number under the radical will be negative, and there is no solution.

$$root = \sqrt{b^2 - c}$$

The two solutions returned are $(-b + \sqrt{b^2 - c}, \ -b - \sqrt{b^2 - c})$.

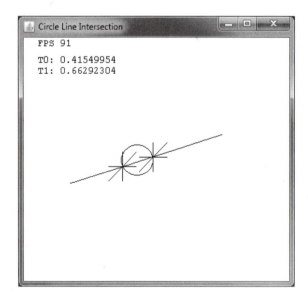

Figure 15.16
Circle-Line Intersection Example.
© 2014 Timothy Wright.

The CircleLineIntersectionExample, shown in Figure 15.16 and located in the javagames.collision package, demonstrates the circle-line intersection algorithm presented previously. The p0 and p1 variables hold the start and end points for the line being tested. The circle is stored with the center and radius variables. The t0 and t1 variables hold the intersection values for the parametric line equation, or null if an intersection does not occur. The plane0 and plane1 variables hold the intersection points for the ray, and the segment0 and segment1 variables hold the intersections for the line segments. The segment variables may be null even if an intersection on the ray is found.

The processInput() method moves the circle center based on the mouse position. The updateObjects() method checks for the intersection between the line and the circle. The p0 point is used as the origin, and the normalized direction vector is computed using this point. The plane variables hold any intersection, while the segment variables are only set if the intersection is within the bounds of the line segment.

The lineCircleIntersection() method is presented previously and is used to calculate the intersection of a ray and a circle. If no intersection is found, it returns null, otherwise it returns an array with the two values for the intersection.

The render() method prints the values of the two t values, as well as draws the line and the circle. The plane intersections and the segment intersections are drawn if they are not null.

```java
package javagames.collision;

import java.awt.*;

import javagames.util.*;


public class CircleLineIntersectionExample extends SimpleFramework {
    private Vector2f p0;
    private Vector2f p1;

    private Vector2f center;
    private float radius;

    private Float t0, t1;

    private Vector2f plane0;
    private Vector2f plane1;
    private Vector2f segment0;
    private Vector2f segment1;

    public CircleLineIntersectionExample() {
        appWidth = 640;
```

```
        appHeight = 640;
        appTitle = "Circle Line Intersection";
        appBackground = Color.WHITE;
        appFPSColor = Color.BLACK;
    }

    @Override
    protected void initialize() {
        super.initialize();

        radius = 0.125f;
        center = new Vector2f();

        p0 = new Vector2f( -0.65f, -0.2f );
        p1 = new Vector2f(  0.50f,  0.2f );

    }

    @Override
    protected void processInput( float delta ) {
        super.processInput( delta );
        center = getWorldMousePosition();
    }

    @Override
    protected void updateObjects( float delta ) {
        super.updateObjects( delta );

        Vector2f d = p1.sub( p0 );
        float len = d.len();
        d = d.norm();

        plane0 = plane1 = null;
        segment0 = segment1 = null;
        t0 = t1 = null;
        float[] intersections =
            lineCircleIntersection( p0, d, center, radius );
        if( intersections != null ) {
            t0 = intersections[0];
            plane0 = p0.add( d.mul( t0 ) );
            if( t0 >= 0.0f && t0 <= len ) {
                segment0 = plane0;
            }
            t1 = intersections[1];
            plane1 = p0.add( d.mul( t1 ) );
            if( t1 >= 0.0f && t1 <= len ) {
                segment1 = plane1;
            }
        }
    }
}
```

```java
private float[] lineCircleIntersection(
    Vector2f O, Vector2f d, Vector2f C, float r ) {

    Vector2f V = O.sub( C );
    float b = d.dot( V );
    float bb = b*b;
    float rr = r*r;
    float VV = V.dot( V );
    float c = VV - rr;
    if( bb < c ) {
        return null;
    }
    float root = (float)Math.sqrt( bb - c );
    return new float[]{ -b - root, -b + root };
}

@Override
protected void render( Graphics g ) {
    super.render( g );
    g.drawString( "T0: " + t0, 20, 35 );
    g.drawString( "T1: " + t1, 20, 50 );

    drawLine( g, p0, p1 );
    drawOval( g, center, radius );
    drawIntersections( g, plane0, segment0 );
    drawIntersections( g, plane1, segment1 );
}

private void drawLine( Graphics g, Vector2f p0, Vector2f p1 ) {
    Matrix3x3f view = getViewportTransform();
    Vector2f p0Cpy = view.mul( p0 );
    Vector2f p1Cpy = view.mul( p1 );
    g.drawLine( (int)p0Cpy.x, (int)p0Cpy.y, (int)p1Cpy.x, (int)p1Cpy.y );
}

private void drawOval( Graphics g, Vector2f center, float radius ) {
    Matrix3x3f view = getViewportTransform();

    Vector2f topLeft =
        new Vector2f( center.x - radius, center.y + radius );
    topLeft = view.mul( topLeft );

    Vector2f bottomRight =
        new Vector2f( center.x + radius, center.y - radius );
    bottomRight = view.mul( bottomRight );

    int circleX = (int)topLeft.x;
    int circleY = (int)topLeft.y;
    int circleWidth = (int)(bottomRight.x - topLeft.x);
```

```java
        int circleHeight = (int)(bottomRight.y - topLeft.y);

        g.drawOval( circleX, circleY, circleWidth, circleHeight );
    }

    private void drawIntersections(
        Graphics g, Vector2f planeIntersection, Vector2f lineIntersection ) {

        Matrix3x3f view = getViewportTransform();

        if( planeIntersection != null ) {
            g.setColor( Color.BLACK );
            Vector2f intCpy = view.mul( planeIntersection );
            g.drawLine(
                (int)intCpy.x-20, (int)intCpy.y,
                (int)intCpy.x+20, (int)intCpy.y
            );
            g.drawLine(
                (int)intCpy.x, (int)intCpy.y-20,
                (int)intCpy.x, (int)intCpy.y+20
            );
        }

        if( lineIntersection != null ) {
            g.setColor( Color.BLUE );
            Vector2f intCpy = view.mul( lineIntersection );
            g.drawLine(
                (int)intCpy.x-20, (int)intCpy.y+20,
                (int)intCpy.x+20, (int)intCpy.y-20
            );
        }
    }

    public static void main( String[] args ) {
        launchApp( new CircleLineIntersectionExample() );
    }

}
```

FINDING A LINE-LINE INTERSECTION

To find the intersection of two lines, a similar approach to the previous examples can be used. If each line is a ray, unless they are parallel, there is an intersection. Using a parametric line equation, and solving for the unknown t values, they can then be verified to be within the range of zero and one. If both values are within the range, then there is an intersection (see Figure 15.17).

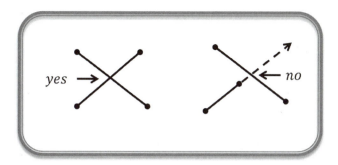

Figure 15.17
Line-Line Intersections.
© 2014 Timothy Wright.

To find the intersection point, one of the properties of the dot product is used.

$$A * B^{\perp} = 0$$

Recall that the dot product of two perpendicular vectors is always zero. This equation is used as a starting point. The parametric line equation is plugged into this equation, which allows the t value to be found. See Figure 15.18.

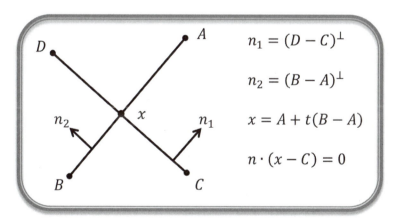

$$n_1 = (D - C)^{\perp}$$

$$n_2 = (B - A)^{\perp}$$

$$x = A + t(B - A)$$

$$n \cdot (x - C) = 0$$

Figure 15.18
Line-Line Components.
© 2014 Timothy Wright.

$$n_1 * (x - c) = 0$$
$$n_1 * [A + t(B - A) - C] = 0$$
$$n_1 * [t(B - A) + (A - C)] = 0$$
$$n_1 * t(B - A) + n_1(A - C) = 0$$
$$n_1 * t(B - A) = -n_1 * (A - C)$$

$$t[n_1 * (B - A)] = n_1 * (C - A)$$

$$t_1 = \frac{n_1 * (C - A)}{n_1 * (B - A)} = \frac{(D - C)^\perp * (C - A)}{(D - C)^\perp * (B - A)}$$

If the lines in the previous example are switched around, then the other t value is:

$$t_2 = \frac{n_2 * (A - C)}{n_2 * (D - C)} = \frac{(B - A)^\perp * (A - C)}{(B * A)^\perp * (D - C)}$$

If either of the denominator values are zero, then the lines are parallel and there can be no intersection:

$$n * (B - A) = 0$$

$$n * (D - C) = 0$$

Also, each t value needs to be checked to see if it is between zero and one. Since these are both between zero and one, there is an intersection:

$$0 \le t_1 \le 1$$

$$0 \le t_2 \le 1$$

You can simplify the algorithm by finding a common denominator value.

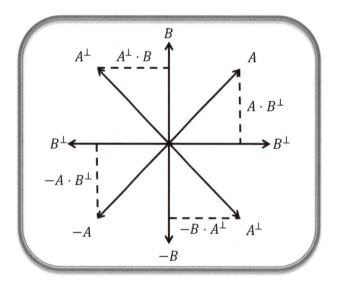

Figure 15.19
Perpendicular Vectors.
© 2014 Timothy Wright.

Looking at the relationships in Figure 15.19, it is evident that:

$$A^\perp * B = -A * B^\perp$$

This relationship can be used to rewrite the t value equation so that they share the same denominator.

$$t_1 = \frac{(D-C)^\perp * (C-A)}{(D-C)^\perp * (B-A)} = \frac{-[(D-C)^\perp * (A-C)]}{-[(D-C)^\perp * (A-B)]} = \frac{(D-C)^\perp * (A-C)}{(D-C)^\perp * (A-B)}$$

$$t_2 = \frac{(B-A)^\perp * (A-C)}{(B-A)^\perp * (D-C)} = \frac{-[(B-A)^\perp * (A-C)]}{-[(B-A)^\perp * (D-C)]} = \frac{(B-A)^\perp * (A-C)}{(D-C)^\perp * (A-B)}$$

Now the following can be used to calculate the intersection values:

$$\text{let } d = (D-C)^\perp * (A-C)$$
$$e = (B-A)^\perp * (A-C)$$
$$f = (D-C)^\perp * (A-B)$$
$$t_1 = d/f$$
$$t_2 = e/f$$

Because division can be an expensive operation, the range can be verified to be between zero and one before the division is performed.

```
if f < 0
    if d < 0 or d > f : no intersection
else
    if d > 0 or d < f : no intersection
```

The same check can be done for the e value. If none of these checks is true, then both intersection values will be between zero and one and an intersection exists. The complete algorithm is as follows:

```
private float[] lineLineIntersection(
    Vector2f A, Vector2f B, Vector2f C, Vector2f D ) {
Vector2f DsubC = D.sub( C );
Vector2f DsubCperp = DsubC.perp();
Vector2f AsubB = A.sub( B );
float f = DsubCperp.dot( AsubB );
if( Math.abs( f ) < EPSILON ) {
    return null; // zero denom
}
```

```
Vector2f AsubC = A.sub( C );
float d = DsubCperp.dot( AsubC );
if( f > 0 ) {
    if( d < 0 || d > f ) return null;
} else {
    if( d > 0 || d < f ) return null;
}
Vector2f BsubA = B.sub( A );
Vector2f BsubAperp = BsubA.perp();
float e = BsubAperp.dot( AsubC );
if( f > 0 ) {
    if( e < 0 || e > f ) return null;
} else {
    if( e > 0 || e < f ) return null;
}
return new float[]{
      d / f, e / f
};
}
```

Figure 15.20
Line-Line Intersection Example.
© 2014 Timothy Wright.

The LineLineIntersectionExample, as seen in Figure 15.20 and located in the javagames.collision package, finds the intersection between two line segments using the algorithm previously described. The EPSILON value is used to see if the determinant is zero, which happens when the two lines are parallel. The vectors A and B form the first line segment, and the vectors C and D form the second line segment. The intersect vector holds the intersection found using the first t value. If no intersection exists, the intersection value is null.

The processInput() method sets the D vector to the mouse position. Left-clicking sets each of the other three line points. Clicking the right mouse button clears all the points. The updateObjects() method finds the intersection of the two lines and then uses the first returned value to compute the intersection. The lineLineIntersection() method takes four vectors, two for each line segment, and returns the intersection values as an array with two values or null if no intersection is found.

The render() method draws the two line segments as well as crosshairs for the intersection location. The drawLine() method and the drawCrossHairs() methods are responsible for drawing the symbols on the screen. The LineLineIntersectionExample code is as follows:

```
package javagames.collision;

import java.awt.*;
import java.awt.event.MouseEvent;

import javagames.util.*;


public class LineLineIntersectionExample extends SimpleFramework {
    private static final float EPSILON = 0.00001f;

    private Vector2f A, B, C, D;
    private Vector2f intersect;

    public LineLineIntersectionExample() {
        appTitle = "Line Line Intersection";
        appBackground = Color.WHITE;
        appFPSColor = Color.BLACK;
    }

    @Override
    protected void processInput( float delta ) {
        super.processInput( delta );

        D = getWorldMousePosition();

        if( mouse.buttonDownOnce( MouseEvent.BUTTON1 ) ) {
            if( A == null ) A = D;
            else if( B == null ) B = D;
            else C = D;
        }
```

```
            if( mouse.buttonDownOnce( MouseEvent.BUTTON3 ) ) {
                A = B = C = D = null;
                intersect = null;
            }
        }

        @Override
        protected void updateObjects( float delta ) {
            super.updateObjects( delta );

            if( !(A == null || B == null || C == null || D == null) ) {
                float[] t = lineLineIntersection( A, B, C, D );
                if( t == null ) {
                    intersect = null;
                } else {
                    intersect = A.add( B.sub( A ).mul( t[0] ) );
                }
            }
        }

        private float[] lineLineIntersection(
            Vector2f A, Vector2f B, Vector2f C, Vector2f D ) {

            Vector2f DsubC = D.sub( C );
            Vector2f DsubCperp = DsubC.perp();
            Vector2f AsubB = A.sub( B );
            float f = DsubCperp.dot( AsubB );
            if( Math.abs( f ) < EPSILON ) {
                return null; // zero denom
            }
            Vector2f AsubC = A.sub( C );
            float d = DsubCperp.dot( AsubC );
            if( f > 0 ) {
                if( d < 0 || d > f ) return null;
            } else {
                if( d > 0 || d < f ) return null;
            }
            Vector2f BsubA = B.sub( A );
            Vector2f BsubAperp = BsubA.perp();
            float e = BsubAperp.dot( AsubC );
            if( f > 0 ) {
                if( e < 0 || e > f ) return null;
            } else {
                if( e > 0 || e < f ) return null;
            }
```

```java
            return new float[]{
                    d / f, e / f
            };
        }

        @Override
        protected void render( Graphics g ) {
            super.render( g );

            g.drawString( "Left Mouse to place points", 20, 35 );
            g.drawString( "Right Mouse to clear points", 20, 50 );

            g.setColor( intersect == null ? Color.RED : Color.GREEN );
            drawLine( g, A, B );
            drawLine( g, C, D );
            drawCrossHairs( g );
        }

        private void drawLine( Graphics g, Vector2f v0, Vector2f v1 ) {
            if( v0 != null ) {
                Matrix3x3f view = getViewportTransform();
                Vector2f va = view.mul( v0 );
                if( v1 == null ) {
                    g.fillRect( (int)va.x, (int)va.y, 1, 1 );
                } else {
                    Vector2f vb = view.mul( v1 );
                    g.drawLine( (int)va.x, (int)va.y, (int)vb.x, (int)vb.y );
                }
            }
        }

        private void drawCrossHairs( Graphics g ) {
            if( intersect != null ) {
                Matrix3x3f view = getViewportTransform();
                Vector2f intView = view.mul( intersect );
                g.setColor( Color.BLACK );
                int x = (int)intView.x;
                int y = (int)intView.y;
                g.drawLine( x, y-20, x, y+20 );
                g.drawLine( x-20, y, x+20, y );
            }
        }

        public static void main( String[] args ) {
            launchApp( new LineLineIntersectionExample() );
        }
    }
}
```

CALCULATING A REFLECTION VECTOR

Once an intersection point is found, a reflection vector can be calculated. This vector is the direction the object would bounce off the line segment. See Figure 15.21.

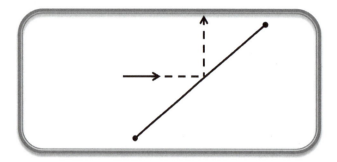

Figure 15.21
Reflection Vector.
© 2014 Timothy Wright.

The intersection point can be found with a line intersection test. All that is needed to calculate the reflection vector is the original vector and a perpendicular vector to the reflection segment. The reflection vector is calculated as follows:

As shown in Figure 15.22, the vector V is the original direction vector. It is reflected off of the line segment AB. The normal is a normalized vector perpendicular to the AB line segment.

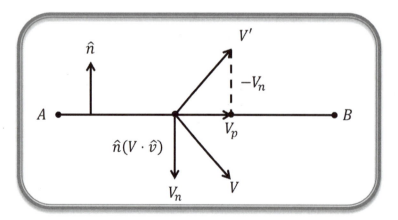

Figure 15.22
Reflection Vector Proof.
© 2014 Timothy Wright.

The reflection vector is calculated as follows:

$$V_n = \hat{n}(V * \hat{n})$$
$$V_p = V - V_n$$
$$V' = V_p - V_n$$

To reflect a direction off a line segment, the intersection point is used to create the original reflection vector, as well as the starting point for the reflection. See Figure 15.23.

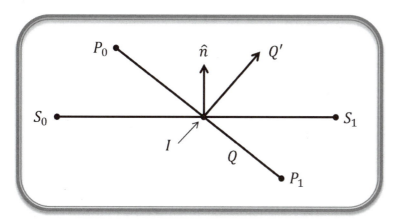

Figure 15.23
Reflection Vector Components.
© 2014 Timothy Wright.

$$S_V = S_1 - S_o$$

$$n = S_v^\perp$$

$$\hat{n} = \frac{n}{\|n\|}$$

I is the intersection of Q and P. $Q = P_1 - I$ and Q' is the reflection.

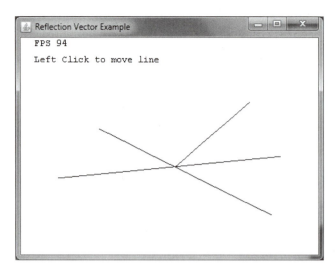

Figure 15.24
Reflection Vector Example.
© 2014 Timothy Wright.

The ReflectionVectorExample, as shown in Figure 15.24 and located in the javagames.collision package, calculates a reflection vector off a line segment. The EPSILON value is used to check for parallel lines. The variables s0, s1, p0, and p1 hold two line segments. The intersection vector holds the intersection point of the two lines, and the reflection vector holds the reflection calculated from the two line segments. The s0 and s1 lines stay in the same place, the p0 point is placed when the left mouse is clicked, and the p1 point follows the mouse.

The updateObjects() method calculates the intersection using the line-line intersection algorithm described earlier. The reflection vector is calculated if an intersection is found. The reflection vector is set to null if there is no intersection.

The getIntersection() method calculates the intersection point, returning a single intersection point instead of two parametric line values. The getReflectionVector() method calculates the reflection given an initial direction vector and a normalized vector perpendicular to the reflection surface.

The render() method draws the usual frame rate and usage information. The drawLine() method transforms and draws the line segment. The ReflectionVectorExample is as follows:

```
package javagames.collision;

import java.awt.*;
import java.awt.event.MouseEvent;

import javagames.util.*;
```

```java
public class ReflectionVectorExample extends SimpleFramework {
    private static final float EPSILON = 0.00001f;

    private Vector2f s0, s1, p0, p1;
    private Vector2f intersection;
    private Vector2f reflection;

    public ReflectionVectorExample() {
        appTitle = "Reflection Vector Example";
        appBackground = Color.WHITE;
        appFPSColor = Color.BLACK;
    }

    @Override
    protected void initialize() {
        super.initialize();

        s0 = new Vector2f( -0.75f, -0.3f );
        s1 = new Vector2f(  0.75f, -0.1f );

        p0 = new Vector2f();
        p1 = new Vector2f();
    }

    @Override
    protected void processInput( float delta ) {
        super.processInput( delta );

        p1 = getWorldMousePosition();
        if( mouse.buttonDownOnce( MouseEvent.BUTTON1 ) ) {
            p0 = new Vector2f( p1 );
        }
    }

    @Override
    protected void updateObjects( float delta ) {
        super.updateObjects( delta );

        intersection = getIntersection( p0, p1, s0, s1 );
        if( intersection != null ) {
            Vector2f Sv = s1.sub( s0 );
            Vector2f n = Sv.perp().norm();
            Vector2f V = p1.sub( intersection );
            Vector2f reflect = getReflectionVector( V, n );
            reflection = intersection.add( reflect );
        } else {
            reflection = null;
        }
    }
```

```java
private Vector2f getIntersection(
    Vector2f A, Vector2f B, Vector2f C, Vector2f D ) {

    Vector2f DsubC = D.sub( C );
    Vector2f DsubCperp = DsubC.perp();
    Vector2f AsubB = A.sub( B );
    float f = DsubCperp.dot( AsubB );
    if( Math.abs( f ) < EPSILON ) {
        return null; // zero denom
    }
    Vector2f AsubC = A.sub( C );
    float d = DsubCperp.dot( AsubC );
    if( f > 0 ) {
        if( d < 0 || d > f ) return null;
    } else {
        if( d > 0 || d < f ) return null;
    }
    Vector2f BsubA = B.sub( A );
    Vector2f BsubAperp = BsubA.perp();
    float e = BsubAperp.dot( AsubC );
    if( f > 0 ) {
        if( e < 0 || e > f ) return null;
    } else {
        if( e > 0 || e < f ) return null;
    }

    return A.add( BsubA.mul( d / f ) );
}

private Vector2f getReflectionVector( Vector2f V, Vector2f n ) {
    Vector2f Vn = n.mul( V.dot( n ) );
    Vector2f Vp = V.sub( Vn );
    return Vp.sub( Vn );
}

@Override
protected void render( Graphics g ) {
    super.render( g );

    g.drawString( "Left Click to move line", 20, 35 );

    drawLine( g, s0, s1 );
    drawLine( g, p0, p1 );

    if( reflection != null ) {
        g.setColor( Color.BLUE );
        drawLine( g, intersection, reflection );
    }
}
```

```
private void drawLine( Graphics g, Vector2f v0, Vector2f v1 ) {
    Matrix3x3f view = getViewportTransform();
    Vector2f v0Cpy = view.mul( v0 );
    Vector2f v1Cpy = view.mul( v1 );
    g.drawLine( (int)v0Cpy.x, (int)v0Cpy.y, (int)v1Cpy.x, (int)v1Cpy.y );
}

public static void main( String[] args ) {
    launchApp( new ReflectionVectorExample() );
}
}
```

BOUNCING A POINT INSIDE A POLYGON

When attempting to bounce an object off the sides of a polygon, there are many ways to handle the collision response. One way is to just calculate the reflection vector and adjust the velocity of the point, as shown in Figure 15.25. This way is simple, but doesn't accurately model the collision.

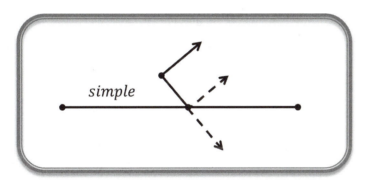

Figure 15.25
Simple Reflection.
© 2014 Timothy Wright.

This simple method calculates the new point position based on the velocity, and if the line segment formed by the start and end point intersects the polygon, the point is left in the starting position and the velocity is updated.

Another way to handle the collision is to calculate the intersection, the reflection vector, and update the position of the object. This is shown in Figure 15.26.

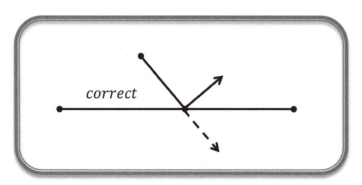

Figure 15.26
Correct Reflection.
© 2014 Timothy Wright.

Unfortunately, both methods have problems. The correct method must accurately adjust the point, and then continue checking for collisions recursively until there are no more collisions or the bounce distance is too small. At that point, the correct method will suffer from some of the same problems as the simple method. To keep it as simple as possible, the simple method will be used.

There are also many problems with the simple method. First, when the point's position is only updated if there is a collision, if the point travels far enough each frame, it will always hit something and the point will never move. See Figure 15.27.

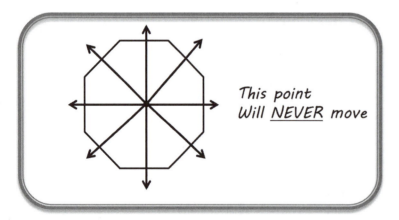

Figure 15.27
Point Will Never Move.
© 2014 Timothy Wright.

The second issue with just leaving the point in its original position happens when the point is very close to the line. If the point starts out touching or almost touching a polygon line, then it will always register a collision, and will get stuck to the line. See Figure 15.28.

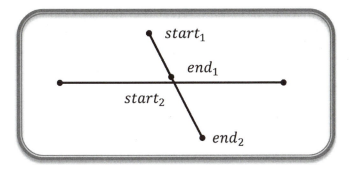

Figure 15.28
Simple Collision Trouble.
© 2014 Timothy Wright.

To keep points that start out touching or almost touching the polygon from getting stuck, they have to be ignored. But this causes another problem. If the new position is almost touching the polygon, it will not intersect the polygon until the next frame, but at that point, since it is so close, it will be ignored, so it does not get stuck. This causes the point, if it stops right before the polygon line, to pass right through it.

```
if end-point really close to the line
    collision has occurred
else if start-point really close to the line
    ignore it, or it will get stuck
```

This pseudocode describes the checks needed to keep the point from sticking to or passing through the polygon line.

The equation shown in Figure 15.29 is used to find the signed perpendicular distance from the point P to the SQ line segment. Remember to normalize the normal vector. This distance value can be used to check if the point is touching or is almost touching a line segment.

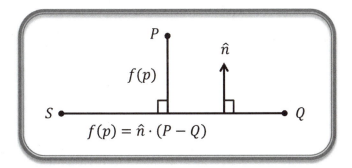

$$f(p) = \hat{n} \cdot (P - Q)$$

Figure 15.29
Perpendicular Point Distance.
© 2014 Timothy Wright.

There are also problems when using the more accurate method that updates the point position after a collision. If the reflection happens in a corner, the new position can jump over lines that should cause collisions. This is shown in Figure 15.30.

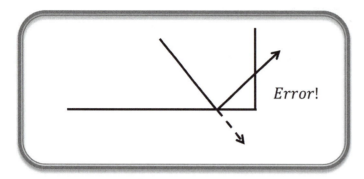

Figure 15.30
Correct Corner Error.
© 2014 Timothy Wright.

Every time a collision is found, the new reflected vector must be checked for collision with the entire polygon. While most items are not moving fast enough for this to be a problem, it can cause a lot of checks around corners.

The second issue with just leaving the point in its original position also can happen with corners, but involves multiple collisions.

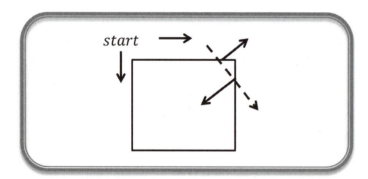

Figure 15.31
Clockwise/Counterclockwise Testing.
© 2014 Timothy Wright.

As seen in Figure 15.31, there are two different collisions. If the polygon sides are checked clockwise or counterclockwise, the first collision point will change. Not only does each collision cause more collision checks, all collisions must check for multiple collisions, measure the distance to each collision, and only use the closest one.

Which method is used depends on the level of accuracy needed. Make sure to handle the weird cases that can occur.

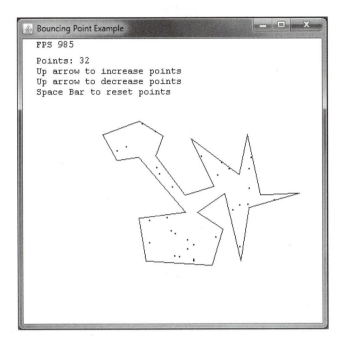

Figure 15.32
Bouncy Point Example.
© 2014 Timothy Wright.

The BouncyPointExample, as seen in Figure 15.32 and located in the javagames.collision package, creates random points with random velocity directions and distances and bounces them around inside a polygon. The EPSILON value is used to check for values very close to zero. The number of points generated can be adjusted. The poylgonCount variable holds the current number of points, and the points and velocities are stored in their own array. The polygon array holds the original polygon and the copy holds the viewport transformed coordinates.

The initialize() method creates the polygon with hard-coded points, as well as creates the initial random points, using the createPoints() method. This method is called whenever the points are reset.

The processInput() method increases or decreases the number of points using the arrow keys, and uses the space bar to restart the points. The clamp() method keeps the points within the MIN_POINTS and MAX_POINTS constants.

The updateObject() method updates each point's position based on its velocity, computing a new velocity if there is a collision. This example used the simple method for collision detection, so the position of each point is updated only if there is no collision. The getNewVelocity() method returns the new velocity for the point if there is a collision with one of the polygon sides. The following code makes sure that the point doesn't pass through or get stuck to the polygon.

```
private boolean hitPolygon(
    Vector2f start, Vector2f end, Vector2f S, Vector2f P ) {
    if( isZero( getPointLineDistance( end, S, P ) ) ) {
        return true;
    } else if( !isZero( getPointLineDistance( start, S, P ) ) ) {
        return lineLineIntersection( start, end, S, P );
    } else {
        return false;
    }
}
```

The getPointLineDistance() method calculates the distance from the given point to the line segment so the distance to each line segment can be used to keep the points from sticking. The lineLineIntersection() method needs to return only if there was an intersection. The actual intersection location is not needed. The calculateReflection() method is used to bounce each point off the polygon sides. Finally, the render() method displays the usual instructions, draws the polygon, and draws each point as a tiny rectangle.

```
package javagames.collision;

import java.awt.Graphics;
import java.awt.event.KeyEvent;
import java.util.Random;

import javagames.util.*;


public class BouncingPointExample extends SimpleFramework {
    private static final float EPSILON = 0.000001f;

    private static final int MAX_POINTS = 4096;
    private static final int MIN_POINTS = 8;
    private static final int MULTIPLE = 2;

    private int pointCount;
    private Vector2f[] points;
    private Vector2f[] velocities;

    private Vector2f[] polygon;
    private Vector2f[] polygonCpy;
```

```java
public BouncingPointExample() {
    appTitle = "Bouncing Point Example";
    appWidth = 640;
    appHeight = 640;
    appSleep = 1L;
    appBackground = Color.WHITE;
    appFPSColor = Color.BLACK;
}
protected void initialize() {
    super.initialize();
    polygon = new Vector2f[] {
        new Vector2f( 0.09233177f, -0.22378719f),
        new Vector2f(-0.21752739f,  0.16431928f),
        new Vector2f(-0.37089205f,  0.14553994f),
        new Vector2f(-0.46478873f,  0.32707357f),
        new Vector2f(-0.21439749f,  0.41784036f),
        new Vector2f(-0.05790299f,  0.31768388f),
        new Vector2f(-0.107981205f, 0.17370892f),
        new Vector2f( 0.08607197f, -0.101721406f),
        new Vector2f( 0.2832551f,  -0.042253494f),
        new Vector2f( 0.12989044f,  0.29577464f),
        new Vector2f( 0.4522692f,   0.042253554f),
        new Vector2f( 0.5054773f,   0.32707357f),
        new Vector2f( 0.5899843f,  -0.098591566f),
        new Vector2f( 0.85289514f, -0.08920181f),
        new Vector2f( 0.5117371f,  -0.18935835f),
        new Vector2f( 0.458529f,   -0.5649452f),
        new Vector2f( 0.3552426f,  -0.08920181f),
        new Vector2f( 0.16744912f, -0.22378719f),
        new Vector2f( 0.33959305f, -0.342723f),
        new Vector2f( 0.26760566f, -0.5962441f),
        new Vector2f(-0.17370892f, -0.56807506f),
        new Vector2f(-0.22065729f, -0.26134586f),
    };
    polygonCpy = new Vector2f[ polygon.length ];
    pointCount = MIN_POINTS;
    createPoints();
}
private void createPoints() {
    Random rand = new Random();
    points = new Vector2f[ pointCount ];
    velocities = new Vector2f[ points.length ];
    for( int i = 0; i < points.length; ++i ) {
        points[i] = new Vector2f();
```

```java
            double rad = Math.toRadians( rand.nextInt( 360 ) );
            double distancePerSecond = rand.nextFloat() + 0.5f;
            float vx = (float)(distancePerSecond * Math.cos( rad ));
            float vy = (float)(distancePerSecond * Math.sin( rad ));
            velocities[i] = new Vector2f( vx, vy );
        }
    }

    protected void processInput( float delta ) {
        super.processInput( delta );

        if( keyboard.keyDownOnce( KeyEvent.VK_SPACE ) ) {
            createPoints();
        }
        if( keyboard.keyDownOnce( KeyEvent.VK_UP ) ) {
            pointCount = clamp( pointCount * MULTIPLE );
            createPoints();
        }
        if( keyboard.keyDownOnce( KeyEvent.VK_DOWN ) ) {
            pointCount = clamp( pointCount / MULTIPLE );
            createPoints();
        }
    }

    private int clamp( int count ) {
        if( count < MIN_POINTS ) return MIN_POINTS;
        if( count > MAX_POINTS ) return MAX_POINTS;
        return count;
    }

    protected void updateObjects( float delta ) {
        super.updateObjects( delta );

        for( int i = 0; i < points.length; ++i ) {
            Vector2f velocity = velocities[i];
            Vector2f start = points[i];
            Vector2f end = start.add( velocity.mul( delta ) );
            Vector2f newVelocity = getNewVelocity( start, end, velocity );
            if( newVelocity != null ) {
                velocities[i] = newVelocity;
            } else {
                points[i] = end;
            }
        }
    }

    private Vector2f getNewVelocity(
        Vector2f start, Vector2f end, Vector2f velocity ) {
```

```
    Vector2f P = null;
    Vector2f S = polygon[ polygon.length - 1 ];
    for( int j = 0; j < polygon.length; ++j ) {
        P = polygon[j];
        if( hitPolygon( start, end, S, P ) ) {
            return calculateReflection( velocity, S, P );
        }
        S = P;
    }
    return null;
}

private boolean hitPolygon(
    Vector2f start, Vector2f end, Vector2f S, Vector2f P ) {

    if( isZero( getPointLineDistance( end, S, P ) ) ) {
        return true;
    } else if( !isZero( getPointLineDistance( start, S, P ) ) ) {
        return lineLineIntersection( start, end, S, P );
    } else {
        return false;
    }
}

private boolean isZero( float value ) {
    return Math.abs( value ) < EPSILON;
}

private float getPointLineDistance( Vector2f P, Vector2f S, Vector2f Q ) {
    Vector2f v = Q.sub( S );
    Vector2f n = v.perp().norm();
    return n.dot( P.sub( Q ) );
}

private boolean lineLineIntersection
        ( Vector2f A, Vector2f B, Vector2f C, Vector2f D ) {

    Vector2f DsubC = D.sub( C );
    Vector2f DsubCperp = DsubC.perp();
    Vector2f AsubB = A.sub( B );
    float f = DsubCperp.dot( AsubB );
    if( Math.abs( f ) < EPSILON ) {
        return false; // zero denom
    }
    Vector2f AsubC = A.sub( C );
    float d = DsubCperp.dot( AsubC );
    if( f > 0 ) {
        if( d < 0 || d > f ) return false;
```

```
      } else {
         if( d > 0 || d < f ) return false;
      }
      Vector2f BsubA = B.sub( A );
      Vector2f BsubAperp = BsubA.perp();
      float e = BsubAperp.dot( AsubC );
      if( f > 0 ) {
         if( e < 0 || e > f ) return false;
      } else {
         if( e > 0 || e < f ) return false;
      }

      return true;
   }
   private Vector2f calculateReflection(
      Vector2f V, Vector2f P0, Vector2f P1 ) {

      Vector2f Pv = P0.sub( P1 );
      Vector2f n = Pv.perp().norm();
      Vector2f Vn = n.mul( V.dot( n ) );
      Vector2f Vp = V.sub( Vn );
      return Vp.sub( Vn );
   }
   protected void render( Graphics g ) {
      super.render( g );

      g.drawString( "Points: " + pointCount, 20, 35 );
      g.drawString( "Up arrow to increase points", 20, 50 );
      g.drawString( "Up arrow to decrease points", 20, 65 );
      g.drawString( "Space Bar to reset points", 20, 80 );

      Matrix3x3f view = getViewportTransform();
      for( int i = 0; i < polygon.length; ++i ) {
         polygonCpy[i] = view.mul( polygon[i] );
      }
      Utility.drawPolygon( g, polygonCpy );

      for( int i = 0; i < points.length; ++i ) {
         Vector2f copy = view.mul( points[i] );
         g.drawRect( (int)copy.x, (int)copy.y, 1, 1 );
      }
   }
   public static void main( String[] args ) {
      launchApp( new BouncingPointExample() );
   }

}
```

RESOURCES AND FURTHER READING

Haines, Eric, "Essential Ray Tracing Algorithms," Chapter 2 in Andrew Glassner, ed., *An Introduction to Ray Tracing,* Academic Press Inc., London, 1989.

Akenine-Moller, Tomas and Eric Haines, *Real-Time Rendering, 2nd Edition*, A K Peters, pp. 568–570 and pp. 664–665, 2002.

Antonio, Franklin, "Faster Line Segment Intersection," in David Kirk, ed., *Graphic Gems III*, Academic Press, pp. 199–202, 1992, http://www.graphicsgems.org/.

PART III

THE COMPLETE GAME

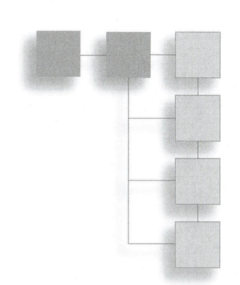

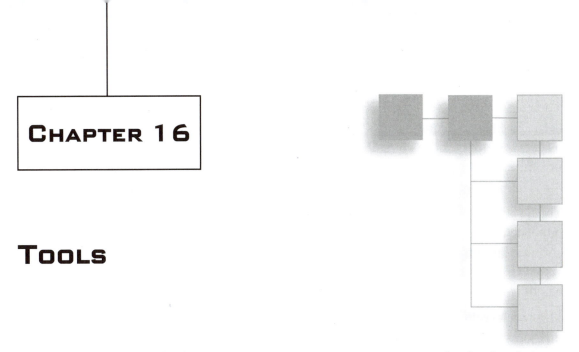

CHAPTER 16

TOOLS

Before you get to the final game, it is necessary to create some tools, the first being a better GameFramework. Although the current framework is fine, the full-screen version doesn't allow for aspect ratio, and it is difficult to add Swing components. After updating the framework, a new editor can be created adding more options with Swing components. Next, a sprite class is created to allow images in pixel space to be used by objects in world space. Finally, a simple particle engine is created to allow for explosions and rocket blasts.

Let's get to it.

CREATING A GAME FRAMEWORK

The GameFramework class, located in the javagames.util package, combines full-screen and window frameworks into a single framework with hooks to allow customization with subclasses. Most of these methods will be familiar, with a few abstract methods and tricks to allow subclasses to perform some low-level tasks. The first thing to notice is the abstract methods:

```
protected abstract void createFramework()
protected abstract void renderFrame(Graphics g)
public abstract int getScreenWidth()
public abstract int getScreenHeight()
```

The first two protected methods allow the subclasses to create the framework and render each frame. The screen width and height methods are necessary because depending on whether the game is a windowed or full-screen game, with or without aspect ratio, the component that contains the actual width and height will vary.

The createAndShowGUI() method passes the creation to the createFramework() method, then disables the cursor and starts the game thread. The new setupInput() method takes a generic component so both full-screen and windowed frameworks can configure input. Also, two overloaded createBuffereStrategy() methods take a Canvas or a Window object.

The setupViewport() method calculates the values for the viewport width, height, and upper-left coordinates. The actual creation of the viewport must be left to the subclasses. getViewportTransform(), getReverseViewportTransform(), getWorldMousePosition(), and getRelativeWorldMousePosition() use the abstract methods to get the screen width and height from the subclasses.

Most of the other methods are the same as the previous frameworks. The renderFrame() method calls the abstract renderFrame(Graphics g) method. The only other method that needs an explanation is the shutdown() method.

```
protected void shutDown() {
    if( Thread.currentThread() != gameThread ) {
        try {
            running = false;
            gameThread.join();
            onShutDown();
        } catch( InterruptedException e ) {
            e.printStackTrace();
        }
        System.exit( 0 );
    } else {
        SwingUtilities.invokeLater( new Runnable() {
            public void run() {
                shutDown();
            }
        });
    }
}

protected void onShutDown() {

}
```

First, the onShutDown() method is not abstract, so children are not required to override it. The second important part is the check for the current thread. The code cannot shut down the game thread and join the thread if the shutdown method is called from the game thread, so it is necessary to only shut down the game thread if you're not on the game thread.

```java
package javagames.util;


import java.awt.*;
import java.awt.event.*;
import java.awt.image.BufferStrategy;

import javax.swing.*;


public abstract class GameFramework extends JFrame implements Runnable {

    private BufferStrategy bs;
    private volatile boolean running;
    private Thread gameThread;

    protected int vx;
    protected int vy;
    protected int vw;
    protected int vh;

    protected FrameRate frameRate;
    protected RelativeMouseInput mouse;
    protected KeyboardInput keyboard;

    protected Color appBackground = Color.BLACK;
    protected Color appBorder = Color.LIGHT_GRAY;
    protected Color appFPSColor = Color.GREEN;
    protected Font appFont = new Font( "Courier New", Font.PLAIN, 14 );
    protected String appTitle = "TBD-Title";
    protected float appBorderScale = 0.8f;
    protected int appWidth = 640;
    protected int appHeight = 640;
    protected float appWorldWidth = 2.0f;
    protected float appWorldHeight = 2.0f;
    protected long appSleep = 10L;
    protected boolean appMaintainRatio = false;
    protected boolean appDisableCursor = false;
    protected int textPos = 0;
```

```java
public GameFramework() {

}

protected abstract void createFramework();
protected abstract void renderFrame( Graphics g );
public abstract int getScreenWidth();
public abstract int getScreenHeight();

protected void createAndShowGUI() {

    createFramework();

    if( appDisableCursor ) {
        disableCursor();
    }

    gameThread = new Thread( this );
    gameThread.start();
}

protected void setupInput( Component component ) {
    keyboard = new KeyboardInput();
    component.addKeyListener( keyboard );

    mouse = new RelativeMouseInput( component );
    component.addMouseListener( mouse );
    component.addMouseMotionListener( mouse );
    component.addMouseWheelListener( mouse );
}

protected void createBufferStrategy( Canvas component ) {
    component.createBufferStrategy( 2 );
    bs = component.getBufferStrategy();
}

protected void createBufferStrategy( Window window ) {
    window.createBufferStrategy( 2 );
    bs = window.getBufferStrategy();
}

protected void setupViewport( int sw, int sh ) {

    int w = (int)( sw * appBorderScale );
    int h = (int)( sh * appBorderScale );
    int x = ( sw - w ) / 2;
    int y = ( sh - h ) / 2;

    vw = w;
    vh = (int)( w * appWorldHeight / appWorldWidth );
```

```
      if( vh > h ) {
         vw = (int)( h * appWorldWidth / appWorldHeight );
         vh = h;
      }

      vx = x + ( w - vw ) / 2;
      vy = y + ( h - vh ) / 2;
   }
   protected Matrix3x3f getViewportTransform() {
      return Utility.createViewport( appWorldWidth, appWorldHeight,
            getScreenWidth(), getScreenHeight() );
   }

   protected Matrix3x3f getReverseViewportTransform() {
      return Utility.createReverseViewport( appWorldWidth, appWorldHeight,
            getScreenWidth(), getScreenHeight() );
   }

   protected Vector2f getWorldMousePosition() {
      Matrix3x3f screenToWorld = getReverseViewportTransform();
      Point mousePos = mouse.getPosition();
      Vector2f screenPos = new Vector2f( mousePos.x, mousePos.y );
      return screenToWorld.mul( screenPos );
   }

   protected Vector2f getRelativeWorldMousePosition() {
      float sx = appWorldWidth / ( getScreenWidth() - 1 );
      float sy = appWorldHeight / ( getScreenHeight() - 1 );
      Matrix3x3f viewport = Matrix3x3f.scale( sx, -sy );
      Point p = mouse.getPosition();
      return viewport.mul( new Vector2f( p.x, p.y ) );
   }

   public void run() {
      running = true;
      initialize();
      long curTime = System.nanoTime();
      long lastTime = curTime;
      double nsPerFrame;
      while( running ) {
         curTime = System.nanoTime();
         nsPerFrame = curTime - lastTime;
         gameLoop( (float)( nsPerFrame / 1.0E9 ) );
         lastTime = curTime;
      }
      terminate();
   }
```

```
protected void initialize() {
    frameRate = new FrameRate();
    frameRate.initialize();
}

protected void terminate() {

}

private void gameLoop( float delta ) {
    processInput( delta );
    updateObjects( delta );
    renderFrame();
    sleep( appSleep );
}

private void renderFrame() {
    do {
        do {
            Graphics g = null;
            try {
                g = bs.getDrawGraphics();
                renderFrame( g );
            } finally {
                if( g != null ) {
                    g.dispose();
                }
            }
        } while( bs.contentsRestored() );
        bs.show();
    } while( bs.contentsLost() );
}

private void sleep( long sleep ) {
    try {
        Thread.sleep( sleep );
    } catch( InterruptedException ex ) {
    }
}

protected void processInput( float delta ) {
    keyboard.poll();
    mouse.poll();
}

protected void updateObjects( float delta ) {

}
```

```
protected void render( Graphics g ) {
    g.setFont( appFont );
    g.setColor( appFPSColor );
    frameRate.calculate();
    textPos = Utility.drawString( g, 20, 0, frameRate.getFrameRate() );
}

private void disableCursor() {
    Toolkit tk = Toolkit.getDefaultToolkit();
    Image image = tk.createImage( "" );
    Point point = new Point( 0, 0 );
    String name = "CanBeAnything";
    Cursor cursor = tk.createCustomCursor( image, point, name );
    setCursor( cursor );
}

protected void shutDown() {
    if( Thread.currentThread() != gameThread ) {
        try {
            running = false;
            gameThread.join();
            onShutDown();
        } catch( InterruptedException e ) {
            e.printStackTrace();
        }
        System.exit( 0 );
    } else {
        SwingUtilities.invokeLater( new Runnable() {
            public void run() {
                shutDown();
            }
        });
    }
}

protected void onShutDown() {

}

protected static void launchApp( final GameFramework app ) {
    app.addWindowListener( new WindowAdapter() {
        public void windowClosing( WindowEvent e ) {
            app.shutDown();
        }
    });
```

```
        SwingUtilities.invokeLater( new Runnable() {
            public void run() {
                app.createAndShowGUI();
            }
        });
    }
}
```

The WindowFramework, located in the same package, extends the GameFramework to provide a game window. The createFramework() method is overridden, creating the Canvas object. The same component listener is used to maintain the aspect ratio. Notice that the setupViewport() method is used with the canvas width and height, and the canvas is passed to both the setupInput() and createBufferStrategy() methods. The renderFrame() method clears the canvas and passes the graphics object to the render() method.

Of the three frameworks, this one is the simplest. The WindowFramework code is as follows:

```
package javagames.util;

import java.awt.*;
import java.awt.event.*;


public class WindowFramework extends GameFramework {

    private Canvas canvas;

    @Override
    protected void createFramework() {

        canvas = new Canvas();
        canvas.setBackground( appBackground );
        canvas.setIgnoreRepaint( true );
        getContentPane().add( canvas );
        setLocationByPlatform( true );

        if( appMaintainRatio ) {
            getContentPane().setBackground( appBorder );
            setSize( appWidth, appHeight );
            setLayout( null );
            getContentPane().addComponentListener( new ComponentAdapter() {
                public void componentResized( ComponentEvent e ) {
                    onComponentResized( e );
                }
            });
```

```
        } else {
            canvas.setSize( appWidth, appHeight );
            pack();
        }

        setTitle( appTitle );
        setupInput( canvas );

        setVisible( true );

        createBufferStrategy( canvas );
        canvas.requestFocus();
    }

    protected void onComponentResized( ComponentEvent e ) {
        Dimension size = getContentPane().getSize();
        setupViewport( size.width, size.height );
        canvas.setLocation( vx, vy );
        canvas.setSize( vw, vh );
    }

    public int getScreenWidth() {
        return canvas.getWidth();
    }

    public int getScreenHeight() {
        return canvas.getHeight();
    }

    @Override
    protected void renderFrame( Graphics g ) {
        g.clearRect( 0, 0, getScreenWidth(), getScreenHeight() );
        render( g );
    }

}
```

The FullScreenFramework, located in the same package, works differently. Not only does it need to change the display mode, it also handles the aspect ratio, which the previous framework did not do. This is accomplished by rendering the screen to a VolatileImage, which can be copied to the buffer strategy very quickly. See Chapter 10, "Images," for more information.

The createFramework() method sets up the frame, saves the current display mode, sets up the input, creates the buffer strategy with the generic methods, changes the display mode, and, if the aspect ratio is maintained, creates the intermediate VolatileImage. Notice the getScreenWidth() and getScreenHeight() methods return either the frame size or the VolatileImage size.

The renderFrame() method either renders the same way the previous full-screen frame-work did, or uses the VolatileImage to maintain the aspect ratio. The onShutDown() method returns the display mode to the original size.

```java
package javagames.util;

import java.awt.*;
import java.awt.image.VolatileImage;


public class FullScreenFramework extends GameFramework {

    private static final int BIT_DEPTH = 32;

    private VolatileImage vi;
    private GraphicsConfiguration gc;
    private DisplayMode currentDisplayMode;

    @Override
    protected void createFramework() {

        setIgnoreRepaint( true );
        setUndecorated( true );

        GraphicsEnvironment ge = GraphicsEnvironment
                .getLocalGraphicsEnvironment();
        GraphicsDevice gd = ge.getDefaultScreenDevice();
        gc = gd.getDefaultConfiguration();
        currentDisplayMode = gd.getDisplayMode();
        if( !gd.isFullScreenSupported() ) {
            System.err.println( "ERROR: Not Supported!!!" );
            System.exit( 0 );
        }

        if( appMaintainRatio ) {
            setBackground( appBorder );
            setupViewport( appWidth, appHeight );
            createVolatileImage();
        } else {
            setBackground( appBackground );
        }

        gd.setFullScreenWindow( this );
        gd.setDisplayMode( new DisplayMode( appWidth, appHeight, BIT_DEPTH,
                DisplayMode.REFRESH_RATE_UNKNOWN ) );

        setupInput( this );
        createBufferStrategy( this );
    }
```

```java
public int getScreenWidth() {
    return appMaintainRatio ? vw : getWidth();
}
public int getScreenHeight() {
    return appMaintainRatio ? vh : getHeight();
}

private void renderVolatileImage( Graphics g ) {
    do {
        int returnCode = vi.validate( gc );
        if( returnCode == VolatileImage.IMAGE_INCOMPATIBLE ) {
            createVolatileImage();
        }
        Graphics2D g2d = null;
        try {
            g2d = vi.createGraphics();
            g2d.setBackground( appBackground );
            g2d.clearRect( 0, 0, getScreenWidth(), getScreenHeight() );
            render( g2d );
        } finally {
            if( g2d != null )
                g2d.dispose();
        }
        g.drawImage( vi, vx, vy, null );
    } while( vi.contentsLost() );
}

private void createVolatileImage() {
    if( vi != null ) {
        vi.flush();
        vi = null;
    }
    vi = gc.createCompatibleVolatileImage(
        getScreenWidth(), getScreenHeight() );
}

@Override
protected void renderFrame( Graphics g ) {
    if( appMaintainRatio ) {
        g.clearRect( 0, 0, getWidth(), getHeight() );
        renderVolatileImage( g );
    } else {
        g.clearRect( 0, 0, getScreenWidth(), getScreenHeight() );
        render( g );
    }
}
```

```
    @Override
    protected void onShutDown() {
        super.onShutDown();
        GraphicsEnvironment ge =
            GraphicsEnvironment.getLocalGraphicsEnvironment();
        GraphicsDevice gd = ge.getDefaultScreenDevice();
        gd.setDisplayMode( currentDisplayMode );
        gd.setFullScreenWindow( null );
    }

}
```

The SwingFramework, located in the same package, is an example of extending the GameFramework and adding Swing components. This framework is used to create a better editor for the game assets. The getScreenWidth() and getScreenHeight() methods return the canvas size, which will be the portion of the GUI with the game rendering. The renderFrame() method is the same as the WindowFramework.

The fun stuff happens in the createFramework() method. First, the look and feel is updated to the Nimbus version. Then a main panel is created. This panel creates a game canvas on another panel, uses a null layout manager to maintain the aspect ratio, and adds the whole thing to the center of the main panel using a BorderLayout. The usual input and buffer strategy are created with the canvas.

Because a null layout is used, whenever the canvas size and location are updated, the repaint() method is called. Also, notice that this framework creates another method to be overridden. The onCreateAndShowGUI() is called after the creation of the Swing component, but before the GUI is visible, so other components can be added. This class will be extended further with the updated PolygonEditor later in the chapter.

```
package javagames.util;

import java.awt.*;
import java.awt.event.*;

import javax.swing.*;


public class SwingFramework extends GameFramework {

    protected Canvas canvas;
    private JPanel mainPanel;
    private JPanel centerPanel;

    protected JPanel getMainPanel() {
        if( mainPanel == null ) {
            mainPanel = new JPanel();
```

```java
            mainPanel.setLayout( new BorderLayout() );
            mainPanel.add( getCenterPanel(), BorderLayout.CENTER );
        }
        return mainPanel;
    }

    private JPanel getCenterPanel() {
        if( centerPanel == null ) {
            centerPanel = new JPanel();
            centerPanel.setBackground( appBorder );
            centerPanel.setLayout( null );
            centerPanel.add( getCanvas() );
        }
        return centerPanel;
    }

    private Canvas getCanvas() {
        if( canvas == null ) {
            canvas = new Canvas();
            canvas.setBackground( appBackground );
        }
        return canvas;
    }

    private void setUpLookAndFeel() {
        try {
            UIManager.setLookAndFeel(
        "com.sun.java.swing.plaf.nimbus.NimbusLookAndFeel"
    );
        } catch( Exception e ) {
            e.printStackTrace();
        }
    }

    protected void onCreateAndShowGUI() {

    }

    @Override
    protected void createFramework() {

        setUpLookAndFeel();
        getContentPane().add( getMainPanel() );
        setLocationByPlatform( true );
        setSize( appWidth, appHeight );
        setTitle( appTitle );

        getContentPane().setBackground( appBorder );
        setSize( appWidth, appHeight );
```

```
    getContentPane().addComponentListener( new ComponentAdapter() {
        public void componentResized( ComponentEvent e ) {
            onComponentResized( e );
        }
    });

    setupInput( getCanvas() );
    onCreateAndShowGUI();

    setVisible( true );
    createBufferStrategy( getCanvas() );
    getCanvas().requestFocus();

}

protected void onComponentResized( ComponentEvent e ) {
    Dimension size = getCenterPanel().getSize();
    setupViewport( size.width, size.height );
    getCanvas().setLocation( vx, vy );
    getCanvas().setSize( vw, vh );
    getCanvas().repaint();
}

@Override
protected void renderFrame( Graphics g ) {
    g.clearRect( 0, 0, getScreenWidth(), getScreenHeight() );
    render( g );
}

@Override
public int getScreenWidth() {
    return getCanvas().getWidth();
}

@Override
public int getScreenHeight() {
    return getCanvas().getHeight();
}

}
```

UPDATING THE POLYGON EDITOR

Before proceeding with the updated polygon editor, there are a few methods you need
to add to the Utility class, located in the javagames.util package. The first, which will
be used in the complete game, adds the ability to draw centered strings instead of sup-
plying the x position. The updated methods take the screen width and calculate the
string width, centering the string in the horizontal direction.

```
public class Utility {
// other methods here…
  public static int drawCenteredString(
    Graphics g, int w, int y, String str ) {
    return drawCenteredString( g, w, y, new String[]{ str } );
  }

  public static int drawCenteredString(
    Graphics g, int w, int y, List<String> str ) {
    return drawCenteredString( g, w, y, str.toArray( new String[0] ) );
  }

  public static int drawCenteredString(
    Graphics g, int w, int y, String... str ) {
    FontMetrics fm = g.getFontMetrics();
    int height = fm.getAscent() + fm.getDescent() + fm.getLeading();
    for( String s : str ) {
      Rectangle2D bounds = g.getFontMetrics().getStringBounds( s, g );
      int x = ( w - (int)bounds.getWidth() ) / 2;
      g.drawString( s, x, y + fm.getAscent() );
      y += height;
    }
    return y;
  }

}
```

The second update transfers the code to scale images up and down to the Utility class and adds a single scale method that determines if the image is being scaled up or down.

```
public class Utility {
// other methods here…
  public static BufferedImage scaleImage(
    BufferedImage toScale, int targetWidth, int targetHeight ) {
    int width = toScale.getWidth();
    int height = toScale.getHeight();
    if( targetWidth < width || targetHeight < height ) {
      return scaleDownImage( toScale, targetWidth, targetHeight );
    } else {
      return scaleUpImage( toScale, targetWidth, targetHeight );
    }
  }

  private static BufferedImage scaleUpImage(
    BufferedImage toScale, int targetWidth, int targetHeight ) {
```

```java
        BufferedImage image =
            new BufferedImage(
                targetWidth, targetHeight, BufferedImage.TYPE_INT_ARGB
            );
        Graphics2D g2d = image.createGraphics();
        g2d.setRenderingHint(
            RenderingHints.KEY_INTERPOLATION, RenderingHints.
            VALUE_INTERPOLATION_BILINEAR
        );
        g2d.drawImage(
            toScale, 0, 0, image.getWidth(), image.getHeight(), null );
        g2d.dispose();
        return image;
    }
    private static BufferedImage scaleDownImage(
        BufferedImage toScale, int targetWidth, int targetHeight ) {
        int w = toScale.getWidth();
        int h = toScale.getHeight();
        do {
            w = w / 2;
            if( w < targetWidth ) {
                w = targetWidth;
            }
            h = h / 2;
            if( h < targetHeight ) {
                h = targetHeight;
            }

            BufferedImage tmp =
                new BufferedImage( w, h, BufferedImage.TYPE_INT_ARGB );
            Graphics2D g2d = tmp.createGraphics();
            g2d.setRenderingHint(
                RenderingHints.KEY_INTERPOLATION,
                RenderingHints.VALUE_INTERPOLATION_BICUBIC
            );
            g2d.drawImage( toScale, 0, 0, w, h, null );
            g2d.dispose();
            toScale = tmp;
        } while( w != targetWidth || h != targetHeight );

        return toScale;
    }
}
```

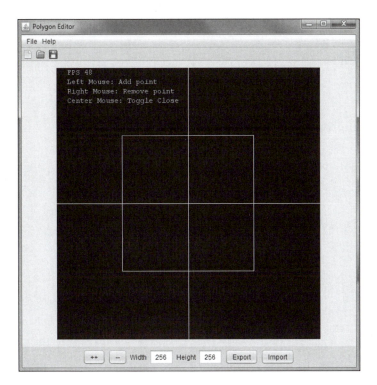

Figure 16.1
Polygon Editor.
© 2014 Timothy Wright.

The first step to updating the PolygonEditor, located in the javagames.tools package and shown in Figure 16.1, is to create a FileFilter class used to filter files from both save and load file dialogs. The following ExampleFileFilter extends Swing's FileFilter, adding a description and a method to filter out unwanted files by the file extension. By passing in a description and list of approved extensions, only approved files will be visible.

```
package javagames.tools;

import java.io.File;

import javax.swing.filechooser.FileFilter;


public class ExampleFileFilter extends FileFilter {

    private String description;
    private String[] filters;
```

```
    public ExampleFileFilter( String description, String[] filters ) {
        this.description = description;
        this.filters = filters;
    }

    @Override
    public boolean accept( File f ) {
        if( f.isDirectory() ) {
            return true;
        }

        String extension = getExtension( f );
        if( extension != null ) {
            for( String filter : filters ) {
                if( extension.equalsIgnoreCase( filter ) ) {
                    return true;
                }
            }
        }
        return false;
    }

    @Override
    public String getDescription() {
        return description;
    }

    public String getExtension( File f ) {
        String ext = null;
        String s = f.getName();
        int i = s.lastIndexOf( '.' );
        if( i > 0 && i < s.length() - 1 ) {
            ext = s.substring( i + 1 ).toLowerCase();
        }
        return ext;
    }
}
```

Armed with the ExampleFileFilter, the new SwingFramework, and the editor code from the prototype chapter, you can upgrade the editor to behave like a real business program (the horror).

The PolygonEditor extends the SwingFramework. Besides setting the usual application properties, it creates two file filters: one for *.png files and one for *.xml files. The onCreateAndShowGUI() method is the new override added by the SwingFramework. It allows other GUI components to be added to the editor. By calling the getMainPanel(), extra components can be added. This method creates and hooks up a lot of controls for the editor.

A File menu is created with an Exit menu item, which closes the application. A Help menu is also created and it launches an About dialog. It also creates a toolbar with buttons for managing the XML files. The following is an example toolbar button to create a new file. Notice the `UIManager.getIcon()` method call to get a platform-specific icon.

```
JToolBar bar = new JToolBar();
bar.setFloatable( false );

JButton b = new JButton(
UIManager.getIcon( "FileChooser.fileIcon" ) );
b.addActionListener( new ActionListener() {
    public void actionPerformed( ActionEvent e ) {
        onNew();
    }
});
bar.add( b );
```

A panel on the bottom is created to import and export a PNG file. The ++ and -- buttons, which control the bounding rectangle, define the area of the editor the loaded PNG file will occupy. The width and height text fields define the size of the exported image. The following `onLoadXML()` method is an example of using the Swing `JFileChooser` for managing, saving, and loading files.

```
protected void onLoadXML() {
    JFileChooser chooser = new JFileChooser( currentDirectory );
    chooser.setFileFilter( xmlFilter );
    int retVal = chooser.showOpenDialog( this );
    if( retVal == JFileChooser.APPROVE_OPTION ) {
        File file = chooser.getSelectedFile();
        currentDirectory = file;
        parseModel( file );
    }
}
```

The format of the model XML is as follows:

```
<model bounds="0.17500022">
    <coord x="-0.04851" y="0.0579" />
    <coord x="-0.07355" y="-0.0425" />
</model>
```

The file chooser has two methods for displaying the dialog: one for loading files and one for saving.

```
JFileChooser.showOpenDialog()
JFileChooser.showSaveDialog()
```

There are a lot of different methods in the JFileChooser class. While the online documentation explains all the details, the two examples of loading and saving both PNG and XML files are a good introduction.

Also, notice that the image scaling updates to the Utility class, the width and height text fields, and the bounding screen rectangle are all necessary to import and export images. Because the images are saved by pixel width and height, but displayed in the editor by world units (in this case, 2 × 2 units), an imported image needs to be scaled to fit into the bounds. Exporting from a 2 × 2 bounding rectangle in screen space needs text fields to specify a width and height for the image size.

One new method to examine is the drawSprite() method:

```
private void drawSprite( Graphics g ) {
    if( sprite == null ) {
        return;
    }

    Vector2f topLeft = new Vector2f( -bounds / 2.0f, bounds / 2.0f );
    Vector2f bottomRight = new Vector2f( bounds / 2.0f, -bounds / 2.0f );

    Matrix3x3f view = getViewportTransform();
    topLeft = view.mul( topLeft );
    bottomRight = view.mul( bottomRight );

    int width = (int)Math.abs( topLeft.x - bottomRight.x );
    int height = (int)Math.abs( topLeft.y - bottomRight.y );

    if( scaled == null || scaled.getWidth() != width
            || scaled.getHeight() != height ) {
        scaled = Utility.scaleImage( sprite, width, height );
    }

    g.drawImage( scaled, (int)topLeft.x, (int)topLeft.y, null );
}
```

This method creates a topLeft and bottomRight vector and scales this rectangle to the screen. This screen size is then used to scale the sprite image to the same screen size. This method is the basis for the Sprite class presented later in the chapter.

The rest of the code for drawing points, polygons, and handling the mouse button input is the same as the previous editor. Except for the new Swing controls, there is nothing in this example that hasn't already been presented.

```java
package javagames.tools;

import java.awt.*;
import java.awt.event.*;
import java.awt.image.BufferedImage;
import java.io.*;
import java.util.ArrayList;

import javagames.util.*;

import javax.imageio.ImageIO;
import javax.swing.*;

import org.w3c.dom.Document;
import org.w3c.dom.Element;


public class PolygonEditor extends SwingFramework {
    private static final float BOUNDS = 0.80f;
    private static final float DELTA = BOUNDS / 32.0f;

    private File currentDirectory;
    private ExampleFileFilter imageFilter;
    private ExampleFileFilter xmlFilter;

    private JTextField widthControl;
    private JTextField heightControl;

    private float bounds = BOUNDS / 2.0f;
    private ArrayList<Vector2f> polygon;
    private Vector2f mousePos;
    private boolean closed;

    private BufferedImage sprite;
    private BufferedImage scaled;

    public PolygonEditor() {

        appBorder = new Color( 0xFFEBCD );
        appBackground = Color.BLACK;
        appFont = new Font( "Courier New", Font.PLAIN, 14 );
        appFPSColor = Color.GREEN;
        appWidth = 640;
        appHeight = 640;
        appSleep = 20L;
        appMaintainRatio = true;
        appBorderScale = 0.95f;
        appTitle = "Polygon Editor";
        appWorldWidth = BOUNDS;
```

```java
        appWorldHeight = BOUNDS;

        imageFilter =
            new ExampleFileFilter( "Image File", new String[] { "png" } );
        xmlFilter =
            new ExampleFileFilter( "Model File", new String[] { "xml" } );
        currentDirectory = new File( "." );

    }

    @Override
    protected void onCreateAndShowGUI() {

        JMenuBar menuBar = new JMenuBar();

        JMenu menu = new JMenu( "File" );
        JMenuItem item = new JMenuItem( new AbstractAction( "Exit" ) {
            public void actionPerformed( ActionEvent e ) {
                PolygonEditor.this.dispatchEvent( new WindowEvent(
                        PolygonEditor.this, WindowEvent.WINDOW_CLOSING )
                );
            }
        });
        menu.add( item );
        menuBar.add( menu );

        menu = new JMenu( "Help" );
        item = new JMenuItem( new AbstractAction( "About" ) {
            public void actionPerformed( ActionEvent e ) {
                JOptionPane.showMessageDialog(
                    PolygonEditor.this, "About this app!!!",
                    "About", JOptionPane.INFORMATION_MESSAGE
                );
            }
        });
        menu.add( item );
        menuBar.add( menu );

        setJMenuBar( menuBar );

        // Lets make a toolbar...
        JToolBar bar = new JToolBar();
        bar.setFloatable( false );

        JButton b =
            new JButton( UIManager.getIcon( "FileChooser.fileIcon" ) );
        b.addActionListener( new ActionListener() {
            public void actionPerformed( ActionEvent e ) {
                onNew();
            }
        });
```

```
bar.add( b );
b = new JButton( UIManager.getIcon( "FileChooser.directoryIcon" ) );
b.addActionListener( new ActionListener() {
    public void actionPerformed( ActionEvent e ) {
        onLoadXML();
    }
});
bar.add( b );
b = new JButton( UIManager.getIcon( "FileChooser.floppyDriveIcon" ) );
b.addActionListener( new ActionListener() {
    public void actionPerformed( ActionEvent e ) {
        onSaveXML();
    }
});
bar.add( b );

getMainPanel().add( bar, BorderLayout.NORTH );

JPanel p = new JPanel();
JButton increase = new JButton( "++" );
increase.addActionListener( new ActionListener() {
    public void actionPerformed( ActionEvent e ) {
        increaseBounds();
    }
});
p.add( increase );
JButton decrease = new JButton( "--" );
decrease.addActionListener( new ActionListener() {
    public void actionPerformed( ActionEvent e ) {
        decreaseBounds();
    }
});
p.add( decrease );

p.add( new JLabel( "Width" ) );
widthControl = new JTextField( 3 );
widthControl.setHorizontalAlignment( JTextField.CENTER );
widthControl.setText( "256" );
p.add( widthControl );

p.add( new JLabel( "Height" ) );
heightControl = new JTextField( 3 );
heightControl.setHorizontalAlignment( JTextField.CENTER );
heightControl.setText( "256" );
p.add( heightControl );
```

```java
        JButton button = new JButton( "Export" );
        button.addActionListener( new ActionListener() {
            public void actionPerformed( ActionEvent e ) {
                exportImage();
            }
        });
        p.add( button );
        button = new JButton( "Import" );
        button.addActionListener( new ActionListener() {
            public void actionPerformed( ActionEvent e ) {
                importImage();
            }
        });
        p.add( button );
        getMainPanel().add( p, BorderLayout.SOUTH );
    }

    protected void onNew() {
        polygon.clear();
        sprite = null;
        scaled = null;
    }

    protected void onLoadXML() {
        JFileChooser chooser = new JFileChooser( currentDirectory );
        chooser.setFileFilter( xmlFilter );
        int retVal = chooser.showOpenDialog( this );
        if( retVal == JFileChooser.APPROVE_OPTION ) {
            File file = chooser.getSelectedFile();
            currentDirectory = file;
            parseModel( file );
        }
    }

    private void parseModel( File file ) {
        FileReader reader = null;
        try {
            reader = new FileReader( file );
            Document root = XMLUtility.parseDocument( reader );
            parseModel( root.getDocumentElement() );
            closed = true;
        } catch( Exception e ) {
            e.printStackTrace();
```

```
      } finally {
         if( reader != null ) {
            try {
               reader.close();
            } catch( Exception e ) {
            }
         }
      }
   }

protected void onSaveXML() {
   JFileChooser chooser = new JFileChooser( currentDirectory );
   chooser.setFileFilter( xmlFilter );
   int retVal = chooser.showSaveDialog( this );
   if( retVal == JFileChooser.APPROVE_OPTION ) {
      File file = chooser.getSelectedFile();
      currentDirectory = file;
      if( file.exists() ) {
         int overwrite = JOptionPane.showConfirmDialog( this,
               "Overwrite existing file?" );
         if( overwrite == JOptionPane.YES_OPTION ) {
            writeXML( file );
         }
      } else {
      writeXML(file);
      }

private void writeXML( File file ) {
   PrintWriter out = null;
   try {
      out = new PrintWriter( file );
      writeXML( out );
   } catch( FileNotFoundException fex ) {
      fex.printStackTrace();
   } finally {
      try {
         out.close();
      } catch( Exception e ) {
      }
   }
}
```

```java
private void writeXML( PrintWriter out ) {
    out.println( "<model bounds=\"" + bounds + "\">" );
    for( Vector2f point : polygon ) {
        out.println(
            "\t<coord x=\"" + point.x + "\" y=\"" + point.y + "\" />"
        );
    }
    out.println( "</model>" );
}

protected void increaseBounds() {
    bounds += DELTA;
    if( bounds > BOUNDS ) {
        bounds = BOUNDS;
    }
}

protected void decreaseBounds() {
    bounds -= DELTA;
    if( bounds < DELTA ) {
        bounds = DELTA;
    }
}

protected void exportImage() {
    JFileChooser chooser = new JFileChooser( currentDirectory );
    chooser.setFileFilter( imageFilter );
    int retVal = chooser.showSaveDialog( this );
    if( retVal == JFileChooser.APPROVE_OPTION ) {
        File file = chooser.getSelectedFile();
        currentDirectory = file;
        if( file.exists() ) {
            int overwrite = JOptionPane.showConfirmDialog( this,
                    "Overwrite existing file?" );
            if( overwrite == JOptionPane.YES_OPTION ) {
                exportImage( file );
            }
        } else {
            exportImage( file );
        }
    }
}

private void exportImage( File file ) {
    int imageWidth = Integer.parseInt( widthControl.getText() );
    int imageHeight = Integer.parseInt( heightControl.getText() );
```

```
        BufferedImage image = new BufferedImage( imageWidth, imageHeight,
            BufferedImage.TYPE_INT_ARGB );

        Matrix3x3f view = Utility.createViewport( bounds, bounds, imageWidth,
            imageHeight );
        Graphics g = image.getGraphics();
        drawPolygon( g, view );
        g.dispose();

        try {
            System.out.println(
                "Export: " + ImageIO.write( image, "png", file )
            );
        } catch( IOException e ) {
            e.printStackTrace();
        }
    }

    protected void importImage() {
        JFileChooser chooser = new JFileChooser( currentDirectory );
        chooser.setFileFilter( imageFilter );
        int retVal = chooser.showOpenDialog( this );
        if( retVal == JFileChooser.APPROVE_OPTION ) {
            File file = chooser.getSelectedFile();
            currentDirectory = file;
            try {
                sprite = ImageIO.read( file );
                scaled = null;
            } catch( IOException e ) {
                e.printStackTrace();
            }
        }
    }

    private void parseModel( Element model ) {
        bounds = Float.parseFloat( model.getAttribute( "bounds" ) );

        polygon.clear();
        for( Element coords : XMLUtility.getAllElements( model, "coord" ) ) {
            float x = Float.parseFloat( coords.getAttribute( "x" ) );
            float y = Float.parseFloat( coords.getAttribute( "y" ) );
            polygon.add( new Vector2f( x, y ) );
        }
    }
```

```java
@Override
protected void initialize() {
    super.initialize();
    polygon = new ArrayList<Vector2f>();
}

@Override
protected void processInput( float delta ) {
    super.processInput( delta );

    mousePos = getWorldMousePosition();

    if( mouse.buttonDownOnce( MouseEvent.BUTTON1 ) ) {
        polygon.add( mousePos );
    }
    if( mouse.buttonDownOnce( MouseEvent.BUTTON2 ) ) {
        closed = !closed;
    }
    if( mouse.buttonDownOnce( MouseEvent.BUTTON3 ) ) {
        if( !polygon.isEmpty() ) {
            polygon.remove( polygon.size() - 1 );
        }
    }
}

@Override
protected void render( Graphics g ) {
    super.render( g );
    ((Graphics2D)g).setRenderingHint( RenderingHints.KEY_ANTIALIASING,
            RenderingHints.VALUE_ANTIALIAS_ON );
    ((Graphics2D)g).setRenderingHint( RenderingHints.KEY_INTERPOLATION,
            RenderingHints.VALUE_INTERPOLATION_BILINEAR );

    textPos = Utility.drawString( g, 20, textPos, "Left Mouse: Add point",
            "Right Mouse: Remove point", "Center Mouse: Toggle Close" );

    drawSprite( g );
    drawAxisLines( g );
    drawPolygon( g, getViewportTransform() );
    drawBoundingBox( g );
}

private void drawSprite( Graphics g ) {
    if( sprite == null ) {
        return;
    }

    Vector2f topLeft = new Vector2f( -bounds / 2.0f, bounds / 2.0f );
    Vector2f bottomRight = new Vector2f( bounds / 2.0f, -bounds / 2.0f );
```

```
        Matrix3x3f view = getViewportTransform();
        topLeft = view.mul( topLeft );
        bottomRight = view.mul( bottomRight );

        int width = (int)Math.abs( topLeft.x - bottomRight.x );
        int height = (int)Math.abs( topLeft.y - bottomRight.y );

        if( scaled == null || scaled.getWidth() != width
                || scaled.getHeight() != height ) {
            scaled = Utility.scaleImage( sprite, width, height );
        }

        g.drawImage( scaled, (int)topLeft.x, (int)topLeft.y, null );
    }
    private void drawAxisLines( Graphics g ) {
        g.setColor( Color.WHITE );
        Vector2f left = new Vector2f( appWorldWidth / 2.0f, 0.0f );
        Vector2f right = new Vector2f( -left.x, 0.0f );
        drawLine( g, getViewportTransform(), left, right );
        Vector2f top = new Vector2f( 0.0f, appWorldHeight / 2.0f );
        Vector2f bottom = new Vector2f( 0.0f, -top.y );
        drawLine( g, getViewportTransform(), top, bottom );
    }
    private void drawPolygon( Graphics g, Matrix3x3f view ) {
        g.setColor( Color.GREEN );

        if( polygon.size() == 1 ) {
            drawPoint( g, view, polygon.get( 0 ) );
        }

        for( int i = 0; i < polygon.size() - 1; ++i ) {
            drawLine( g, view, polygon.get( i ), polygon.get( i + 1 ) );
        }

        if( closed && polygon.size() > 1 ) {
            Vector2f P = polygon.get( polygon.size() - 1 );
            Vector2f S = polygon.get( 0 );
            drawLine( g, view, S, P );
        }
        if( !( polygon.isEmpty() || closed ) ) {
            Vector2f P = polygon.get( polygon.size() - 1 );
            Vector2f S = mousePos;
            drawLine( g, view, S, P );
        }
    }
}
```

```
    private void drawPoint( Graphics g, Matrix3x3f view, Vector2f v ) {
        Vector2f s = view.mul( v );
        g.drawRect( (int)s.x, (int)s.y, 1, 1 );
    }

    private void drawLine(
        Graphics g, Matrix3x3f view, Vector2f v0, Vector2f v1 ) {
        Vector2f S = view.mul( v0 );
        Vector2f P = view.mul( v1 );
        g.drawLine( (int)S.x, (int)S.y, (int)P.x, (int)P.y );
    }

    private void drawBoundingBox( Graphics g ) {
        Vector2f[] bb = { new Vector2f( -bounds / 2.0f, bounds / 2.0f ),
                new Vector2f( bounds / 2.0f, bounds / 2.0f ),
                new Vector2f( bounds / 2.0f, -bounds / 2.0f ),
                new Vector2f( -bounds / 2.0f, -bounds / 2.0f ), };

        Matrix3x3f view = getViewportTransform();
        for( int i = 0; i < bb.length; ++i ) {
            bb[ i ] = view.mul( bb[ i ] );
        }
        g.setColor( Color.WHITE );
        Utility.drawPolygon( g, bb );
    }

    public static void main( String[] args ) {
        launchApp( new PolygonEditor() );
    }

}
```

DRAWING A SPRITE

The Sprite class is added to the javagames.util package to handle drawing images in pixel size to rectangles in world space. Just like the drawSprite() method in the PolygonEditor, the Sprite class has a top-left and bottom-right vector defining the bounding rectangle in world space.

The sprite can be drawn with an optional rotation. The render method first calculates the screen size of the rectangle and then, if the scaled image isn't the correct size, the original image is scaled. The AffineTransform with a bilinear interpolation from Chapter 10 is used to render the image. Remember that the AffineTransform class is column major, so the transformations are in reverse order. The image is translated to the center, rotated by the negative of the rotation angle (to take into account the flipped y-axis in screen space), and finally transformed to the screen position.

There is also an extra `scaleImage()` method to scale the image before rendering it, which can save time by performing the scaling when the sprite image is first loaded. As long as the world-to-screen viewport matrix can be created when the sprite's image is loaded, this method will scale the image to the correct size before the first image is rendered.

```java
package javagames.util;

import java.awt.*;
import java.awt.geom.AffineTransform;
import java.awt.image.BufferedImage;


public class Sprite {

    private BufferedImage image;
    private BufferedImage scaled;
    private Vector2f topLeft;
    private Vector2f bottomRight;

    public Sprite(
        BufferedImage image, Vector2f topLeft, Vector2f bottomRight ) {
        this.image = image;
        this.topLeft = topLeft;
        this.bottomRight = bottomRight;
    }

    public void render( Graphics2D g, Matrix3x3f view ) {
        render( g, view, new Vector2f(), 0.0f );
    }

    public void render(
        Graphics2D g, Matrix3x3f view, Vector2f position, float angle ) {
        if( image != null ) {
            Vector2f tl = view.mul( topLeft );
            Vector2f br = view.mul( bottomRight );
            int width = (int)Math.abs( br.x - tl.x );
            int height = (int)Math.abs( br.y - tl.y );
            if( scaled == null ||
                width != scaled.getWidth() ||
                height != scaled.getHeight() ) {
                scaled = Utility.scaleImage( image, width, height );
            }

            g.setRenderingHint(
                RenderingHints.KEY_INTERPOLATION,
                RenderingHints.VALUE_INTERPOLATION_BILINEAR
            );
```

```
        Vector2f screen = view.mul( position );
        AffineTransform transform =
            AffineTransform.getTranslateInstance( screen.x, screen.y );
        transform.rotate( -angle );
        transform.translate(
            -scaled.getWidth() / 2, -scaled.getHeight() / 2 );
        g.drawImage( scaled, transform, null );
    }
}

    public void scaleImage( Matrix3x3f view ) {
        Vector2f screenTopLeft = view.mul( topLeft );
        Vector2f screenBottomRight = view.mul( bottomRight );
        int scaledWidth = (int)Math.abs(screenBottomRight.x - screenTopLeft.x);
        int scaledHeight =
          (int)Math.abs(screenBottomRight.y - screenTopLeft.y);
        scaled = Utility.scaleImage( image, scaledWidth, scaledHeight );
    }
}
```

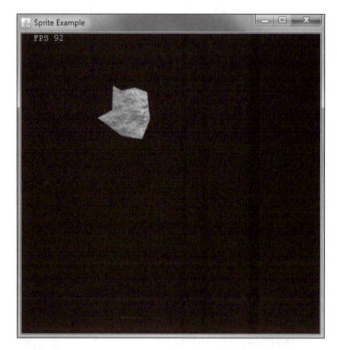

Figure 16.2
Sprite Example.
© 2014 Timothy Wright.

The SpriteExample, as shown in Figure 16.2 and located in the javagames.tools package, is a quick test of using the sprite class to draw images to rectangles in world space. The initialize() method loads a rock sprite and creates the sprite class. The updateObjects() method performs simple screen collision. Finally, the render() method creates the rotating sprite.

```java
package javagames.tools;

import java.awt.*;
import java.awt.image.BufferedImage;
import java.io.InputStream;

import javagames.util.*;

import javax.imageio.ImageIO;


public class SpriteExample extends WindowFramework {

    private Sprite sprite;
    private Vector2f pos;
    private Vector2f vel;
    private float rot;
    private float rotDelta;

    public SpriteExample() {
        appTitle = "Sprite Example";

        pos = new Vector2f();
        vel = new Vector2f( 0.25f, -0.3f );
        rotDelta = (float)Math.toRadians( 90.0 );
    }

    @Override
    protected void initialize() {
        super.initialize();
        InputStream in = ResourceLoader.load( SpriteExample.class,
            "res/assets/images/large0.png",
            "/images/large0.png"
        );
        try {
            BufferedImage image = ImageIO.read( in );
            Vector2f topLeft = new Vector2f( -0.25f, 0.25f );
            Vector2f bottomRight = new Vector2f( 0.25f, -0.25f );
            sprite = new Sprite( image, topLeft, bottomRight );
        } catch( Exception e ) {
            e.printStackTrace();
        }
    }
```

```java
@Override
protected void updateObjects( float delta ) {
    super.updateObjects( delta );

    pos = pos.add( vel.mul( delta ) );
    if( pos.x < -appWorldWidth / 2.0f ) {
        pos.x = -appWorldWidth / 2.0f;
        vel.x = -vel.x;
    } else if( pos.x > appWorldWidth / 2.0f ) {
        pos.x = appWorldWidth / 2.0f;
        vel.x = -vel.x;
    }
    if( pos.y < -appWorldHeight / 2.0f ) {
        pos.y = -appWorldHeight / 2.0f;
        vel.y = -vel.y;
    } else if( pos.y > appWorldHeight / 2.0f ) {
        pos.y = appWorldHeight / 2.0f;
        vel.y = -vel.y;
    }

    rot += rotDelta * delta;
}

@Override
protected void render( Graphics g ) {
    super.render( g );

    g.setColor( Color.GREEN );
    g.drawRect( 0, 0, getScreenWidth() - 1, getScreenHeight() - 1 );

    sprite.render( (Graphics2D)g, getViewportTransform(), pos, rot );
}

public static void main( String[] args ) {
    launchApp( new SpriteExample() );
}

}
```

CREATING A SIMPLE PARTICLE ENGINE

A particle system is just a fancy way to keep track of each particle in an explosion, including fire, smoke effects, liquid droplets, or anything else that can be modeled as a collection of tiny elements. Each particle in the system maintains its own physics variables, and each particle is updated every frame. As you can imagine, these systems can become quite complex. For the purposes of this text, a very simple particle system is created just to give you a taste of what is possible.

The TestParticle class, located in the javagames.tools package, is a simple class that represents a particle. The radius is the rendered size of the circle, and the color fills the circle. The vector has an angle and direction, along with a lifespan in seconds. The update() method updates the time the particle has been alive and updates its current position. The render() method draws the little circle scaled to the screen (it can be really small), and the hasDied() method checks if the lifespan has expired.

```java
package javagames.tools;

import java.awt.Color;
import java.awt.Graphics2D;

import javagames.util.Matrix3x3f;
import javagames.util.Vector2f;

public class TestParticle {

    private Vector2f pos;
    private Vector2f curPos;
    private Vector2f vel;
    private Vector2f curVel;
    private Color color;
    private float lifeSpan;
    private float time;
    private float radius;

    public TestParticle() {

    }

    public void setPosition( Vector2f pos ) {
        this.pos = pos;
    }

    public void setRadius( float radius ) {
        this.radius = radius;
    }

    public void setVector( float angle, float r ) {
        vel = Vector2f.polar( angle, r );
    }

    public void setColor( Color color ) {
        this.color = color;
    }

    public void setLifeSpan( float lifeSpan ) {
        this.lifeSpan = lifeSpan;
    }
```

```
public void update( float delta ) {
    time += delta;
    curVel = vel.mul( time );
    curPos = pos.add( curVel );
}

public void draw( Graphics2D g, Matrix3x3f view ) {

    g.setColor( color );
            Vector2f topLeft =
                new Vector2f( curPos.x - radius, curPos.y + radius );
            topLeft = view.mul( topLeft );

            Vector2f bottomRight =
                new Vector2f( curPos.x + radius, curPos.y - radius );
            bottomRight = view.mul( bottomRight );

            int circleX = (int)topLeft.x;
            int circleY = (int)topLeft.y;
            int circleWidth = (int)(bottomRight.x - topLeft.x);
            int circleHeight = (int)(bottomRight.y - topLeft.y);

            g.fillOval( circleX, circleY, circleWidth, circleHeight );
}

public boolean hasDied() {
    return time > lifeSpan;
}

}
```

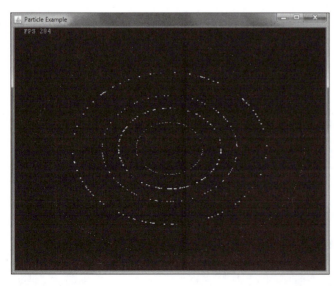

Figure 16.3
Particle Example.
© 2014 Timothy Wright.

The ParticleExample, as shown in Figure 16.3 and located in the javagames.tools package, demonstrates creating particles and rendering them as explosions. These effects, while simple, add to the final game by simulating explosions and rocket blasts.

The initialize() method creates a list of random colors for the circle explosions, as well as a list of particle colors. The getRandomPosition() method generates random positions for the particle events. The createParticleRings() method creates five rings with velocities and life spans. These explosions are used for the player ship in the complete game. The createRandomParticle() method creates bursts in all directions and is the explosion used for the space rocks. The updateObjects() method generates random particle events, draws each particle, and, if the particle has died, removes it from the list. Finally, the render() method loops through the particle list and draws each individual particle.

```
package javagames.tools;

import java.awt.*;
import java.util.*;

import javagames.util.Vector2f;
import javagames.util.WindowFramework;


public class ParticleExample extends WindowFramework {

    private float elapsedRing;
    private float ringTime;
    private float elapsedBurst;
    private float burstTime;
    private Random random;
    private Vector<Color> colors;
    private Vector<TestParticle> particles;

    public ParticleExample() {
        appWidth = 640;
        appHeight = 480;
        appSleep = 1L;
        appTitle = "Particle Example";
    }

    @Override
    protected void initialize() {
        super.initialize();

        random = new Random();
        particles = new Vector<TestParticle>();
```

```
        colors = new Vector<Color>();
        colors.add( Color.WHITE );
        colors.add( Color.RED );
        colors.add( Color.YELLOW );
        colors.add( Color.ORANGE );
        colors.add( Color.PINK );
    }

    private Vector2f getRandomPosition() {
        float x = -0.5f + random.nextFloat();
        float y = -0.5f + random.nextFloat();
        return new Vector2f( x, y );
    }

    private void createParticleRings() {

        for( int ring = 0; ring < 5; ++ring ) {

            float velocity = 0.25f + random.nextFloat() * 1.0f;
            float lifeSpan = 1.0f + random.nextFloat() * 1.0f;
            float radius = 0.003f + random.nextFloat() * 0.003f;

            for( int i = 0; i < 100; ++i ) {
                TestParticle p = new TestParticle();
                p.setPosition( new Vector2f() );
                p.setRadius( radius );
                p.setLifeSpan( lifeSpan );
                p.setColor( colors.get( random.nextInt( colors.size() ) ) );
                float angle = (float)Math.toRadians( random.nextInt( 360 ) );
                p.setVector( angle, velocity );
                particles.add( p );
            }
        }
    }

    private TestParticle createRandomParticle( Vector2f pos ) {
        TestParticle p = new TestParticle();
        p.setPosition( pos );
        p.setRadius( 0.002f + random.nextFloat() * 0.004f );
        p.setLifeSpan( random.nextFloat() * 1.0f );
        switch( random.nextInt( 4 ) ) {
            case 0: p.setColor( Color.WHITE ); break;
            case 1: p.setColor( Color.GRAY ); break;
            case 2: p.setColor( Color.LIGHT_GRAY ); break;
            case 3: p.setColor( Color.DARK_GRAY ); break;
        }
        float angle = (float)Math.toRadians( random.nextInt( 360 ) );
        float velocity = random.nextFloat() * 2.0f;
```

```
            p.setVector( angle, velocity );
            return p;
        }

        @Override
        protected void updateObjects( float delta ) {
            super.updateObjects( delta );

            elapsedBurst += delta;
            elapsedRing += delta;

            if( elapsedBurst > burstTime ) {
                Vector2f pos = getRandomPosition();
                for( int i = 0; i < 150; ++i ) {
                    particles.add( createRandomParticle( pos ) );
                }
                elapsedBurst = 0.0f;
                burstTime = 0.1f + random.nextFloat() * 1.5f;
            }
            if( elapsedRing > ringTime ) {
                elapsedRing = 0.0f;
                createParticleRings();
                ringTime = 2.5f + random.nextFloat() * 2.5f;
            }

            Iterator<TestParticle> it = particles.iterator();
            while( it.hasNext() ) {
                TestParticle p = it.next();
                p.update( delta );
                if( p.hasDied() ) {
                    it.remove();
                }
            }
        }

        @Override
        protected void render( Graphics g ) {
            super.render( g );

            g.setColor( Color.GREEN );
            g.drawRect( 0, 0, getScreenWidth() - 1, getScreenHeight() - 1 );
            Graphics2D g2d = (Graphics2D)g;
            g2d.setRenderingHint(
                RenderingHints.KEY_ANTIALIASING,
                RenderingHints.VALUE_ANTIALIAS_ON
            );
```

```
        for( TestParticle particle : particles ) {
            particle.draw( g2d, getViewportTransform() );
        }
    }

    public static void main( String[] args ) {
        launchApp( new ParticleExample() );
    }
}
```

This chapter covered a lot of tools needed for the final task: creating a complete game. Make sure you explore and understand the tools presented in this chapter before moving on to making the complete game, because there is a lot of ground to cover. Onward ho…

RESOURCES AND FURTHER READING

"Getting Started with Swing," http://docs.oracle.com/javase/tutorial/uiswing/start/index.html.

"Using Swing Components," http://docs.oracle.com/javase/tutorial/uiswing/components/.

CHAPTER 17

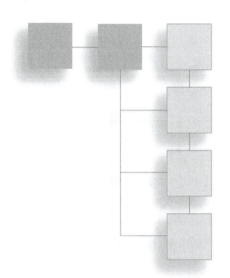

SPACE ROCKS

Now, taking everything covered so far, this chapter presents a complete game. Through all my years reading forum posts about game programming, I've come to realize that finishing a game is a huge stumbling block for a lot of people. The reason for this may have something to do with the fact that to code a complete game, there is a ton of stuff to learn, and most of the code is boring. As you examine the code for this complete game, notice that the actual gameplay (the fun part) is a very small part of the entire codebase. Most of the code is framework, input handling, or dealing with sound and image resources. Very little of the code is what a beginner imagines it takes to make a game.

Although the game is "complete," there is still a lot of polish that could be added. I didn't want to just throw up thousands of lines of code, but I also didn't want to end the book without an idea of what it takes to finish a game. The game that follows, called "Space Rocks," contains all the parts and pieces of a finished game. Granted, it is not very big, it's not very fun, and isn't that difficult—but it is a game.

The game contains the following:

- Build script
- Input handling
- Collision detection
- Particle system
- Physics (flying ship)
- Sound

- Sprites
- XML model files
- Generic state framework
- Loading screen
- Attract mode with multiple screens
- Gameplay
- High score persistence

This is a lot of code to cover. Fortunately, the entire rest of the book goes into great detail about the inner workings of all these parts and pieces, so there isn't a lot of new information. In fact, other than the GameState and the GameController objects, everything should be familiar. All of the code is located in the javagames.completegame package, or other packages within this base package. The code listings all contain the package declaration, so you can always refer back to the code examples if you are having trouble finding the source.

Let's finish a game…

THE BULLET CLASS

The Bullet class is the only previous class that remains unchanged (except for the package name).

```
package javagames.completegame.object;


import java.awt.Color;
import java.awt.Graphics2D;

import javagames.util.*;


public class Bullet {
    private Vector2f velocity;
    private Vector2f position;
    private Color color;
    private float radius;

    public Bullet( Vector2f position, float angle ) {
        this.position = position;
        velocity = Vector2f.polar( angle, 1.0f );
        radius = 0.006f;
        color = Color.GREEN;
    }
```

```
    public Vector2f getPosition() {
        return position;
    }

    public void draw( Graphics2D g, Matrix3x3f view ) {

        g.setColor( color );
        Vector2f topLeft =
            new Vector2f( position.x - radius, position.y + radius );
        topLeft = view.mul( topLeft );

        Vector2f bottomRight = new Vector2f( position.x + radius, position.y
                - radius );
        bottomRight = view.mul( bottomRight );

        int circleX = (int)topLeft.x;
        int circleY = (int)topLeft.y;
        int circleWidth = (int)( bottomRight.x - topLeft.x );
        int circleHeight = (int)( bottomRight.y - topLeft.y );

        g.fillOval( circleX, circleY, circleWidth, circleHeight );
    }

    public void update( float time ) {
        position = position.add( velocity.mul( time ) );
    }
}
```

THE POLYGONWRAPPER CLASS

The PolygonWrapper class adds the wrapPosition() method that not only takes a polygon, but also the center position for that polygon, along with a list of wrapped positions. If any portion of the polygon is off-screen, the center of the polygon needs to be wrapped, even though the center is still on the screen. This adds the ability to wrap sprites.

```
package javagames.completegame.object;

import java.util.List;

import javagames.util.Matrix3x3f;
import javagames.util.Vector2f;


public class PolygonWrapper {

    private float worldWidth;
    private float worldHeight;
    private Vector2f worldMin;
    private Vector2f worldMax;
```

```java
public PolygonWrapper( float worldWidth, float worldHeight ) {
    this.worldWidth = worldWidth;
    this.worldHeight = worldHeight;
    worldMax = new Vector2f( worldWidth / 2.0f, worldHeight / 2.0f );
    worldMin = worldMax.inv();
}

public boolean hasLeftWorld( Vector2f position ) {
    return position.x < worldMin.x || position.x > worldMax.x ||
        position.y < worldMin.y || position.y > worldMax.y;
}

public Vector2f wrapPosition( Vector2f position ) {
    Vector2f wrapped = new Vector2f( position );
    if( position.x < worldMin.x ) {
        wrapped.x = position.x + worldWidth;
    } else if( position.x > worldMax.x ) {
        wrapped.x = position.x - worldWidth;
    }
    if( position.y < worldMin.y ) {
        wrapped.y = position.y + worldHeight;
    } else if( position.y > worldMax.y ) {
        wrapped.y = position.y - worldHeight;
    }
    return wrapped;

}

public void wrapPolygon( Vector2f[] poly, List<Vector2f[]> renderList ) {
    Vector2f min = getMin( poly );
    Vector2f max = getMax( poly );

    boolean north = max.y > worldMax.y;
    boolean south = min.y < worldMin.y;
    boolean west = min.x < worldMin.x;
    boolean east = max.x > worldMax.x;

    if( west ) renderList.add( wrapEast( poly ) );
    if( east ) renderList.add( wrapWest( poly ) );
    if( north ) renderList.add( wrapSouth( poly ) );
    if( south ) renderList.add( wrapNorth( poly ) );
    if( north && west ) renderList.add( wrapSouthEast( poly ) );
    if( north && east ) renderList.add( wrapSouthWest( poly ) );
    if( south && west ) renderList.add( wrapNorthEast( poly ) );
    if( south && east ) renderList.add( wrapNorthWest( poly ) );

}

public void wrapPositions( Vector2f[] poly, Vector2f position,
    List<Vector2f> centerList ) {
```

```java
        Vector2f min = getMin( poly );
        Vector2f max = getMax( poly );

        boolean north = max.y > worldMax.y;
        boolean south = min.y < worldMin.y;
        boolean west = min.x < worldMin.x;
        boolean east = max.x > worldMax.x;

        if( west ) centerList.add(
            position.add( new Vector2f( worldWidth, 0.0f ) ) );
        if( east ) centerList.add(
            position.add( new Vector2f( -worldWidth, 0.0f ) ) );
        if( north ) centerList.add(
            position.add( new Vector2f( 0.0f, -worldHeight ) ) );
        if( south ) centerList.add(
            position.add( new Vector2f( 0.0f, worldHeight ) ) );
        if( north && west )
            centerList.add(
                position.add( new Vector2f( worldWidth, -worldHeight ) )
            );
        if( north && east )
            centerList.add(
                position.add( new Vector2f( -worldWidth, -worldHeight ) )
            );
        if( south && west )
            centerList.add(
                position.add( new Vector2f( worldWidth, worldHeight ) )
            );
        if( south && east )
            centerList.add(
                position.add( new Vector2f( -worldWidth, worldHeight ) )
            );
    }

    private Vector2f getMin( Vector2f[] poly ) {
        Vector2f min = new Vector2f( Float.MAX_VALUE, Float.MAX_VALUE );
        for( Vector2f v : poly ) {
            min.x = Math.min( v.x, min.x );
            min.y = Math.min( v.y, min.y );
        }
        return min;
    }

    private Vector2f getMax( Vector2f[] poly ) {
        Vector2f max = new Vector2f( -Float.MAX_VALUE, -Float.MAX_VALUE );
        for( Vector2f v : poly ) {
```

```java
            max.x = Math.max( v.x, max.x );
            max.y = Math.max( v.y, max.y );
        }
        return max;
    }

    private Vector2f[] wrapNorth( Vector2f[] poly ) {
        return transform( poly, Matrix3x3f.translate( 0.0f, worldHeight ) );
    }

    private Vector2f[] wrapSouth( Vector2f[] poly ) {
        return transform( poly, Matrix3x3f.translate( 0.0f, -worldHeight ) );
    }

    private Vector2f[] wrapEast( Vector2f[] poly ) {
        return transform( poly, Matrix3x3f.translate( worldWidth, 0.0f ) );
    }

    private Vector2f[] wrapWest( Vector2f[] poly ) {
        return transform( poly, Matrix3x3f.translate( -worldWidth, 0.0f ) );
    }

    private Vector2f[] wrapNorthWest( Vector2f[] poly ) {
        return transform(
            poly, Matrix3x3f.translate( -worldWidth, worldHeight )
        );
    }

    private Vector2f[] wrapNorthEast( Vector2f[] poly ) {
        return transform(
            poly, Matrix3x3f.translate( worldWidth, worldHeight )
        );
    }

    private Vector2f[] wrapSouthEast( Vector2f[] poly ) {
        return transform(
            poly, Matrix3x3f.translate( worldWidth, -worldHeight )
        );
    }

    private Vector2f[] wrapSouthWest( Vector2f[] poly ) {
        return transform(
            poly, Matrix3x3f.translate( -worldWidth, -worldHeight )
        );
    }

    private Vector2f[] transform( Vector2f[] poly, Matrix3x3f mat ) {
        Vector2f[] copy = new Vector2f[ poly.length ];
```

```
        for( int i = 0; i < poly.length; ++i ) {
            copy[i] = mat.mul( poly[i] );
        }
        return copy;
    }

}
```

THE PARTICLE CLASS

The Particle class represents a single element in the various explosions in the game.

```
package javagames.completegame.object;


import java.awt.Color;
import java.awt.Graphics2D;

import javagames.util.Matrix3x3f;
import javagames.util.Vector2f;


public class Particle {

    private Vector2f pos;
    private Vector2f curPos;
    private Vector2f vel;
    private Vector2f curVel;
    private Color color;
    private float lifeSpan;
    private float time;
    private float radius;

    public Particle() {

    }

    public void setPosition( Vector2f pos ) {
        this.pos = pos;
    }

    public void setRadius( float radius ) {
        this.radius = radius;
    }

    public void setVector( float angle, float r ) {
        vel = Vector2f.polar( angle, r );
    }

    public void setColor( Color color ) {
        this.color = color;
    }
```

```
    public void setLifeSpan( float lifeSpan ) {
        this.lifeSpan = lifeSpan;
    }

    public void update( float delta ) {
        time += delta;
        curVel = vel.mul( time );
        curPos = pos.add( curVel );
    }

    public void draw( Graphics2D g, Matrix3x3f view ) {

        g.setColor( color );
        Vector2f topLeft =
            new Vector2f( curPos.x - radius, curPos.y + radius );
        topLeft = view.mul( topLeft );

        Vector2f bottomRight =
            new Vector2f( curPos.x + radius, curPos.y - radius );
        bottomRight = view.mul( bottomRight );

        int circleX = (int)topLeft.x;
        int circleY = (int)topLeft.y;
        int circleWidth = (int)( bottomRight.x - topLeft.x );
        int circleHeight = (int)( bottomRight.y - topLeft.y );

        g.fillOval( circleX, circleY, circleWidth, circleHeight );
    }

    public boolean hasDied() {
        return time > lifeSpan;
    }

}
```

THE ASTEROID CLASS

The Asteroid class is updated by adding a sprite, and only uses the polygon for collision detection. Remember, however, that the polygon still needs to be translated and
rotated. Instead of using the PolygonWrapper to wrap only the polygon, the sprite positions are also wrapped so both the sprite and the polygon can wrap from one side of
the screen to the other.

```
package javagames.completegame.object;


import java.awt.Graphics2D;
import java.util.*;

import javagames.util.*;
```

```java
public class Asteroid {
    public enum Size {
        Large, Medium, Small;
    }

    private PolygonWrapper wrapper;
    private Size size;

    private Sprite sprite;

    private float rotation;
    private float rotationDelta;

    private Vector2f[] polygon;
    private Vector2f position;
    private Vector2f velocity;
    private ArrayList<Vector2f[]> collisionList;
    private ArrayList<Vector2f> positionList;

    public Asteroid( PolygonWrapper wrapper ) {
        this.wrapper = wrapper;
        collisionList = new ArrayList<Vector2f[]>();
        positionList = new ArrayList<Vector2f>();
        velocity = getRandomVelocity();
        rotationDelta = getRandomRotationDelta();
    }

    private Vector2f getRandomVelocity() {
        float angle = getRandomRadians( 0, 360 );
        float radius = getRandomFloat( 0.06f, 0.3f );
        return Vector2f.polar( angle, radius );
    }

    private float getRandomRadians( int minDegree, int maxDegree ) {
        int rand = new Random().nextInt( maxDegree - minDegree + 1 );
        return (float)Math.toRadians( rand + minDegree );
    }

    private float getRandomRotationDelta() {
        float radians = getRandomRadians( 5, 45 );
        return new Random().nextBoolean() ? radians : -radians;
    }

    private float getRandomFloat( float min, float max ) {
        float rand = new Random().nextFloat();
        return rand * ( max - min ) + min;
    }
```

```java
    public void setSprite( Sprite sprite ) {
        this.sprite = sprite;
    }

    public Sprite getSprite() {
        return sprite;
    }

    public void setPolygon( Vector2f[] polygon ) {
        this.polygon = polygon;
    }

    public Vector2f[] getPolygon() {
        return polygon;
    }

    public void setPosition( Vector2f position ) {
        this.position = position;
    }

    public Vector2f getPosition() {
        return position;
    }

    public void setSize( Size size ) {
        this.size = size;
    }

    public Size getSize() {
        return size;
    }

    public void update( float time ) {
        position = position.add( velocity.mul( time ) );
        position = wrapper.wrapPosition( position );

        rotation += rotationDelta * time;

        collisionList.clear();
        Vector2f[] world = transformPolygon();
        collisionList.add( world );
        wrapper.wrapPolygon( world, collisionList );

        positionList.clear();
        positionList.add( position );
        wrapper.wrapPositions( world, position, positionList );

    }

    private Vector2f[] transformPolygon() {
        Matrix3x3f mat = Matrix3x3f.rotate( rotation );
        mat = mat.mul( Matrix3x3f.translate( position ) );
```

```
        return transform( polygon, mat );
    }

    private Vector2f[] transform( Vector2f[] poly, Matrix3x3f mat ) {
        Vector2f[] copy = new Vector2f[ poly.length ];
        for( int i = 0; i < poly.length; ++i ) {
            copy[ i ] = mat.mul( poly[ i ] );
        }
        return copy;
    }

    public void draw( Graphics2D g, Matrix3x3f view ) {

        for( Vector2f pos : positionList ) {
            sprite.render( g, view, pos, rotation );
        }

    }

    public boolean contains( Vector2f point ) {
        for( Vector2f[] polygon : collisionList ) {
            if( pointInPolygon( point, polygon ) ) {
                return true;
            }
        }
        return false;
    }

    private boolean pointInPolygon( Vector2f point, Vector2f[] polygon ) {
        boolean inside = false;
        Vector2f start = polygon[ polygon.length - 1 ];
        boolean startAbove = start.y >= point.y;
        for( int i = 0; i < polygon.length; ++i ) {
            Vector2f end = polygon[ i ];
            boolean endAbove = end.y >= point.y;
            if( startAbove != endAbove ) {
                float m = ( end.y - start.y ) / ( end.x - start.x );
                float x = start.x + ( point.y - start.y ) / m;
                if( x >= point.x ) {
                    inside = !inside;
                }
            }
            startAbove = endAbove;
            start = end;
        }
        return inside;
    }

}
```

Tip

Don't forget that you can get the full source code on the book's website at http://www.indiegameprogramming.com.

THE ASTEROIDFACTORY CLASS

The AsteroidFactory class has been updated to parse an XML file to create the asteroids instead of using hard-coded values. This way, you can use the files created by the Swing GUI in Chapter 16, "Tools." The XML format is as follows:

```xml
<?xml version="1.0"?>
<models>
    <model bounds="0.5859375" size="Large" sprite="large0.png">
        <coord x="-0.029733956" y="0.283255100" />
        <coord x="-0.183098610" y="0.111111104" />
    </model>
<models>
```

The base model file comes from saving the XML file from the polygon editor. The models saved from the editor were just pasted into this file, and the size and sprite image were added. Either importing an image and drawing the polygon shape, or exporting the polygon shape and filling it with a sprite will work for creating the rock sprites and model file. If you want, you can grab the sprites and model files from the download section of the book's website.

```java
package javagames.completegame.object;


import java.awt.image.BufferedImage;
import java.io.InputStream;
import java.util.*;

import javagames.completegame.object.Asteroid.Size;
import javagames.util.*;

import javax.imageio.ImageIO;

import org.w3c.dom.Element;

public class AsteroidFactory {

    private Vector<Asteroid> small;
    private Vector<Asteroid> medium;
    private Vector<Asteroid> large;

    private float worldWidth;
    private PolygonWrapper wrapper;
    private Random rand;
```

```java
public AsteroidFactory( PolygonWrapper wrapper, float worldWidth ) {
    this.worldWidth = worldWidth;
    this.wrapper = wrapper;
    small = new Vector<Asteroid>();
    medium = new Vector<Asteroid>();
    large = new Vector<Asteroid>();
    rand = new Random();
}

public void loadModels( Element root ) {
    for( Element model : XMLUtility.getAllElements( root, "model" ) ) {
        parseModel( model );
    }
}

private void parseModel( Element model ) {
    Asteroid asteroid = new Asteroid( wrapper );

    Vector<Vector2f> polygon = new Vector<Vector2f>();
    String modelSize = model.getAttribute( "size" );
    String image = model.getAttribute( "sprite" );
    String bounds = model.getAttribute( "bounds" );

    for( Element coords : XMLUtility.getAllElements( model, "coord" ) ) {
        float x = Float.parseFloat( coords.getAttribute( "x" ) );
        float y = Float.parseFloat( coords.getAttribute( "y" ) );
        polygon.add( new Vector2f( x, y ) );
    }

    asteroid.setPolygon( polygon.toArray( new Vector2f[ 0 ] ) );

    BufferedImage bi = null;
    InputStream stream = ResourceLoader.load( AsteroidFactory.class,
            "res/assets/images/" + image, "/images/" + image );
    try {
        bi = ImageIO.read( stream );
    } catch( Exception e ) {
        e.printStackTrace();
    }

    float bound = Float.parseFloat( bounds );
    Vector2f topLeft = new Vector2f( -bound / 2.0f, bound / 2.0f );
    Vector2f bottomRight = new Vector2f( bound / 2.0f, -bound / 2.0f );

    Sprite sprite = new Sprite( bi, topLeft, bottomRight );
    asteroid.setSprite( sprite );

    Size size = Size.valueOf( modelSize );
    asteroid.setSize( size );
```

```
         if( size == Size.Large ) {
            large.add( asteroid );
         } else if( size == Size.Medium ) {
            medium.add( asteroid );
         } else if( size == Size.Small ) {
            small.add( asteroid );
         }
      }

      public Asteroid getLargeAsteroid() {
         return getLargeAsteroid( getAstroidStartPosition() );
      }

      public Asteroid getLargeAsteroid( Vector2f position ) {
         return copy( getRandomAsteroid( large ), position );
      }

      public Asteroid getMediumAsteroid() {
         return getMediumAsteroid( getAstroidStartPosition() );
      }

      public Asteroid getMediumAsteroid( Vector2f position ) {
         return copy( getRandomAsteroid( medium ), position );
      }

      public Asteroid getSmallAsteroid() {
         return getSmallAsteroid( getAstroidStartPosition() );
      }

      public Asteroid getSmallAsteroid( Vector2f position ) {
         return copy( getRandomAsteroid( small ), position );
      }

      public Asteroid copy( Asteroid template, Vector2f position ) {
         Asteroid asteroid = new Asteroid( wrapper );
         asteroid.setPosition( position );
         asteroid.setSprite( template.getSprite() );
         asteroid.setSize( template.getSize() );
         asteroid.setPolygon( template.getPolygon() );
         return asteroid;
      }

      private Vector2f getAstroidStartPosition() {
         float angle = (float)Math.toRadians( rand.nextInt( 360 ) );
         float minimum = worldWidth / 4.0f;
         float extra = rand.nextFloat() * minimum;
         float radius = minimum + extra;
         return Vector2f.polar( angle, radius );
      }
```

```
    private Asteroid getRandomAsteroid( List<Asteroid> asteroids ) {
        return asteroids.get( rand.nextInt( asteroids.size() ) );
    }

}
```

THE ASTEROIDEXPLOSION CLASS

The AsteroidExplosion class uses the Particle class to create a gray burst of particles, as demonstrated in Chapter 16.

```
package javagames.completegame.object;


import java.awt.*;
import java.util.*;

import javagames.util.*;


public class AsteroidExplosion {
    private static final int MAX_PARTICLES = 150;

    private Vector<Particle> particles;
    private Random random = new Random();
    private Vector2f pos;

    public AsteroidExplosion( Vector2f pos ) {
        this.pos = pos;
        createParticles();
    }

    private void createParticles() {
        particles = new Vector<Particle>();
        for( int i = 0; i < MAX_PARTICLES; ++i ) {
            particles.add( createRandomParticle() );
        }
    }

    private Particle createRandomParticle() {
        Particle p = new Particle();
        p.setPosition( pos );
        p.setRadius( 0.002f + random.nextFloat() * 0.004f );
        p.setLifeSpan( random.nextFloat() * 1.0f );
        switch( random.nextInt( 4 ) ) {
            case 0:
                p.setColor( Color.WHITE );
                break;
```

```
            case 1:
                p.setColor( Color.GRAY );
                break;
            case 2:
                p.setColor( Color.LIGHT_GRAY );
                break;
            case 3:
                p.setColor( Color.DARK_GRAY );
                break;
        }
        float angle = (float)Math.toRadians( random.nextInt( 360 ) );
        float velocity = random.nextFloat() * 2.0f;
        p.setVector( angle, velocity );
        return p;
    }

    public void update( float time ) {
        Iterator<Particle> it = particles.iterator();
        while( it.hasNext() ) {
            Particle p = it.next();
            p.update( time );
            if( p.hasDied() ) {
                it.remove();
            }
        }
    }

    public void render( Graphics2D g, Matrix3x3f view ) {
        for( Particle p : particles ) {
            p.draw( g, view );
        }
    }

    public boolean isFinished() {
        return particles.size() == 0;
    }

}
```

THE SHIP CLASS

The Ship class keeps the functionality from the prototype game and adds support for
sprites. The Ship uses two sprites, one regular, and one when it is invincible. There are
methods to get the width and height of the ship to help the rendering of the lives in the
upper-left corner of the screen. The update() method wraps both the collision polygon

and the sprite position. The Ship also adds particles for the rocket blasts when the ship is flying.

```java
package javagames.completegame.object;

import java.awt.*;
import java.util.*;

import javagames.util.*;


public class Ship {

    private static final int MAX_PARTICLES = 300;

    private float angle;
    private float acceleration;
    private float friction;
    private float maxVelocity;
    private float rotationDelta;
    private float curAcc;

    private Vector2f position;
    private Vector2f velocity;

    private ArrayList<Particle> particles;
    private Random random;
    private PolygonWrapper wrapper;

    private boolean alive;
    private boolean invincible;
    private float invincibleDelta;

    private Sprite ship;
    private Sprite glow;

    private Vector2f[] polygon;
    private ArrayList<Vector2f[]> collisionList;
    private ArrayList<Vector2f> positionList;

    public Ship( PolygonWrapper wrapper ) {

        this.wrapper = wrapper;

        friction = 0.25f;
        rotationDelta = (float)Math.toRadians( 180.0 );
        acceleration = 1.0f;
        maxVelocity = 0.5f;
        velocity = new Vector2f();

        position = new Vector2f();

        particles = new ArrayList<Particle>();
```

```java
        random = new Random();
        collisionList = new ArrayList<Vector2f[]>();
        positionList = new ArrayList<Vector2f>();
    }

    public void setPolygon( Vector2f[] polygon ) {
        this.polygon = polygon;
    }

    public void setShipSprite( Sprite ship ) {
        this.ship = ship;
    }

    public void setGlowSprite( Sprite glow ) {
        this.glow = glow;
    }

    public float getWidth() {
        float min = Float.MAX_VALUE;
        float max = -Float.MAX_VALUE;
        for( Vector2f v : polygon ) {
            min = Math.min( min, v.x );
            max = Math.max( max, v.x );
        }
        return Math.abs( min ) + Math.abs( max );
    }

    public float getHeight() {
        float min = Float.MAX_VALUE;
        float max = -Float.MAX_VALUE;
        for( Vector2f v : polygon ) {
            min = Math.min( min, v.y );
            max = Math.max( max, v.y );
        }
        return Math.abs( min ) + Math.abs( max );
    }

    public void setAlive( boolean alive ) {
        this.alive = alive;
    }

    public boolean isAlive() {
        return alive;
    }

    public void setPotition( Vector2f position ) {
        this.position = position;
    }
```

```java
public void rotateLeft( float delta ) {
    angle += rotationDelta * delta;
}

public void rotateRight( float delta ) {
    angle -= rotationDelta * delta;
}

public void reset() {
    setAlive( true );
    setPotition( new Vector2f() );
    setAngle( 0.0f );
    positionList.clear();
    collisionList.clear();
    velocity = new Vector2f();
    particles.clear();
}

public void setThrusting( boolean thrusting ) {
    if( isAlive() ) {
        curAcc = thrusting ? acceleration : 0.0f;
        if( thrusting ) {
            while( particles.size() < MAX_PARTICLES ) {
                particles.add( createRandomParticle() );
            }
        }
    }
}

public void setAngle( float angle ) {
    this.angle = angle;
}

public Bullet launchBullet() {
    Vector2f bulletPos = position.add( Vector2f.polar( angle, 0.0325f ) );
    return new Bullet( bulletPos, angle );
}

public void update( float delta ) {
    if( isAlive() ) {
        updatePosition( delta );
        updateInvincible( delta );
        updateParticles( delta );
        collisionList.clear();
        Vector2f[] world = transformPolygon();
        collisionList.add( world );
        wrapper.wrapPolygon( world, collisionList );
```

```java
            positionList.clear();
            positionList.add( position );
            wrapper.wrapPositions( world, position, positionList );
        }
    }

    private Vector2f[] transformPolygon() {
        Matrix3x3f mat = Matrix3x3f.rotate( angle );
        mat = mat.mul( Matrix3x3f.translate( position ) );
        return transform( polygon, mat );
    }

    private void updatePosition( float time ) {
        Vector2f accel = Vector2f.polar( angle, curAcc );
        velocity = velocity.add( accel.mul( time ) );
        float maxSpeed = Math.min( maxVelocity / velocity.len(), 1.0f );
        velocity = velocity.mul( maxSpeed );
        float slowDown = 1.0f - friction * time;
        velocity = velocity.mul( slowDown );
        position = position.add( velocity.mul( time ) );
        position = wrapper.wrapPosition( position );
    }

    private Vector2f[] transform( Vector2f[] poly, Matrix3x3f mat ) {
        Vector2f[] copy = new Vector2f[ poly.length ];
        for( int i = 0; i < poly.length; ++i ) {
            copy[i] = mat.mul( poly[i] );
        }
        return copy;
    }

    public void draw( Graphics2D g, Matrix3x3f view ) {
        if( isAlive() ) {

            for( Vector2f pos : positionList ) {
                if( isInvincible() ) {
                    glow.render( g, view, pos, angle );
                } else {
                    ship.render( g, view, pos, angle );
                }
            }

            for( Particle p : particles ) {
                p.draw( g, view );
            }

        }
    }
}
```

```java
public Vector2f isTouching( Asteroid asteroid ) {
    if( isAlive() ) {
        for( Vector2f[] poly : collisionList ) {
            for( Vector2f v : poly ) {
                if( asteroid.contains( v ) ) {
                    return v;
                }
            }
        }
    }
    return null;
}

public boolean isInvincible() {
    return invincible;
}

public void setInvincible() {
    invincible = true;
}

private void updateInvincible( float time ) {
    if( isInvincible() ) {
        invincibleDelta += time;
        if( invincibleDelta > 3.0f ) {
            invincibleDelta = 0.0f;
            invincible = false;
        }
    }
}

private Particle createRandomParticle() {
    Particle p = new Particle();
    p.setRadius( 0.002f + random.nextFloat() * 0.004f );
    p.setLifeSpan( random.nextFloat() * 0.5f );
    switch( random.nextInt( 5 ) ) {
        case 0: p.setColor( Color.WHITE ); break;
        case 1: p.setColor( Color.RED ); break;
        case 2: p.setColor( Color.YELLOW ); break;
        case 3: p.setColor( Color.ORANGE ); break;
        case 4: p.setColor( Color.PINK ); break;
    }
    int thrustAngle = 100;
    float a = (float)Math.toRadians(
        random.nextInt( thrustAngle ) - ( thrustAngle / 2 )
    );
```

```
        float velocity = random.nextFloat() * 0.375f;
        Vector2f bulletPos =
            position.add( Vector2f.polar( angle, -0.0325f ) );
        p.setPosition( bulletPos );
        p.setVector( angle + (float)Math.PI + a, velocity );
        return p;
    }

    private void updateParticles( float delta ) {
        Iterator<Particle> part = particles.iterator();
        while( part.hasNext() ) {
            Particle p = part.next();
            Vector2f bulletPos =
                position.add( Vector2f.polar( angle, -0.0325f ) );
            p.setPosition( bulletPos );
            p.update( delta );
            if( p.hasDied() ) {
                part.remove();
            }
        }
    }

}
```

THE SHIPFACTORY CLASS

The ShipFactory class parses the ship model file:

```
<model bounds="0.075" sprite="Ship.png" glow="ShipGlow.png">
    <coord x="0.0325" y="0.0" />
    <coord x="-0.0325" y="0.0325" />
    <coord x="0.0" y="0.0" />
    <coord x="-0.0325" y="-0.0325" />
</model>
```

There are two sprites, a regular one and a green glow sprite for invincible mode. There is also a convenience method for creating new Ship objects.

```
package javagames.completegame.object;

import java.awt.image.BufferedImage;
import java.io.InputStream;
import java.util.Vector;

import javax.imageio.ImageIO;
```

```java
import javagames.util.*;

import org.w3c.dom.Element;

public class ShipFactory {

    private PolygonWrapper wrapper;
    private Vector2f[] polygon;
    private Sprite shipRegular;
    private Sprite shipGlow;

    public ShipFactory( PolygonWrapper wrapper ) {
        this.wrapper = wrapper;
    }

    public void loadFactory( Element xml ) {
        Vector<Vector2f> points = new Vector<Vector2f>();
        String spritePath = xml.getAttribute( "sprite" );
        String glowPath = xml.getAttribute( "glow" );
        String bounds = xml.getAttribute( "bounds" );

        for( Element coords : XMLUtility.getAllElements( xml, "coord" ) ) {
            float x = Float.parseFloat( coords.getAttribute( "x" ) );
            float y = Float.parseFloat( coords.getAttribute( "y" ) );
            points.add( new Vector2f( x, y ) );
        }

        polygon = points.toArray( new Vector2f[0] );

        float bound = Float.parseFloat( bounds );
        Vector2f topLeft = new Vector2f( -bound / 2.0f, bound / 2.0f );
        Vector2f bottomRight = new Vector2f( bound / 2.0f, -bound / 2.0f );

        BufferedImage image = loadSprite( spritePath );
        shipRegular = new Sprite( image, topLeft, bottomRight );

        image = loadSprite( glowPath );
        shipGlow = new Sprite( image, topLeft, bottomRight );

    }

    public Ship createShip() {
        Ship ship = new Ship( wrapper );
        ship.setAlive( true );
        ship.setPolygon( polygon );
        ship.setGlowSprite( shipGlow );
        ship.setShipSprite( shipRegular );
        return ship;
    }
```

```
        private BufferedImage loadSprite( String path ) {
            InputStream stream = ResourceLoader.load(
                ShipFactory.class,
                "res/assets/images/" + path,
                "/images/" + path
            );
            try {
                return ImageIO.read( stream );
            } catch( Exception e ) {
                e.printStackTrace();
            }
            return null;
        }


    }
```

THE SHIPEXPLOSION CLASS

The ShipExplosion class creates particle ring explosions when the ship is destroyed.

```
package javagames.completegame.object;

import java.awt.*;
import java.util.*;

import javagames.util.*;


public class ShipExplosion {
    private static final int MAX_PARTICLES = 150;
    private static final int MAX_RINGS = 5;

    private Vector<Particle> particles;
    private Random random = new Random();
    private Vector2f pos;
    private Vector<Color> colors;

    public ShipExplosion( Vector2f pos ) {
        this.pos = pos;
        createColors();
        createParticles();
    }

    private void createColors() {
        colors = new Vector<Color>();
        colors.add( Color.WHITE );
        colors.add( Color.RED );
```

```java
            colors.add( Color.YELLOW );
            colors.add( Color.ORANGE );
            colors.add( Color.PINK );
    }
    private void createParticles() {
        particles = new Vector<Particle>();
        for( int ring = 0; ring < MAX_RINGS; ++ring ) {

            float velocity = 0.25f + random.nextFloat() * 1.0f;
            float lifeSpan = random.nextFloat() * 1.0f;
            float radius = 0.003f + random.nextFloat() * 0.003f;

            for( int i = 0; i < MAX_PARTICLES; ++i ) {
                Particle p = new Particle();
                p.setPosition( pos );
                p.setRadius( radius );
                p.setLifeSpan( lifeSpan );
                p.setColor( colors.get( random.nextInt( colors.size() ) ) );
                float angle = (float)Math.toRadians( random.nextInt( 360 ) );
                p.setVector( angle, velocity );
                particles.add( p );
            }
        }
    }

    public void update( float time ) {
        Iterator<Particle> it = particles.iterator();
        while( it.hasNext() ) {
            Particle p = it.next();
            p.update( time );
            if( p.hasDied() )
                it.remove();
        }
    }
    public void render( Graphics2D g, Matrix3x3f view ) {
        for( Particle p : particles ) {
            p.draw( g, view );
        }
    }
    public boolean isFinished() {
        return particles.size() == 0;
    }
}
```

ADDING GAME CONSTANTS

The usual game constants have been placed into a class that can eventually be loaded from a configuration file. For now, constants work just fine.

```
package javagames.completegame.admin;

import java.awt.Color;


public class GameConstants {

    public static final Color APP_BORDER = Color.DARK_GRAY;
    public static final int APP_WIDTH = 1680;
    public static final int APP_HEIGHT = 1050;
    public static final long APP_SLEEP = 10L;
    public static final String APP_TITLE = "Complete Game";
    public static final float WORLD_WIDTH = 2.0f;
    public static final float WORLD_HEIGHT = 2.0f;
    public static final float BORDER_SCALE = 0.95f;
    public static final boolean DISABLE_CURSOR = true;
    public static final boolean MAINTAIN_RATIO = true;

}
```

THE ACME CLASS

The Acme class is the game version of the Utility class, and holds all the necessary helper methods that don't need a brand new class, but need somewhere to go.

```
package javagames.completegame.admin;

import java.awt.*;

import javagames.completegame.CompleteGame;
import javagames.completegame.object.Ship;
import javagames.util.*;


public class Acme {

    private CompleteGame app;
    private Ship ship;

    public Acme( CompleteGame app ) {
        this.app = app;
    }

    public void setShip( Ship ship ) {
        this.ship = ship;
    }
```

```java
public void drawScore( Graphics2D g, int score ) {
    g.setRenderingHint(
        RenderingHints.KEY_TEXT_ANTIALIASING,
        RenderingHints.VALUE_TEXT_ANTIALIAS_ON
    );
    String toShow = "" + score;
    while( toShow.length() < 6 ) {
        toShow = "0" + toShow;
    }
    g.setFont( new Font( "Arial", Font.BOLD, 20 ) );
    g.setColor( Color.GREEN );
    Utility.drawCenteredString( g, app.getScreenWidth(), 0, toShow );
}

public void drawLives( Graphics2D g, Matrix3x3f view, int lives ) {
    float w = ship.getWidth();
    float h = ship.getHeight();
    float x = -0.95f + w;
    float y = 1.0f - h / 2.0f;
    for( int i = 0; i < lives; ++i ) {
        x += w * i;
        ship.setAngle( (float)Math.toRadians( 90 ) );
        ship.setPotition( new Vector2f( x, y ) );
        ship.update( 0.0f );
        ship.draw( g, view );
    }
}

}
```

THE GAMESTATE CLASS

The GameState class will keep track of the current level, the number of remaining lives, and the current score while the game is running. This state object is passed around the different state objects while the game is playing, but not while the attract screens are looping.

```java
package javagames.completegame.state;


import javagames.completegame.object.Asteroid.Size;


public class GameState {

    private int level;
    private int lives;
    private int score;
```

```
public void setLevel( int level ) {
    this.level = level;
}

public int getLevel() {
    return level;
}

public void setLives( int lives ) {
    this.lives = lives;
}

public int getLives() {
    return lives;
}

public int getScore() {
    return score;
}

public void updateScore( Size size ) {
    switch( size ) {
        case Small: score += 500; break;
        case Medium: score += 300; break;
        case Large: score += 100; break;
    }
}

}
```

THE SCORE CLASS

The Score class is a simple Comparable<> object used to sort the score objects stored in the high-score file.

```
package javagames.completegame.state;

public class Score implements Comparable<Score> {
    public String name = "";
    public int score = 0;

    public Score( String name, int score ) {
        this.name = name;
        this.score = score;
    }

    public int compareTo( Score o ) {
        if( score == o.score )
            return 0;
```

```
            if( score < o.score )
                return -1;
            return 1;
        }
    }
}
```

THE QUICKLOOPER CLASS

The QuickLooper class is an updated sound loop event that can be opened and closed only once, instead of every time the sound is played. This reduces the latency for the sound event. Also, there is an addition to the processEvent() method that keeps taking events off of the queue. This prevents loop events from getting backed up when the sound is used for multiple start and stop events from rapid keypresses. Because there is a 50ms buffer, there can be a delay from starting and stopping the sound in quick succession.

```
package javagames.completegame.admin;

import javagames.sound.AudioStream;
import javagames.sound.SoundEvent;


public class QuickLooper extends SoundEvent {

    public static final String STATE_CLOSED = "closed";
    public static final String STATE_WAITING = "waiting";
    public static final String STATE_RUNNING = "running";

    public static final String EVENT_FIRE = "fire";
    public static final String EVENT_DONE = "done";
    public static final String EVENT_OPEN = "open";
    public static final String EVENT_CLOSE = "close";

    private String currentState;

    public QuickLooper( AudioStream audio ) {
        super( audio );
        currentState = STATE_CLOSED;
    }

    public void open() {
        put( EVENT_OPEN );
    }

    public void close() {
        put( EVENT_CLOSE );
    }
```

```java
public void fire() {
    put( EVENT_FIRE );
}

public void done() {
    put( EVENT_DONE );
}

protected void processEvent( String event ) throws InterruptedException {
    while( queue.peek() == EVENT_DONE || queue.peek() == EVENT_FIRE ) {
        event = queue.take();
    }
    if( currentState == STATE_CLOSED ) {
        if( event == EVENT_OPEN ) {
            audio.open();
            currentState = STATE_WAITING;
        }
    } else if( currentState == STATE_WAITING ) {
        if( event == EVENT_CLOSE ) {
            audio.close();
            currentState = STATE_CLOSED;
        }
        if( event == EVENT_FIRE ) {
            audio.loop( AudioStream.LOOP_CONTINUOUSLY );
            currentState = STATE_RUNNING;
        }
    } else if( currentState == STATE_RUNNING ) {
        if( event == EVENT_CLOSE ) {
            audio.stop();
            audio.close();
            currentState = STATE_CLOSED;
        }
        if( event == EVENT_DONE ) {
            audio.stop();
            currentState = STATE_WAITING;
        }
    }
}
}
```

THE QUICKRESTART CLASS

The QuickRestart class is similar to the last sound event update, allowing the sound to be opened and closed only once, instead of every time the sound is played. This class does not need the extra while loop to pull out events because the sound is restarted, which doesn't cause any queue issues.

```java
package javagames.completegame.admin;

import javagames.sound.AudioStream;
import javagames.sound.SoundEvent;


public class QuickRestart extends SoundEvent {
    public static final String STATE_CLOSED = "closed";
    public static final String STATE_WAITING = "waiting";
    public static final String STATE_RUNNING = "running";

    public static final String EVENT_FIRE = "fire";
    public static final String EVENT_DONE = "done";
    public static final String EVENT_OPEN = "open";
    public static final String EVENT_CLOSE = "close";

    private String currentState;

    public QuickRestart( AudioStream stream ) {
        super( stream );
        currentState = STATE_CLOSED;
    }

    public void open() {
        put( EVENT_OPEN );
    }

    public void close() {
        put( EVENT_CLOSE );
    }

    public void fire() {
        put( EVENT_FIRE );
    }

    protected void processEvent( String event ) throws InterruptedException {
        System.out.println( "Quick Restart Got: " + event );
        System.out.println( "Current State: " + currentState );
        if( currentState == STATE_CLOSED ) {
            if( event == EVENT_OPEN ) {
                audio.open();
                currentState = STATE_WAITING;
            }
```

```
        } else if( currentState == STATE_WAITING ) {
            if( event == EVENT_CLOSE ) {
                audio.close();
                currentState = STATE_CLOSED;
            }
            if( event == EVENT_FIRE ) {
                audio.start();
                currentState = STATE_RUNNING;
            }
        } else if( currentState == STATE_RUNNING ) {
            if( event == EVENT_FIRE ) {
                audio.restart();
            }
            if( event == EVENT_CLOSE ) {
                audio.stop();
                audio.close();
                currentState = STATE_CLOSED;
            }
            if( event == EVENT_DONE ) {
                currentState = STATE_WAITING;
            }
        }

        System.out.println( "New State: " + currentState );

    }

    @Override
    protected void onAudioFinished() {
        put( EVENT_DONE );
    }

}
```

THE HIGHSCOREMGR CLASS

HighScoreMgr is responsible for saving and loading the top ten high scores in a data file. If the file is not found when the game is started, then a default file is written. The file, spacerocks.dat has the following format:

```
<hs>
    <player name="Dad" score="220600"/>
    <player name="" score="51700"/>
    <player name="B0B3ar" score="50000"/>
    <player name="U" score="45000"/>
    <player name="Lilly" score="42900"/>
    <player name="Awe" score="33240"/>
    <player name="Woowoo" score="31000"/>
```

```
    <player name="Loopy" score="27600"/>
    <player name="Coco" score="26700"/>
    <player name="AAA" score="14200"/>
</hs>
```

This file is saved in the user's home directory. This also uses the Score class presented previously to sort the scores from highest to lowest.

```java
package javagames.completegame.admin;


import java.io.*;
import java.text.*;
import java.util.*;

import javagames.completegame.state.GameState;
import javagames.completegame.state.Score;
import javagames.util.XMLUtility;

import javax.swing.JOptionPane;
import org.w3c.dom.*;


public class HighScoreMgr {
    private static final String HIGH_SCORE_FILE_NAME = "spacerocks.dat";
    private static final String[][] DEFAULT_SCORES = {
        { "BOB3ar", "50000" },
        { "Lilly", "42900" },
        { "Tiger", "40000" },
        { "Coco", "36000" },
        { "Loopy", "30100" },
        { "Woowoo", "27800" },
        { "Orange Foot", "23400" },
        { "Groovy", "18300" },
        { "Guitar God", "11100" },
        { "Daddy", "7800" },
    };
    private Vector<Score> scores = new Vector<Score>();
    private NumberFormat format = null;

    public HighScoreMgr() {
        format = new DecimalFormat();
        format.setMaximumFractionDigits( 0 );
        format.setMinimumFractionDigits( 0 );
        format.setGroupingUsed( true );
        format.setParseIntegerOnly( true );
    }
```

```java
public void loadHighScores() {
    try {
        File file = getHighScoreFile();
        if( !file.exists() ) {
            createDefaultFile( file );
        }
        parseHighScoreFile( file );
    } catch( Exception e ) {
        e.printStackTrace();
        handleFileError();
    }

}

private void createDefaultFile( File file ) throws IOException {
    if( !file.createNewFile() ) {
        throw new IOException();
    }

    String xml = "<hs>\n";
    for( String[] score : DEFAULT_SCORES ) {
        xml += "<player name=\"" + score[ 0 ] + "\" score=\"" + score[ 1 ]
                + "\"/>\n";
    }
    xml += "</hs>";

    PrintWriter out = new PrintWriter( new FileWriter( file ) );
    out.write( xml );
    out.flush();
    out.close();
}

private void handleFileError() {
    JOptionPane.showMessageDialog(
        null,
        "Could not create High Score File"
        + "\nWill not be able to save high scores", "Error",
        JOptionPane.ERROR_MESSAGE
    );

    // Something went wrong, so add scores so the
    // game won't crash...
    for( String[] score : DEFAULT_SCORES ) {
        scores.add(
            new Score( score[ 0 ], Integer.parseInt( score[ 1 ] ) )
        );
    }
}
```

```java
private File getHighScoreFile() {
    return new File(
        System.getProperty( "user.home" ), HIGH_SCORE_FILE_NAME );
}

private void parseHighScoreFile( File file ) {
    try {
        Document document =
            XMLUtility.parseDocument( new FileReader( file ) );
        Element root = document.getDocumentElement();
        for( Element player : XMLUtility.getElements( root, "player" ) ) {
            parsePlayer( player );
        }
    } catch( Exception e ) {
        e.printStackTrace();
    }
}

private void parsePlayer( Element player ) {
    String name = player.getAttribute( "name" );
    int score = Integer.parseInt( player.getAttribute( "score" ) );
    scores.add( new Score( name, score ) );
}

private String getFormattedScore( int index, Score score ) {
    String str = "" + ( index + 1 ) + ". " + score.name;
    str += " - " + format( score.score );
    return str;
}

public String format( int score ) {
    return format.format( score );
}

public String[] getHighScores() {
    Vector<String> hs = new Vector<String>();
    hs.add( "H I G H   S C O R E S" );
    hs.add( "--------------------------" );
    for( int i = 0; i < scores.size(); ++i ) {
        hs.add( getFormattedScore( i, scores.get( i ) ) );
    }
    return hs.toArray( new String[ 0 ] );
}

public boolean newHighScore( GameState state ) {
    return getLowestScore() < state.getScore();
}
```

```java
    private int getLowestScore() {
        return scores.lastElement().score;
    }

    public void addNewScore( Score newScore ) {
        scores.add( newScore );
        Collections.sort( scores );
        scores.remove( scores.firstElement() );
        Collections.reverse( scores );

        try {
            File file = getHighScoreFile();
            PrintWriter out = new PrintWriter( new FileWriter( file ) );
            String xml = "<hs>\n";
            for( Score score : scores ) {
                xml += "<player name=\"" +
                    score.name +
                    "\" score=\"" + score.score +
                    "\"/>\n";
            }
            xml += "</hs>";
            out.write( xml );
            out.flush();
            out.close();
        } catch( Exception e ) {
            e.printStackTrace();
        }
    }
}
```

MANAGING THE STATE

The complete game is a little over-engineered for such a small game, but I wanted to include some kind of state management. When a game gets very large, even this simple state and state-controller pattern would not be enough to keep things organized. The State class is the basis for each game state. There are methods that correspond to the game loop, an enter() method, and an exit() method.

```java
package javagames.completegame.state;


import java.awt.Graphics2D;

import javagames.completegame.CompleteGame;
import javagames.util.Matrix3x3f;
```

```java
public class State {

    protected StateController controller;
    protected CompleteGame app;

    public void setController( StateController controller ) {
        this.controller = controller;
        app = (CompleteGame)controller.getAttribute( "app" );
    }

    protected StateController getController() {
        return controller;
    }

    public void enter() {

    }

    public void processInput( float delta ) {

    }

    public void updateObjects( float delta ) {

    }

    public void render( Graphics2D g, Matrix3x3f view ) {

    }

    public void exit() {

    }

}
```

THE STATECONTROLLER CLASS

The StateController class is the key class in the entire game. This class handles the transition from one state to another, passes all the game loop calls to the current state, and contains a map of game objects referenced by name. This is a very simple way to pass resources around, and new objects can be added and retrieved without adding any extra methods to the controller. As long as a class knows the name of the resource and the type of the object, that object can be accessed.

```java
package javagames.completegame.state;


import java.awt.*;
import java.util.*;
```

```java
import javagames.util.Matrix3x3f;

public class StateController {

    private Map<String, Object> attributes;
    private State currentState;

    public StateController() {
        attributes =
            Collections.synchronizedMap( new HashMap<String, Object>() );
    }

    public void setState( State newState ) {

        if( currentState != null ) {
            currentState.exit();
        }

        if( newState != null ) {
            newState.setController( this );
            newState.enter();
        }

        currentState = newState;
    }

    public void processInput( float delta ) {
        currentState.processInput( delta );
    }

    public void updateObjects( float delta ) {
        currentState.updateObjects( delta );
    }

    public void render( Graphics2D g, Matrix3x3f view ) {
        g.setRenderingHint( RenderingHints.KEY_ANTIALIASING,
                RenderingHints.VALUE_ANTIALIAS_ON );
        currentState.render( g, view );
    }

    public Object getAttribute( String name ) {
        return attributes.get( name );
    }

    public Object removeAttribute( String name ) {
        return attributes.remove( name );
    }
```

```
    public void setAttribute( String name, Object attribute ) {
        attributes.put( name, attribute );
    }
    public Set<String> getAttributeNames() {
        return attributes.keySet();
    }
}
```

THE COMPLETEGAME CLASS

The CompleteGame class is the extension of the GameFramework. This is the class that is launched when the game is first started. However, there isn't much for this class to do, because all of the game items are loaded during the loading screen. The application's properties are set with the GameConstants and the StateController is created. Various items are created and added as named attributes in the controller. The processInput(), updateObjects(), and render() methods pass control to the controller, and other than shutting down the sound threads, this class does little else.

```
package javagames.completegame;


import java.awt.*;

import javagames.completegame.admin.*;
import javagames.completegame.object.*;
import javagames.completegame.state.*;
import javagames.sound.*;
import javagames.util.*;


public class CompleteGame extends WindowFramework {

    private StateController controller;

    public CompleteGame() {

        appBorder = GameConstants.APP_BORDER;
        appWidth = GameConstants.APP_WIDTH;
        appHeight = GameConstants.APP_HEIGHT;
        appSleep = GameConstants.APP_SLEEP;
        appTitle = GameConstants.APP_TITLE;
        appWorldWidth = GameConstants.WORLD_WIDTH;
        appWorldHeight = GameConstants.WORLD_HEIGHT;
```

```
        appBorderScale = GameConstants.BORDER_SCALE;
        appDisableCursor = GameConstants.DISABLE_CURSOR;
        appMaintainRatio = GameConstants.MAINTAIN_RATIO;
    }

    @Override
    protected void initialize() {
        super.initialize();

        controller = new StateController();

        controller.setAttribute( "app", this );
        controller.setAttribute( "keys", keyboard );
        controller.setAttribute( "ACME", new Acme( this ) );
        controller.setAttribute( "wrapper", new PolygonWrapper( appWorldWidth,
                appWorldHeight ) );
        controller.setAttribute( "viewport", getViewportTransform() );

        controller.setState( new GameLoading() );
    }

    public void shutDownGame() {
        shutDown();
    }

    @Override
    protected void processInput( float delta ) {
        super.processInput( delta );
        controller.processInput( delta );
    }

    @Override
    protected void updateObjects( float delta ) {
        controller.updateObjects( delta );
    }

    @Override
    protected void render( Graphics g ) {
        controller.render( (Graphics2D)g, getViewportTransform() );
        super.render( g );
    }

    @Override
    protected void terminate() {
        super.terminate();
```

```java
        QuickRestart event =
          (QuickRestart)controller.getAttribute( "fire-clip" );
        if( event != null ) {
            System.out.println( "Sound: fire-clip" );
            event.close();
            event.shutDown();
            System.out.println( "Done: fire-clip" );
        }

        LoopEvent loop = (LoopEvent)controller.getAttribute( "ambience" );
        if( loop != null ) {
            System.out.println( "Sound: ambience" );
            loop.done();
            loop.shutDown();
            System.out.println( "Done: ambience" );
        }

        QuickRestart[] explosions =
          (QuickRestart[])controller.getAttribute( "explosions" );
        for( int i = 0; i < explosions.length; ++i ) {
            System.out.println( "Sound: explosions: " + i );
            explosions[ i ].close();
            explosions[ i ].shutDown();
            System.out.println( "Done: explosions" );
        }

        QuickLooper thruster =
          (QuickLooper)controller.getAttribute( "thruster-clip" );
        if( thruster != null ) {
            System.out.println( "Sound: thruster-clip" );
            thruster.close();
            thruster.shutDown();
            System.out.println( "Done: thruster-clip" );
        }
    }
    public static void main( String[] args ) {
        launchApp( new CompleteGame() );
    }
}
```

THE GAMELOADING STATE

The GameLoading state, as shown in Figure 17.1, is the first state the game enters.

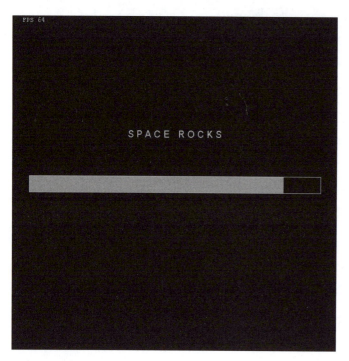

Figure 17.1
Game Loading.
© 2014 Timothy Wright.

This state loads all the game resources using the thread pool method demonstrated in Chapter 12, "Threads." The items loaded are:

- Background image
- High score file
- Asteroid models and sprites
- Ship model and sprites
- Thruster, explosions, and missile sounds

The updateObjects() method checks the progress of all the resource loading and updates the load percentage. The render() method draws the loading progress. When all the game resources are loaded, the state transitions to the PressSpaceToPlay state. Remember, for the ambient sound, there are differences depending on which version of Java you are using.

```java
package javagames.completegame.state;

import java.awt.*;
import java.awt.image.BufferedImage;
import java.io.*;
import java.util.*;
import java.util.List;
import java.util.concurrent.*;

import javagames.completegame.admin.*;
import javagames.completegame.object.*;
import javagames.sound.*;
import javagames.util.*;

import javax.imageio.ImageIO;
import javax.xml.parsers.ParserConfigurationException;

import org.w3c.dom.*;
import org.xml.sax.SAXException;


public class GameLoading extends State {

    private String[] explosions = { "EXPLOSION_large_01.wav",
            "EXPLOSION_large_02.wav", "EXPLOSION_large_03.wav",
            "EXPLOSION_large_04.wav", "EXPLOSION_large_05.wav",
    };

    private ExecutorService threadPool;
    private List<Callable<Boolean>> loadTasks;
    private List<Future<Boolean>> loadResults;

    private int numberOfTasks;
    private float percent;
    private float wait;

    @Override
    public void enter() {
        threadPool = Executors.newCachedThreadPool();

        loadTasks = new ArrayList<Callable<Boolean>>();
        loadTasks.add( new Callable<Boolean>() {

            @Override
            public Boolean call() throws Exception {
                InputStream stream = ResourceLoader.load( GameLoading.class,
                        "res/assets/images/space_background_600x600.png",
                        "/images/space_background_600x600.png" );
                BufferedImage image = ImageIO.read( stream );
```

```java
                Vector2f worldTopLeft = new Vector2f(
                        -GameConstants.WORLD_WIDTH / 2.0f,
                        GameConstants.WORLD_HEIGHT / 2.0f );
                Vector2f worldBottomRight = new Vector2f(
                        GameConstants.WORLD_WIDTH / 2.0f,
                        -GameConstants.WORLD_HEIGHT / 2.0f );
                Sprite sprite =
                    new Sprite( image, worldTopLeft, worldBottomRight );

                Matrix3x3f viewport =
                    (Matrix3x3f)controller.getAttribute( "viewport" );
                sprite.scaleImage( viewport );
                controller.setAttribute( "background", sprite );
                return Boolean.TRUE;
            }
        });
        loadTasks.add( new Callable<Boolean>() {

            @Override
            public Boolean call() throws Exception {
                HighScoreMgr mgr = new HighScoreMgr();
                mgr.loadHighScores();
                controller.setAttribute( "score", mgr );
                return Boolean.TRUE;
            }
        });
        loadTasks.add( new Callable<Boolean>() {

            @Override
            public Boolean call() throws Exception {
                PolygonWrapper wrapper =
                    (PolygonWrapper)controller.getAttribute( "wrapper" );
                AsteroidFactory factory = new AsteroidFactory( wrapper,
                        GameConstants.WORLD_WIDTH );
                factory.loadModels( loadXML( "new_asteroids.xml" ) );
                controller.setAttribute( "factory", factory );
                return Boolean.TRUE;
            }
        });
        loadTasks.add( new Callable<Boolean>() {

            @Override
            public Boolean call() throws Exception {
                PolygonWrapper wrapper =
                    (PolygonWrapper)controller.getAttribute( "wrapper" );
                ShipFactory factory = new ShipFactory( wrapper );
```

```
            Element xml = loadXML( "ship.xml" );
            factory.loadFactory( xml );
            controller.setAttribute( "ship-factory", factory );

            Acme acme = (Acme)controller.getAttribute( "ACME" );
            acme.setShip( factory.createShip() );
            return Boolean.TRUE;
        }
});
loadTasks.add( new Callable<Boolean>() {

    @Override
    public Boolean call() throws Exception {
        byte[] soundBytes = loadSound( "DRONE9RE.WAV" );
        QuickLooper clip =
            new QuickLooper( new BlockingDataLine( soundBytes ) );
        clip.initialize();
        clip.open();
        controller.setAttribute( "thruster-clip", clip );
        return Boolean.TRUE;
    }
});
loadTasks.add( new Callable<Boolean>() {

    @Override
    public Boolean call() throws Exception {
        byte[] soundBytes = loadSound( "WEAPON_scifi_fire_02.wav" );
        QuickRestart restartClip =
            new QuickRestart( new BlockingDataLine(
                soundBytes
        ));
        restartClip.initialize();
        restartClip.open();
        controller.setAttribute( "fire-clip", restartClip );
        return Boolean.TRUE;
    }
});
loadTasks.add( new Callable<Boolean>() {

    @Override
    public Boolean call() throws Exception {
        ArrayList<QuickRestart> explosion =
            new ArrayList<QuickRestart>();
        for( String path : explosions ) {
            byte[] soundBytes = loadSound( path );
```

```java
                    QuickRestart restartClip = new QuickRestart(
                            new BlockingDataLine( soundBytes ) );
                    restartClip.initialize();
                    restartClip.open();
                    explosion.add( restartClip );
                }
                controller.setAttribute( "explosions",
                        explosion.toArray( new QuickRestart[ 0 ] ) );
                return Boolean.TRUE;
            }
        });
        loadTasks.add( new Callable<Boolean>() {

            @Override
            public Boolean call() throws Exception {
                byte[] soundBytes = loadSound( "AMBIENCE_alien.wav" );

                // Java 7.0
                LoopEvent loopEvent = new LoopEvent(
                    new BlockingClip( soundBytes ) );

                // Java 6.0
                // LoopEvent loopEvent = new LoopEvent(
                //     new BlockingDataLine(
                //     soundBytes ) );

                loopEvent.initialize();
                controller.setAttribute( "ambience", loopEvent );
                return Boolean.TRUE;

        loadResults = new ArrayList<Future<Boolean>>();
        for( Callable<Boolean> task : loadTasks ) {
            loadResults.add( threadPool.submit( task ) );
        }

        numberOfTasks = loadResults.size();
        if( numberOfTasks == 0 ) {
            numberOfTasks = 1;
        }
    }

    private Element loadXML( String path ) throws IOException, SAXException,
            ParserConfigurationException {
        InputStream model = ResourceLoader.load( GameLoading.class,
                "res/assets/xml/" + path, "/xml/" + path );
        Document document = XMLUtility.parseDocument( model );
        return document.getDocumentElement();
    }
```

```
private byte[] loadSound( String path ) {
    InputStream in = ResourceLoader.load( GameLoading.class,
            "res/assets/sound/" + path, "/sound/" + path );
    return readBytes( in );
}

private byte[] readBytes( InputStream in ) {
    try {
        BufferedInputStream buf = new BufferedInputStream( in );
        ByteArrayOutputStream out = new ByteArrayOutputStream();
        int read;
        while( ( read = buf.read() ) != -1 ) {
            out.write( read );
        }
        in.close();
        return out.toByteArray();
    } catch( IOException ex ) {
        ex.printStackTrace();
        return null;
    }
}

@Override
public void updateObjects( float delta ) {

    // remove finished tasks
    Iterator<Future<Boolean>> it = loadResults.iterator();
    while( it.hasNext() ) {
        Future<Boolean> next = it.next();
        if( next.isDone() ) {
            try {
                if( next.get() ) {
                    it.remove();
                }
            } catch( Exception ex ) {
                ex.printStackTrace();
            }
        }
    }

    // update progress bar
    percent = ( numberOfTasks - loadResults.size() ) / (float)numberOfTasks;

    if( percent >= 1.0f ) {
        threadPool.shutdown();
        wait += delta;
    }
```

```
        if( wait > 1.0f && threadPool.isShutdown() ) {
            LoopEvent loop = (LoopEvent)controller.getAttribute( "ambience" );
            loop.fire();
            getController().setState( new PressSpaceToPlay() );
        }
    }

    @Override
    public void render( Graphics2D g, Matrix3x3f view ) {
        super.render( g, view );
        g.setRenderingHint( RenderingHints.KEY_TEXT_ANTIALIASING,
                RenderingHints.VALUE_TEXT_ANTIALIAS_ON );
        g.setFont( new Font( "Arial", Font.PLAIN, 20 ) );
        g.setColor( Color.GREEN );
        String message = "S P A C E    R O C K S";
        Utility.drawCenteredString( g, app.getScreenWidth(),
                app.getScreenHeight() / 3, message );

        int vw = (int)( app.getScreenWidth() * .9f );
        int vh = (int)( app.getScreenWidth() * .05f );
        int vx = ( app.getScreenWidth() - vw ) / 2;
        int vy = ( app.getScreenWidth() - vh ) / 2;

        // fill in progress
        g.setColor( Color.GRAY );
        int width = (int)( vw * percent );
        g.fillRect( vx, vy, width, vh );

        // draw border
        g.setColor( Color.GREEN );
        g.drawRect( vx, vy, vw, vh );
    }

}
```

THE ATTRACTSTATE CLASS

The AttractState class is any state that the game is in while waiting for the user to start a new game or exit the application. The enter() method pulls all the necessary objects from the StateController and creates some random rocks to fly around. There is an abstract method, getState(), that subclasses supply, returning the transition game state. The getWaitTime() returns the number of seconds to stay in the current state before transitioning.

The processInput() overrides the timed transition, exiting the game on an Esc key, or starting the game on a spacebar event. The render() method draws the stars, planet background, and floating rocks.

```java
package javagames.completegame.state;

import java.awt.Graphics2D;
import java.awt.event.KeyEvent;
import java.util.*;

import javagames.completegame.admin.*;
import javagames.completegame.object.*;
import javagames.util.*;


public abstract class AttractState extends State {
    private List<Asteroid> asteroids;
    private float time;
    private Sprite background;
    private AsteroidFactory factory;

    protected Acme acme;
    protected KeyboardInput keys;
    protected HighScoreMgr highScoreMgr;

    public AttractState() {

    }

    public AttractState( List<Asteroid> asteroids ) {
        this.asteroids = asteroids;
    }

    @Override
    public void enter() {

        highScoreMgr = (HighScoreMgr)controller.getAttribute( "score" );
        keys = (KeyboardInput)controller.getAttribute( "keys" );
        background = (Sprite)controller.getAttribute( "background" );
        factory = (AsteroidFactory)controller.getAttribute( "factory" );
        acme = (Acme)controller.getAttribute( "ACME" );

        if( asteroids == null ) {
            asteroids = new Vector<Asteroid>();
            asteroids.add( factory.getLargeAsteroid() );
            asteroids.add( factory.getMediumAsteroid() );
            asteroids.add( factory.getSmallAsteroid() );
        }
        time = 0.0f;
    }

    @Override
    public void updateObjects( float delta ) {
        time += delta;
```

```
        if( shouldChangeState() ) {
           AttractState state = getState();
           state.setAsteroids( asteroids );
           getController().setState( state );
           return;
        }
        for( Asteroid a : asteroids ) {
           a.update( delta );
        }
     }

     protected boolean shouldChangeState() {
        return time > getWaitTime();
     }

     protected float getWaitTime() {
        return 5.0f;
     }

     private void setAsteroids( List<Asteroid> asteroids ) {
        this.asteroids = asteroids;
     }

     protected abstract AttractState getState();

     public List<Asteroid> getAsteroids() {
        return asteroids;
     }

     @Override
     public void processInput( float delta ) {
        if( keys.keyDownOnce( KeyEvent.VK_ESCAPE ) ) {
           app.shutDownGame();
        }
        if( keys.keyDownOnce( KeyEvent.VK_SPACE ) ) {
           GameState state = new GameState();
           state.setLevel( 1 );
           state.setLives( 2 );
           getController().setState( new LevelStarting( state ) );
        }
     }

     @Override
     public void render( Graphics2D g, Matrix3x3f view ) {
        background.render( g, view );
        for( Asteroid a : asteroids ) {
           a.draw( g, view );
        }
     }
  }
```

THE PRESSSPACETOPLAY MODE

The `PressSpaceToPlay` mode, as shown in Figure 17.2, is the first of the attract game modes entered when the game starts.

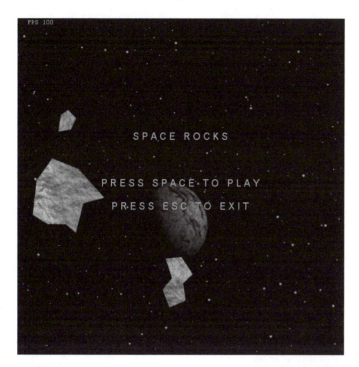

Figure 17.2
Press Space to Play.
© 2014 Timothy Wright.

The `render()` method displays some text. The `super.render()` method allows the base class to draw the background and the floating rocks. When the default five seconds has elapsed, the state transitions to the `HighScore` state.

```
package javagames.completegame.state;


import java.awt.*;

import javagames.util.Matrix3x3f;
import javagames.util.Utility;


public class PressSpaceToPlay extends AttractState {

    @Override
    protected AttractState getState() {
```

```
            return new HighScore();
    }

    public void render( Graphics2D g, Matrix3x3f view ) {
        super.render( g, view );
        int width = app.getScreenWidth();
        int height = app.getScreenHeight();
        g.setRenderingHint( RenderingHints.KEY_TEXT_ANTIALIASING,
                RenderingHints.VALUE_TEXT_ANTIALIAS_ON );
        g.setFont( new Font( "Arial", Font.PLAIN, 20 ) );
        g.setColor( Color.GREEN );
        String[] msg = { "S P A C E   R O C K S", "", "", "",
                "P R E S S   S P A C E   T O   P L A Y", "",
                "P R E S S   E S C   T O   E X I T" };
        Utility.drawCenteredString( g, width, height / 3, msg );
    }

}
```

THE HIGHSCORE STATE

The HighScore state, as shown in Figure 17.3, displays the high scores for the top ten players.

Figure 17.3
High Score.
© 2014 Timothy Wright.

This state increases the wait time to seven seconds so people can marvel at their awesome high score. When this state is done, it transitions to the GameInformationState.

```java
package javagames.completegame.state;


import java.awt.*;
import java.awt.geom.Rectangle2D;

import javagames.util.Matrix3x3f;
import javagames.util.Utility;


public class HighScore extends AttractState {

    @Override
    protected AttractState getState() {
        return new GameInformationState();
    }

    @Override
    public void render( Graphics2D g, Matrix3x3f view ) {
        super.render( g, view );
        String[] hs = highScoreMgr.getHighScores();

        g.setRenderingHint( RenderingHints.KEY_TEXT_ANTIALIASING,
                RenderingHints.VALUE_TEXT_ANTIALIAS_ON );
        g.setFont( new Font( "Arial", Font.PLAIN, 20 ) );
        g.setColor( Color.GREEN );

        Rectangle2D bounds = g.getFontMetrics().getStringBounds( hs[ 0 ], g );
        int x = ( app.getScreenWidth() - (int)bounds.getWidth() ) / 2;
        Utility.drawString( g, x, app.getScreenHeight() / 3, hs );
    }

    @Override
    protected float getWaitTime() {
        return 7.0f;
    }
}
```

THE GAMEINFORMATIONSTATE CLASS

The GameInformationState class, as shown in Figure 17.4, is the last of the attract modes. It displays a "Thank You" message to various people for helping me (or putting up with me) during the development of the game.

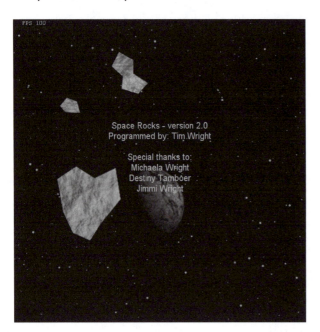

Figure 17.4
Game Information.
© 2014 Timothy Wright.

When this state transitions, it goes back to the starting state. These attract states will continue to loop through each other until the game is shut down, or the spacebar is pressed, starting a new game.

```
package javagames.completegame.state;


import java.awt.*;

import javagames.util.Matrix3x3f;
import javagames.util.Utility;


public class GameInformationState extends AttractState {

    private static final String[] gameInfo = {
      "Space Rocks - version 2.0",
       "Programmed by: Tim Wright",
       "",
      "Special thanks to:",
       "Michaela Wright",
       "Destiny Tamboer",
       "Jimmi Wright",
    };
```

```
    @Override
    protected AttractState getState() {
        return new PressSpaceToPlay();
    }

    @Override
    public void render( Graphics2D g, Matrix3x3f view ) {
        super.render( g, view );
        g.setRenderingHint( RenderingHints.KEY_TEXT_ANTIALIASING,
                RenderingHints.VALUE_TEXT_ANTIALIAS_ON );
        g.setFont( new Font( "Arial", Font.PLAIN, 20 ) );
        g.setColor( Color.GREEN );

        Utility.drawCenteredString( g, app.getScreenWidth(),
                app.getScreenHeight() / 3, gameInfo );
    }

}
```

THE LEVELSTARTING STATE

The LevelStarting state, as shown in Figure 17.5, starts the game. The current level is presented, transitioning to the LevelPlaying state after a few seconds.

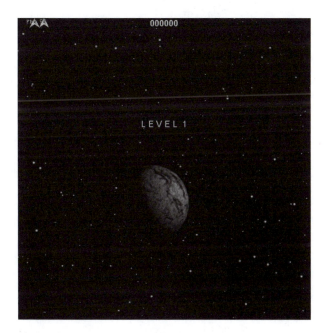

Figure 17.5
Level Starting.
© 2014 Timothy Wright.

Notice that both this state and the LevelPlaying state use the GameState class, which holds the current level, number of lives, and current score.

```
package javagames.completegame.state;


import java.awt.*;
import javagames.completegame.admin.Acme;
import javagames.util.*;


public class LevelStarting extends State {
    double time;
    private Sprite background;
    private GameState state;
    private Acme acme;

    public LevelStarting( GameState state ) {
        this.state = state;
    }

    @Override
    public void enter() {
        background = (Sprite)controller.getAttribute( "background" );
        acme = (Acme)controller.getAttribute( "ACME" );
        time = 0.0;
    }

    @Override
    public void updateObjects( float delta ) {
        time += delta;
        if( time > 2.0 ) {
            getController().setState( new LevelPlaying( state ) );
        }
    }

    @Override
    public void render( Graphics2D g, Matrix3x3f view ) {
        super.render( g, view );
        background.render( g, view );

        acme.drawScore( g, state.getScore() );
        acme.drawLives( g, view, state.getLives() );

        g.setRenderingHint( RenderingHints.KEY_TEXT_ANTIALIASING,
                RenderingHints.VALUE_TEXT_ANTIALIAS_ON );
        g.setFont( new Font( "Arial", Font.PLAIN, 20 ) );
        g.setColor( Color.GREEN );
```

```
        Utility.drawCenteredString( g, app.getScreenWidth(),
            app.getScreenHeight() / 3, "L E V E L  " + state.getLevel() );
    }
}
```

THE LEVELPLAYING STATE

The LevelPlaying game state, as shown in Figure 17.6, is the meat of the game.

Figure 17.6
Level Playing.
© 2014 Timothy Wright.

The enter() method pulls all the needed attributes from the controller. The process Input() method fires a bullet on a spacebar press, as well as kicks off a laser sound event. The left and right arrow keys rotate the ship. The up arrow activates the ship's thruster, draws the rocket blast particles, and activates the thruster sound. The updateObjects() method updates the rocks, bullets, ship, explosions, and checks for the level won condition.

When each bullet is updated, it is checked for collision with any asteroid. If an asteroid is hit, the bullet is removed, the asteroid is split into smaller asteroids, an asteroid explosion particle event is created, and an explosion sound is kicked off. Because there are multiple explosion sounds, a random sound is chosen.

When the ship is updated, it is also checked for collision with all the asteroids. If the ship is currently invincible, the asteroid is destroyed just as if it was hit by a bullet. If the ship is not invincible, it's marked as dead, the thruster sound is turned off, and a ship explosion is generated. After the ship explosion is finished, if there are any more lives available, the ship is placed in the middle of the screen in invincible mode so it doesn't die if it's placed on top of an asteroid. The life count is decremented and play continues.

If the ship manages to destroy all the flying rocks, a new level is started by transitioning back to the LevelStarting event. Notice, in the enter() method, that the number of random asteroids created is generated from the level number; the higher the level, the more asteroids and the harder it is to stay alive.

If the ship has no remaining lives, the game transitions to the GameOver state.

```
package javagames.completegame.state;


import java.awt.Graphics2D;
import java.awt.event.KeyEvent;
import java.util.*;

import javagames.completegame.admin.*;
import javagames.completegame.object.*;
import javagames.completegame.object.Asteroid.Size;
import javagames.util.*;


public class LevelPlaying extends State {

    private ArrayList<AsteroidExplosion> explosions;
    private ArrayList<Asteroid> asteroids;
    private ArrayList<Bullet> bullets;

    private double respawn = 0.0;
    private Sprite background;
    private AsteroidFactory factory;
    private Acme acme;

    private QuickLooper thruster;
    private QuickRestart laser;
    private QuickRestart[] explosion;
    private Random rand = new Random();
```

```
    private ShipExplosion shipExplosion;
    private ShipFactory shipFactory;
    private Ship ship;
    private boolean thrusting;
    private GameState state;
    private PolygonWrapper wrapper;
    private KeyboardInput keys;

    public LevelPlaying( GameState state ) {
        this.state = state;
    }

    @Override
    public void enter() {

        background = (Sprite)controller.getAttribute( "background" );
        factory = (AsteroidFactory)controller.getAttribute( "factory" );
        keys = (KeyboardInput)controller.getAttribute( "keys" );
        laser = (QuickRestart)controller.getAttribute( "fire-clip" );
        explosion = (QuickRestart[])controller.getAttribute( "explosions" );
        thruster = (QuickLooper)controller.getAttribute( "thruster-clip" );
        shipFactory = (ShipFactory)controller.getAttribute( "ship-factory" );
        wrapper = (PolygonWrapper)controller.getAttribute( "wrapper" );
        acme = (Acme)controller.getAttribute( "ACME" );

        ship = shipFactory.createShip();
        ship.setAngle( (float)Math.toRadians( 90 ) );

        explosions = new ArrayList<AsteroidExplosion>();
        asteroids = new ArrayList<Asteroid>();
        bullets = new ArrayList<Bullet>();

        // generate random
        for( int i = 0; i < state.getLevel(); ++i ) {
            asteroids.add( factory.getLargeAsteroid() );
            asteroids.add( factory.getMediumAsteroid() );
            asteroids.add( factory.getSmallAsteroid() );
        }

        createShip( false );
    }

    private void createShip( boolean invincible ) {
        ship.reset();
        if( invincible ) {
            ship.setInvincible();
        }
    }
```

```java
@Override
public void processInput( float delta ) {

    if( ship.isAlive() ) {
        if( keys.keyDownOnce( KeyEvent.VK_SPACE ) ) {
            bullets.add( ship.launchBullet() );
            laser.fire();
        }

        if( keys.keyDown( KeyEvent.VK_LEFT ) ) {
            ship.rotateLeft( delta );
        }

        if( keys.keyDown( KeyEvent.VK_RIGHT ) ) {
            ship.rotateRight( delta );
        }

        if( keys.keyDown( KeyEvent.VK_UP ) ) {
            ship.setThrusting( true );
            if( !thrusting ) {
                thruster.fire();
                thrusting = true;
            }
        } else {
            ship.setThrusting( false );
            if( thrusting ) {
                thruster.done();
                thrusting = false;
            }
        }
    }
}

@Override
public void updateObjects( float delta ) {

    updateAsteroids( delta );
    updateBullets( delta );
    updateShip( delta );
    updateAsteroidExplosions( delta );
    updateShipExplosion( delta );
    checkForLevelWon();

}

private void updateShip( float delta ) {
    if( shouldRespawn() ) {
```

```
                processRespawnShip( delta );
        } else {
            ship.update( delta );
            ArrayList<Asteroid> ast = new ArrayList<Asteroid>( asteroids );
            for( Asteroid asteroid : ast ) {
                Vector2f collision = ship.isTouching( asteroid );
                if( collision != null ) {
                    if( ship.isInvincible() ) {
                        explosions.add( new AsteroidExplosion( collision ) );
                        explosion[ rand.nextInt( explosion.length ) ].fire();
                        remove( asteroid );
                    } else {
                        shipExplosion = new ShipExplosion( collision );
                        explosion[ rand.nextInt( explosion.length ) ].fire();
                        ship.setAlive( false );
                        thruster.done();
                        thrusting = false;
                    }
                }
            }
        }
    }

    private void updateAsteroids( float delta ) {
        for( Asteroid a : asteroids ) {
            a.update( delta );
        }
    }

    private void updateBullets( float delta ) {
        ArrayList<Bullet> copy = new ArrayList<Bullet>( bullets );
        for( Bullet bullet : copy ) {
            updateBullet( delta, bullet );
        }
    }

    private void updateBullet( float delta, Bullet bullet ) {
        bullet.update( delta );
        if( wrapper.hasLeftWorld( bullet.getPosition() ) ) {
            bullets.remove( bullet );
        } else {
            ArrayList<Asteroid> ast = new ArrayList<Asteroid>( asteroids );
            for( Asteroid asteroid : ast ) {
                if( asteroid.contains( bullet.getPosition() ) ) {
```

```java
                remove( asteroid );
                bullets.remove( bullet );
                explosions.add(
                    new AsteroidExplosion( bullet.getPosition() )
                );
                explosion[ rand.nextInt( explosion.length ) ].fire();
            }
        }
    }
}

private void remove( Asteroid asteroid ) {
    asteroids.remove( asteroid );
    state.updateScore( asteroid.getSize() );
    spawnBabies( asteroid );
}

private void spawnBabies( Asteroid asteroid ) {
    if( asteroid.getSize() == Size.Large ) {
        asteroids.add(
            factory.getMediumAsteroid( asteroid.getPosition() )
        );
        asteroids.add(
            factory.getMediumAsteroid( asteroid.getPosition() )
        );
    }
    if( asteroid.getSize() == Size.Medium ) {
        asteroids.add( factory.getSmallAsteroid( asteroid.getPosition() ) );
        asteroids.add( factory.getSmallAsteroid( asteroid.getPosition() ) );
    }
}

private boolean shouldRespawn() {
    return !ship.isAlive() && shipExplosion == null;
}

private void processRespawnShip( double delta ) {
    respawn += delta;
    if( respawn > 1.0 ) {
        if( state.getLives() > 0 ) {
            respawn = 0.0;
            state.setLives( state.getLives() - 1 );
            createShip( true );
        } else {
```

```
            getController().setState( new GameOver( asteroids, state ) );
        }
    }
}

private void checkForLevelWon() {
    if( asteroids.isEmpty() && explosions.isEmpty() ) {
        state.setLevel( state.getLevel() + 1 );
        thruster.done();
        getController().setState( new LevelStarting( state ) );
    }
}

private void updateAsteroidExplosions( float delta ) {
    for( AsteroidExplosion explosion : new ArrayList<AsteroidExplosion>(
            explosions ) ) {
        explosion.update( delta );
        if( explosion.isFinished() ) {
            explosions.remove( explosion );
        }
    }
}

private void updateShipExplosion( float delta ) {
    if( shipExplosion != null ) {
        shipExplosion.update( delta );
        if( shipExplosion.isFinished() ) {
            shipExplosion = null;
        }
    }
}

@Override
public void render( Graphics2D g, Matrix3x3f view ) {
    background.render( g, view );

    ship.draw( g, view );

    for( Asteroid a : asteroids ) {
        a.draw( g, view );
    }

    for( AsteroidExplosion ex : explosions ) {
        ex.render( g, view );
    }
```

```
        for( Bullet b : bullets ) {
            b.draw( g, view );
        }

        if( shipExplosion != null ) {
            shipExplosion.render( g, view );
        }

        acme.drawLives( g, view, state.getLives() );
        acme.drawScore( g, state.getScore() );

    }
}
```

THE GAMEOVER STATE

The GameOver state, as shown in Figure 17.7, is entered when the player runs out of lives.

Figure 17.7
Game Over.
© 2014 Timothy Wright.

If the score is large enough to make it into the top ten, the EnterHighScoreName state is reached. Otherwise, the HighScore attract state is entered and the attract state loop continues until the player starts another game or quits the application.

```
package javagames.completegame.state;


import java.awt.Graphics2D;
import java.util.List;

import javagames.completegame.object.*;
import javagames.util.Matrix3x3f;
import javagames.util.Utility;


public class GameOver extends AttractState {

    GameState state;

    public GameOver( List<Asteroid> asteroids, GameState state ) {
        super( asteroids );
        this.state = state;
    }

    @Override
    protected float getWaitTime() {
        return 3.0f;
    }

    @Override
    protected AttractState getState() {
        if( highScoreMgr.newHighScore( state ) ) {
            return new EnterHighScoreName( state );
        } else {
            return new HighScore();
        }
    }

    @Override
    public void render( Graphics2D g, Matrix3x3f view ) {

        super.render( g, view );
        acme.drawScore( g, state.getScore() );
        Utility.drawCenteredString( g, app.getScreenWidth(),
                app.getScreenHeight() / 3, "G A M E   O V E R" );

    }

}
```

THE ENTERHIGHSCORENAME STATE

The EnterHighScoreName state, as shown in Figure 17.8, presents a list of characters, just like the example in Chapter 11, "Text." The enter() method adds all the available characters and measures each one to find the maximum width to space the letters.

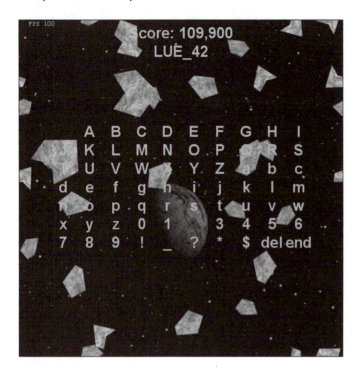

Figure 17.8
Enter High Score Name.
© 2014 Timothy Wright.

The processInput() method moves the selected character around with the arrow keys and sets the value with the spacebar.

The updateHeldKey() and resetHeldKey() methods keep track of the arrow keys if they are held down. Instead of just zipping the selected character as fast as possible, this slows it down to the STEP value, which is a tenth of a second. That way it doesn't scroll too fast.

The render() method draws the score, the entered name, and the character list, rendering the selected character as red with a box around it.

```
package javagames.completegame.state;


import java.awt.*;
import java.awt.event.*;
import java.util.Vector;

import javagames.util.Matrix3x3f;
```

```java
public class EnterHighScoreName extends AttractState {
    class GameLetter {
        public String letter;
        public int width;

        public GameLetter( String letter, int width ) {
            this.letter = letter;
            this.width = width;
        }
    }

    private static final long STEP = (long)0.10E9;
    private static final int FONT_SIZE = 32;

    private int maxWidth;
    private GameLetter[] letters;
    private int rowCount;
    private int colCount;
    private String name = "";
    private long heldDown = 0;
    private long last = 0;

    private int selectedRow = 0;
    private int selectedCol = 0;

    private GameState state;
    private boolean finished = false;

    public EnterHighScoreName( GameState state ) {
        this.state = state;
    }

    @Override
    public void enter() {
        super.enter();

        Font font = new Font( "Arial", Font.BOLD, FONT_SIZE );
        FontMetrics fm = app.getFontMetrics( font );
        Vector<GameLetter> temp = new Vector<GameLetter>();
        maxWidth = Integer.MIN_VALUE;

        maxWidth = addLetter( fm, " ", maxWidth, temp );
        maxWidth = addLetters( fm, (int)'A', (int)'Z', maxWidth, temp );
        maxWidth = addLetters( fm, (int)'a', (int)'z', maxWidth, temp );
        maxWidth = addLetters( fm, (int)'0', (int)'9', maxWidth, temp );

        maxWidth = addLetter( fm, "!", maxWidth, temp );
        maxWidth = addLetter( fm, "_", maxWidth, temp );
        maxWidth = addLetter( fm, "?", maxWidth, temp );
```

```
        maxWidth = addLetter( fm, "*", maxWidth, temp );
        maxWidth = addLetter( fm, "$", maxWidth, temp );
        maxWidth = addLetter( fm, "del", maxWidth, temp );
        maxWidth = addLetter( fm, "end", maxWidth, temp );
        letters = temp.toArray( new GameLetter[ 0 ] );

        colCount = 10;
        rowCount = letters.length / colCount;
    }

    private int addLetters( FontMetrics fm, int start, int end, int maxWidth,
            Vector<GameLetter> letters ) {
        for( int i = start; i <= end; ++i ) {
            maxWidth = addLetter( fm, "" + (char)i, maxWidth, letters );
        }
        return maxWidth;
    }

    private int addLetter( FontMetrics fm, String letter, int max,
            Vector<GameLetter> letters ) {
        int strWidth = fm.stringWidth( letter );
        max = Math.max( max, strWidth );
        letters.add( new GameLetter( letter, strWidth ) );
        return max;
    }

    @Override
    public void processInput( float delta ) {

        if( keys.keyDownOnce( KeyEvent.VK_LEFT ) ) {
            selectedCol = roll( selectedCol - 1, 0, colCount - 1 );
            resetHeldKey();
        }
        if( keys.keyDown( KeyEvent.VK_LEFT ) && updateHeldKey() ) {
            selectedCol = roll( selectedCol - 1, 0, colCount - 1 );
        }
        if( keys.keyDownOnce( KeyEvent.VK_RIGHT ) ) {
            selectedCol = roll( selectedCol + 1, 0, colCount - 1 );
            resetHeldKey();
        }
        if( keys.keyDown( KeyEvent.VK_RIGHT ) && updateHeldKey() ) {
            selectedCol = roll( selectedCol + 1, 0, colCount - 1 );
        }
        if( keys.keyDownOnce( KeyEvent.VK_UP ) ) {
            selectedRow = roll( selectedRow - 1, 0, rowCount - 1 );
            resetHeldKey();
        }
```

```java
    if( keys.keyDown( KeyEvent.VK_UP ) && updateHeldKey() ) {
        selectedRow = roll( selectedRow - 1, 0, rowCount - 1 );
    }
    if( keys.keyDownOnce( KeyEvent.VK_DOWN ) ) {
        selectedRow = roll( selectedRow + 1, 0, rowCount - 1 );
        resetHeldKey();
    }
    if( keys.keyDown( KeyEvent.VK_DOWN ) && updateHeldKey() ) {
         selectedRow = roll( selectedRow + 1, 0, rowCount - 1 );
    }
    if( keys.keyDownOnce( KeyEvent.VK_SPACE ) ) {
        int selected = getSelectedIndex( selectedRow, selectedCol );
        updateHighScoreRecord( letters[ selected ].letter );
    }
}

private void resetHeldKey() {
    last = System.nanoTime();
    heldDown = -STEP;
}

private boolean updateHeldKey() {
    long current = System.nanoTime();
    heldDown += current - last;
    last = current;
    if( heldDown > STEP ) {
        heldDown -= STEP;
        return true;
    }
    return false;
}

@Override
public void render( Graphics2D g, Matrix3x3f view ) {
    super.render( g, view );

    g.setColor( Color.GREEN );
    g.setRenderingHint( RenderingHints.KEY_TEXT_ANTIALIASING,
            RenderingHints.VALUE_TEXT_ANTIALIAS_ON );
    Font font = new Font( "Arial", Font.BOLD, FONT_SIZE );
    g.setFont( font );
    FontMetrics fm = g.getFontMetrics();
    int sh = fm.getAscent() + fm.getDescent() + fm.getLeading();

    // draw the score
    String score = "Score: " + highScoreMgr.format( state.getScore() );
     int scoreX =
        (( app.getScreenWidth() - fm.stringWidth( score ) ) / 2);
```

```
            int scoreY = sh;
            g.drawString( score, scoreX, scoreY );

            // draw the name
            int nameX = (( app.getScreenWidth() - fm.stringWidth( name ) ) / 2 );
            int nameY = scoreY + sh;
            g.drawString( name, nameX, nameY );

            // lets center the whole thing...
            int xStart = ( app.getScreenWidth() - ( maxWidth * colCount ) ) / 2;
            int x = xStart;
            int y = ( app.getScreenHeight() - ( fm.getAscent() * rowCount ) ) / 2;

            int count = 0;
            for( int i = 0; i < letters.length; ++i ) {
                GameLetter letter = letters[ i ];
                boolean selected =
                    i == getSelectedIndex( selectedRow, selectedCol );
                g.setColor( selected ? Color.RED : Color.GREEN );
                int xp = x + ( maxWidth - letter.width ) / 2;
                g.drawString( letter.letter, xp, y );
                if( selected ) {
                    g.drawRect( x, y - fm.getAscent(), maxWidth, sh );
                }
                x += maxWidth;
                count++;
                if( count % colCount == 0 ) {
                    y += sh;
                    x = xStart;
                }
            }
        }
    }

    private void updateHighScoreRecord( String letter ) {
        if( letter.equalsIgnoreCase( "end" ) ) {
            highScoreMgr.addNewScore( new Score( name, state.getScore() ) );
            finished = true;
        } else if( letter.equalsIgnoreCase( "del" ) ) {
            if( !name.isEmpty() ) {
                name = name.substring( 0, name.length() - 1 );
            }
        } else {
            name += letter;
        }
    }
```

```
    private int roll( int value, int min, int max ) {
        if( value < min )
            return max;
        if( value > max )
            return min;
        return value;
    }

    private int getSelectedIndex( int row, int col ) {
        return row * colCount + col;
    }

    @Override
    protected AttractState getState() {
        return new HighScore();
    }

    @Override
    protected boolean shouldChangeState() {
        return finished;
    }
}
```

CREATING A BUILD SCRIPT

Finally, the last file you need is a build script. This file imports the common.xml base script developed in Chapter 14, "Deplyoment with ANT." The common.classpath and jar.mainclass properties are both set before the common file is imported. Once the default JAR is created, the sound, images, and XML folders are added to the JAR so all of the resources are available from inside the JAR file, and the game consists of just that single file.

```xml
<?xml version="1.0" encoding="UTF-8"?>

<project name="complete-game" default="default">

    <description>
        Building Space Rocks
    </description>

    <property name="common.classpath" value="custom.classpath"/>
    <property name="jar.mainclass"
        value="javagames.completegame.CompleteGame"/>

    <import file="res/assets/xml/common.xml"/>

    <path id="custom.classpath">
        <pathelement location="${basedir}/bin"/>
    </path>
```

```
<target name="default" depends="build, signjar"
   description="--> This builds my first real game"/>

<target name="jar" depends="common.jar">
   <jar update="true"
      destfile="lib/${ant.project.name}.jar">
      <fileset dir="res/assets"
         includes="sound/**,images/**,xml/**"/>
   </jar>
</target>

</project>
```

RESOURCES AND FURTHER READING

Adams, Ernest, *Fundamentals of Game Design,* 3rd Edition, New Riders, 2013.

Rogers, Scott, *Level Up!: The Guide to Great Video Game Design*, Wiley, 2010.

Salen, Katie and Eric Zimmerman, *Rules of Play: Game Design Fundamentals*, The MIT Press, 2003.

Schell, Jesse, *The Art of Game Design: A Book of Lenses*, CRC Press, 2008.

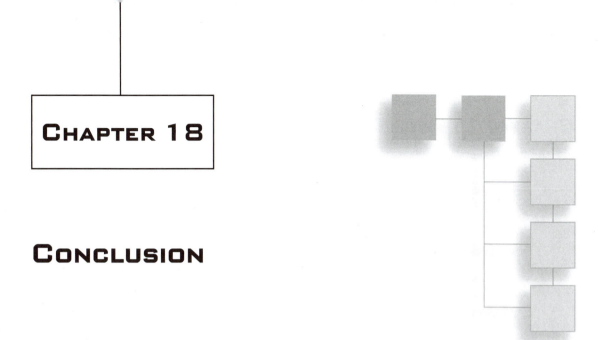

CHAPTER 18

CONCLUSION

That was a lot of information to cover, and it doesn't even scratch the surface of game programming today. This is one of the reasons why game programming appeals to so many people. Much like the Wild West, developers are on the outskirts, blazing trails, continuing to push the boundaries between movies, fiction, games, and interactive media. With all the different platforms available, indie game resources, websites, competitions, and communities, as well as the success of mobile development, crowdsource funding, self-publishing, and ability for a single person to make an impact, the industry has not been this exciting since the late '80s, when anything was possible.

Many aspects of game programming were not covered in this text. From third-party tools, 3D graphics, mobile development, multiplayer network games, artificial intelligence, and game design—the topics of study for games continues to grow at an exciting rate.

It is also important to remember, while you develop your own games, that the technology aspect (the coding) is only part of the puzzle. There is an art to making a game "fun." Game programming is hard. Hopefully, given the amount of detail in this book, you have lost any assumptions you had that making games is easy. But all the coding and math in the world is not enough to make a game fun to play. So keep that in mind while you craft the next great game. It takes a lot of work.

All the code examples in the text serve as a method for exploring different situations that may come up during your travels. The utility library code gives you the necessary tools to start making your own test programs, proof-of-concept applications, and prototype games. Even if you plan on targeting some other platforms or languages, these tools allow for quick prototype experiments.

The following sections list all the example code presented in each chapter. Use this list as a reference to find a specific example.

CHAPTER 1—"HELLO WORLD"

- The `FrameRate` class has been used throughout the book to measure the application speed.

- The `HelloWorldApp` is the first game window example, but uses passive rendering to update the display.

- The `RenderThreadExample` is a simple example of using threads to create a custom game loop.

- The `ActiveRenderingExample` is the active rendering game window with a custom game loop thread.

- The `DisplayModeExample` allows the user to switch to full-screen display mode. This is also the first example using Swing components.

- The `FullScreenRenderingExample` combines active rendering and changing the display mode to create a full-screen game window.

CHAPTER 2—"INPUT"

- The `SimpleKeyboardInput` and `SimpleKeyboardExample` classes demonstrate polling the keyboard during the game loop.

- The `KeyboardInput` improves upon the example by adding the `keyDown()` and `keyDownOnce()` methods.

- The `SimpleMouseInput` and `SimpleMouseExample` classes are the initial examples of polling the mouse the same way the keyboard is polled.

- The `RelativeMouseInput` and `RelativeMouseExample` classes add and demonstrate the ability to keep the mouse cursor from leaving the game window, adding relative mouse movement.

CHAPTER 3—"TRANSFORMATIONS"

- The `Vector2f` class is introduced. Used in `VectorGraphicsExample`, simple translation, rotation, and shearing are explained.

- The `PolarCoordinateExample` converts from Cartesian coordinates to polar coordinates and back.

- The `Matrix3x3f` class is introduced, along with the `MatrixMultiplicationExample`, which rotates planets around the sun.

CHAPTER 4—"TIME AND SPACE"

- The `TimeDeltaExample` demonstrates adding the tick count to the game loop to perform animation not dependent on the frame rate.

- The `ScreenMappingExample` class uses normalized device coordinates and maps these values to the screen with transformations.

- The `ViewportRatioExample` class maintains the world ratio and centers the viewport in the game window.

- The `CannonExample` class uses the tick count and world coordinates to implement the physics and gravity to simulate a cannon and a cannonball.

CHAPTER 5—"SIMPLE GAME FRAMEWORK"

- The `Utility` class is added to the `javagames.util` package. This class is updated throughout the rest of the book with helper methods.

- The `SimpleFramework` class is introduced. The class wraps up all the common code into a framework that can be used to simplify the rest of the examples in the book.

- The `SimpleFrameworkTemplate` class is an example of using the framework as a starting point for future code examples.

CHAPTER 6—"VECTOR2F UPDATES"

The following methods are added to the `Vector2f` class to aid with intersection testing.

- `inv()`—Computes the inverse vector
- `add()`—Adds two vectors
- `sub()`—Subtracts two vectors
- `mul()`—Multiplies a vector with a scalar
- `div()`—Divides a vector with a scalar
- `perp()`—Computes a perpendicular vector
- `dot()`—Calculates the dot product from two vectors
- `angle()`—Returns the angle created by the vector

- `polar()`—Converts a polar angle to a vector
- `toString()`—Converts the vector to a `"(x,y)"` string.

CHAPTER 7—"INTERSECTION TESTING"

- The `PointInPolygonExample` class demonstrates testing the point-in-poly algorithm and is the first example to use the `SimpleFramework` code.
- The `OverlapExample` class demonstrates `AABB` and circle-intersection testing as well as testing the mouse to see if it is inside the shapes.
- The `LineLineOverlapExample` class uses the separating axis test to detect when two lines overlap.
- The `RectRectOverlapExample` class uses the separating axis test to detect when two rectangles overlap.

CHAPTER 8—"GAME PROTOTYPE"

- The `PolygonWrapper` class wraps the game polygons from one side of the game window to the other, and the `ScreenWrapExample` tests out the new code.
- The `PrototypeAsteroid` class represents the rocks flying about in the game.
- The `PrototypeEditor` class is the first example of using Swing to create game tools.
- The `PrototypeAsteroidFactory` class creates random rocks at runtime, and the `RandomAsteroidExample` demonstrates using the factory.
- The `PrototypeBullet`, `PrototypeShip`, and `FlyingShipExample` classes test flying the ship around and shooting weapons.
- The `PrototypeGame` extends `SimpleFramework` and uses everything so far to create a prototype game.

CHAPTER 9—"FILES AND RESOURCES"

- The `FilesAndDirectories` example demonstrates traversing a file tree.
- The `ReadingDataFromFiles` and `WritingDataToFiles` classes demonstrate basic file I/O.
- The `ClasspathResources` class shows different ways to load a resource at runtime.
- The `ResourceLoader` and `ResourceLoaderExample` classes add the helper class to the utility package and show its usage.

- The `PrintSystemProperties` example enumerates all the Java system properties.

- The `SavingPropertyFiles` and `PropertyFileExample` classes show examples for using Java properties.

- The `SaveXMLExample` and `LoadXMLExample` classes demonstrate using XML files.

- The `XMLUtility` class is added to the utility package to help with parsing XML documents.

CHAPTER 10—"IMAGES"

- The `ImageCreatorExample` class saves and loads images to the hard drive in *.GIF, *.BMP, *.JPG, and *.PNG formats.

- The `ColorInterpolationExample` class shows linear interpolation of colors and how to access the raw pixel values of an image.

- The `ImageSpeedTest` class shows how to use `VolatileImage` to increase rendering speed.

- The `TransparentImageExample` class presents the code to create an image with a transparent background.

- The `AlphaCompositeExample` class demonstrates the different alpha blending modes.

- The `FlyingSpritesExample` class shows how to draw sprites with different configuration options to control speed and quality.

- The `ScaleImageExample` and `ScaleUpImageExample` classes demonstrate the various ways to scale images for speed and quality.

CHAPTER 11—"TEXT"

- `BoxedTextProblem` and `BoxedTextSolution` demonstrate how to calculate font sizes at runtime.

- `UtilityDrawStringExample` shows how to incorporate the updates to the `Utility` class to draw strings.

- `TextMetricExample` presents all the different properties available for a font.

- `TextLayoutExample` shows how to lay out letters in a retro high-score example program.

- `ConsoleOverlayExample` combines text rendering and transparency to create a text console overlay.

- The `SafeKeyboardInput` class is added to the utility package to process typed keys without missing any. The `SafeKeyboardInputExample` demonstrates using the updates.

CHAPTER 12—"THREADS"

- `CallableTaskExample` introduces using a thread pool. `FileLoadingExample` uses a thread pool to simulate loading resources on startup.

- `FakeHardware`, `FakeHardwareListener`, and `FakeHardwareEvent` are created to allow exploring threads with classes under your control.

- `WaitNotifyExample` demonstrates suspending and resuming threads using the `wait()` and `notify()` methods.

- `BlockingHardware` and `BlockingHardwareListener` demonstrate wrapping a non-blocking class with a blocking class.

- The `BlockingQueueExample` shows how to pass messages between threads.

- `OneShotEvent`, `LoopEvent`, and `RestartEvent` show how to use the `BlockingHardware` class in a state machine.

- `MultiThreadEventExample` explains how to use the state machines in the game loop.

CHAPTER 13—"SOUND"

- `PlayingClipsExample` explores some of the problems with the sound support in Java.

- `AudioStream`, `BlockingAudioListener`, and `SoundException` form the base classes of the custom audio library.

- The `BlockingClip` class wraps a `Clip` object with a blocking class that can be used with the game code.

- `AudioDataLine` and `BlockingDataLine` create a blocking version of a data line for streaming sounds.

- `SoundEvent` uses a blocking queue so the sound library can be used in the game loop.

- `OneShotEvent`, `LoopEvent`, and `RestartEvent` create state machines to provide basic sound capabilities.

- `SoundPlayerExample` demonstrates using the sounds in a game loop.

- `SoundControlsExample` uses updates to the sound library to add pan and volume controls to the classes and demonstrates their usage.

CHAPTER 14—"DEPLOYMENT WITH ANT"

- The `common.xml` file is an example of an extendable build script that can be customized to compile, package, and deploy game code for a user.

- The `CustomBuild.xml` file is an example of extending the `common.xml` file for a specific game.

CHAPTER 15—"COLLISION DETECTION"

- `BouncingBallsExample` creates random balls that bounce around the screen.

- `LineRectIntersectionExample` places a spinning rectangle in the middle of the screen and computes the intersection of a line with a rectangle.

- `CircleLineIntersectionExample` shows how to compute the intersection of (you guessed it) a circle and a line.

- `LineLineIntersectionExample` computes the exact intersection point of two line segments.

- `ReflectionVectorExample` calculates the reflection vector off a line segment.

- `BouncyPointExample` bounces random points around a closed polygon.

CHAPTER 16—"TOOLS"

- `GameFramework`, `WindowFramework`, `FullScreenFramework`, and `SwingFramework` demonstrate a more generic framework for the game code.

- The `Utility` class is updated with more `String` rendering, as well as the code to scale images.

- `PolygonEditor` is used along with the `ExampleFileFilter` to create a better polygon editor that saves and loads files.

- The `Sprite` class is added to the utility package to easily draw sprites in the game. The `SpriteExample` demonstrates the new class.

- `TestParticle` and `ParticleExample` explore a simple particle engine.

CHAPTER 17—"SPACE ROCKS"

The game objects consist of:

- `Bullet`—Bullets fired from the ship
- `PolygonWrapper`—Utility class to wrap objects
- `Particle`—A single particle entity
- `Asteroid`—A space rock
- `AsteroidFactory`—Creates random space rocks
- `AsteroidExplosion`—Uses the particles to create the explosion
- `Ship`—Represents the flying ship object
- `ShipFactory`—Creates new ship objects
- `ShipExplosion`—Ship explosion when the ship is destroyed

Administration classes are as follows:

- `GameConstants`—All game constants in one class
- `Acme`—Helper methods without a home (cue sad music)
- `QuickLooper`—Only loads sound once
- `QuickRestart`—Only loads sound once
- `HighScoreMgr`—Deals with the high-score file

Game state classes are as follows:

- `GameState`—Keeps track of the current level, score, and lives
- `Score`—A `Comparable<>` object to sort the scores
- `State`—Base class for the state management state machine
- `StateController`—Key class for the entire game

Complete game classes are as follows:

- `CompleteGame`—Game framework with the `main()` method
- `GameLoading`—Game state to load resources
- `AttractState`—Base class for various attract screens
- `PressSpaceToPlay`—Spacebar starts the game
- `HighScore`—Displays the top ten scores

- `GameInformationState`—Displays a "Thank You" message to friends and family
- `LevelStarting`—Displays the current level and lets the player catch their breath
- `LevelPlaying`—The meat of the game (this is the only part a beginner thinks there is to making a game)
- `GameOver`—All good things come to an end
- `EnterHighScoreName`—Lets the user enter his name for his score

There is also a `build.xml` build script for packaging the complete game.

RESOURCES AND FURTHER READING

I also recommend the following books that have been referenced in various chapters throughout the book. They are full of bits of wisdom.

Akenine-Moller, Tomas, Eric Haines, *Real-Time Rendering*, 2nd Edition, A K Peters, 2002.

Ericson, Christer, *Real-Time Collision Detection*, Focal Press, 2004.

Goetz, Brian, *Java Concurrency in Practice*, Addison-Wesley, Upper Saddle River, 2006.

Oaks, Scott, Henry Wong, *Java Threads*, 3rd Edition, O'Reilly, Sebastopol, CA, 2004.

Adams, Ernest, *Fundamentals of Game Design*, (3rd Edition), New Riders, 2013.

Rogers, Scott, *Level Up!: The Guide to Great Video Game Design*, Wiley, 2010.

Schell, Jesse, *The Art of Game Design: A book of lenses*, CRC Press, 2008.

Salen Katie and Eric Zimmerman, *Rules of Play: Game Design Fundamentals*, The MIT Press, 2003.

I am of the belief that if a prototype game or core idea is not fun, no amount of polish will make it fun. The only way to find that fun game is to experiment and fail many times. This is the spirit of game development: the courage to try new things and strive not to repeat the same old game, but to create something fresh and new.

This is why I have no problem giving away this knowledge instead of keeping it to myself. After all, if other people aren't making great games, what am I going to play in my spare time? The wonderful thing about computer games is that there is always room for another great one!

Now that you have some tools necessary to create a game, get busy…

INDEX